Metaethics

YORK COLLEGE

Metaet
ethics
most r
referen
there,
that pe
essenti
it? Hov
Each c
further

Mark
Lincol
in the
express

Routledge Contemporary Introductions to Philosophy
Series editor: Paul K Moser, Loyola University of
Chicago

This innovative, well-structured series is for students who have already done an introductory course in philosophy. Each book introduces a core general subject in contemporary philosophy and offers students an accessible but substantial transition from introductory to higher-level college work in that subject. The series is accessible to non-specialists and each book clearly motivates and expounds the problems and positions introduced. An orientating chapter briefly introduces its topic and reminds readers of any crucial material they need to have retained from a typical introductory course. Considerable attention is given to explaining the central philosophical problems of a subject and the main competing solutions and arguments for those solutions. The primary aim is to educate students in the main problems, positions, and arguments of contemporary philosophy rather than to convince students of a single position.

Ancient Philosophy
2nd Edition
Christopher Shields

Classical Modern Philosophy
Jeffrey Tlumak

Continental Philosophy
Andrew Cutrofello

Epistemology
3rd Edition
Robert Audi

Ethics
2nd Edition
Harry J. Gensler

Metaethics
Mark van Roojen

Metaphysics
3rd Edition
Michael J. Loux

Moral Psychology
Valerie Tiberius

Philosophy of Art
Noël Carroll

Philosophy of Biology
*Alex Rosenberg and Daniel
W. McShea*

Philosophy of Economics
Julian Reiss

Philosophy of Language
2nd Edition
William G. Lycan

Metaethics

A Contemporary Introduction

Mark van Roojen

Routledge
Taylor & Francis Group

NEW YORK AND LONDON

First published 2015
by Routledge
711 Third Avenue, New York, NY 10017

and by Routledge
2 Park Square, Milton Park, Abingdon, Oxon OX14 4RN

Routledge is an imprint of the Taylor & Francis Group, an informa business

Library of Congress Cataloging-in-Publication Data
   Van Roojen, Mark Steven.
   Metaethics : a contemporary introduction /
Mark van Roojen. — 1 [edition].
      pages cm. — (Routledge contemporary introductions to philosophy)
   1. Metaethics. I. Title.
   BJ1012.V36 2015
   170'.42—dc23
   2014046808

ISBN: 978-0-415-89441-8 (hbk)
ISBN: 978-0-415-89442-5 (pbk)
ISBN: 978-1-315-69705-5 (ebk)

Typeset in Garamond Pro and Gill Sans
by Apex CoVantage, LLC

For my metaethics teachers, Gil, Michael, Jamie, and Mark, and for Jenny and Joe, who always come through when needed

Contents

Acknowledgments

I have a number of people to thank. So many that I'm probably forgetting someone. I apologize for that.

This book is an attempt to summarize and give shape to a tremendous amount of work by a huge number of people in metaethics. My understanding of that work depends in turn on the understanding of various other people who taught me a lot. Gil Harman, Michael Smith, Jamie Dreier, Mark Schroeder, Mark Kalderon, Mark Johnston, Peter Railton, Frank Jackson, and David Lewis all changed how I think of metaethics. At some points in the book the debts will be obvious, but the less evident debts are just as important.

Various readers for the press gave hugely helpful input at several stages, from the first proposal and drafts of several early chapters to comments on a version of the whole manuscript. Most of them remain anonymous to me, but I know that Mark Timmons and Simon Kirchin each gave me tremendously helpful feedback on the early chapters. Tristram McPherson and a second reader gave me generous comments on a completed draft this past summer. Both readers made crucial suggestions that changed the structure of the book in important ways and clarified what I had to say at many points. Tristram's extremely helpful and sympathetic comments were even more impressive for having been returned only a week after getting the draft.

Thanks are due to the UNL philosophy department and to Greg Snow, then of the Arts and Sciences College dean's office, for a semester-long course reduction while I worked on this and another project.

A number of other people read various parts of the manuscript and gave me their helpful reactions at various stages. These include Aaron Elliot, Guy Fletcher, Shane George, Ben Henke, Robert Johnson, Jason Lemmon, Katerina Psaroudaki, Chelsea Richardson, Adam Thompson, and Preston Werner. Jason also kindly proofread the entire first draft. Aaron and Ben were extremely helpful in working on and suggesting options for the charts. In addition, my undergraduate ethical theory class in spring 2013 and my graduate seminar for fall 2013 each read several chapters in the course of the term, and their reactions provided useful feedback.

Conversations (some via e-mail) with a number of people helped me figure things out as I was writing. Aaron Bronfman, John Brunero, Al Casullo, Jonathan Dancy, Julia Driver, Bill FitzPatrick, John Gibbons, Jennifer Haley, Reina Hayaki, David Henderson, Harry Ide, Simon Kirchin, Jennifer Mc-Kitrick, Colin McLear, Tristram McPherson, Joe Mendola, Hille Paakkun-ainen, Sarah Raskoff, Connie Rosati, Mark Schroeder, Daniel Star, Nick Sturgeon, Dan Threet, Mark Timmons, and Pekka Vayrynen served as useful sounding boards and offered helpful advice.

My editor, Andrew Beck, was a pleasure to work with. The whole project was his idea, and he cleverly sent me several of the other books in the Routledge Contemporary Introductions to Philosophy series to aid in my deliberations. I wound up reading William Lycan's philosophy of language volume, and it so impressed me that I agreed to try my hand at a metaethics text. Andy's understanding and encouragement along the way were important to letting me enjoy much of the process despite insecurities and missed deadlines.

Joe Mendola and Jennifer Haley read each chapter, sometimes more than once. Their comments saved many a passage from incoherence and helped me figure out what I should be trying to say. They also lent needed perspective. Without their help, this all would have been much more difficult.

1 A Brief Introduction

1.1. What Metaethics Is

When people talk about ethics, they are most often talking about normative ethics.[1] That is, they are talking about what is right and wrong, good and bad, valuable or disvaluable. They may have in mind some very specific issue of this sort—whether lying is always wrong, for example. Or they may have something more general in mind—whether right actions always aim at the good. Most of us have considered such issues at one time or another. Meta-ethics also concerns ethics, but it looks at ethics in an even more general and more reflexive way than we do when we're thinking only about such normative questions. Rather than focusing on more particular normative issues within ethics—issues about which actions are right or wrong, or which things are valuable or disvaluable, for example—our primary concern will be with some of the most abstract questions regarding ethics in general. You are likely familiar with 'meta' as a prefix used to designate topics that involve reflection on the subject named by the term to which it is prefixed.[2] So metaethics involves reflecting on the nature of ethics. For instance, some people think that there are no ethical truths, or that all ethical truths are relative to the believer. Metaethics talks about issues like these.

As it turns out it will be very hard to say anything uncontroversial about the nature of ethics, and metaethics reflects that difficulty. That's partly what makes metaethics interesting—a characterization of ethics is one of the things metaethics aims to provide and controversy is inherent in that project. For instance, some people think that ethics has a lot to do with religion, whereas others think there is no special connection between the two. Some think that it involves social conventions; others think conventions have nothing to do with basic ethical matters. It is precisely because there isn't an obviously correct, uniquely plausible way of picking out ethics and its nature that metaethics is part of philosophy. The topic itself leaves room for the sort of wonder, disagreement, and puzzlement that characterize philosophical topics. This book will start from some puzzles about ethics and from there go on to examine the range of positions in metaethics people wind up advocating as a result of reacting to them.

Metaethical enquiry arises very naturally out of normative ethical enquiry and isn't necessarily distinct from it. You likely sometimes disagree with friends about the permissibility of some particular course of action. Sometimes such disagreements are pretty easy to resolve, or at least it is pretty easy to figure out what the two of you would need to know to resolve it. Some debates about health care policy may be like that. Both of you think the issue turns on whether the actions in question make people healthier or unhealthier. If you found out the effects of the law on human health and agreed on what they were, your dispute would be resolved.

But other disagreements seem more recalcitrant. It can seem that these disagreements go "all the way down." And these can very quickly lead to higher order reflection on ethics itself, that is to metaethics. For example, suppose you disagree with someone about the permissibility of legally banning gestation crates for pigs. You and your friend agree on many of the empirical facts. You agree that the crates are roughly 2 foot by 7 foot pens that many large hog farm operations use to house pregnant sows. You agree that they allow sows, who can weigh several hundred pounds, little freedom of movement and that the pens are too small for the sows to turn around in. You both know that many sows spend most of their lives in such pens.[3] And neither of you has any doubt that animals feel emotions including pain, discomfort, fear, and unhappiness. Yet one of you thinks it would be wrong to ban such pens as some states have done, whereas the other thinks that morality requires legislation to outlaw the practice. The two of you present each other with arguments, first one way and then the other. You argue that hogs are intelligent animals capable of frustration and depression. Your friend agrees, but argues that our moral obligations don't extend to species far from our own. Furthermore, your friend suggests, it is wrong of the government to interfere with people's choices absent serious concerns about the well-being of other humans. The conversation goes on for quite a while. The discussion makes clear that each of you has both a consistent set of moral commitments and a reasonable grasp of the empirical facts about commercial farming, pigs, the pens at issue, farm regulations, and so on. And yet neither party changes her or his mind.

Situations like this naturally lead many people to wonder about the nature of morality and our beliefs about it. It might seem that you and your friend have a fundamental disagreement about the nature of morality. Perhaps you are talking past one another because each of you has a different idea of what morality is about. You think it involves the treatment of all living things and your friend thinks ethics is silent on the treatment of animals. Perhaps knowing the true nature of moral obligation, rightness, and wrongness would help you settle the matter. If you each agreed on the subject matter perhaps you could also agree on what relevant evidence would settle the issue. Or perhaps there aren't further facts about the subject matter of ethics that would help settle matters. Perhaps instead moral rightness is relative to a moral outlook. Insofar as each of you has a different coherent outlook fitting with your judgement about gestation crates, maybe your judgements are true—that is true relative to the outlook you each accept. Or perhaps instead it isn't that these issues are the sorts of issues about which there can be facts of the matter, even relative facts. Maybe what we take to be moral beliefs are really just complex pro or con attitudes themselves incapable of being assessed for correctness. Maybe our moral words just express emotions in the way that 'boo!' and 'hurrah!' express emotions. Maybe it's just the fact that these attitudes clash that explains why we can seem to disagree despite the absence of facts to settle the disagreement. When faced with fundamental moral disagreement such thoughts are very natural. They ask us to put ethics itself under the microscope and figure out what it is, how it works, and what it is about.

1.2.   The Plan of Approach to the Topic

Comprehensive metaethical theories aim to provide answers to these sort of questions in a consistent and coherent way. This book should provide an overview of the main approaches providing general answers to the question of what ethics is, the reasons at least some people find these approaches plausible, and the difficulties they face. One good way to understand meta-ethical theories is to see them as offering solutions to puzzles that arise in the course of more abstract reflection on the nature of ethics. Accordingly the first several chapters of this book will rehearse some intuitive ideas that lead to philosophical difficulties. In particular the first three chapters introduce three sets of loosely related puzzles that most metaethical theories will address in one way or another. I should emphasize that the puzzles in each chapter are *loosely* related to one another. They are grouped together for expository purposes and each of the three chapters discusses more than one kind of worry. There may be some underlying unity to be found, but then again there may not.

I've talked about the puzzle sets without yet introducing them. I should give a brief summary here—one that the next three chapters fill out. Every well-developed metaethical theory will offer (a) an account of the subject matter of ethics, (b) an explanation of ethical judgement's practical action-guiding role in people's lives, and (c) an account of how we can come to know what it is we do know about ethics and morals. Most such theories will structure their account of the subject matter so as to facilitate the latter two explanatory tasks. As it turns out, each of the tasks—explaining the subject matter, explaining the practicality of morality, and explaining how we come to know what we know—is made more difficult by features that seem to be part and parcel of ethical thinking and ethical reality. (1) It is difficult to be confident of the subject matter of ethics and perhaps even to be confident that it has a subject matter because of widespread moral disagreement about many important ethical issues, as well as a lack of consensus about the nature of the subject. (2) It is hard to account for the practicality that seems distinctive to ethics without taking on board either relativism about ethics or controversial commitments in the philosophy of mind and action. And (3) it is hard to provide an adequate epistemology of moral knowledge given the ways in which empirical evidence seems to under-determine normative theory choice.

In the next three chapters these issues and related issues in the vicinity will be developed in more detail. From there we'll survey the range of meta-ethical positions that result partly or mainly from trying to confront one or more of the puzzles.

1.3. Charting the Territory

Metaethical theories can be taxonomized in various ways and no one typol-ogy is best for all purposes. Still it is useful to have some sense of the terrain before embarking on our tour. Accordingly I offer Chart 1.1 as a very rough guide. It classifies standard metaethical positions by the ways in which they answer important theoretical questions over which metaethical theories divide. Since I'm introducing the chart before we've discussed any particular position in detail, I don't expect readers to fully grasp the details of any view on the chart. The chart can help a reader get a rough idea of the alternatives—an idea that will be further filled in as we study the positions in more detail. Hopefully the chart will also come in handy as we delve deeper into the different positions in subsequent chapters.

The branching tree structure charted offers one way to think of metaeth-ics. At each node there is some question about which metaethicists disagree, and then below it two or more ways to answer. These then yield subdivisions that can be divided yet further. The resulting positions are labeled with standard names, except for a few for which I have had to come up with the labels. We begin with a divide that is usually marked using the terms 'cog-nitivism' and 'noncognitivism.' But what separates the classic variants is actually disagreement about two different questions, one about language and the other about thought. Old-fashioned cognitivists and noncognitivists gave each question the same answer, but recently fictionalists have given a mixed answer. This then generates three branches at the beginning of our taxonomy. From there we get further subdivisions based on yet further questions. I trust the structure will be made relatively clear from the diagram, although the exact nature of each question may remain somewhat unclear until we discuss the variants in subsequent chapters.

Chart 1.1 includes a set of claims I am calling "minimal realism." That's my term and because the position is minimal few writers would call it a genuinely realist position. I have it on the chart because I use the claims definitive of the position to develop various issues in forthcoming chapters. The positions below it on the chart commit to further things beyond the minimal commitments and thus aren't as minimal.

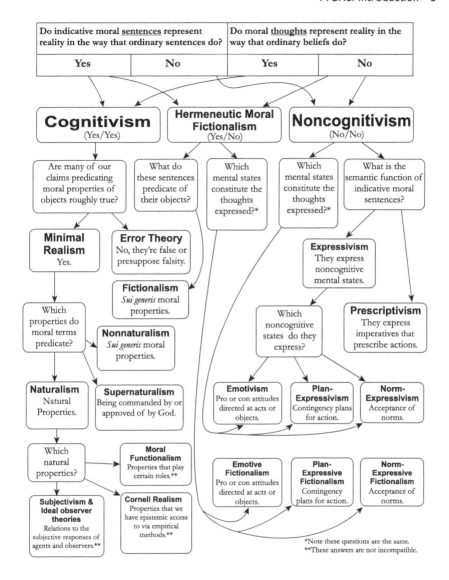

Do indicative moral <u>sentences</u> represent reality in the way that ordinary sentences do?		Do moral <u>thoughts</u> represent reality in the way that ordinary beliefs do?	
Yes	No	Yes	No

Cognitivism
(Yes/Yes)

Hermeneutic Moral Fictionalism
(Yes/No)

Noncognitivism
(No/No)

Are many of our claims predicating moral properties of objects roughly true?

What do these sentences predicate of their objects?

Which mental states constitute the thoughts expressed?*

Which mental states constitute the thoughts expressed?*

What is the semantic function of indicative moral sentences?

Minimal Realism
Yes.

Error Theory
No, they're false or presuppose falsity.

Expressivism
They express noncognitive mental states.

Fictionalism
Sui generis moral properties.

Which properties do moral terms predicate?

Nonnaturalism
Sui generis moral properties.

Which noncognitive states do they express?

Prescriptivism
They express imperatives that prescribe actions.

Naturalism
Natural Properties.

Supernaturalism
Being commanded by or approved of by God.

Emotivism
Pro or con attitudes directed at acts or objects.

Plan-Expressivism
Contingency plans for action.

Norm-Expressivism
Acceptance of norms.

Which natural properties?

Moral Functionalism
Properties that play certain roles.**

Emotive Fictionalism
Pro or con attitudes directed at acts or objects.

Plan-Expressive Fictionalism
Contingency plans for action.

Norm-Expressive Fictionalism
Acceptance of norms.

Subjectivism & Ideal observer theories
Relations to the subjective responses of agents and observers.**

Cornell Realism
Properties that we have epistemic access to via empirical methods.**

*Note these questions are the same.
**These answers are not incompatible.

1.4. Why Do Metaethics?

Readers of previous drafts have suggested I address this question—why should you, or anyone, pursue metaethics even for a semester? Typically when someone asks for a reason to do something they're asking for an answer that shows the enquirer how, from her own point of view, she has a reason to do whatever she's asking about. And typically there are two sorts of answers we can give to this sort of question. (1) The subject matter could be *intrinsically* worth pursuing regardless of how it connected with other aims the enquirer might or should have. Or (2) studying metaethics could be *instrumentally* valuable to you insofar as it serves goals unrelated to the intrinsic worth or interest of the subject. I can provide one rationale for studying metaethics of the instrumental sort, and two related rationales of the first intrinsic sort, answers that may satisfy you or not depending on what you as a potential reader already think and understand about philosophy.

Let's start with the easier but more prosaic answer. Insofar as metaethics involves thinking about issues from just about all the domains of philosophy—metaphysics, philosophy of mind, philosophy of language, moral psychology, and normative ethical theory—and insofar as doing philosophy in general can help you build skills you can use either in other philosophical domains or in other more general intellectual domains, a class in metaethics can help you work on these skills. Since this book is intended for use in more advanced philosophy classes, I take it that you already see the point of learning some of these skills (writing well, thinking through problems systematically, looking for assumptions in one's thought that may be leading one astray, etc.) or you just find philosophy interesting. Or—more pessimistically—you don't think that the earlier mentioned skills will do you any good, but the class meets a requirement and fits your schedule. In either case the class does meet goals you have. So you have instrumental reason to study metaethics.

Perhaps the following two answers, aimed at bringing out the possible intrinsic value of the pursuit, will carry some weight. Some of you reading this book already like philosophy as subject matter—I presume most students in upper-level classes enjoy philosophy to some degree or other. You may not like all of philosophy, but you likely are engaged with one or more of the subfields of philosophy, metaphysics, philosophy of mind, philosophy of language, normative ethics, and so on. And as I've already said metaethics involves all of these. Or to put it in a way I once heard it put, metaethics is aggressively intersubdisciplinary. To do it you have to think about other parts of philosophy. A lot. So at least at some points we will be talking about things near and dear to your heart so long as you have some interest in some aspect of philosophy or other. Whether this counts as showing that metaethics is intrinsically worthwhile will of course depend on whether your prior interest in philosophy reflects facts about the value of philosophy. That is both a normative and a metaethical issue. After all, on some views of the property of being worthwhile it just is the property of fitting into an agent's affective and desiderative psychology in some way. So then, you could consider the rest of the argument of this book part of the answer to the question.

And that brings me to the second reason to think metaethics has intrinsic value. This is the answer I want to put the most weight on, but also the answer that won't really be convincing when it is given. Sometimes the best way to show that something is worth doing is to show people how to do it.

Dancing seems to be like this. Woodworking does as well. I suspect most things of ultimate interest are like this. They reveal their main attractions only after some work. For these kinds of things we may be able to point to instrumental reasons we might have for choosing to do them. And we may be able to point out that others who have tried them found them fulfilling. But to understand the attraction from the inside, to know what's valuable about doing these sorts of activities, you have to do them and maybe you even need to do them tolerably well. If that's right, I can't just tell you that it is worthwhile for its own sake. Or I can tell you, but I don't have much to say if you don't believe me. If you've got a certain kind of curiosity and it bothers you when several things that seem obvious to you can't all be true, you are very likely the sort of person who upon understanding the issues will come to enjoy thinking about how to resolve them.

There may be one other way to go a bit further to answer the "Why do metaethics?" question. That is to foreshadow just a little. The next several chapters rehearse a series of problems and puzzles concerning ethics, as a way to set up most substantive metaethical positions as responses to those problems and puzzles. We've already glanced at a bit of one problem—that it sometimes looks difficult or impossible to settle some ethical controversies, even among highly informed people. Some philosophers think this problem and others like it serious enough that they become moral skeptics. They think that it is literally true that nothing is right and that nothing is wrong. Moral ideas are mistaken and our sense that some actions are wrong and others not is an illusion. To accept these conclusions is to accept error theory.

Many people, myself included, would find it very troubling if error theory were true. But error theory has very sophisticated defenders. We'd be engaging in wishful thinking if we dismissed it without investigating further. If error theory isn't true it would have to be because some metaethical alternative to error theory did a satisfactory job handling all of the issues that make skepticism a live option. Figuring out whether that's so requires engaging with a good swath of metaethics, examining the assumptions that lead to such skepticism and also the ways that various non-skeptical theories come to grips with the skeptical arguments. If you are troubled that all of morality might be a big mistake—that nothing might be right and nothing might be wrong—you have reason to think much more about metaethics.

1.5. Some Cautions and Encouragement

That brings me to a few words of caution about how to read and use this book. I'm starting with metaethical problems because I think philosophy often starts with quandaries that arise when all of what one believes about some matter cannot all be true at once. But that means that one appropriate response to the first several chapters is to be unsure what to think. This can be disconcerting if you are used to having your bearings in a subject. So I want to advise you not to worry too much about it. When we get to the various more developed theoretical responses to the domain, the particular metaethical theories we will survey, you will be exploring a range of possible responses to the issues that at first lead to appropriate confusion. By getting a sense of the ways previous thinkers have resolved their uncertainties about these issues you'll wind up with a better sense of the underlying motivations that lead to the worries and a better sense of how to respond to them. You might even want to go back to the puzzle chapters and get more out of them after you are familiar with some of the more systematic responses outlined in the chapters covering the major theoretical alternatives in metaethics. My main point here is just to say that being confused is part of doing philosophy. Don't let it discourage you. Nothing is obvious.

I also have a more prosaic caution. I myself learned to write philosophy by modeling my writing on what I read. I should caution you that pedagogical writing is somewhat lighter on footnoting than most professional writing is and should be. Because this is a textbook and I am trying to streamline the prose, my citation practices are not good models for your own writing in philosophy. This book is an attempt to convey a lot of thought by a lot of people who themselves are reacting to a lot of thought by still other people. If there were notes for every intellectual debt there would be one for every paragraph. I do use parenthetical notes for many important sources and provide suggestions for further reading at the end of each chapter, and the bibliography is rather comprehensive.

Notes

1 Throughout this book I will use 'ethics' and 'morality' to mean the same thing. Different authors in the literature might favor one or the other term, but there is no widely recognized difference between them on which all agree.

2 Hence the use of the term in blogs as a tag for threads that take the blog as its own subject matter.

3 Stephanie Strom, "McDonald's Set to Phase Out Suppliers' Use of Sow Crates," *New York Times* (February 14, 2012), p. B2.

2 A Subject Matter for Ethics?

A natural place to start in any philosophical domain is with a characterization of what it's about: an account of the subject matter. Insofar as thinking about metaethics is thinking about ethics, it would be natural to want an explanation of the subject matter or ethics. But that is itself a controversial metaethical question. So instead of answering it in a forthright way, I will try to explain why it is difficult to provide an account of the sort we might expect for any domain that genuinely has a subject matter. The difficulties have led some theorists to deny that ethics is a genuine subject, while it has led others to propose various divergent and incompatible accounts of the subject matter. This chapter and the two that follow are all part of that explanation. This chapter sets out what it would be to provide an account of the subject matter that treats ethics as similar to other domains with a genuine subject matter to "be about." And it endeavors to show how several different phenomena related to disagreement and to lack of agreement cause trouble for providing such a story. On the one hand we have disagreement, where one person affirms what another denies. The amount of ethical disagreement among intelligent people grounds an argument for doubting that they are talking about a common topic. At a different level, that people can rationally doubt any informative characterization of the nature of that topic provides further reason to wonder whether they all speak of the same reality. And then we notice that the possibility of genuine disagreement seems to require us to address common topics about which we disagree. If so an otherwise plausible relativism also seems to be ruled out by the fact of disagreement of the first sort.

I'll begin the explanation by abstractly sketching one simple way of providing an account of ethical subject matter, one that could be filled out in a variety of more particular ways. The sketch treats moral thought and talk as essentially continuous with thought and language in other domains that we take to have a real subject matter about which we know something. It is meant to be a kind of default approach for any representational subject matter. I call the approach "minimal realism" to signify that the approach is meant to be metaphysically unambitious and only to build in assumptions needed to treat moral language as representational in the same way that talk of redness and roundness is representational. As it turns out, the suggestion that we could be even minimally realist about ethical language runs into difficulties when we confront the diversity of views about ethics at every level, even among those who seem to be perfectly capable of thinking about moral matters. We often have deep and substantive disagreement about which things are good, bad, right, wrong, virtuous, vicious, and so on. At a more abstract level even the most thoughtful moralists have trouble offering an account of what they are saying in an informative way. And if they do manage to offer a plausible informative account some other equally thoughtful moralist can reasonably doubt it. You might think that this would cause us to lose confidence that we are talking about any one thing. And yet we regularly use moral terminology to dispute all sorts of issues, confident that we are not talking past one another.

These different phenomena each complicate matters for anyone who hoped to offer even a minimally realist account of what rightness or goodness is, and of what we are doing when we call something "right" or "good." And that is where the interest in our otherwise boring initial sketch comes in. Minimal realism about morality has two things going for it: (1) The resulting view allows us to unify our understanding of language and thought to explain how each relate to their subject matter in similar ways. And (2) the same features that make minimal realism attractive for ordinary descriptive domains show up in the moral domain and make an extension to morality very attractive. Sketching the minimally realist view allows me to show how the attempt to accommodate the disagreement and lack of agreement we find in ethics while retaining at least a minimal commitment to such realism generates a number of metaethical positions. It also allows me to show how other positions are generated by rejecting the minimally realist picture in the face of difficulties dealing with these issues. Raising these issues in this chapter will thus allow subsequent chapters to present diverse metaethical positions as reactions to these problems, though reactions of very different sorts.

2.1. A Simple Minimally Realist View

Suppose you were to be asked to give an account of our use of some ordinary predicate, such as 'red,' 'round,' or 'smart' as it is used in simple predications but also in more complex constructions such as conditionals and belief reports. And suppose that you were asked as part of offering this account to explain when it was appropriate to use these terms in those ways, and what people were communicating when they used the terms. One way to go about answering this request would be to give an explanation of the meaning of the target term, a characterization of the truth conditions and contents of the sentences containing the target term, and an account of the states of mind expressed by simple and complex uses of the target predicates.

Let's start with *semantics*[1]—an account of what the terms mean. It is plausible that the meanings of the terms partly determine what speakers are able to communicate with them. And since speakers are able to understand new sentences in which terms they understand occur, it is also plausible to think that they contribute a constant meaning to each of the sentences of which they form a part. Since the target terms are predicates it would be very natural to start with the suggestion that each one stands for a property and that it contributes that property to the meaning of the sentences in which it occurs. 'Red' stands for the property of redness, 'round' for 'roundness,' and 'smart' for smartness. This wouldn't yet be very helpful to tell someone who did not already know the terms 'redness,' 'roundness,' and 'smartness,' but we could remedy that by giving them a more specific sense of which properties we were talking about. We might explain that red is a color and point to relevant samples until our audience had an idea of which property we had in mind. We might tell them round is a shape and then point to round shapes, or we might give them a definition in geometric terms. And we might explain what we take smartness to be, possibly by using some examples. Or we might try characterizing the property in a complex definition. In each of these ways we would hope to pass on our understanding of the target terms as standing for some property or other.

We could then go on to explain the truth conditions of sentences containing each term by explaining that a simple indicative sentence such as 'the ball is red' is true when the subject of the sentence has the property we just specified. The sentence will be true when the facts are as the sentence represents them to be—in this case when the ball is in fact red. And similarly for our other target terms 'round' and 'smart.' We could extend the story to more complex sentences by explaining that sentences such as 'The brick is round and the brick red' is true when the brick that is the subject of the sentence is both round and red. 'The brick is round or the brick is red' will similarly be true when the brick is either round or red. Actually, we probably would not need to give our audience these explanations, provided they already understood what 'and' and 'or' mean. But if we did give the explanation it would be correct. Conditional sentences containing the terms, such as 'If the ball is red then Sally is smart,' would be a little more difficult, but the difficulty would come from the 'If . . . then' construction and not from the predicates in those sentences. Our views about how 'if . . . then' works will largely determine what we say when one or another of the simpler sentences is part of such a compound sentence. For example, if you think the conditional in question is a material conditional, you'll think the sentence is true whenever the ball is not red or Sally is smart. It is thus very natural to think of all of the indicative sentences of the sorts so far discussed as representing that the world is a certain way and to think of their contents as the propositions they assert to be true. 'The ball is red' is true just in case the *proposition* that the ball is red is true or obtains. And that proposition—the proposition that the ball is red—will be the *content* of the sentence. (If propositions talk is opaque to you, don't worry too much about it. The important thing here is to grasp the big picture—that we can explicate the contents of simple and complex sentences containing predicates in a systematic way if we accept the idea that predicates represent properties that are predicated of subjects.)

Suppose now that we want to extend our account further to extend to sentences containing "that" clauses, such as the following:

> Amanda *believes* that the ball is round.
> Amanda *doubts* that the ball is round.
> Tyrone *wishes* that the ball was new.
> Gunther *regrets* that the ball is flat.

The most straightforward extension of the story about simple indicative sentences to attitude reports using "that" clauses would say that people can stand in various mental states that relate them to propositions that are their content and that these sentences serve to tell us about those states. They do this by telling us both the general kind of mental state the person is in and the proposition that it is directed toward as the state's content. On this way of thinking, the belief that the ball is round has the same content as the sentence, "the ball is round." And when someone uses that sentence in an assertion we might go on to say that the use of the sentence expresses a belief with that content. Thus, 'Amanda believes that the ball is round' attributes to Amanda a belief with the content that the ball is round. That belief is true just in case the proposition that the ball is round is true, just as the sentence 'The ball is round' is true just in case the proposition that the ball is round is true. Both the sentence and the belief represent the ball as round. And if that proposition is true it is a *fact* that the ball is round. More generally, the content of an arbitrary belief that P represents P as true, as one of the facts about how things are. An indicative sentence has the same content as the belief it expresses, so an indicative sentence 'P' would have the content P. And beliefs of the form 'so and so believes P' attribute a belief with the content P to the person under discussion.

The other attitude reports employing "that" clauses get treated in a parallel way. Just as 'Amanda believes that the ball is round' is true just in case Amanda stands in the believing relation to the proposition that the ball is round, 'Amanda doubts that the ball is round' is true just in case she doubts that proposition. And similarly for wishing, regretting, and other propositional attitudes.

Finally there are certain other sentences employing "that" clauses that we'd like to bring into the overall picture:

> It is possible that the ball is defective.
> It is likely that the ball is defective.
> It is certain that the ball is defective.

It is a fact that the ball is defective.
It is false that the ball is defective.

These can be folded into the account so far if we think of them as saying something about the proposition picked out by the "that" clause. The first sentence says that the proposition that the ball is defective could be true. The second says that it is likely. The third says that it is certain. The fourth says that it is true, whereas the fifth says that it is false.

The account on offer would have to be extended beyond indicative sentences, to include questions, commands, and so on. We would want to explain how questions relate to the propositions that might be their answers, and perhaps bring in a theory of mood as a sort of force indicator. 'Is the ball red?' highlights the same content or proposition that 'The ball is red' asserts, but asks whether it is the case in virtue of a difference in mood. And so on.

Let's name views of this sort about a given predicate *minimal realism* about that predicate. To summarize, minimal realism about an arbitrary predicate 'P' holds roughly that:

1. 'P' represents a property (for convenience I will use *P* to represent this property here).
2. The sentence 'X is P' represents X as having the property *P*.
3. The content of 'X is P' is that X is *P*. And this content is the proposition that X is *P*.
4. An assertion of 'X is P' expresses the belief that X is *P*.
5. The belief that X is *P* represents things to be just the way the sentence 'X is P' represents them to be; they both represent X as having the property *P* and they both represent the proposition that X is *P* as true.
6. The belief that X is *P*, the sentence 'X is P,' and the proposition that X is *P* are true when X in fact has the property *P*.
7. A sentence of the form 'B believes that X is P' attributes the attitude of believing that X is *P* to B.
8. At least some indicative sentences of the form 'X is P' do in fact represent the world correctly and these sentences turn out to be true in virtue of representing things correctly.

The last provision is necessary to capture the realist thought that some things really have the properties spoken of by our target predicates.

Some of these claims could be omitted without straying too far from the basic minimally realist view—for example some philosophers think we don't need to talk about propositions as the contents of thought and talk. But I have included the preceding claims because they are typically endorsed as a package. It's not important to remember all of the details. The important takeaway idea is just that the package is one concrete way of filling out the idea that predicates represent properties and that it allows us to paint a systematic and somewhat unified picture of thought and language and their commonalities.

The minimal realism of interest for our purposes is minimal realism about morality and moral predicates. Minimal realism about morality treats moral predicates such as 'right,' 'wrong,' 'good' and 'bad,' in the way that the preceding sketch treated 'round,' 'red,' 'flat,' 'new,' and 'defective.' It treats the terms as labels for real properties that can be had by certain sorts of objects. And it treats these properties as represented in (or constituents of) the contents of moral thought and talk naturally expressed with moral predicates. Minimal realism about morality is *realist* insofar as it involves the following claims: (a) That indicative moral sentences represent the world to be some way or other (in brief, that they are representational). That (b) moral *beliefs* are also representational. That (c) there are *properties* corresponding to the predicates used in making these moral claims that serve as the part of the contents of the claims. And (d) that at least some of the ethical claims made are true or correct—that things sometimes are as ethical thoughts or sentences represent them to be. The first two claims are constitutive of *cognitivism*[2] and the third is an elaboration of that kind of view. The fourth asserts what error theorists deny—that some of our moral judgements correspond to reality. Commitment to these four theses merits the label *realism* insofar as it says there really are ways that things might be morally speaking and that our thoughts and sentences do sometimes correctly represent that reality.

Minimal realism about morality is minimal insofar as it doesn't require more than this. For example, minimal realism doesn't commit to any heavy-duty metaphysical claims about the nature of the properties represented. It doesn't say that they must be natural properties, or that they must be *nonsubjective* or *response-independent* properties.[3] These claims can consistently be added to the core minimal realist claims to generate a more robust form of realism. Many self-described realists about morality will want to do just that. They may commit to more specific claims about the properties in question, for example that they are objective, response independent, incompatible with moral relativism, or whatever. Given the stipulated characterization of minimal realism, these added claims will make the resulting realism nonminimal. These less than minimal realist views are compatible with minimal realism but they go beyond it.

Some robust realists may refuse to call views without those additional commitments realist at all. For example, many metaethicists won't call relativism a realist view, despite the fact that most relativists can and do accept the main claims of minimal realism. There may be a point to such insistence in many contexts. For purposes of illustrating some of the difficulties with finding a subject matter for ethical thought and talk we don't need to go that far. The main puzzles arise whether we take on board the further commitments or not. So for now I'll leave those further claims out of the discussion and out of the minimally realist package. We'll be looking at them soon enough in the chapters that examine various positions in more detail.

Minimal realism about morality is a fairly natural view. The same features that made realism plausible for 'red' and 'round' recur when we talk and think about goodness, badness, rightness, wrongness, permissibility, and so on. Simple moral sentences such as 'Polly is good' or 'Stealing is wrong' seem similar in content to others such as 'Sally is smart.' They contain a noun and a verb phrase of the form 'is _____,' where the blank is filled in with an adjective. On their face such sentences predicate a property of their subject, the property picked out by the adjective. 'Sally is smart' says of Sally that she is smart, where that entails that she has the property of being smart. 'Polly is good' seems analogously to say of Polly that she has the property of being good. And 'Stealing is wrong' seems to say of an act-type (stealing) or perhaps a class of actions (those that involve stealing) that they have a property, the property of wrongness. These sentences are true when their subjects are as the sentences say they are and false when they're not.

People who believe moral claims can disagree with one another just as people can disagree over nonmoral claims. Someone who thinks Polly is not good disagrees with the person who thinks that she is good, just as a person who thinks Sally is not smart disagrees with those who know that she is. Whether our disagreement is moral or not we can express that disagreement by labeling conflicting claims 'false,' just as we can express agreement using 'true.' Minimal realism about morality takes these parallels between simple ethical or moral sentences and simple predications of other sorts rather seriously. It explains the parallels as due to a common representational function: All indicative sentences are about something; they all say something about their subject; and they are true or false depending on whether their subjects are as the sentences say they are.

There are further possible parallels between ethical judgements and others. Someone can think or believe that Sally is smart without uttering the sentence and without even having the sentence in mind. Some believers don't speak English. And yet that's what they believe as evidenced by actions such as going to Sally for advice. Here is a simple story about how this might work. Like language, thought can be about things and represent its subject as having properties. Beliefs are such representational states of mind. A belief will be true if things are as the belief represents them to be. A belief is false if it misrepresents the world. The belief that Sally is smart represents the world to be the way that the sentence 'Sally is smart' represents it to be. But a person can have that belief by thinking it in German, perhaps even by using the words "Sally ist klug" in thought. Or she can think it some other way. The thoughts and the sentences have the same content because what they require of the world in order to be correct or true is the very same thing—that Sally is smart. Our simple minimally realist theory generalizes these ideas to moral discourse and thought. For either the sentence, 'Sally is good,' or the thought that she's good, to be true Sally must be as they represent her to be—namely good. And so on for other moral predicates.

So minimal realism is a pretty natural view to accept for most simple moral or normative predicates.[4] Suppose we accept it on that basis; what would it then be to give a relatively complete account of the subject matter of ethics? We might begin by offering an account of the meanings of our central moral terms taken one at a time. In other words we would try to produce a semantic theory for moral terms that enables us to see what our sentences and judgements enable us to say about the world. On the realist picture we are provisionally working with we would try to assign properties to the central moral predicates such as 'right,' 'wrong,' 'good,' 'bad,' and so on. Most straightforwardly we'd assign rightness to 'right,' wrongness to 'wrong,' goodness to 'good,' and so on. These properties would then be constituents of the meanings of the sentences that employ the target terms and constituents of the contents of thought about moral matters. We would also need to offer an account of *how* these predicates come to stand for these properties—an account of what has to be the case for a particular predicate to represent a particular property. These issues are *metasemantic* (that means they are about how the terms get their semantics/meanings) and often among the most interesting features of metaethical theorizing about moral semantics. We'll pay special attention to metasemantics in chapters 11 and 12.

But moral semantics is not the whole of metaethics, at least not on this minimally realist conception. Metaethics also concerns the *nature* of the properties predicated by moral judgements. Just knowing which predicates pick out which properties doesn't yet tell us very much about that nature. So metaethics will engage the metaphysics of ethics—attempting to discern the real nature of the properties in question. We'll want to know what an action would have to be like to be wrong, or what a person would have to be like to be good or virtuous. If we are lucky we might find a characterization of rightness or goodness that might enable us to recognize instances of these properties when we encounter them. Or if we're not so lucky, we'll at least want an explanation of why no such account can be given. We'll also want to know which moral properties are relational properties and which are not. These questions go well beyond moral semantics.

We may also want something further yet. We may want to understand why we think of the judgements in question as moral or ethical judgements. This is not so much a question about the individual moral judgements taken one by one as it is about the bunch together. Why is it natural to treat these properties (rightness, goodness, virtue) as a group, that is to treat them all as paradigm instances of moral properties? Here a realist might give a more abstract characterization of the subject matter of ethics in general. The aim would be to explain how the properties are similar to one another and to answer why the bunch of them together enable us to make judgements about some common domain. It might identify certain ethical properties as explanatorily basic and then explain how other ethical properties are built up out of these.

Each of these tasks is a reasonable project if one accepts the minimally realist picture. But not every metaethicist is even minimally a realist. There are various reasons for this. Some of these will derive from the contestability of ethical matters, both at the substantive normative level and at a higher level on which competent moral thinkers seem capable of doubting every nontrivial characterization of our subject. We'll survey some of the motivating concerns in what follows.

2.2. Disagreement According to Minimal Realism

Morality, like many other topics, can be something over which we disagree. If I say and believe that Fred's callous disregard of his daughter's feelings is wrong and you say and believe it is not wrong, we disagree. And disagreement requires more than a mere difference of opinion or state of mind. If I think raptors are more common than they used to be and you're not sure about that we don't yet have a disagreement. Nor do we have one when I think raptors are fast and you think they are graceful. The same distinction can be made about moral beliefs and sentences. If I say Marvel's pride in her daughter's work is virtuous, and you say that you aren't sure, we don't share the same state of mind, but we don't thereby disagree. Nor must you disagree with me if you go on to say that Marvel's pride is hard to maintain, or that it isn't unnatural. Not every difference in belief, moral or otherwise, is a disagreement.

A minimally realist model will have a story to tell about what separates mere difference of opinion from genuine disagreement of the more robust sort. In order to be disagreeing when we make simple judgements of this sort we must both be talking about the same thing and I have to believe something about it that you deny. With simple predicative statements of the form 'such-and-such is thus-and-so,' and 'such-and-such is not thus-and-so,' the two sentences disagree if they are about the same thing and the property predicated is the same. The 'such-and-such' clause must be about the same thing and the 'thus-and-so' clause must pick out the same property. That they involve the same words is not sufficient. If I say it is raining and you say it is not raining we'll disagree only if we are talking about the same place. If we're on the phone and I'm in Seattle and you are in Phoenix there need be no disagreement at all. If I aim to disagree with you about the nature of bank deposits I won't succeed if one of us is talking about financial matter and the other about streamside minerals. If I want to deny what you assert when you say Hal is funny, I won't really be doing so if you claim only that he's odd and I claim only that he is not amusing.

That minimal realism in a domain can offer this sort of explanation of a distinction we already recognize is a point in its favor. So it counts in favor of minimal realism about ethics that we recognize the distinction between *difference* and *disagreement* in ethics as well as in other domains. But it is a commitment of the explanation that moral terms picked out the same property in the mouths of disputants. So a minimally realist position will be in trouble if it can't deliver that result. And it will have the same difficulty if the thought that something is right has one content—that is attributes one property—when I think it, but has a different content involving a different property when you do. Such thoughts would be like the judgement that Hal is funny in our earlier example.

2.3.   Disruptive Disagreement and Disruptive Doubt

Widespread difference and disagreement over moral matters can upset our minimal realist picture if it makes it difficult to assign common properties to moral predicates. There are various ways this might happen. The fact of actual widespread disagreement can be used to call into question the very idea that there is something we are all talking about when we make ethical judgements. This could be true either if there is nothing we're talking about, or if different people in fact are talking about different things. The first alternative is a kind of *error theory*—moral talk purports to be about a common subject matter but there is nothing for it to be about. The second is a version of *relativism*—moral talk is about different properties in different people's mouths. Consider, for example, what would happen if 'right' in a speaker's mouth designated the property of fitting with that particular speaker's moral commitments. Distinct speakers would then use the terms to pick out distinct properties. A single action can fit with my moral commitments and not fit with yours. And so it might be right relative to me and not right relative to you.

Another phenomenon, one that concerns doubt rather than disagreement, can also destabilize our confidence that our common moral terms pick out the same thing. Take any informative characterization of the properties we predicate when we make a moral judgement.

Both competent thinkers of thoughts employing those predicates and competent users of the relevant moral terms can doubt the correctness of that informative characterization. One person thinks ethics is concerned with the promotion of human well-being. Another thinks it has to do with following God's commands. Yet another thinks it is grounded in conventional social norms. There seems to be no informative characterization of the general subject matter of ethics that must be shared by all competent moral thinkers. You might think that there must be some understanding of the meaning of a term shared by competent speakers who use a term univocally. If so, such disagreement delivers grounds to doubt that we all use moral terms to address a common topic.

Both of these lines of argument provide some motivation for relativism, since relativism is a natural response to certain kinds of differences in meaning. If a predicate 'Z' in my mouth predicates a certain relation to me while the same predicate in yours predicates that relation to you, my assertions and your denials that lying is **Z** can both be true. Lying could be related to me in the way that '**Z**' indicates but not related to you in the '**Z**' way. So moral disagreement would not be a ground for thinking that either party was or both parties were failing to track reality. 'Entertaining' may be a predicate like this—golf may be entertaining for you even though it thoroughly bores me. A moral relativist might explain my doubting your characterization of the subject matter of ethics as reflecting the fact that moral terms in my mouth predicate a different property of their targets than the same terms in your mouth. Suppose, for example, that the property designated is the property of comporting with the speaker's moral commitments. Then two speakers could each affirm sentences the other denies and yet speak truly. Because minimal realism itself takes no stand on relativism, a minimal realist might then think that relativism is the best reaction to these worries.

However, unfortunately for relativism, disagreement also raises a problem for relativism. We just noted that it was a point in favor of minimal realism that it could make a distinction between real disagreement and mere differences of opinion. Minimal realism suggests that we have genuine disagreement only when disputing parties use their moral terms to affirm and deny the presence of the same property. Subjects deploying predicates to pick out *different* properties will not so easily disagree when they deny what their opponents affirm. If we think that most moral disputes are instances of genuine disagreement that counts against a relativist analysis of their moral vocabulary. Each of these three ideas corresponds to an important line of argument propounded by influential metaethical theorists. Sections 2.4–2.6 in this chapter fill out those arguments.

2.4. Mackie's Argument From Disagreement

John Mackie (1977, chapter 1, §8) famously argued for moral error theory—roughly the theory that holds that all moral judgements are false.[5] One of his main arguments is known as the *argument from disagreement*. It is a sophisticated development of a commonsense line of thought about ethics.

People disagree about all sorts of things, moral and nonmoral. But from a certain perspective it can seem that ethics and morals are more deeply controversial than other matters. For almost any substantial moral claim it seems we can find some person, now living or dead, who would call it into question and disagree with it. Most historical events we regard as atrocities were perpetrated by people who thought their actions were right and proper. Matters that earlier generations regarded as of crucial importance strike us as trivial. Various anthropologists have pointed to cultures in diverse places that deny ethical claims we think stand at the center of morality. For example:

> Courtesy, modesty, good manners, conformity to definite ethical standards are universal, but what constitutes courtesy, modesty, good

> manners, and ethical standards is not universal. It is instructive to know that standards differ in the most unexpected ways. (F. Boaz in preface to Mead, 1954)

Even within our own present culture we have seen political conflicts generated by disagreements over sexual morality, war, civil rights, and torture. What one side takes to be beyond the pale another takes to be required. And these are no mere passing disputes. People have devoted their lives to one side or the other. People have died and waged wars over these issues. They have sacrificed their lives refusing to give up beliefs that others took as deeply mistaken. These all seem to be disputes over which things are right and wrong, which are obligatory, permitted, and forbidden.

People who think a lot about the nature of ethics often disagree in a further way. They disagree not simply about which things are right or wrong, but also about what it amounts to for something to be right or wrong. That is they disagree about the metaphysics of ethics. And that is to disagree about metaethics. If you ask several people for an account of the subject matter of morality you should be prepared for different answers about its nature. Where I live several respondents will suggest a version of divine command theory—the property rightness just is the property of being what is commanded by God. Yet others will say that such a theory just cannot be correct, for it would entail the rightness of heinous acts in circumstances where God or gods had certain desires. The disagreement here seems very deep in that it concerns not only which things are right, but also the nature of rightness itself.

If this sketch is not overdrawn, there may be no belief about ethics or morality that a person has to accept in order to have views about ethics or morality. Somehow knowing enough about ethics to have ethical opinions is consistent with being as wrong as you like about any particular ethical claim and perhaps about most of them. It is also consistent with being wrong about any particular more abstract metaethical claim. To give these ideas a name, call them the no-common-ground hypothesis. At its most general it is the thought that there is no common ground at any level about morality, not concerning which things are right, what makes them right, nor concerning what it is to be right.

As I said, Mackie's argument is a sophisticated development of this line of thought into a skeptical worry about ethics in general. The sophistication lies in casting the argument as an inference to the best explanation. Various epistemologists and philosophers of science have championed such inferences as a method for justifying the choice of theories based on evidence of various sorts. It combines two simple ideas. First, we are justified in believing a theory if it best explains some range of phenomena for which we have evidence. Second, whether a theory best explains some phenomenon depends both on how well it explains that phenomenon, but also on how badly rival theories do at the same task. Putting these ideas together and elaborating we get the following. We are often faced with some range of phenomena that seem to require an explanation. From there we might construct more or less complex theories that might explain the phenomena in need of an explanation. These competing explanations will differ from one another in various ways. Some will be more complex; others simple. Some will explain a wider range of phenomena than others. Some will more closely predict phenomena that we can test. And so on. Some explanations can be better than others in virtue of these differences, even when they all explain the thing we want to explain.

Theories can be better in one way, but not better in all ways. One theory might explain more than another, but also predict data that isn't forthcoming. Another theory may be simpler than another but not fit as well with other facts we take ourselves to know. If a single theory is better in enough relevant ways it might be the best theory overall. And if it is best overall it might be reasonable to take it seriously and perhaps even believe it. That is what advocates of *inference to the best explanation* think. If the best theory posits some entity, the story goes, we are justified if we believe in that entity on that basis. Similarly, if the best explanation requires some fact, we are justified in believing in that fact. And so on. Some fans of inference to the best explanation think that all justified beliefs involve a process like this.

Mackie suggests that the fact of widespread moral disagreement cries out for explanation. And he thinks there are two general sorts of explanation one can give. If one is a realist one will think that disagreement stems from errors introduced by our differential access to a common subject matter. Anti-realists, on the other hand, can offer explanations of disagreement that involve no commitment to a common subject matter at all. Rather, their argument might go, we can explain disagreement as falling out of the practical import of morality. Insofar as a person prefers to live in a particular way, that might be reason for that person to wish that morality favored that way of living. For then they could live as they liked without doing anything that warrants criticism or censure. We already notice that people diverge widely in the ways they would like to live. And we know from other domains that people often wind up believing what they hope to be true, not through conscious choice but through less voluntary psychological mechanisms. There is thus good reason to think that similar mechanisms might be at work in explaining moral diversity. Disagreement about morality then can be explained as a version of wishful thinking, with each person believing that morality favors the ways of living that she herself prefers.

Having canvassed the two candidate explanations, Mackie thinks we can see that the second is better. It doesn't require that we postulate anything radically new—we already know about wishful thinking and that people favor different ways of life. Our belief in these is independent of our moral commitments, and we would believe in wishful thinking and the diversity of people's lifestyle preferences even if they did not explain moral disagreement. By contrast the realist explanation requires us to postulate genuine moral properties that we respond to, and fallible epistemic mechanisms to guide us in our responses to those properties. Independent of our moral commitments we don't have any reason to think there are such partially reliable mechanisms. Thus, Mackie suggests, the former explanation is better than the latter. We have no need to posit a common subject matter about which we disagree.

The argument then has something like the following form:

a.   There is widespread moral disagreement between communities who make moral judgements. (Premise)
b.   This disagreement might be explained by differential access to a common moral reality. (Premise)
c.   This disagreement might instead be explained by people approving of their own actual ways of life due to wishful thinking. (Premise)
d.   The latter explanation is better than the former because it doesn't require postulating anything over and above what we already accept. (Premise, supported by further argument)
e.   There are no other plausible explanations for the disagreement.

From these premises an inference to the best explanation might then justify:

(Conclusion) Therefore, we should accept the explanation offered by (c) rather than that offered by (b).

As it stands the challenge is schematic. Neither the wishful thinking explanation nor the realist alternative is worked out in much detail. To carry the day each side will have to fill in their explanatory stories, and fill them in consistently with what we already know. Realists who wish to resist Mackie's challenge will want to fill in detail that shows how our epistemic abilities could give us fallible access to some realm of moral facts. They will want to explain how some judgements turn out to be closer to the truth than others because of the kind of access we have. This will require investigations into moral epistemology and moral psychology. We will need to know something about how people in fact come to make moral judgements and we will have to examine whether those ways of judging could give us more or less reliable access to some domain, a domain that is plausibly of concern when we engage in ethical thinking. By the same token, devotees of Mackie's challenge will have to engage these more detailed accounts to challenge their adequacy. And they'll also want to delve into moral psychology to explain why it matters to people whether morality favors their favorite ways of life.

Still, we got the challenge off the ground without too many controversial assumptions about the nature of morality. And that makes it a fairly powerful challenge. Mackie does assume that morality has a practical upshot that most people care about. But this argument doesn't presuppose any particular account of the meanings of moral terms or the nature of the properties that the realist explanation makes use of.[6] As a result the argument has some force against a wide range of minimally realist positions that share very little beyond a commitment to the representational nature of ethical thought and language and the claim that sometimes we get ethical matters right.

2.4.1. Convergence

You might not be so troubled by actual disagreement if you thought that there were rational methods for resolving the disagreements and that over time existing disagreements would be resolved by those methods. Our arrival at a verdict regarding previously controversial moral claims via these rational methods might vindicate the thought that we were on to something all along, even if at first we have only a cloudy view of what that something is. Realists who find this idea plausible can argue that we should be optimistic that many of the issues we disagree about can be rationally resolved through the appropriate methods. Just as Mackie's putative best explanation needs filling out, so will this realist rival. A convincing version of this line of argument will have to tell us a good bit about what these methods are, and also about why these methods give us epistemic access to the ethical subject matter, whatever it is. These desiderata will likely put constraints on the suggested account of the subject matter. The subject will have to be one about which the methods in question could tell us something.

This line of resistance to the argument from disagreement puts a lot of weight on epistemic issues of the sort we approach again as the main focus of chapter 3.

2.5. The Open Question Argument

There's another well-known argument that starts with a certain kind of diversity of thought and that can end with doubts about a common ethical subject matter. This is G. E. Moore's *Open Question Argument* (hereafter sometimes abbreviated the OQA; Moore, 1903, chapter 1, §13). While Moore himself used it only to argue against any substantial analysis of ethical properties, many have taken it to undermine the idea that ethics aims to represent reality at all. It doesn't do that all by itself, however, because the upshot of Moore's argument is not that moral predicates don't pick out properties—just that they don't pick out properties of a certain sort. Furthermore, the diversity of thought Moore needs—the possibility that we can doubt all substantial characterizations of ethical properties—isn't disagreement in a strong sense even if it is a difference of opinion. So there may be something a bit forced in discussing it together with robust disagreement as a source of trouble for minimal realism. I am in fact associating two different sorts of non-agreement with one another partly for expository purposes.

Still, both phenomena do create difficulties for generating an account of the subject matter of ethics. I've just laid out one way that full-blooded disagreement can cause such trouble. The argument that the Open Question Argument too generates difficulties is more complex, and the steps are all controversial. The Open Question Argument is supposed to rule out any substantial characterization of the properties putatively predicated by moral discourse. If that's right it leaves only Moore's own response to the argument—that moral predicates pick out irreducibly moral properties—as an option for minimal realists. The irreducible nature of the properties in question would make it more difficult to be confident that we are all in fact talking about the same thing. And yet the phenomenon of genuine disagreement, coupled with the minimal realist picture of what such disagreement must be, doesn't sit well with relativism about the subject matter. Thus the doubts exploited by the OQA can combine with the disagreement we have already noted to cause even more trouble than each could by itself.[7] In any case, the Open Question Argument is of interest on its own terms. It is probably the most widely deployed argument in metaethics over the course of many, many years. And, even those who doubt its conclusion often find it hard to explain exactly how it goes wrong. So let's look at what it is and how it works.

Moore is well known to have denied that the most fundamental moral property, goodness as he thought, could be defined in natural or supernatural terms. In *Principia Ethica* Moore wrote:

> The hypothesis that disagreement about the meaning of good is disagreement with regard to the correct analysis of a given whole, may be most plainly seen to be incorrect by consideration of the fact that, whatever definition may be offered, it may always, be asked, with significance, of the complex so defined, whether it is itself good. To take, for instance, one of the more plausible, because one of the more complicated of such proposed definitions, it may easily be thought, at first sight, that to be good may mean to be that which we desire to desire. Thus if we apply this definition to a particular instance and say "When we think that A is good, we are thinking that A is one of the things which we desire to desire," our proposition may seem quite plausible. But, if we carry the investigation further, and ask ourselves "Is it good to desire to desire A?" it is apparent, on a little reflection, that this question is itself as intelligible, as the original question, "Is A good?"—that we are, in fact, now asking for exactly the same information about the desire to desire A, for which we formerly asked with regard to A itself. But it is also apparent that the meaning of this second question cannot be correctly analyzed into "Is the desire to desire A one of the things which we desire to desire?": we have not before our minds anything so complicated as the question "Do we desire to desire to desire to desire A?" Moreover any one can easily convince himself by inspection that the predicate of

this proposition—"good"—is positively different from notion of "desiring to desire" which enters into its subject: "That we should desire to desire A is good" is not merely equivalent to "That A should be good is good." It may indeed be true that what we desire to desire is always good; perhaps, even the converse may be true: but it is very doubtful whether this is the case, and the mere fact that we understand very well what is meant by doubting it, shews clearly that we have two different notions before our mind. (1903, §13)

This passage contains the Open Question Argument. It can be read in many different ways, and surrounding pages suggest more than one way to understand the argument. I'm going to focus on two relatively powerful reconstructions of the OQA. They each take some particular proposal about the nature of goodness and argue against it. But in each case the point is supposed to be general and independent of the particular proposals under discussion. That's because the arguments turn on nothing particular to the proposed specifications of goodness. Moore intended his readers to think of each proposal as an instance of a type all of which were vulnerable to the same objection, and that is also how my reconstructions of his argument are supposed to be viewed.

2.5.1. A First Reconstruction of the OQA

Here's a first way to understand the argument. Consider the proposal that the property of goodness is the property of being what we desire to desire. Moore suggests that the following line of argument should be sufficient to rule this proposal out:[8]

1. We can meaningfully ask, "Is that which we desire to desire good?" (Premise)
2. We could not meaningfully ask, "Is what we desire to desire what we desire to desire?" (Premise)
3. An analysis of a concept captures the contribution of that concept to the contents of thoughts in which they occur. (Premise)
4. If we analyze good or goodness as what we desire to desire, the question in 1 should be analyzed as asking something equivalent to, "Is what we desire to desire what we desire to desire?" (From 1 and 3)
5. If one can meaningfully use a sentence to express a thought, one can meaningfully use any sentence that would be used in giving a correct analysis of the contents expressed by the first sentence to express the same thought. (Premise)
6. Thus, "Is what we desire to desire what we desire to desire?" is not a correct analysis of "Is what we desire to desire good?" (From 4 and 5)
7. Thus also, that such-and-such is good is not the same thought as the thought that such-and-such is what we desire. (From 3 and 6)

From this argument Moore generalizes to all other analyses of thoughts predicating goodness, and sentences containing 'good.' As I already noted, if the argument has any force, that generalization should be fair enough since this version does not seem to turn on the particular analysis on offer.

So far the conclusion is about thought contents and the meanings of the terms in question, in particular the predicate 'good.' But Moore at times seems to want to go further than the claim about meaning to a claim about the property goodness. Moore doesn't make it obvious exactly how this transition is supposed to go. One way it might be warranted would be if the entire meaning of a predicate were just the property it picks out. On that assumption, two predicates with different meanings would have to pick out different properties. Sentences employing the different predicates would in that case ascribe different properties to their targets.

2.5.2. Distinguishing Sense and Reference

But the assumption underlying this reasoning is controversial. Consistent with the thought that predicates contribute properties to the meanings of the sentences they are constituents of, they can do more than this. One influential theory of how this might work was suggested by Gottlob Frege in the nineteenth century. His basic idea was that each referential term of language contributes both a referent (the thing it stands for) and a sense—a way of thinking about the referent or of picking it out. On Frege's (1892) view the sense of a referring expression determines its referent. There are various more or less sophisticated ways of developing the approach, and one can accept it for some classes of terms while denying it for others. But as a way of getting the hang of the basic idea you could think of Frege's senses as descriptions that uniquely describe the referent. A term with a given referent will have that referent because the referent satisfies the description that is the sense of the term.

If you like this picture, you might use it to resist the move from Moore's conclusions about meanings and analysis to the conclusion that there can be no substantial true identity claims identifying properties with one another. For Moore's requirement that analyses capture the contents of the thoughts expressed would require two terms to have the same senses in order to have the same meanings. Merely sharing a referent would not then be sufficient for sameness of meaning. Two predicates, each of which contributed the same property to the truth conditions of sentences in which they occur, won't have to share the same sense and hence won't mean the same or be adequate analyses of each other's meaning. Thus Fregeans about predicates have room to maneuver around the argument against property identity. For they can agree with Moore that the terms have different meanings and that the thoughts expressed have different contents without agreeing that they also have different referents.[9]

2.5.3. A Second Reconstruction of the OQA

Moore's passage might also inspire a different reading of the argument. It is of interest because it seems to survive confrontation with the Fregean distinction between sense and reference. Thus if this reading of the argument works, it would reinstate the claim that there is no substantive way to uniquely characterize the common subject matter of ethics. Consider:[10]

A. Moore wonders whether pleasure is good. (Premise)
B. When you wonder whether something is good you don't believe that it is good. (Premise)
C. Moore does not believe pleasure is good. (From A and B)
D. Moore believes that goodness is good. (Premise)
E. So, goodness and pleasantness differ in respect of what Moore believes about them. (He believes that one is good, but he isn't sure about the other.)
F. But by the principle of the indiscernibility of identicals, if **X** is identical with **Y**, then **X** and **Y** are indiscernible, that is they have all their properties in common. (Premise—sometimes known as *Leibniz's Law*)
G. Thus goodness and pleasantness are distinct. (From E and F)

Again, the argument is supposed to generalize to all identity claims involving goodness. Indeed, many of those moved by one or the other of these arguments have taken it to apply more broadly yet to all general ethical or normative terms such as 'bad,' 'right,' 'wrong,' and so on.

Unlike the first reconstruction, this version doesn't invoke controversial premises about the nature of analysis, meaning, and so on. So the distinction between sense and reference doesn't seem to offer a simple way out of the conclusion that goodness is distinct from any naturalistically characterizable property. And that, to my mind, makes it harder to resist this version of the Open Question Argument. (Though things may not be as they seem.) Step F does involve Leibniz's Law, also known as the *Principle of the Indiscernibility of Identicals*, which as stated seems fairly abstract and hence potentially controversial. But really the thought is pretty commonsensical. When we identify an item using one term with an item picked out using another term we aren't really identifying one thing with another different thing. We're identifying it with itself under another name. We're explaining that there's just one thing there. But then if there is just one thing there to talk about, anything we truly say about it will be true of it, whatever we call it. If **X** and **Y** are one and the same thing, anything true of **X** will be true of **Y**. If **X** has some particular property, then **Y** has it too. If I'm thinking of **X** and **X** just is **Y**, then I'm thinking of **Y** perhaps in a way I don't recognize. So I would urge you to look elsewhere if you want to reject one of the premises of the argument.

(I want to pause here for a side comment to readers new to metaethics. I'm not saying that either of these reconstructions of the argument is sound, or that the second is and the first is not or vice versa. I am saying that these lines of argument have importantly influenced philosophers' thinking about the nature of ethics for over a century and that it isn't easy to see whether or where they go wrong. You aren't missing anything if you don't fully understand how these arguments work, whether they're sound, or what might be problematic about them. Moore's text has engaged many of the best philosophical minds, and it is unlikely that it would have done so if there was not something difficult to get a definitive grip on.)

2.5.4.   Slight Digression About Naturalism

The Open Question Argument has been extremely influential. For much of the twentieth century the prevailing view seems to have been that Moore had established that those who identify moral properties with "natural" or nonmoral properties committed the "*naturalistic fallacy.*" This name is somewhat puzzling as fallacies are errors of reasoning, not the mere acceptance of (allegedly) false beliefs. Moore himself used the phrase as a name for a way of reaching the conclusion that good or goodness is identical to a property picked out in other terms, but most later users of the phrase seem to think the fallacy consists in identifying moral properties with natural properties, however the claim is supported.[11] The important point is about the influence of the argument. Many philosophers found Moore's argument persuasive, enough that this use of the phrase was widespread and not ironic. Most philosophers nowadays recognize that the argument has some problems, problems that come out when you try to generalize it to other identity claims, such as that between water and H_2O.[12] Even so, many still think that the attractiveness of the OQA indirectly vindicates an anti-naturalist upshot deriving from independent reasons to accept the conclusion. So the argument is still influential.

It is worth pausing here to consider what a natural property is supposed to be. Moore himself might be able to answer that natural properties are the nonmoral (or nonnormative) properties that are not supernatural. It seemed most important to Moore just to indicate that moral and normative properties were in a class of their own and he explicitly meant to include supernatural properties along with the natural properties as the target for his argument. But there is a use of 'natural property' and 'naturalism' by philosophers that is supposed to mean a bit more than that. Philosophers often use these terms to indicate a commitment to a kind of unity among the natural properties that makes them fall into a unified class. We'll spend a good bit of time filling out these ideas in the chapters on scientific naturalism later in the book, but I think it makes sense to connect the underlying thought with a philosophically popular way of viewing the world and also to explain how Moore's nonnaturalism seems to conflict with it.

It is very attractive to view the last 400 years of intellectual history starting roughly with the scientific revolution as one in which we have gone from a superstitious, enchanted, or magical view of how the world works to a natural and scientific view of its basic operations. Seemingly random and hard to systematically explain processes and events have yielded to various sorts of law-governed or at least generalizable explanation as various sciences have gotten up and running. We can think of the discoveries of Newton and Copernicus as setting the process on its course. By the twentieth century physics and astronomy were joined by chemistry, biology, psychology, sociology, and so on as sciences that offered explanations of events and processes at different levels of description. Phenomena that might previously have gone unexplained or which were explained only in what you might think of as spooky and hence unsystematic ways came to be viewed as the normal operations of a world governed by various sorts of scientific laws. We can use this way of viewing the world to suggest what is at stake for a lot of philosophers when they say they are naturalists. They are stating their commitment to a picture of the basic order that is compatible with this view of nature and the world. They think that the only properties that there are are those that could comfortably fit within this picture. And these are the natural properties. This is why many who try to get more precise about what it is to be "natural" often look to science in formulating their definitions of 'natural' and 'naturalism.'

Even those philosophers who aren't thoroughgoing naturalists tend to find something attractive in the picture and subscribe to much of it. Theistic philosophers think that over and above natural phenomena there is a deity (or are deities) of some sort, but most of them don't think that deity interferes much in the operation of a world much like the one naturalists accept. Even most contemporary ethical nonnaturalists will want nonnatural moral properties to be able to exist in a world that is *otherwise* natural. They are not immune to the attractions of the scientific picture of the natural world. Even so, many committed naturalists will find such nonnaturalist positions unacceptably double-minded. On one way of thinking about it, given the successes of science in explaining previously mysterious phenomena, things that might lead you to doubt the naturalness of any real phenomenon should justify no such inference.

That anyway is my sketch of philosophical naturalism. I've no doubt oversimplified things enormously and slighted alternative conceptions. But I do think the sketch here represents a powerful current underlying contemporary philosophical naturalism. Moore's anti-naturalist conclusion put him at odds with this popular current in philosophical thought. To admit a range of properties fundamentally unlike the properties we get access to via various sciences is, to this way of thinking, to fall away from an appropriately scientific world view. So naturalists in philosophy will see it as a point in favor of any metaethical theory if its metaphysics is naturalistic. And this will mean that naturalism puts a further constraint on acceptable answers to our questions about the subject matter of ethics. We'll consider several views that reject naturalism in the remainder of the book, though in the remainder of this chapter I leave the issue aside. But we should note that many philosophers treat metaphysical naturalism—a commitment to the existence of only natural properties—as a constraint on theorizing.

2.5.5.   How Would We Get a Common Subject Matter If Moore Were Right?

Moore himself intended his argument to exclude supernatural properties as well as natural properties. And if you look back at either version of the argument, the naturalness of the candidate allegedly identical properties plays no role in the argument. So it looks like the intended conclusion is that goodness is not identical with any property predicated by other *nonmoral* terms whether natural in any interesting sense or not.

Suppose that's right. Where does that leave our search for an ethical subject matter? There seem to be three possibilities: (1) 'Good' picks out a property that we can also pick out using other nonnormative terms. (2) 'Good' picks out a unique property that can only be picked out using normative terms. Or (3) 'good' picks out no property at all. From the perspective of realism, only the first two options are on the table. Option 3 denies that moral predicates pick a property and predicating a property just is what predicates do on the realist view. Moore's argument purports to rule out option one. So realists who accept Moore's verdict are left with option two: 'good' picks out a property, but it is an unanalyzable normative property that is distinct from any property predicable using natural or supernatural terms.

That theoretical option puts restrictions on how we might determine whether we address a *common* subject matter for ethical discussions. We can't provide an analysis or translation of what we are saying that all accept as correct. For such translations will either use normative words or they won't. If they do, we can raise the same issue with respect to those normative words and we haven't shown we pick out the same properties unless we settle the issue for those terms. And by accepting Moore's conclusion, we have agreed that one couldn't use nonnormative words to provide an analysis or translation of normative talk. So it looks like the resulting view is going to make it harder to demonstrate sameness of meaning for moral terms, at least until we have some reason to believe that there is one and only one property that is a candidate for the referent of any given moral term. Normally, when our grip on a property is recognitional (rather than mediated by a description) our grounds for thinking that others co-refer is that we mostly agree about the extension of the property in question. I think that your word 'yellow' picks out the same property that mine does because 'we apply it to the same things.'[13] But the widespread disagreement about morality that grounds Mackie's argument undercuts just this move. Different people, even in the same community let alone across communities, do not agree on which things are good, right, wrong, and so on.

2.6.   Speaker Relativism

One reaction to all of this might be to retain the minimal realism but give up on common properties as the things we think and talk about, and as what we predicate with that thought and talk. There are different ways to fill this out. Least plausible would be the suggestion that each moral term picks out a unique property in the mouth of each person. The implausibility comes in that the proposal would make communication using such terms very difficult if not impossible. If what 'right' means in my mouth is different from what it means in yours or anyone else's it is going to be very difficult for you to know what I mean to convey when I call some option right. Relatedly, it will also be difficult for us to express disagreement using our moral terms. If I say that something is right and you say it is not but our terms pick out different properties, we could be making consistent claims. We might be like two people who seem to disagree about the nature of bank deposits but who really aren't because one is talking about financial matters and the other about streamside minerals. So we would prefer a view that allows for some commonality of meaning and the ability to express disagreement using a common word that comes along with it.

That would suggest a group relative set of meanings for moral terms. If members of a group share a common meaning for their moral terms they would be able to communicate and disagree with one another by using those terms. If the cases of moral diversity that make the most trouble for finding a candidate meaning for our most general moral terms are the differences between members of different groups or societies, such a view might offer a solution. For it could admit that people were not in fact predicating the same properties in just those instances where there was the most divergence in moral view. Those with one view of moral matters would be predicating a property that they and those in their home group (whom we might suppose share a common moral sensibility) use their moral term to pick out, whereas those with a different view would be predicating a different property, one to which their sensibilities are better attuned. On such a view intragroup communication would be in good shape, and members of the same group could communicate their disagreements using common moral words. But between groups there would remain problems with communication and with disagreement.

Many people who emphasize moral diversity are relatively happy to take this view. The popularity of anthropological arguments for relativism reflect this. And it is not hard to get in a frame of mind where it seems plausible that my disagreement with ancient Greek writers about morality shows that we just have different moral concepts. So some will find this a comfortable theoretical refuge.

2.7.   Hare-Style Translation Arguments

There is a worry that remains. The upshot about disagreements between members of sufficiently different groups is not as easy to live with as some relativists might wish. There are powerful arguments that we *can* disagree with those in foreign communities and that we can express that disagreement using our most general terms of moral appraisal such as 'good,' 'bad,' 'right,' 'wrong,' and their translations. If the very minimal realism we start from forces us to relativism and that relativism makes such disagreement impossible, we must give up that minimal realism rather than accept the no-disagreement conclusion. Or so say the progenitors of the arguments we will now examine.

The *locus classicus* for the challenge is R. M. Hare's introduction of the "Missionaries and Cannibals" argument in his first book, *The Language of Morals* (1952, p. 148). Hare imagines two communities (Missionaries and Cannibals), each of which has a most general term of commendation that they apply to all sorts of things. Let's suppose the term used by one group is 'bood' and that used by the other is 'gad.'[14] People in each community typically choose things that they take to be "bood" or "gad" over things that aren't. They are generally somewhat moved to emulate those who are "bood" or "gad," and so on. In these ways the two groups use their respective terms similarly. However, they do not generally apply the terms to the same kinds of objects. The first group favors actions that are fierce, people who are stoic, and things that give one an advantage over others. So they apply 'bood' to these things. The second favors actions that are meek, people who are sympathetic, and things that enable people to lead comfortable lives. They apply 'gad' to these. Sometimes the extensions of the two predicates will overlap, but not as a regular pattern. Or, so as not to beg any questions, it would at least seem that way to an outsider who judges the extension by observing what the insiders apply the terms to. Hare suggests that we should see the two groups as in disagreement about a moral issue when the one group insists that meekness is "gad" and members of the other the other tell us that meekness is "not bood." One group contradicts what the other affirms, even though they use different phoneme. And this is reason to think that 'gad' means 'bood.' I contradict you only if what I negate is something you assert.[15]

We can now ask whether we would translate their two terms using any term of our own language and if so, which ones. It is natural, the argument goes, to translate each of their terms, 'bood' and 'gad' with our term 'good.' For we would seem to be joining the dispute on one side or the other if we claimed that meekness was either good or not good. Correct translations preserve the meanings of the expressions they translate. If this translation is correct all three predicates, 'bood,' 'gad,' and our own 'good' must have the same meaning. Yet (Hare's assumption is) they don't share an extension. So the meanings of the terms cannot be constituted by the extension they share. Nor, Hare thinks, could they all predicate the same property, for if they all predicated one and the same property they would have the same extension. As the example has been constructed, the thing all of the predicates have in common is that they are normally used to commend the things to which they are applied. So, Hare concludes, their common meaning must involve this common commendatory use and not their having a common extension or predicating a common property. And since our own 'good' is one of these terms, our term would seem not to represent a property, contrary to the realist picture. That anyway is what Hare thinks we should conclude.

Whether we follow Hare to that conclusion, the thought experiment causes trouble for relativism. It seems that we think it possible to express real disagreement with our moral terms, even when we don't agree on the extension of their correct application. And we can express that disagreement even across great gulfs in ways of seeing the normative world and to members of different social groups with such very different views. That cuts against the speaker-relativist suggestion that we should think divergent groups' terms differ in meaning, designate different properties, and have different truth conditions.

One way to avoid the speaker-relativist conclusion that the groups designate different properties with 'gad' and 'bood' is to become an absolutist and insist that the property designated by any group's most general term of commendation pick out the same property. But Hare thinks that's implausible. The lack of overlap between the judgements that employ 'gad' and those of the other group that employ 'bood' are stipulated to be very great. How then would they pick out one and the same property? So Hare suggests we give up on the idea that moral terms designate properties. They are instead, at least in the first instance, linguistic devices for a certain sort of speech act, one of moral commendation. And this move is to give up on most of the central tenets of minimal realism. It is to treat moral language as (primarily) nonrepresentational, and to treat it as fundamentally different from ordinary language employing ordinary predicates such as 'red,' 'round,' 'smart,' and so on.

There has been a good bit of development in semantic theory since Hare first deployed this argument. Some of this development has included theories that allow for wide divergence between the actual extension of a predicate and the extensions that even competent users of the terms would assign them. Advocates of such theories can resist the conclusion that the two predicates have different extensions. For they will argue that differences in the way speakers apply the predicates don't reflect differences in actual extension because the extensions of predicates are determined in ways that don't depend on what people believe about their extensions. This line of argument has met vigorous resistance from Hare's intellectual descendants, Terry Horgan and Mark Timmons, who offer their "Moral Twin-Earth" argument as an adaptation of Hare's argument suited to undermine such up-to-date theories. We'll look at both the new semantic theories and this response when we consider scientific naturalism in later chapters.

2.8. Concluding Summary

We have three different arguments that begin with some sort of failure to agree. Our first (Mackie's) argued from widespread actual ethical disagreement to the hypothesis that there is not one common subject matter for differing moral views to represent and to answer to. The second (the OQA) started from our ability to doubt any hypothesis about the nature of ethical reality to the claim that no substantive characterization of that subject matter is possible. And that upshot, together with the kind of disagreement cited by the first argument, might leave us with no way to show that each of us predicates the same property when we use moral terms such as 'right' and 'good.' From there the third argumentative strategy (Hare's) used the possibility of genuine ethical disagreements about which things are right or good to argue that even disparate communities must be able to use moral terms with the same meaning.

The arguments are importantly distinct. And they push in opposite directions. Thus putting them together can cause even more trouble. The first two suggest that any view that takes commonality of meaning to require moral predicates to contribute a common property or relation to sentences in which they occur will have difficulty finding plausible properties for that role, given that people disagree about all of morality as much as they do, and given that all substantive characterizations of the candidate properties are open to doubt and dispute. The third argument suggests that moral terms do in fact have common meanings. Putting them together thus puts pressure on the representational conception of predicate meaning built into minimal realism. This is not to say that those who adhere to such realism have no way to respond. But it is to say that it will be instructive to view features of their positive theories as responses to these pressures.

But these are not the only considerations that have shaped extant meta-ethical theories. The next two chapters explore two other sets of motivating ideas—ideas that can explain yet more features of the theories we'll canvass in more detail in subsequent chapters.

Questions

Comprehension

C1. What explanation does Mackie offer of persistent moral disagreement?

C2. What assumption does the first version of the Open Question Argument make about the ways we think of moral properties and their nature?

C3. What feature of our use of general moral terms does Hare think is essential to their meaning what they do?

Extension

E1. How would you explain the persistence of widespread moral disagreement?

E2. Construct an argument like the Open Question Argument to show that buckets are not pails. What does this tell you about the OQA as a valid form of argument?

E3. Can you explain why the principle of the indiscernibility of identicals (Leibniz's Law) is plausible?

E4. How could someone use the sense/reference distinction to respond to the second version of the Open Question Argument?

Reading

Read along with: Mackie (1977, chapter 1, §8, pp. 36–38), Moore (1903, chapter 1), and Hare (1952, pp. 148–149).

Further reading: Kalderon (2004) has a nice discussion of the Open Question Argument. Sarah McGrath (2008; 2011) has interesting things to say about moral disagreement. Loeb (1998) is also about disagreement. David Merli (2007) is all about the subject of this chapter. Readers might benefit from some extra background in the philosophy of language. I think that William Lycan's (2008) book is an excellent exposition aimed at the same audience I'm aiming at with this book. The second and third chapters are especially relevant to this chapter.

Notes

1   I will italicize relatively unfamiliar terms as they occur throughout the book, and italicize them again if I haven't used them for a while in the main text. I will also collect many such terms in the glossary.

2   We will learn more about cognitivism in the course of encountering noncognitivist theories in chapter 8. For now, the twin claims embodied in (a) and (b)—that moral thought and talk are representational and thus apt for truth if they represent things correctly and falsity when they misrepresent reality—will serve to get the main cognitivist idea across.

3   The italicized words will be better defined in chapter 7, but for now we can say that subjective or response-dependent properties have an essential connection to the responses of subjects to the things that have them. Being funny is subjective and response dependent in this sense, insofar as it is essentially connected to human amusement.

4   And it seems relatively straightforward to extend it to more complex predicates as well. "The ball is made of NaOH arranged in a lattice structure" can get a parallel treatment even though the predicate in that sentence is a complex one made up of more simple terms. We would assign this sentence the content that the ball is made of NaOH arranged in a lattice structure, we think it is true if the ball is so composed, and we would say that Amanda has a belief with that content if she has a belief that represents the ball as being made up of NaOH arranged in a lattice structure.

5   This view is anti-realist because it rejects the fourth of our minimal realist claims, that some of our moral judgements are true, or more carefully that some of our positive moral judgements are true. Though that is the upshot of Mackie's overall argument, I think this particular argument, "the argument from disagreement," is neutral between that and other anti-realist conclusions.

6   This is easy to miss if you pay too much attention to Mackie's overall positive view because Mackie did use a conception of the meanings of moral terms in formulating the

error theory he supported with the argument from disagreement. But the argument from disagreement in the first instance targets the claim that there is a common moral reality we're all talking about, and that doesn't require any story about what moral terms mean or even refer to.

7 If this still seems at best an associative connection to the topic we started with, I won't argue. My overall goal is to efficiently canvass arguments that have motivated the wide range of positions we find in metaethics.

8 This is inspired by ". . . whatever definition be offered, it may always be asked, with significance, of the complex so defined, whether it is itself good," in the long quotation from Moore in section 2.5.

9 There may be other ways to justify Moore's transition from claims about analysis to claims about property identity or lack thereof that elude this response.

10 The inspiration here is ". . . whoever will attentively consider with himself what is actually before his mind when he asks the question 'Is pleasure (or whatever it may be) after all good?' can easily satisfy himself that he is not merely wondering whether pleasure is pleasant" (Moore, 1903, §13). I owe this interpretation to Jamie Dreier long ago. Kalderon (2004) also has a nice treatment.

11 I think it fairly clear from Moore's texts that he reserved "the naturalistic fallacy" for reasoning that traded on an ambiguity in the word 'is' as between using it to predicate a property on the one hand and using it to make an identity claim on the other. So in his use the fallacy lies in how one comes to the conclusion that the properties are identical, not in accepting the conclusion itself. The passages in §12 of *Principia*—where he notes it would be fallacious to conclude that yellowness and sweetness were identical on the basis that oranges are both— support this reading of Moore, as does his caution not to think that 'I am pleased' is an identity.

12 Question E2 at the end of the chapter is aimed at formulating an objection based on this issue. I urge readers to attend to it even if they aren't otherwise working through the questions at the end of each chapter.

13 Moore has some interesting things to say about how we might cotton on to such a property if there was one (1903, chapter 1, §10), but the story seems to presuppose that there is only one candidate in the running.

14 Hare frames the example using 'bad' and 'good' but that prejudices the translation, so I opt for these replacements, which also show up in Dreier (1990) in a different but related context.

15 It is actually tricky how to put the crucial idea without overstating the case since I can contradict what you say by disagreeing with part of what you say.

3 Moral Epistemology and the Empirical Underdetermination of Ethical Theory

It counts in favor of a comprehensive metaethical theory that it gives an account of how we come to know the things we seem to know in ethics. Parallel thoughts are not unfamiliar with respect to any domain of which philosophy tries to give an account of its subject. We want our account of personal identity to fit with the things people ordinarily pay attention to when they track who is whom. We want our account of numbers to license using mathematical methods to discover their properties. Similarly we want our theories about the nature of rightness and wrongness to make sense of our using the methods we do to discover which actions are right and which are wrong, which things are good and which are bad. And so on.

Many metaethicists however think there is a special problem about providing a convincing story where ethics is concerned. There probably isn't just a single reason they think this. Some are worried about how widespread fundamental disagreement among seemingly reasonable people is compatible with our being in a position to know the truth about ethical matters. Others, perhaps convinced by Moore's Open Question argument, think that moral properties are distinct from all of the more familiar natural properties to which our senses give us access, and then worry that leaves us with no route to acquaint ourselves with the properties in question. Still others have the sense that fundamental moral conclusions won't be settled by natural science and empirical evidence, and that this makes moral enquiry different from other sorts of investigation. Some of these thoughts depend on prior metaethical commitments. This means that the lines of thought I'll be exploring here do not and perhaps should not bother everybody. Some merely regard the issues raised as good reasons to avoid competing views. That's fine. The ideas under discussion still help to explain a lot about how metaethics looks.

3.1. Empirical Underdetermination

Many suspect that ethical enquiry is different from more standard empirical investigations because the adequacy of a moral position is not ultimately a matter of how it fits with our empirical evidence. The kind of evidence we have for much of what we believe—evidence that we get from our senses through observation and experiment—doesn't determine what we should think about ethics, either directly or by ordinary reasoning on the basis of such evidence. This thought lies behind Mackie's accusation that authoritative ethical reasoning must rely on a distinctive input that cannot be underwritten by "our ordinary accounts of sensory perception or introspection," among other things (1977, p. 39). The worry is worth taking seriously. Perhaps moral theory is empirically underdetermined. Perhaps any body of empirical evidence is compatible with any number of different and even conflicting comprehensive moral views.

Here's one illustration. Malcolm and Meena disagree about the morality of abortion without disagreeing about the relevant empirical facts in the neighborhood. Both agree that conception occurs when an egg and sperm combine to form a one-celled zygote that starts to divide. And they agree that the resulting blastocyst takes about a week to attach to the wall of the uterus. They agree that a placenta forms and the embryo now starts growing in size as its cells differentiate into different types of cells. They agree that the embryo develops into a fetus that has precursors of all the major organs after about the eighth week of development and that the fetus is able to move at about three months of age when it is about 6 inches long. They agree that by the sixth month the brain has begun to develop rapidly and that by the ninth month the fetus has become a baby, normally able to survive outside the womb.[1] They also agree on the health effects of pregnancy and abortion, the possible diseases of both fetus and mother that might affect the health of either one, and much more besides.

Still Malcolm thinks it is always morally wrong to decide to abort an embryo or fetus, whereas Meena thinks it is sometimes the right choice for a woman to make. Malcolm further believes that abortion should be made illegal because it is wrong, whereas Meena thinks that the law should protect women who decide to have abortions up until the fetus is very well along in its development, certainly into the sixth month of pregnancy.

Meena and Malcolm have a fundamental moral disagreement about the moral status of abortion. While there may be further differences in their other beliefs that explain why they disagree about abortion, it does not have to be like that. Perhaps Malcolm is a dualist and thinks people have immaterial souls capable of thinking and feeling and that this soul is implanted at conception, whereas Meena thinks sentience develops over time along with the organs that support mental activity. But not everyone who agrees with Malcolm about abortion is such a dualist. And furthermore the dualist metaphysical view doesn't seem to be the sort of theory we could subject to empirical test. What evidence could there be for it? If it is true, perhaps fetuses have such evidence, but insofar as no one remembers what things were like as a fetus, it would be a fact beyond *our* ability to determine empirically.

Malcolm may defend his view by claiming that fetuses are persons and that it is always wrong to kill a person. Meena may, in turn, deny that fetuses are persons and go on to argue that it is permissible to kill another person in self-defense anyway. The disagreement, here again, does not seem to be about empirical matters. Meena does not deny that fetuses are living organisms of the same species as she is. She denies that they have a certain moral status—the status that entitles them to the same treatment as other persons. In that sense, intelligent nonhuman space aliens similar to us might be persons. So again, the dispute seems not to be over empirical matters. Nor is the dispute about the correct view of self-defense one over empirical matters. No doubt each of them can say various things to bolster their view of matters. Malcolm can try to use their agreement that babies are people and not permissibly harmed to argue that earlier stages in human development should get the same protection as babies. But Meena can respond that developmental differences underlying differences in the abilities of young fetuses and babies are morally relevant.

We all know people like Meena and people like Malcolm. In fact, we have many real-life examples of people who disagree about morality where the disagreement does not come down to different views about the truth of relevant empirically discoverable facts. The dispute over gestation crates discussed in the Introduction may be another example of a disagreement that can't be fully settled by empirical claims alone.

A third example will be familiar to you from normative ethics classes. *Consequentialists* such as utilitarians believe that the rightness or wrongness of an action turns on relative goodness of its effects, where goodness is assessed from a standpoint with no particular relationship to the agent. Others who are *deontologists* or *non-consequentialists* think factors besides the value of the outcome can be relevant to the rightness or wrongness of an action. Many think that there are certain act-types that are wrong to perform, even when the consequences will be better than the consequences of alternative courses of action. They may, for example, agree with Elizabeth Anscombe that "procuring the judicial execution of the innocent should be quite excluded from consideration" (1958, p. 17), whatever the benefits. Other non-consequentialists think that we are required to look after our own friends and family, even when abandoning them may have better overall consequences. There is a genuine disagreement here between consequentialists and their opponents, for the theories render conflicting verdicts about correct action. Even when all empirical uncertainties are resolved, both sides of the dispute seem to hold coherent positions. Neither side seems to contradict itself. And that seems to show that the empirical facts are not going to be relevant to settling who is right and who is wrong. When consequentialists take one view and non-consequentialists take the opposing view, each of them is going beyond anything logically entailed by their empirical evidence. Such examples seem to show that at least some moral issues cannot be settled purely on the basis of empirical evidence. The parties to these disputes are making a further substantive claim over and above anything settled by that evidence, a claim that depends for its validation on something other than that evidence.

3.2.   Coherence as the Ultimate Criterion?

You might think that all it takes to be justified in one's moral views is that the overall package of such views fit together in a coherent way, both internally so that one's moral beliefs cohere and also with one's nonmoral beliefs and any claims connecting them to observation. If you think harming others is wrong, you should think that cutting off the fingers of a typist is wrong. It would be incoherent not to. And if you think your cousin Amanda is a moral expert, and Amanda says that harming other is wrong, your beliefs would be more coherent if you agreed with her about that than if you didn't, so other things equal you have reason to agree. Coherence of this sort is clearly relevant to justification.

But it is hard to see how coherence alone could lead to convergence in what we should believe, morally speaking, if we start from different moral assumptions and if no other input constrains our reasoning or our starting points. Meena and Malcolm have perfectly coherent sets of beliefs but they disagree about morality. If coherence is the only resource each has for persuading the other, they can remain in disagreement forever so long as neither already believes, nor comes to adopt, a judgement that coheres better with the opposing position than her or his own.

Beliefs about the ordinary physical world don't seem to be like this insofar as our sensory experience pretty directly leads to beliefs, beliefs to which we must adjust our beliefs about the physical world. If my sensory experience overlaps enough with yours, coherence with that experience will push our beliefs in a similar direction. We should then expect our beliefs about the physical world to converge over time. For example, when you and I are in front of a statue and not visually impaired we will usually both come to believe there is a statue in front of us. Now that we have this belief in common, there will be at least one common commitment that each of us will have to take into account in modifying what we believe so as to be more coherent. It is, of course, possible that we give it up in order to achieve coherence. But in real life this is not the only visually caused belief we are likely to have in common. Once we get enough overlap, changes of belief in the direction of greater coherence for each of us will be liable to make us more similar.

That, anyway, is how things are likely to go for beliefs about the physical world. It isn't obvious that the pressure for convergence will extend to moral beliefs. I've told the story of Meena and Malcolm so that they each have perfectly coherent moral beliefs. Suppose they wind up sharing the same nonnormative beliefs about the empirical world. To keep the story simple, let's suppose they are responding to the same empirical evidence and have wound up with the same ordinary factual and scientific beliefs. Do we have reason to think that adding this feature must introduce some incoherence to Meena's or Malcolm's overall views?

It *could*, if one or the other of them has a commitment that connects the nonmoral with the moral in such a way that they now have reason to add a new moral belief to their stock of beliefs and if this new moral belief contradicts an existing moral belief. If Malcolm believes that abortion is wrong because it always causes pain to the fetus, and then he comes to find out that 2-month-old fetuses don't have a sufficiently developed nervous system to feel pain, he should give up that moral belief (though he might consistently continue to think it wrong for other reasons). Our sketch of Meena and Malcolm didn't include any linking beliefs of that sort. I did my best to make their moral views each consistent with what we know and what we are likely to find out about the medical realities surrounding abortion. If I succeeded, we can add any likely nonmoral empirical beliefs to the thoughts of either Meena or Malcolm without generating any additional incoherence, at least with regards to their beliefs involving abortion.

As I've filled out the story, Meena and Malcolm have done the best they can in working with the resources they have to make their total worldview as coherent as possible. If all there is to justification is coherence, or coherence plus appropriate responses to empirical evidence, each of them is fully justified in what they believe. If one of them is wrong it will be through no fault of her or his own. Whoever it is will have done as much as could be expected in determining the moral facts with respect to the relevant domain. He or she will just have been unlucky that his or her views don't reflect the moral truth. There is no further way she or he could have responded to her or his evidence that would have made her or his view more reasonable and more justified.

But that suggests an unsettling thought—neither Meena nor Malcolm can have knowledge in this domain. Even if one of their views is correct, it won't be knowledge. The unsettling thought gets its grip due to a compelling idea about knowledge. True beliefs that just happen to be true don't count as knowledge, even when one has a good justification for holding them. An example from the Gettier (1963) problem literature makes the point. A broken clock stuck at 4 o'clock will get the time right twice a day (Russell, 1948, pp. 170–171). Suppose you look at it and correctly conclude that it is 4 p.m. Your belief will be true, and you may even be justified in believing it, given that normally checking a clock is a good way to come to know the time. But if the clock is broken your lucky belief doesn't count as knowledge. Similarly, if Meena's moral views are correct and coherent, her beliefs will be true and justified by the best methods we have for ascertaining moral truths. But they won't count as knowledge.

This is troubling. We seem to have a very general argument that none of us knows anything about morality. No matter how coherent our moral opinions and no matter how accurate our nonmoral beliefs, we seem to be able to imagine someone who coherently denies what we affirm. That one of us also gets it right will have been an accident. Try as we might, we can't then know anything about morality.

As I remarked, the view is unsettling. So you could see why someone might resist and go back to reexamine the assumptions that led to this point. There seem to be three options for doing that: (1) You could accept relativism about moral truth, so that each party to the disagreement is right if we understand what they are saying in the right way. Or (2) you might argue that empirical evidence can in fact settle basic moral matters. Or (3) posit some non-empirical source of substantive moral knowledge that constrains correct moral theorizing.

We'll spend a good bit of time on relativism at various points later in the book, but let me just sketch how the relativist response might be worked out. You might think that true moral judgements capture facts about the relations of agents or judges to various types of action. Here's one way to work that out: A person's judgement to the effect that such and such an action is wrong would express the judgement that the action was inconsistent with that person's own deepest moral commitments. On this view Meena's judgement that abortion is morally permissible would be expressing the thought that permitting abortion fits with her deepest moral commitments. Malcolm's judgement that it is not permissible would express the thought that permitting abortion would not fit with *his* deepest moral commitments. Both of those claims could be true, for instance when Meena and Malcolm have *different* basic moral commitments. More would need to be said to defend the view and to explain how it fits with the kind of moral disagreement highlighted by Hare's Missionaries and Cannibals argument in chapter 2.

Alternatively, if you don't like relativism, you might resist the fundamental claim about the underdetermination of theory by evidence. That is, you might think that empirical evidence really can settle even basic normative matters. To support this thought you might argue that our problem is just that my sketches, however realistic, were incomplete. I was simply insufficiently imaginative in coming up with relevant empirical evidence to decide between Meena and Malcolm's positions on abortion or to settle the debate between consequentialism and deontology. Perhaps certain empirical facts could settle the status of one-celled zygotes as persons or nonpersons. Similarly, perhaps there is some further bit of empirical evidence (or better yet a truckload of such evidence) that would—if we had it—settle the debates over consequentialism. Those who favor this mode of resistance thus deny that moral theory is empirically underdetermined.

A third way to resist would be to postulate a source of knowledge distinct from but analogous to sense experience with which our justified moral beliefs must cohere. Theory choice would then be governed by coherence with all of what one accepts, including what one accepts on the basis of this distinct epistemic faculty. This is the position championed by *ethical intuitionists,* who are usually also Moorean nonreductionists about ethical properties. We'll examine the intuitionist option in some detail after a discussion of reductive naturalism and supervenience as resources for those who want to deny empirical underdetermination.

3.3.   Reductive Naturalism

Reductive naturalists think that moral properties just are natural properties. There are at least two ways this idea might be worked out. You could think that a target moral property such as goodness was identical to a particular natural property in our acquaintance, such as happiness. That is, you could think that these two properties are one and the same thing. Somewhat less simply, you could think that the target property was not identical to any natural property we have a word for, but that it was a property made up of or composed of natural properties. On the assumption that properties made up solely of natural properties are themselves natural, this would be sufficient to show that the target property also was natural. If goodness were the complex property of either promoting happiness or promoting healthiness we might have an example of this. Since the distribution of such properties is an empirical matter, it looks like reductive naturalism can elude the problem by making empirical evidence relevant to settling even the disputes that seem not to involve empirical matters. Suppose that rightness just is the property that actions have when they promote the greatest amount of total happiness. If we knew this we would have a way to find out which actions are right. Happiness can be studied empirically and psychology can tell us what makes people happy. Other sciences can contribute by telling us the best ways to bring about the things that make people happy. Doing those things would then be right. Meena and Malcolm could consult this research or do some of their own to resolve their disagreement. Empirical evidence would, after all, settle the issues allegedly left undetermined.

This result is sometimes cited by reductive naturalists as reason to accept their views. Naturalists can tell a story about how we can come to know many of the moral truths we take ourselves to know. And this story doesn't require any further faculties beyond our five senses, whereas non-naturalists seem to require such a faculty, as I'll shortly explain. We might then consider this a point in favor of reductive naturalism, at least as opposed to any sort of nonnaturalism.

But there is still some unfinished explanatory business for the naturalist. We supposed that moral properties were identical to natural properties accessible to science, or composed of such properties. But we also supposed that we knew which property or properties were to make up or be identical to the moral properties in question. And that assumption was crucial to our being in a position to use empirical evidence to determine the distribution of moral properties. Having stipulated that we knew that rightness was identical with happiness promotion, we could find out which actions are right by tracking how they affect happiness. But that stipulation should not be something we just help ourselves to when we think of our actual situation. Meena and Malcolm might themselves not accept reductive naturalism. If they don't, naturalism's truth won't seem to help them settle their disagreement.

Suppose they agree that reductive naturalism is true. Absent agreement about which natural property or set of properties composes or is identical to rightness, they will continue to disagree. Two people can accept reductive naturalism in general without having any idea which natural property or properties are which moral properties. Two people can also be more opinionated reductive naturalists with firm but conflicting ideas about the natural property or properties that are to be identified with rightness. In either case, their disagreement will persist even in the face of empirical agreement.

So the reductive thesis needs supplementation to explain how empirical evidence could put us in a position to settle disputes like those of Malcolm and Meena or the one dividing consequentialists and non-consequentialists. That supplementation should provide some story about how we could come to know that what seem to be two properties, goodness and happiness in our example, turn out to be one and the same property. With that story in hand we might be on our way to settling moral issues empirically. As we'll see in subsequent chapters, some metaethical naturalists do offer semantic models that aim to explain how it could be that normative properties could just be natural properties and how we could learn of such identities after being ignorant of them.

3.4. Supervenience

Reductive naturalism is probably still a minority view in metaethics, partly due to the continued influence of the Open Question Argument and to the influence of the related Moral Twin-Earth argument to be discussed more fully in chapters 11 and 12. So even if such naturalism can be worked out in such a way as to allow empirical methods to settle moral disputes, the issue of underdetermination will be relevant for those resistant to naturalism's charms. It is thus worth investigating whether there are other resources that might allow us to rationally choose from among various consistent moral positions.

One place to look is at the claim that the distribution of moral properties *supervenes* on the distribution of nonmoral properties. *Supervenience* is a metaphysical relation linking the extension of one property with the extension of another. One set of properties supervenes on another set of properties if the extension of the first supervenient set cannot be different unless the extension of the second subvenient set is also different. So, for example, if the rightness or wrongness of actions supervene on their nonmoral features, and we know what these nonmoral features are, we might use that knowledge to figure out whether they are right or wrong.

Supervenience is a somewhat complicated relation, so we should look at some examples to get the hang of the idea. The pictorial properties of a video display supervene on the illumination properties of the pixels making up the display. Two otherwise identical screens won't differ in what they depict unless the pixels that are illuminated on one screen differ from the pixels illuminated on the other. Another possibly familiar example shows up in the philosophy of mind. Many philosophers believe that the mental states of people supervene on their physical states. That is to say that two physical duplicates will have the same mental lives. And two people who differ in their thinking must (if this supervenience thesis is true) also differ physically. Supervenience theses come in different varieties and different strengths. They can be local or global. You might think that the distribution of one set of properties supervenes on the distribution of a relatively local set of properties, so that the distribution of subvening properties in other locations would not be relevant to the distribution of the supervening properties around here. For example, what's going on with the illumination of the other TV does not influence what this TV depicts. But you might think that the distribution of some supervening properties depends on the distribution of the subvening properties wherever they occur. With respect to the relationship of the mind to the physical world, some people argue that the physical properties on which the mental supervenes are all internal to the body or brain. Others think they include relational states as well and in principle might extend to any physical fact anywhere in the universe. The former view postulates local supervenience, the latter global. Supervenience claims can vary in modal strength depending on why we think they hold. By this we mean that the "cannot" in the claim that there cannot be a difference in one set of properties without a difference in the other might be stronger or weaker depending on why they cannot. If people can't differ in their mental states without differing in their brain states, this seems to be because of biology and evolutionary history. Had we had a different evolutionary history, it could have been that some other organ did some of our thinking. So to the extent this claim is necessary, it is necessary given our biology, but not necessary given any possible biology. It is what philosophers sometimes call a *nomological necessity*—something that is necessary given the scientific laws of our universe. On the other hand, that bachelorhood supervenes on gender, age, and marital status is arguably conceptually necessary and hence must remain so even if all the physical laws of our world were different.

Most metaethical theorists[2] believe that the distribution of moral or normative properties in the world supervenes on the distribution of the rest and that this is probably at least conceptually necessary. It is very plausible that there could not be two people, one virtuous and the other not, who differed in no other way. Similarly, it is very plausible that two actions identical in all of their intrinsic and relational nonmoral properties would also have exactly the same normative properties. If one action is right the other must be as well. If one is required in a circumstance then the other would be required in any otherwise identical circumstance. And so on. This is a global supervenience claim because the relational properties include relations to things anywhere in the universe. Most philosophers who have considered the issue think that the supervenience thesis is true, and furthermore that we have *a priori* justification for accepting it.

A supervenience claim is weaker than an identity claim; identity entails supervenience (every property supervenes on itself) but not the other way around. Thus the supervenience of the moral on the nonmoral is something a non-naturalist can endorse. Most nonnaturalists and nonreductive naturalists have followed G. E. Moore in doing just that.[3] This might then allow non-naturalists to put supervenience to epistemic work, much as naturalists hope to put their identity claim to work. If the extension of moral properties can vary only if the nonmoral properties do, and if we have empirical access to extension of the nonmoral properties, perhaps we could use that to figure out the extension of moral properties of interest.

But here again we face nearly the same problem we faced in using reductive naturalism as a bridge from the empirical to the moral. To be able to infer the distribution of the moral properties from the distribution of the subvenient nonmoral properties, we need to know more than just that they supervene. We'd also need to know how they supervene on the nonmoral properties, that is, which pattern of nonmoral property instantiation makes for which pattern of moral property instantiation. And knowing just that the two sets of properties are related so that the former cannot vary without variation in the latter does not give us that information. In fact, it is often the exact contours of the relationship that is at issue in conflicts over normative theories. Does the instantiation of lying always bring with it the instantiation of wrongness? Not if the consequences are good, says the consequentialist. Always, says Kant (1797). The parties can agree that the moral supervenes on the nonmoral without agreeing on the moral status of lying in general. So it looks like knowing that normative or moral properties supervene on nonnormative properties is not sufficient for knowing which actions are right and which things are good.

The problem here is very much parallel to that raised about the epistemic relevance of reductive naturalism. The mere fact that property A is linked with property B (either by supervenience or by identity) won't help you use your knowledge about the former to find out about the latter unless you know the nature of the link.

3.5. Intuitionism

Many philosophers have suggested that we might have a faculty, which they call '*intuition*,' that gives us access to moral truths in a way distinct from our five senses. These philosophers are epistemic *intuitionists*.[4] The name makes the view sound rather superstitious but its proponents can argue that there must be something of this sort if we are to have justified beliefs about morality.

Suppose for a moment that Moore was correct—moral properties are genuine but *sui generis* and therefore irreducible to properties of any other kind. What might an adequate epistemology for such properties involve? The natural properties to which we have perceptual access through sight, hearing, touch, taste, and smell are, according to such nonnaturalism, distinct from the moral property we are trying to track. That an action is right is a further fact about it, beyond the facts about the nonmoral properties it instantiates. If we think people have access to this kind of further fact, we are going to have to credit them with a genuine ability to decide when it is there and when it is not, an ability over and above their ability to discover and recognize the nonmoral facts. This ability had better not be some independent extra sensory faculty alongside the usual five senses. On that sensory model moral properties would be the proper objects of this extra sense, much as the colors are the proper objects of vision, and scents the proper objects of our sense of smell. It would be like having a third "eye" in the middle of one's forehead that "saw" only moral properties located in space. Such a totally independent faculty would make any confidence that the normative supervenes on the nonnormative a rash postulation with no serious justification. Any confidence in the supervenience of the moral on the nonmoral would be like the confidence that no two objects could differ in respect of how they smell without also differing in respect of how they look. It could be true, but it would be hard to see how we could get any confidence about the matter in the absence of experiential evidence for it.

Theorists who postulate intuitive access to moral properties would do better to make the faculty in question be a faculty of judgement, that is, an ability to reach verdicts about the moral status of targets of moral appraisal on the basis of the other properties of the target of appraisal. The faculty would be an ability to compute the moral status of an action (say) on the basis of its nonmoral properties. To call it a 'faculty' would simply be to credit it as a genuine epistemic *ability*. Since this faculty would operate on the outputs of empirical judgement but go beyond the contents of the judgements from which it starts, it would be an *a priori* faculty of judgement. Judgements about any particular action would be partly empirical as they would depend on evidence from the senses for much of their support, but their content would go beyond anything purely empirical insofar as they would rest on judgements about which nonmoral properties generate which normative verdicts, and such judgements go beyond what is given by our five senses. Furthermore these judgements would be substantive and not trivial consequences of the meanings of our terms. Insofar as we're following the nonnaturalist in supposing that moral properties are *sui generis* and therefore indefinable in nonmoral terms, they would not come by their *a priori* status as a consequence of any analytic entailment. Intuitionists of this sort would then be committed to an endorsement of *synthetic a priori* knowledge. ('Synthetic' is a philosopher's term for substantive truths as contrasted with stipulative truths or claims that are true by definition or solely because of the meanings of the terms involved in stating them.)

3.6.   Does Evolution Undermine Intuitive Knowledge?

There is a high profile line of argument that can be used to undermine the thought that our intuitive judgements about moral matters reliably reflect moral reality. As I've been articulating the idea of moral intuition, those who rely on it should think of it as a faculty of judgement that yields (largely) correct judgements about some particular matters of moral judgement based in part on nonmoral information. Intuition adds to that information by guiding judgements about how moral matters sit, given the relevant empirical information. These judgements would depend on something like bridge principles, whether particular or general. These bridge principles would take us from nonmoral descriptions of some state of affairs or proposition to claims about the appropriate moral verdict to render, or the appropriate moral proposition to adopt based on that nonmoral state characterization of the affairs or proposition. The bridge principles are bridges that take us from nonmoral propositions to moral propositions of some sort. But the principles need not be explicitly relied upon by those deploying the intuitive faculty. It would be enough if the faculty tracked the function from moral propositions to nonmoral propositions that the correct bridge principles would articulate. We might then think of a veridical faculty of moral intuition as a disposition to judge in accordance with these principles. People who rely on such intuition for knowledge embody those dispositions to judge to a greater or lesser degree. And if all goes well, those whose intuitions don't lead them astray wind up with knowledge generated by a reliable faculty of intuition.

If this kind of view is to help vindicate actual moral reasoning that relies on such an intuitive faculty, a person's dispositions to judge must be largely reliable. That is required if people are to know what they're talking about where morality is concerned. And it is at just this point that Sharon Street (2006) has effectively raised a challenge based in evolutionary theory. As she rightly points out, our dispositions to judge are to a greater or lesser degree influenced by our patterns of emotional and evaluative response. And these patterns, while conditioned by our own past experiences, are themselves a function of how those experiences have trained up certain biological emotional propensities. These propensities, in turn, are the result of a process of natural selection for traits that are connected with greater reproductive fitness. Emotional propensities that made our ancestors less fit than similar ancestors without those traits would have been selected against. And those that generated greater reproductive fitness would have tended to persist and been passed down to us. Had different available propensities been more adaptive, people would likely have wound up with those. And different propensities would combine with different training to yield different intuitive judgements. So, in some sense, the content of the intuitive judgements upon which intuitionists wish to rely depends on contingent facts of human evolutionary history.[5]

Street suggests that any account of the subject matter of morality must make it not a giant coincidence that the processes that selected for greater reproductive fitness also selected for the dispositions that are part and parcel of reliable moral intuition.[6] Had reproductive success not been linked to such reliable judgements, our moral judgements would instead have tracked the unreliable but reproductively helpful dispositions we would have wound up with instead. Street concludes that if the subject matter of morality is independent of us and our nature, it is hard to see how our propensities would have helped us track a moral truth entirely independent of us and our nature. If other available emotional propensities would have been better for having lots of offspring, we likely would have had those propensities. And then we would have had different response dispositions grounding our intuitive judgements and found different intuitive verdicts plausible. Why think that the actual direction of evolutionary selection tracked the facts about morality, when those facts are independent of facts about us?

Many metaethicists have found this challenge quite powerful. It seeks to undermine one way of dealing with the underdetermination of putative moral reality by empirical evidence by postulating a reliable faculty able to compute the moral facts on the basis of the nonmoral empirically accessible facts.

3.7.   Skepticism About the *Synthetic A Priori*

Many of the developments of twentieth-century philosophy were driven by skepticism about synthetic *a priori* knowledge. The *Logical Positivists* of the mid-century, with A. J. Ayer (an important noncognitivist) a prominent member, divided propositions into two sorts—one class that is *tautologous* (roughly true by definition) insofar as the members fall out of the meanings of the terms with which they are expressed, and another that involves empirical matters of fact verifiable or falsifiable by sense experience. They took themselves to be following in Hume's shoes when they used the verifiability criterion to separate sense from meaningless nonsense. Non-tautologies that lacked verification conditions were regarded as meaningless. If the argument of the beginning of this chapter is correct substantive ethical claims are not true by definition. And yet they are not confirmed just on the basis of empirical evidence either. I might learn that what Julius did was wrong by noting that he slapped Maurice, but I also need to know that slapping people is wrong. That last component doesn't seem to get its confirmation by observation. So Ayer concluded that moral claims do not meet the two-pronged test for meaningful language. They are neither tautologies nor empirically verifiable.

Yet it sure looks like ethical claims are meaningful. So Ayer postulated an alternative expressive role for moral language to explain away the impression of meaning. To the extent that moral language has meaning it was supposed to be "*expressive*" or "*emotive meaning*." Rather than functioning to describe the world as the sentences that express beliefs typically do, moral claims were alleged to express noncognitive attitudes. Or so believed Ayer and many other positivists. We'll look at such *noncognitivist* views in more detail in chapter 8. The point to note here is just how quickly the epistemic concerns about morality can lead to a kind of skepticism. Even many non-positivists have some sympathy with positivist repudiations of substantial *a priori* knowledge.

3.8.   Inference to the Best Explanation

It turned out to be very hard to give a precise definition of verifiability that is not too strict to rule out scientifically respectable claims of various sorts. Partly as a result, positivism is no longer as dominant as it once was. Verificationism as a criterion of meaningfulness, or even as a criterion for justifiability, is no longer a consensus position. Many philosophers grant that inference to the best explanation is a perfectly legitimate means of coming to believe in the existence of some entity or property, even if that entity is not strictly entailed by one's empirical evidence. This would mean that the inference is *ampliative*. The conclusion we accept based on the empirical evidence has more to it, is committed to more, than what we commit to when we accept the evidence we rely on. It is thus worth considering whether that sort of inference could generate our warrant for some or all of our moral beliefs. If it could then ethics would be no more problematic than other beliefs based on inference to the best explanation. They would not strictly be entailed by any of our sensory experience but they would, through an explanatory inference, be legitimated by experience.

Gilbert Harman has long been a proponent of inference to the best explanation as a fundamental epistemic method (Harman, 1965). Yet a comparison he deploys to launch a classic introductory metaethics book seems to undercut using such inferences to determine the moral facts. Harman (1977, chapter 1) suggests we compare the way moral beliefs might be supported by moral observations and the way a scientist's beliefs are supported by her observations. When we consider a trained scientist looking at a streak in a cloud chamber and saying to herself, "There goes a proton" (Harman, 1977, p. 6), we have an example of someone whose visual evidence supports but does not entail the truth of her conclusion. This is so because the full explanation of her observation, along with her training, the underlying workings of cloud chambers, her beliefs about physics, protons and cloud chambers, and much more besides, also includes reference to a proton flying through the chamber and creating a visible trail. Since the proton is one part of that full explanation we have reason to think the proton is actually there. If it wasn't, we would not have a good explanation of the streak.

What of a parallel case of moral observation? Harman suggests we might come upon some hoodlums torturing a cat and immediately conclude that something very wrong is going on before us. Our first thought might be, "That's so wrong!" and we might give voice to it almost reflexively. Harman suggests we are not justified in concluding that our observation—that the action is wrong—is supported by what we see in the same way the scientist's observation is supported by what she sees. And he claims this is because the best explanation of what we observe—that the action is wrong—does not require us to make reference to any wrongness anywhere. Rather, he claims, all we need to explain our observation is facts about cats and hoodlums and gasoline, and facts about our psychology. Given that we have a mindset that easily empathizes with a burning cat and dispositions to judge actions that cause pain to those with whom we empathize, and given that the kids were lighting the cat on fire, our reaction is fully explained by our psychological makeup, our ability to see what was happening, and the physical events involved in the hoodlums' torture of the cat. No further fact about wrongness is needed.

Harman's discussion has generated a good deal of literature. Moral realists of various stripes have countered with candidate moral explanations in which the instantiation of a moral property is doing substantial explanatory work. I won't go into that debate here. But I do want to stress several features of Harman's example. First, as Harman sets it up, the target is those who, like Moore, think that moral properties are not reducible to natural properties. If wrongness is in some sense identical to causing great pain to another for no benefit, then wrongness will figure in our explanation of our observation—we were reacting to seeing just that. A second thing worth noticing is that you can be led astray if you think Harman is arguing that there is a huge difference between the scientist and a horrified witness to torture. It is because of what the observation explanations have *in common* that we can't use *either one of them* to justify an inference to a moral conclusion. So, just as our psychological makeup was part of the explanation of our moral verdict, the scientist's psychology entered into her verdict regarding protons. For it was because she was trained in observing cloud chambers that she could make such an immediate perceptual judgement. And interestingly, just as fully explaining her observation committed us to the existence of protons, a full explanation of our moral observation also commits us to protons, at least if we delve further into the micro-level explanation of the events we observed. Cats and hoodlums are partly made of protons, and so a full explanation of the events of the day would involve postulating protons playing certain roles.

Given that Harman's claims are controversial, we should not close off the possibility that he is wrong. But if he's right, adding inference to the best explanation to our repertoire of justificatory methods won't help us elude epistemological worries about moral knowledge unless we are willing to reduce ethical properties, propositions, and facts to facts of a more familiar naturalistic sort. We would be left with two options for vindicating moral knowledge. Either we have a faculty that enables us to respond to synthetic but *a priori* truths about how the moral supervenes on the nonmoral, or Moore was wrong and moral properties can be reduced to naturalistically acceptable properties. This last option, by itself, doesn't yet vindicate actual moral knowledge absent a story about which natural properties moral properties reduce to, as well as a further story about how our everyday ways of making up our minds morally gives us access to the properties in question. Either way then, realists who think we know something about morality have some work to do.

To be fair, so do non-realists and skeptics. They need to explain something too. They should explain how we have come to talk of moral knowledge and to confidently judge that some moral claims are true and others false. Whenever a philosophical theory postulates widespread error in common practice, we can reasonably ask for an explanation of how the error came to be, and of why it (often) seems very natural to keep doing what the theory tells us is a mistake. Alternatively, they can argue that we have misunderstood our own practices of making claims to moral knowledge and judgements about moral truths. They can offer a redescription of what we're doing that reinterprets such claims in a manner that makes them compatible with the underlying skeptical or anti-realist verdicts. We'll see responses of each kind in the chapters that follow.

Every metaethical theory has to get its epistemic story straight.

Questions

Comprehension

C1. Explain briefly why coherence by itself can't settle certain moral disagreements.

C2. How does Harman explain the moral observation that something wrong is going on when an animal is being mistreated? Is it different than the explanation of an observation of a proton in a cloud chamber?

Extension

E1. Could we get evidence of the reliability of a way of finding things out even when we knew that it was a complete accident that we were able to use that method? What would that evidence look like?

Reading

Read along with: Gilbert Harman (1977, chapter 1) and/or Sharon Street (2006).

Further reading: Katia Vavova (2015) gives a nice organizing overview of debunking arguments and their force. Elizabeth Tropman (2009), Mike Huemer (2005), Simon Kirchin (2005), and all of Stratton-Lake (2002) are all good sources about intuitionism.

Notes

1   Many of the details here come from Wikipedia's entry on prenatal development at http://en.wikipedia.org/wiki/Prenatal_development.

2   There are dissenters (Sturgeon, 2009), and the exact formulation will vary with the other commitments of the theorists holding the view.

3   "[T]wo things cannot differ in quality [employed as a term for intrinsic value] without differing in intrinsic nature" (Moore, 1922, p. 263).

4   Epistemic intuitionism should not be confused with a different view associated with W. D. Ross (1930) that sometimes gets the same label, one that says that ethical truths are determined by the correct balance of various *prima facie* moral principles applying to a case or set of cases. Some such intuitionists are also epistemic intuitionists, but epistemic intuitionists—for example, Sidgwick (1875/1966)—can deny that claim about the content of morality.

5   This is no doubt an oversimplification of a more complex and subtle story, but it provides a simplified account to work with. The crucial point is that our actual dispositions to judge one way rather than another, in the circumstances when our judgements seem to be the sort of intuitive judgements upon which realist intuitionists rely, are what they are because of an evolutionary selection process. And this effects the output of such "intuition." Had the outputs been different, much of what we believe about morality would also have been different.

6   This theme is further developed and targeted at intuitionism by Matt Bedke in his paper "Intuitive Non-naturalism Meets Cosmic Coincidence" (2009).

4 The Practicality of Morality and the Humean Conception of Reason and Motivation

Nearly everyone agrees that judgements of rightness and wrongness, and even of goodness and badness, have some kind of relatively tight connection with action and reasons for action—a connection that is distinctive of moral and normative judgements. Moral judgements are supposed to be practical in a way that judgements about theoretical physics or agriculture or kitchen appliances are not. It's not that these other judgements can't play a role in reasoning about what to do, or in motivating someone to act. But they don't regularly do so for most people. On the other hand most people, whether theoretical physicists or cooks, will regard the moral status of an action as relevant to choosing to do or not do it. People often seem to act on moral considerations and it is not uncommon to explain why someone chose one way rather than another by citing their belief that they chose rightly or that the outcome would be good. This might show that such moral beliefs can motivate people to act either alone or in conjunction with other mental states.

The thought that the ability of moral judgements to provide reasons for and to motivate action is fundamental to understanding the nature of ethics underlies the thinking of *metaethical internalists*.[1] Metaethical internalists believe that there is a very strong either necessary or conceptual (or both) connection between moral judgements and/or their contents on the one hand, and reasons for action and/or motives for action on the other. Internalists come in many varieties. Some think that the rightness of an action provides reasons to act, others that its rightness consists in there being reasons of the right sort. Some think that believing something to be right requires having some sort of positive motivating attitude toward it. Others think that not everyone is so motivated but that people will be motivated if they are rational, coherent, or sensible. So there's lots of variation in what internalists think. We'll soon introduce some order to the variety by distinguishing kinds of internalism. Still, it is helpful to get a handle on metaethical internalism by starting with the general notion that ethics is essentially practical and then see various more specific internalist claims as ways of cashing out that idea.

Of course some ways of cashing out the idea fall short of genuine internalism. Someone could deny that moral judgements have any *necessary or conceptual* connection to reasons and motives for acting and give some other explanation of the sense in which ethics is practical. These people would not be internalists; they'd be *externalists*, as we label those who deny internalism. Nevertheless they could still be trying to explain what it was that made internalism seem plausible and thereby give the practicality of morality its due. Much metaethical ink has been spilt by defenders of each position. Since both internalists and sophisticated externalists aim to explain the practicality of morality you might wonder what the fuss is about. If sophisticated members of both camps each try to capture the practicality of morality, why is so much made of the split between those who think the connection is necessary or conceptual and those who don't? The answer, I think, comes from noting how necessary and conceptual claims will combine with relatively common *Humean*[2] views about reasons and motives to support anti-realist metaethical theses.

The overall purpose of this chapter is to explain how this is so. To do that well I will need to lay out a range of different internalist theses and introduce some order into the variation. I will need to survey arguments for several of these positions in order to explain why many find them powerful enough to use as premises of further arguments about the nature of ethics. Then I'll go on to explain how these combine with Humean views to cause troubles for certain constituents of the minimally realist position discussed in the previous chapter. In particular, I'll show how they cause trouble for the thesis that moral judgement/moral beliefs are cognitive states with representational content and for the thought that moral judgements are true or correct absolutely. Finally, I'll briefly explain how many positions in metaethics are partly motivated by various strategies to avoid the resulting tensions.

4.1. Varieties of Internalism

A necessary connection is in one way as tight as a connection can be. If **A** is necessary to **B**, then **B** cannot exist without **A**. If trade is necessary to an economy the economy can't exist without trade. If parents are necessary to children then we can't have children with no parents. Athletes necessarily exercise; a person can't be an athlete without exercising. You get the idea. So if moral judgements necessarily motivate agents then no agent could make such a judgement without being motivated. If moral truths necessarily provide reasons to act then no judgement could be true without also providing such a reason. Yet there can be variation in the nature of the alleged necessary connection. And this variation can make the connection stronger or weaker, not by becoming unnecessary but by changing what exactly is supposed to be necessary to what. An internalist might think it necessary that a person who accepts a moral judgement feels some motivation to act on it. Or she might think that the nature of the connection is such that the person must actually be motivated *enough to act*. The latter claim is in this way stronger than the former, even though both claims are alleged to be necessary. Similarly, views that require moral judgements *to motivate* are stronger than those that require only that they *can motivate*.

On many theories of concepts, conceptual truths are necessary. If the concept of an electron tells you what it takes to be an electron, then electrons will have to be as the conceptual truths about electrons say they are. Not every theory of concepts has this upshot; some theories of mental content deny that the referent of a term must fit the user's conception of it. But most metaethical theorists who formulate internalism as a conceptual claim also think that the postulated conceptual connection would be necessary in virtue of being conceptual. Thus I'll construct my taxonomy of internalist positions around variations in the kind of necessary connection the various positions postulate. By surveying the range of variation and suggesting a name for each variety we'll be in a position to more carefully track which theses have upshots for more comprehensive metaethical positions.[3]

The taxonomy combines three dimensions of variation. We can vary what (moral judgements, reasons, or motives) is necessary to what (moral judgements or reasons). We can vary the kind of connection that's necessary. And we can vary whether it is the judgements themselves or their contents that stand in the necessary relations. These three dimensions of variation cut across each other to produce many varieties of internalism. Luckily they also help organize the kinds of variation and help us come up with labels to keep straight what we are talking about. In the end none of this is all that hard to keep in mind once you get the systematic nature of the variability. Let me explain in more detail.

The term 'internalism' was first used as a thesis about *moral* judgements or *moral* truths, but it has also come to be used as a term for a related view about *reasons* or judgements about *reasons* analogous to internalist views about moral truths and moral judgements.[4] Because analogous views about reasons often lead to views about moral judgements, we want our taxonomy and our terminology to cover both. So we have three *relata*—morality, reasons, and motives. These can be related to one another by three sorts of necessary connections that might be of interest. Morals might necessarily involve reasons in some way; morals might necessarily involve motives; and reasons might necessarily involve motives. We can use Steve Darwall's slash-names to indicate what is alleged to be necessary to what.[5] *Morals/reasons internalism* postulates that morals must have a connection with reasons. *Morals/motives internalism* postulates a necessary connection between morality and motives. And *reasons/motives internalism* postulates a similar connection between reasons and motives. So on our first dimension of variation there are three basic options. Each option is picked out by a slash-name that tells us what is connected to what. There's one more thing the names help us to keep track of. Necessary connection may be asymmetric; the order of the names indicates which thing must be connected to which. For example, morals/reasons internalism says something about what is necessary to morality—a connection with reasons. It does not say that reasons must all be connected with morality.

Along a different axis we should note another kind of possible variation. You might think that moral judgements, that is psychological states, must have a connection with motivation. Or you might think that moral facts, the states of the world that judgements are about, need to be so connected. We need to distinguish these, and again Darwall has introduced some useful terminology. '*Judgement internalism*' will be our name for the view that connects the psychological states with reasons or motives. '*Existence internalism*' will be a name for the internalist claim applied to moral truths or facts. So *morals/reasons judgement internalism* says that it is necessary to moral judgements that they bear a certain sort of connection with reasons. And *reasons/motives existence internalism* requires that true claims about reasons entail facts about motivation—for example that they should be able to motivate people to act on them. So along this dimension of variation we have two options: we might be existence internalists of one sort or another or we might be judgement internalists.

The third dimension of variation has to do with the nature of the necessary connection. A necessary connection is in one way as tight as a connection can be. If **A** is necessary to **B**, then **B** cannot exist without **A**. So if moral judgements have a necessary connection with motives, no moral judgement could lack the connection. Yet the alleged necessary connection can be stronger or weaker not by being less necessary, but by varying the nature of the thing that is claimed to be necessary and the conditions under which it is made manifest. To put the point another way, some versions of internalism require not that motivation invariably accompany moral judgement, but only under particular conditions, absent defeaters, and so on (Korsgaard, 1986). That there is such a connection is still necessary, but we'll only get the motivational response when the defeaters are absent. Thus a further important divide is between *defeasible* internalism and *indefeasible* internalism. Here is an example to illustrate the idea. An *indefeasible morals/ motives judgement internalist* might think that moral judgements would motivate anyone who makes them. That is they hold that there are no conditions that would defeat motivation in those who hold such judgements. By contrast someone might think that motivation must obtain *only absent some defeating conditions such as irrationality*. Such defeasible internalists think that moral judgements necessarily motivate *rational* agents. Since some people are irrational, the irrational people might accept a moral judgement and yet remain unmoved. Irrationality would then be a defeating condition for the manifestation of the motivational requirement. Other defeating conditions yield yet further varieties of *defeasible internalism*. We should note that an internalist claim can be defeasible even without containing any explicit clause stating the conditions under which it is defeated. The view that moral judgements must motivate rational individuals is defeasible in the relevant sense, however we express it, because it is consistent with someone (an irrational person) making a judgement and remaining unmotivated. Similarly, the view that moral judgements must necessarily be able to motivate action counts as defeasible in the relevant sense because judgements that can motivate don't always have to motivate. The availability of defeasible internalist theses will be important when we assess externalist objections to internalism that rest on the possibility of amoralism.

We thus have three different important dimensions of variation for internalist theses. When we combine these dimensions of variation into a two-dimensional representation of the varieties of internalism we get 12 possible combinations that we can represent as shown in the following table.

Each of these possibilities is a variety of internalism. Each has its champions in metaethics whose arguments we'll find throughout the literature. There are logical relations among these varieties that generate supporting relationships between them. For example, if you think moral truths must generate reasons for action by the agents to whom they apply, and you think reasons must be able to motivate rational people, you can put those claims together to argue that moral truths must be able to generate motivation in rational people. This means that an argument for one species of internalism

Varieties of Internalism		
(Answers to questions unitalicized; names of the resulting kind of internalism given in *italics*)		
What must be connected to what? (Answer above; name in *italics*.)	Is the connection about the judgement or about the truth of its content? (Answer above; name in *italics*.)	Is the connection defeasible or not defeasible? (The names themselves answer the question, so no separate answer given to question.)
Morals with motivation. *Morals/Motives Internalism*	The judgement. *Morals/Motives Judgement Internalism*	*Defeasible Morals/Motives Judgement Internalism*
		Indefeasible Morals/Motives Judgement Internalism
	Truth of the content. *Morals/Motives Existence Internalism*	*Defeasible Morals/Motives Existence Internalism*
		Indefeasible Morals/Motives Existence Internalism
Morals with reasons. *Morals/Reasons Internalism*	The judgement. *Morals/Reasons Judgement Internalism*	*Defeasible Morals/Reasons Judgement Internalism*
		Indefeasible Morals/Reasons Judgement Internalism
	Truth of the content. *Morals/Reasons Existence Internalism*	*Defeasible Morals/Reasons Existence Internalism*
		Indefeasible Morals/Reasons Existence Internalism
Reasons with motivation. *Reasons/Motives Internalism*	The judgement. *Reasons/Motives Judgement Internalism*	*Defeasible Reasons/Motives Judgement Internalism*
		Indefeasible Reasons/Motives Judgement Internalism
	Truth of the content. *Reasons/Motives Existence Internalism*	*Defeasible Reasons/Motives Existence Internalism*
		Indefeasible Reasons/Motives Existence Internalism

can also be part of a longer argument for another variety. This is an important point we will exploit later on.

Each of these varieties of internalism can also be denied. Those denials generate 12 externalist positions corresponding to each internalist claim. While there are connections between the varieties as I note earlier, a person might reasonably be an internalist of one sort while taking the externalist side in debates about another possible connection.

4.2.   Motivating Some Important Varieties of Internalism

Taxonomy is of little interest for its own sake, although a good map of related philosophical positions sometimes can be really helpful. Such a map is useful when the territory itself is worth paying attention to. And we'll find reason to pay attention here when we look at some of the reasons many internalists accept the theses and also some arguments that proceed from them. In the next section we'll survey the arguments for the most important varieties of internalism. I've already noted that some arguments take us from one internalist thesis to another whereas others start from independent premises. It makes sense to consider the independent arguments first since the others will only be well supported if the varieties of internalism they take as premises are themselves well supported.

4.2.1.   Direct Arguments for Morals/Motives Internalism

An Argument from the Epistemology of Moral Attitude Attribution

R. M. Hare began his classic, *The Language of Morals*, thus:

> If we were to ask of a person "What are his moral principles?" the way in which we could be most sure of a true answer would be by studying what he did. He might, to be sure, profess in his conversation all sorts of principles, which in his actions he completely disregarded; but it would be when, knowing all the relevant facts of a situation, he was faced with choices or decisions between alternative courses of action, between alternative answers to the question "What shall I do?", that he would reveal in what principles of conduct he really believed. (Hare, 1952, p. 1)

Insofar as this idea is plausible, it suggests that there must be a very strong connection between believing something to be morally right or morally required and being disposed to act as one believes one ought. Not every tight connection is necessary, but if Hare is right, we could explain the nature of our attribution practices by postulating a constitutive connection between moral judgements and motivating attitudes or the disposition to have motivating attitudes. Depending on how one developed this last thought, the resulting view would underwrite a defeasible or indefeasible morals/motives judgement internalism. You could think that accepting a moral judgement that some action is right consists (partly) in being positively motivated toward that action. In that case you'd accept indefeasible morals/motives judgement internalism. Or you might think it involved states that disposed one to have such attitudes, perhaps in certain conditions. That thought would naturally lead to an indefeasible version. Getting to either of these conclusions would require further substantive argument. Insofar as the proposals involve something like inference to the best explanation, an externalist could resist by offering alternative, contingent explanations of the reliability of action as a guide to judgement. We'll see some of that later on.

Translation Arguments

Hare's Missionaries and Cannibals argument, discussed in chapter 2 (as well as its Moral Twin-Earth successors we'll explore in chapters 11 and 12) can be given an internalist upshot. Recall the strategy. First Hare describes two communities, each of which uses some term as a very general term of positive appraisal to commend the things to which the word is applied. He then crafts the story so that other commonalities in the terms' usage—commonalities that might ground a sameness of meaning claim—are ruled out. Hare suggests that we'd still want to translate each of these commendatory terms with our term 'good,' and to take their divergent judgements using the terms to be in genuine disagreement with one another. Insofar as we're inclined to treat the terms as equivalent in meaning, we seem forced to tie that meaning to the commendatory force of the target terms. For he has set up the case to give the terms little else in common. But we also wish to equate the meaning of these terms with the meaning of our own term 'good.' So the meaning of 'good' must be just as closely tied to commendatory force. The commendatory force of 'good' is thus essential to its meaning.

So far we have a necessary connection between sincere use of certain sentences and a positive attitude, at least if we go on to assume that commendation requires a positive attitude toward the object of commendation. From that conclusion we can go further. So far we have:

a. Sincere assertive uses of 'Φ is good' commend Φ. (Upshot of Missionaries and Cannibals argument)
b. It is linguistically appropriate sincerely to commend Φ, only if one approves of Φ. (Plausible assumption)

Proper assertions require sincerity and sincerity comes to accepting what you assert, so we might also accept:

c. Sincere assertive uses of 'Φ is good' are linguistically appropriate if and only if one judges that Φ is good.

And now it looks like this condition (which is both necessary and sufficient) must include satisfaction of any appropriateness conditions on commendation, and hence include the requirement that one approve of the object of commendation. And that could be true only if judging that Φ is good either is (among other things) approving of Φ or requires approval of Φ. This generates an indefeasible form of morals/motives judgement internalism.

Externalists will want to resist. Indefeasible internalist claims are very strong and thus open to counterexamples. David Brink (1986, p. 30) suggests that we find such counterexamples in the person of amoralists such as Dickens's Uriah Heep and Plato's Thrasymachus—figures who seem unmoved by moral considerations. It is important to these examples that the figures in question don't in any way seem to doubt that certain things are good or just. Thrasymachus, for example, agrees that justice requires obeying certain laws. But he doubts whether we have good reason to obey those laws. He thinks that justice serves the interests of the lawmakers and hence may not serve the interests of those who must obey those laws. Thus, he concludes, we often have no reason to do what justice and morality require (Plato, tr. 2004, Book I). If moral judgements must motivate those who hold them, real analogues of Thrasymachus would be impossible, and yet they seem not to be.

Internalists who agree with Hare often reply by denying that the judgements of such figures are genuine. Amoralists, they allege, accept the relevant moral judgements only in an "inverted commas sense." Rather than believing that an action is bad or wrong they only believe that they are "bad" or "wrong," where the quotation marks indicate a certain distance from the perspective that supplies the label. On one version of the idea, the inverted commas judgement has roughly the content that actions of this sort are classified as bad or wrong from a perspective rejected by the amoralist. The amoralist might be indicating that community standards would label the actions wrong.

There is much more to say on both sides of this debate. I raise it here only to point out that an internalist could use translation arguments to support weaker defeasible internalist claims—claims that would not be so vulnerable to putative counterexamples. Someone might think these arguments show that the meaning of 'good' requires it to be apt for commendation. From that hypothesis we can argue as follows: It is plausible that a predicate would retain its meaning as a commendatory term only if those who use it normally approve of the objects to which they apply the term. So we would expect those who use the term normally to approve of the target of evaluation. Then if sincere use of a sentence of the form 'Φ is good' expresses the judgement that Φ is good, that judgement will normally be accompanied by approval of Φ. Insofar as this falls out of constraints that underlie the term's meaning, the constraint will be necessary though defeasible.

Internalists can also make a case for a similar conclusion more directly. They can construct a thought experiment, as Horgan and Timmons (1991, 1992a) do, to build in that the target terms are normally used by those with positive attitudes, while stipulating away any other commonality in use of the terms. That would leave only the term's use to express these attitudes as the feature in virtue of which we translate the terms in the same way. A term would mean what our term 'good' means only because both terms are normally used by people who are reliably motivated to do what they judge to be "good." Thus the attitude expressed by such judgements must be reliably connected to such motivation. To postulate a reliable but not indefeasible connection of this sort is to accept a version of defeasible internalism.[6]

An Argument From Motivational Change

Michael Smith (1994, pp. 6–7) points out that we normally expect someone to change her goals and behavior along with her beliefs when she changes her mind about basic moral views. This shows up in the way we interact with our friends when we think they're acting wrongly. If I think a friend is doing something morally objectionable, I might try to convince that friend of the error of her ways. If she winds up agreeing with me about her former course of conduct, I would expect her to act differently in similar situations from now on. Smith argues that this expectation is better explained by facts about the nature of moral judgement than it would be by postulating the existence of further contingently present psychological states—states such as a general desire to do whatever one believes right. Smith (1994, p. 75) suggests that morally good people don't do what is right in order to do what's right. Rather they act on the consideration that makes the action in question right. But more specific desires of this sort won't be able to explain why people act in the ways they regard as right both before and after they change their minds about what is right, at least in cases where they change their mind about the reason why it is right. A person can come to see a feature of a course of action as a right-making feature and come to believe it right for that reason. And yet they might have known all along that the course of action had that feature. Insofar as we are trying to explain a motivational change, a desire for that feature won't be able to play the right role to explain why change of motivation accompanies that sort of change of mind.

Falk's Argument for Morals/Motives Existence Internalism as the Best Explanation of Judgement Internalism

The three previous arguments have a judgement internalist upshot—those who accept a moral judgement must be motivated by it, at least in certain conditions. W. D. Falk (who, together with William Frankena, is responsible for the 'internalism' label) suggests that judgement internalism supports existence internalism—the claim that true moral judgements about an agent require some connection with the agent's motivational psychology:

. . . [W]hen we try to convince another that he ought to pay his bills, we expect our argument if accepted to effect some change of heart in him, though it may still not change his outward actions. Discussions about moral problems are commonly carried on in the belief that in proving our point, and having it assented to, we shall provide one another with motives or "exciting reasons" (Hutcheson) for doing what otherwise we should not have been ready to do. We should think it odd to receive the answer: "Yes, I know now *that* and *why* I ought to pay my bills, but I am still without any incentive for doing so, and I, therefore, have as little cause for paying them as I had before I knew I ought to."

But the fact that this answer appears odd is evidence that judgements about moral obligations bring to light some internal necessity of acting, and not merely the existence of a state of affairs external to ourselves. For only such judgements can essentially have an influence on people's readiness to act, while the latter have such influence if at all only incidentally. (Falk, 1945, p. 141)

The idea seems to be that we could explain the reliability of the connection between changes in moral beliefs and parallel changes in motivation only if the content of such judgements required a connection with psychological features of the agent that could explain motivation. Michael Smith's influential 1994 book *The Moral Problem* is a sophisticated extension of this strategy of argument. There, Smith argues that we must understand moral judgements as judgements about what would motivate agents in certain conditions, in order to explain the morals/motives judgement internalism he thinks we have independent reason to accept.

4.2.2. Arguments for Morals/Reasons Existence Internalism

Falk's argument closely parallels a commonsense reason to think that true moral judgements provide reasons to act as they commend. When a friend asks for a reason to pursue a course of action, it is appropriate and not obtuse to explain that the course of action is morally right and to offer an explanation of why it is right. No further answer to the question would normally appear to be needed to provide a satisfactory answer. Although our friend might not agree with us, our answer is clearly relevant and to the point. This suggests that moral claims are apt to play a reason-giving role in our justificatory practices, and it isn't too much of a stretch to think this is because such claims are reasons or depend for their truth on reasons.

Relatedly, one standard way of explaining action is to cite the reasons on which a person acted. On one understanding of that sort of explanation, certain facts are apt for the explanation of human action because those facts make it rational or sensible for a person to take that course of action. On the assumption that people are somewhat rational and sensible, this will make it unsurprising if an agent acts because of the facts that make the action sensible, and we can cite those facts—her reasons—as part of the explanation of why she acted. Such action explanations often cite moral facts. The kindness of an action was such that it made it the right action to do, and this explained why our friend did it, despite some hardship in accomplishing the goal. This kind of explanation is perfectly ordinary, and the fact that it is ordinary supports the thought that true moral claims connect tightly with reasons for agents to act.

If one accepts these arguments for morals/reasons internalism, one would expect that many of the constraints on reasons would also have application to moral judgements or truths. In particular, you would expect moral judgements to inherit a necessary connection to motives if moral judgements themselves were necessarily reason giving and reasons themselves had necessary connections to motives. This makes it worth spending some time with an influential argument for internalism about reason claims.

4.2.3. Two Arguments for Reasons/Motives Existence Internalism

Bernard Williams's Argument From the Dual Role of Reasons

In an influential paper, Bernard Williams (1980) begins with the idea that reasons play two different roles in our thinking. On the one hand, we think about our reasons when we deliberate about what it makes sense for us to do with an eye on settling what we will choose to do. On the other, we use reasons to explain what people have done and have chosen, and also to predict what they will do and will choose. Williams thinks that the question, "What do I have reason to do?" in an agent's mouth and "What does she have reason to do?" in a bystander's have the same content and ask for the same information. And that information must then be apt for offering the agent normative guidance and the bystander something that would serve to explain what the agent winds up doing if she acts on that reason. Reasons must be able both to explain and to justify action (Williams, 1980, p. 103; see also Johnson, 1999). We would have something that could play both roles if it turned out that reasons were considerations that a rational agent deliberating on the basis of her current correct information and her rational motives would act on if she deliberated correctly. Such reasons would justify the courses of action they recommend insofar as they display actions as beyond rational criticism, either due to incorrect reasoning or due as a response to incorrect information. And they would explain an action done on the basis of a reason if we assume that people mostly or often are rational in the sense that they deliberate correctly on the basis of well-grounded beliefs that are often true. On the assumption that people are often rational in this sense, it will be unsurprising that a given person does what she has reason to do, at least if reasons are what Williams suggests they are.

So far the argument supports a defeasible version of reasons/motives existence internalism. An agent has a sufficient reason to φ only if sound deliberation from her current motives would lead her to intend to φ. And reasons in general will be considerations that would be sufficient to justify action, absent countervailing reasons. The connection is defeasible because people don't always deliberate correctly. And those who deliberate incorrectly or from incorrect assumptions may well not be motivated by the reasons they have. This kind of reasons/motives existence internalism also would explain why thinking that one had a reason might itself motivate action favored by the reason one took oneself to have. To think that one has a reason of this sort just is to think that you would do the action for which you have such reason if you thought about the matter correctly and responded rationally to the available true facts, given one's actual current psychology. So Williams's first internalist claim has a good bit going for it. And its defeasible status makes it relatively immune to clear counterexample. When we find someone unmoved by reasons we can decide that they are misinformed or reasoning badly relative to their information.

Williams, however, wanted more from his argument than this. He wanted to show not only that reasons must be able to motivate after sound deliberation, but also that they can do so because reasons presuppose motivating attitudes that are already part of an agent's psychology. Here the argument turns crucially on his acceptance of a broadly *instrumentalist* or *Humean* conception of reasons. Such conceptions limit reasoning about what to do to a certain sort of hypothetical structure. Very roughly, on such conceptions reasons for acting in one way or another must be based on ends one already has or goals toward which one is already favorably disposed. Williams clarifies the approach by introducing the notion of an agent's motivational set—a set consisting of desires, tastes, and dispositions of evaluation that capture the agent's current motivational tendencies and pro-attitudes. Williams suggests these can all be thought of as kinds of desire, broadly construed. From there, he suggests we can stipulate a notion of "internal reason," where internal reasons are those whose existence depends on one or more of the elements in the agent's motivational set. For each internal reason an agent has, there must be some element or set of elements in the set that, if removed, would make it the case that the agent no longer had that reason. One has an internal reason to do some action only if it in some way facilitates achieving goals to which one is committed by one's motivational set.

Williams then argues that all reasons must be internal in this stipulated sense. The idea seems to be that one can fail to reason correctly only if one fails to make an inference that is required by something one already accepts or if one accepts something on the basis of a false belief. If that idea is correct, someone could not be rationally criticized for failing to reason on the basis of something she neither accepts nor is committed to accepting by what she already accepts. Williams concludes that there can be no true statements predicating external (as opposed to internal) reasons:

. . . the external reasons statement itself will have to be taken as roughly equivalent to . . . the claim that if the agent rationally deliberated, then, whatever motivations he originally had, he would come to be motivated to φ.

But if this is correct, there does indeed seem great force in Hume's basic point, and it is plausible to suppose that all external reason statements are false. For, **ex hypothesi**, there is no motivation for the agent to deliberate **from**, to reach new motivation. Given the agent's earlier existing motivations, and this new motivation, what has to hold for external reason statements to be true, on this line of interpretation, is that the new motivation could in some way be rationally arrived at, granted the earlier motivations. Yet at the same time it must not bear to the earlier motivations the kind of rational relation which we considered . . . for in that case an internal reason statement would have been true in the first place. I see no reason to suppose that these conditions could possibly be met. (1980, p. 109)

In this way Williams argues from the somewhat weaker defeasible internalist claim that reasons must be able to motivate to the stronger claim that reasons must depend on an existing desire. As the argument is presented the crucial move is more a challenge to provide a non-Humean account of the relevant rational relation between one's prior motivational set and the new one that includes the new motivation to **φ**. Those who see no reason to accept the Humean conception of reasons may then respond by explaining their rival conception of good reasoning.

The Humean Theory of Motivation

Still, many philosophers have thought that we can argue in favor of a Humean conception of reasons from the *Humean Theory of Motivation*. The Humean Theory of Motivation accepts a particular gloss on Hume's claim that "reason alone can never be a motive to any action of the will" (*Treatise*, Book II, Part 3, Section 3). Whether or not Hume himself accepted the claim, motivational Humeans believe that motives must bottom out in desires that are themselves not motivated by anything else. In other words, they think that in order to avoid a regress of motives there must be some basic motive and this must be constituted by an existent desire. Michael Smith formulates the view thus:

R at t constitutes a motivating reason of agent A to φ iff there is some Ψ such that R at t constitutes a desire of A to Ψ and a belief that were he to φ he would Ψ. (Smith, 1987, p. 36)

The idea is not the trivial point that being motivated involves wanting to do what one is motivated to do. It is rather that motivation must have its *source* in a desire or set of desires. On the intended reading, the desires involved are not themselves motivated by belief without further desire. Williams's weaker internalist claim required only that correct deliberation be able to motivate action. But according to the Humean Theory of Motivation, we can only get motivation from some preexisting desire. So the upshot of putting them together is the claim on which Williams relied—deliberation to a new desire must always be supported by a desire of the agent not itself motivated by belief alone.

Hume's own argument for this idea seemed to begin from his conception of what reason could produce, because reason was the mental faculty productive of beliefs. If one accepts Hume's conception of the mind, Humean skepticism about the motivating powers of belief seems to follow. Not everyone shares that conception, so contemporary Humeans have offered arguments for his conclusions about motivation that are supposed to be independent of Hume's philosophy of mind. Michael Smith (1987), for example, has argued that we must adopt the Humean view because reasons explanations are a species of teleological explanation that explain phenomena as necessary for the achievement of some goal. Desires are the mental states that constitute an agent's goals, so teleological motivating reason explanations require the agent to desire something that is the goal to which the action is necessary. Part of his argument also turns on showing that no belief can play the goal-providing role desire must play. I won't go into the details of his argument here or pronounce a verdict. But whether persuaded by Smith or for other reasons, many theorists accept the Humean Theory of Motivation.

However the Humean Theory of Motivation is supported, it combines with Williams's weaker internalist claim to support the stronger claim about correct deliberation, that it must depend on a desire the agent has independent of the deliberation in question. The thought is this: According to Williams's weak internalist claim, an agent has a reason to φ only if she would be motivated to φ after correct deliberation from her existing psychological makeup. That motivation has to come from somewhere and if it is to be relied upon it must be the predictable result of the correct deliberation posited. But the Humean Theory of Motivation tells us that motivations must have their source partly in preexisting desires. And it tells us that these desires are not themselves the products of belief alone, unaided by desire. So deliberation can only generate the required motivation if it involves some desire that exists already, independent of the beliefs that go into the deliberative process. That in turn means that the agent will only have a reason to φ if she already has some desire not itself supported by reasoning from which, by correct reasoning, she can reach the desire to φ. In this way we get to a Humean conception of rationality or good reasoning, from a Humean Theory of Motivation.

Schroeder's Argument for Hypotheticalism

Mark Schroeder (2007) suggests a different strategy to support a similar strong *hypotheticalist* conclusion. Humean theories of reasons are *hypothetical* in the sense that one's reasons depend on one's existing motivational state. *Categorical* reasons, by contrast, are reasons that one has no matter how one is antecedently motivated. A broadly Humean conception of reasons promises to unify the domain of practical reasons insofar as we already think some of our reasons fit the hypothetical model. For example, two people can differ in what they have reason to do insofar as they would differ in what they would enjoy doing. If I enjoy dancing and you don't, I will have a reason to dance that you lack. The difference in reasons is explained by an underlying difference in our motivational sets. This much is common sense.

If all practical reasons were like this it would simplify and unify our conception of practical reasons. There are various obstacles to be overcome before such an account is plausible. Schroeder offers several ingenious strategies Humeans can employ to blunt arguments arising from these obstacles. The point to note is simply that *if such obstacles can be overcome*, it might then be reasonable to accept hypotheticalism as providing a unifying conception of practical reasons. And we might have further reason to accept hypotheticalism if the conception explains many of the features we take all practical reasons to have—another thing Schroeder hopes to show.

4.2.4. From Morals/Reasons and Reasons/Motives Internalism to Morals/Motives Internalism

If one thing is necessarily connected to another thing that is itself necessarily connected to a third thing, the first thing is necessarily indirectly connected to the third. If moral truths entail that there are reasons to do what the truths commend, and if practical reasons require something of an agent's motivation, moral truths will also require something about that motivation. This general idea supplies another way to argue for morals/motives internalism. One can use morals/reasons internalism together with reasons/motives internalism to argue for morals/motives internalism. The exact upshot of this way of arguing depends on the specific varieties of morals/reasons and reasons/motives internalism employed in following out the strategy of argument. We don't have space to look at every variation. But I will fill out two different version corresponding to Williams's weaker and stronger reasons/motives internalist claims. As we'll see, we can generate correspondingly stronger and weaker morals/motives internalist conclusions.

Here's an argument for a variety of defeasible morals/motives existence internalism—one that takes as a premise Williams's weaker version of reasons/motives internalism:[7]

1. A person has a moral obligation to φ, only if she has a reason to φ. (Morals/reasons existence internalism.)

2. A person has a reason to φ, only if she would wind up with a motivation to φ were she to reason correctly on the basis of true premises. (Defeasible reasons/motives existence internalism.)

Therefore:

3. A person has a moral obligation to φ, only if she would wind up with a motivation to φ were she to reason correctly on the basis of true premises. (Defeasible morals/motives existence internalism.)

If Williams is right to think that sound practical reasoning must be grounded in existing desire, the second premise would entail a stronger claim:

2'. A person has a reason to φ, only if she has some desire the satisfaction of which would be promoted by φ-ing. (Indefeasible reasons/motives existence internalism.)

And we could substitute it for (2) in the preceding argument to get:

1. A person has a moral obligation to φ, only if she has a reason to φ. (Morals/reasons existence internalism.)
2'. A person has a reason to φ, only if she has some desire the satisfaction of which would be promoted by φ-ing. (Indefeasible reasons/motives existence internalism.)

Therefore:

3'. A person has a moral obligation to φ, only if she has some desire the satisfaction of which would be promoted by φ-ing. (Indefeasible morals/motives existence internalism.)

These two related arguments illustrate how we can construct indirect arguments for morals/motives internalism by putting together premises drawn from other sorts of internalist conclusions. They also illustrate how the conclusions of such indirect arguments can inherit their strength from the varieties of morals/reasons and reasons/motives internalism employed as premises. Defeasibility in the premises will generate defeasibility in the conclusion.

There is much more that can be said both for and against each of the internalist positions we have surveyed. We'll eventually discuss some of these arguments when we look at particular positions with commitments involving internalism. That means I will continue to ignore most of the arguments against internalism, remedying the slight only when we discuss externalist versions of naturalism in later chapters. What I want to do next is to show how the alleged inconsistency of internalism with a set of other plausible metaethical commitments has motivated a number of comprehensive meta-ethical theories and arguments.

4.3. Internalism Is In Tension With Other Plausible Claims About Morality

Morals/motives existence internalism coupled with Humean/hypotheticalist conceptions of rationality will cause trouble for metaethical theories that include non-relativism among their commitments. Thus we can see why various competing metaethical theories find adherents by noticing how they each propose a different way of resolving the tensions between internalism, Humean conceptions of reasons, and more realist claims such as the denial of error theory and relativism. The following claims are in tension with one another:

1. A moral judgement to the effect that an action is morally required of an agent can be correct only if that agent has a pro-attitude toward the action in question. (Strong morals/motives existence internalism)
2. There are many correct moral judgements applying requirements to agents. (Denial of systematic error with respect to moral requirements)
3. Agents differ significantly in their motivating attitudes so that for any such motive there can and will be an agent lacking that motive. (Plausible psychological claim)
4. Correct moral judgements applying to one moral agent in a situation will correctly apply to any other agent in the same situation. (Moral anti-relativism, or *absolutism*)

If we took these claims as premises in an argument we could reason as follows:

5. There are many agents who are in fact required to do some particular action and each such agent has the required pro-attitude toward the action she is required to do. (From 1 and 2)
6. For at least some of these agents, we will be able to find another similarly situated agent who lacks any relevant pro-attitude. (From 3 and 5. 5 suggests that there are a number of agents subject to moral requirements. Given that, along with the number of agents in the world, we should be able to find other agents in situations similar to the agents with the obligations; 3 suggests that some of these other agents are likely to lack the pro-attitude the first has.)
7. Though similarly situated, this agent will not be required to do the action required of her counterpart. (From 1 and 6)
8. But this contradicts 4, which requires that similarly situated agents have the same obligations applying to them.

From here it isn't hard to see how a number of standard metaethical positions are motivated to resolve the tension by rejecting one or another of the claims generating the incoherence. Robust realists, who defend the nonrelative correctness of a large class of moral judgements but who find the empirical claim about human motivational diversity plausible, typically reject the internalism of the first premise to protect their absolutist commitments. Many of the most powerful objections to internalism come from this quarter because internalism would seem to require rejection of one of the other three claims, and the empirical claim about motivation seems well supported by psychological evidence. *Agent relativists*,[8] by contrast, think that the least plausible of our incoherent set is (4) that moral truth and correctness aren't relative. We'll often find them arguing from internalist premises to relativist conclusions. The preceding internalist claim is specifically about agents, so it should be no surprise to find agent relativists relying on some premise of this sort in their main arguments. Finally, *error theorists* embrace a nihilist upshot. They often argue that both internalism and non-relativism are conceptual truths about morality. These conceptual truths plus the well-supported claim about diverse motivation entail that no positive claims about agents being morally required to act are true. According to them we were mistaken to think that there are any such truths. *Hermeneutic fictionalists*[9] can agree with them about the impossibility of true moral claims and for the same reasons. They deny that our ordinary judgements expressed belief in those claims, as opposed to a willingness to treat them as if they were true.

It is worth asking whether the tension between these four claims also motivates *noncognitivism*—roughly the view that moral judgements are not beliefs and that their contents are not representational. It can seem like it should. Had we substituted 'true' for 'correct' in each of the preceding steps, we would have essentially the same tension as exhibited in the earlier argument. One way of resolving the tension in the set when revised to substitute 'true' for correct would be to reject its second premise, which would say that there are true judgements of obligation. Insofar as first generation noncognitivists introduced their position as the view that moral judgements were neither true nor false, they denied that there were any true judgements about moral requirements. So it is tempting to think some of them might have been moved by this line of thought.

On the other hand, they need not have accepted noncognitivism for that reason, and it might have been a mistake if they did. First of all, they could avoid the tension by rejecting another of the four claims. Insofar as noncognitivism is committed to a close connection between a speaker's attitudes and the judgements speakers make, they are more committed to some version of judgement internalism than to the sort of existence internalism captured in the first claim. Furthermore, one doesn't get very far away from the underlying ideas that generate the tension just by denying that moral claims can be true. After all our original formulation doesn't advert to truth at all and we still have the tension. If noncognitivists use a notion of correctness of any sort, and many of them will, they must choose a member of the set to reject other than the second. In fact many present day noncognitivists happily countenance the idea that claims can be correct and even true. They explain such judgements as involving a minimal conception of truth according to which sentences of the form 'X is true' say no more than what the sentence 'X' would say. Such noncognitivists won't deny our second claim, even substituting 'true' for 'correct.' So it is hard to see that their noncognitivism gets its primary support from existence internalism along with the other claims.

Noncognitivists will however draw sustenance from judgement internalism together with the Humean Theory of Motivation:

NC1.   Sincere semantically competent use of an indicative sentence to the effect that some target is right or good requires the speaker making the judgement to have a pro-attitude toward the target. (Strong morals/motives judgement internalism)

NC2.   There are no cognitive states that are themselves identical to or constituted by pro-attitudes, nor are there any that are capable of motivating pro-attitudes. (Humean claim)

NC3.   Therefore sincere and semantically competent use of such sentences must involve pro-attitudes that don't depend upon any beliefs they express.

NC4.   When the sincere and semantically appropriate use of a sentence requires an attitude be present, that sentence expresses that attitude. (One way of understanding the sincerity conditions on speech acts.)

NC5.   Therefore moral sentences express noncognitive pro-attitudes.

If we couple the conclusion about sentences with the thought that an indicative sentence to the effect that ϕ-ing is right (or good) expresses the belief that ϕ-ing is right (or good), it seems plausible that the belief that ϕ-ing is right (or good) either is that pro-attitude or has that attitude as a constituent. The first option is just what old fashioned non-hybrid noncognitivists accept, and the latter generates a version of hybrid expressivism. We should note that judgement internalism most naturally requires an attitude on the part of the speaker or thinker, not of the agent. And that was in fact the way NC1, the judgement internalist claim, was constructed. This puts speaker-relativist views in a good position to accept this variety of judgement internalism and to use it to motivate a cognitivist position consistent with it. They can deny the fourth premise and give an account on which the speaker's noncognitive attitudes play a role in determining the truth or the content of a moral sentence.

We'll look at some of these issues more closely when we survey many of the particular kinds of comprehensive metaethical theory in the chapters to come. But at this stage we should already see how these issues explain the diversity of metaethical approaches that continue to have adherents.

Questions

Comprehension

C1. Explain what the difference between existence and judgement internalism is supposed to be. Give an example of each.

C2. Explain the difference between defeasible and indefeasible internalisms. Give an example of defeasible morals/motives judgement internalism and of indefeasible morals/motives judgement internalism.

Extension

E1. Do you find the practicality thought persuasive? Can you state what you think the idea is in its best form?

E2. How many different kinds of internalism can you use the amoralist to argue against? How do these different arguments work?

Reading

Read along with: Bernard Williams (1980), Christine Korsgaard (1986), Michael Smith (1987) or (1994, chapter 4).

Further reading: Richard Falk (1947) gives a very nice sense of the motivations for internalism. Michael Smith (1994, chapter 3) argues for morals/motives internalism. R. M. Hare (1952) contains several arguments for morals/motives judgement internalism, especially in chapters 1 and 9. David Brink (1984) and Sigrún Svavarsdottir (1999) argue forcefully against internalism of several sorts. Connie Rosati (1996) suggests that there is an internalism requirement on 'good' as when we talk about a person's good. Michael Smith (1987) defends the Humean Theory of Motivation, as does Neil Sinhababu (2009). For more critical views, see van Roojen (1995, 2002), Melissa Barry (2007), Daniel Bromwich (2010), and Steve Swartzer (2013). Sobel and Copp (2001) address the use of "direction of fit" to argue for it. Thomas Nagel (1978) is an important paper discussed by Smith. Smith (1995b) nicely discusses the puzzles generated by accepting motivational internalism. Tresan (2006) is very interesting but will be more understandable after you've read the next four chapters.

Notes

1 The name is somewhat unfortunate insofar as several philosophical subdisciplines have appropriated 'internalism' to label various unrelated views. This can cause confusion as one moves from metaethics to philosophy of language, philosophy of mind, and epistemology. Use of the term in metaethics goes back to the 1940s and 1950s, so it seems futile to try to substitute a different word at this late date.

2 Humeans as I'm using the term are people who accept the thesis that an agent's reasons or motives must be based in an independent or preexisting desire. The view is arguably attributable to David Hume in his *Treatise*. I'll explain in more detail later.

3 The basic way of cutting things up comes from Darwall (1983, pp. 54–55) and Darwall (1997, pp. 305–312).

4 Falk (1945, 1947) and Frankena (1958) introduce the terminology in a discussion of morality. Williams (1980) uses the same internal/external vocabulary to make analogous points about reasons.

5 Darwall (1997) introduces this naming convention. It is widely but not universally used to distinguish the terms of the relation that internalists think necessary. It has the great virtue of reminding readers of what is supposed to be necessary to what.

6 Dreier (1990) does an especially nice job defending this kind of conclusion.

7 The arguments here draw on my entry on motivational internalism for the *International Encyclopedia of Ethics*, LaFollette, Deigh & Stroud (Eds.) (Wiley, 2012).

8 Agent relativists are relativists who maintain that moral claims can vary in truth from agent to agent.

9 Hermeneutic fictionalists think that our current use of moral talk is fictive. They contrast with *revolutionary fictionalists* who deny that our current use is fictive, but propose from here on to use moral talk as a useful fiction.

5 Error Theory

With this chapter we begin a survey of the main varieties of relatively comprehensive metaethical theories. And we start our overall survey with *error theory*, the view that ethics is all a big mistake. Error theorists about morality believe about the moral roughly what atheists believe about the divine. Just as atheists think it is mistaken to predicate being loved by God or gods of anything, error theorists think there is a mistake in predicating rightness or wrongness of any action, or moral goodness or badness of any thing.

Except for one crucial commitment—to the claim that no moral judgements are really true—error theorists would fully be minimal realists. They are cognitivists: they think that moral judgements are beliefs, that moral sentences typically express these beliefs, and that the meaning of such moral sentences is representational. So they believe that sentences deploying moral predicates like 'right,' 'wrong,' 'good,' and so on, have truth conditions, predicate properties, and express propositions. These judgements and sentences would be true if the world were as these judgements and sentences represent it to be. Error theorists share each of these commitments with any minimally realist view. Yet they are not minimal realists because they think moral judgements fundamentally *misrepresent* reality. The inaccuracy is alleged to be deep enough that run-of-the-mill moral beliefs fail to be true. Some error theorists express this thought by suggesting that all moral claims are false. Others endorse a more qualified but still comprehensive thesis, that all *positive* moral claims are false. They limit their thesis to positive claims because they find it natural to express their acceptance of error theory by claiming that nothing is right, good, morally required or permitted, bad, or impermissible. But not every error theorist likes that way of stating the view. Some error theorists avoid calling any moral claims true or false because they think that the underlying problem prevents moral terms from being straightforwardly truth assessable. Such error theorists think that a claim that presupposes a falsity is for that reason itself neither true nor false. Finally, it is at least possible for error theorists to think the problems go beyond false presupposition, to something like failure to pick out a subject matter at all. On such views ethical judgements purport to represent the world, but fail.[1] Error theorists say one or all of these things to express the view that moral thought and talk is deeply in error. We'll look at these divergent ways of expressing an error theory more closely later in the chapter.

But first I want to motivate the view by developing several lines of argument for it. These arguments will invoke claims familiar from the previous chapters, in effect claiming that the puzzles presented there raise insuperable problems for even minimal realism about morality. The fact that there are real flesh and blood error theorists who find themselves driven by some of these puzzles to the nihilist conclusion that all morality is an illusion underlines the importance of these lines of argument.

5.1. Arguments for Error Theory

5.1.1. Two Metaphysical Lines of Argument for Error Theory

It is hard to talk about error theory without beginning with John Mackie, whose 1977 book, *Ethics: Inventing Right and Wrong*, is the focus of much contemporary discussion.[2] We've already explicitly discussed his *argument from disagreement* in chapter 2, and the two arguments that follow are inspired by Mackie's *argument from queerness*. This famous argument might more aptly be called his "*arguments* from queerness," since Mackie presses several issues at once under the queerness banner. There is an epistemic argument, arising out of concerns about intuitionism canvassed in our chapter 3. And there are two metaphysical arguments. One of these is about the explanation of supervenience, an issue we will look at more closely when we consider nonnaturalism in chapter 13. The other metaphysical argument is rooted in concerns about the practicality of morality, where this is interpreted as an objective feature of moral values or reasons themselves. We'll take this argument from queerness as our jumping-off point because it is rich, suggestive, and underdeveloped; Mackie says many things about the allegedly queer nature of moral properties that probably don't all amount to the same thing. This is good for our purposes; it allows us to tease out related but different lines of argument, each leading to error theory and each connected to some issue or other that we surveyed in chapter 4.

Mackie puts the core objection thus:

> Plato's Forms give a dramatic picture of what objective values would have to be. The Form of the Good is such that knowledge of it provides the knower with both a direction and an overriding motive; something's being good both tells the person who knows this to pursue it and makes him pursue it. A objective good would be sought by anyone who was acquainted with it, not because of any contingent fact that this person, or every person, is so constituted that he desires this end, but just because the end has to-be-pursuedness somehow built into it. Similarly, if there were to be objective principles of right and wrong, any wrong (possible)

course of action would have not-to-be-doneness somehow built into it. (Mackie, 1977, p. 40)

Mackie calls the postulated to-be-pursuedness "*objective prescriptivity*," and we might understand it in several ways. I will consider two and use each to generate an error-theoretic argument.

On a natural reading of the passage, to claim objective prescriptivity for a moral property such as rightness would be to make a claim about the motivational powers of those properties. Moral rightness, on this interpretation, would be a property that has the power to motivate people to do what is right without help from any contingent features of the people so motivated, including features of their psychology such as their tastes, desires, propensities to act, and so on. Mere acquaintance with it would be enough to get people to act rightly, no matter what their antecedent psychologies must be like. This is a very strong version of morals/motives existence internalism. Mackie suggests that this strong internalist claim is in some sense built into our notion of rightness and other moral properties. "[The claim of] objective prescriptivity . . . is embedded in ordinary moral thought and language" (p. 42). But the embedded claim is very likely false. No belief is such that it is capable of motivating people *no matter what they are like*. There are various more or less contentious ways of reaching this verdict. One contentious line of argument begins with the Humean Theory of Motivation (abbreviated 'HTM'), which suggests that motivation must be grounded in an independent desire. Given that people's desires are contingent features of people's psychology, some people might lack those that are necessary for moral motivation. Hence no property can be such that merely apprehending it is sufficient to supply motivation for right action. Less contentiously, even if Hume is wrong, there must be some psychological conditions that block, defuse, or defeat motivation, including motivation grounded in the apprehension of any moral property. Relatedly, the real possibility of actual amoralists makes it likely that knowledge of moral truths doesn't by itself suffice for motivation.

Mackie's passage so interpreted suggests the following simple line of argument:

1. Moral judgements predicate properties that are capable of motivating those who apprehend them, just in virtue of being recognized.
2. No beliefs are such that they must motivate anyone without cooperation from other contingent features of the agent's psychology.
3. Thus the properties predicated by moral judgements are not instantiated.
4. And thus the judgements predicating these properties are false or suffer from presupposition failure.

We could give the idea a more obviously Humean spin if we explicitly relied on the HTM to support premise 2, and thereby made clearer the relevance of the Humean theory to the issue. The argument would then be something like this:

1'. Moral judgements predicate properties that are capable of motivating those who apprehend them, just in virtue of being recognized (and not dependent on contingent desires).
2'. No belief is capable of motivating anything absent the presence of an appropriately related desire.
3'. Beliefs and desires are distinct existences, so no belief is such as to require the presence of any desire.
4'. Apprehension is a kind of belief.
5'. Thus no property is such that mere apprehension of it is capable of motivating a person who doesn't have the appropriate desire.
6'. Thus judgements predicating moral properties predicate properties of a sort that could never be instantiated.
7'. Thus the judgements predicating these properties are false or suffer from presupposition failure.

Motivational Humeans, whose view commits them to the second and third premises, must take this argument seriously, at least if Mackie is right to think that objective prescriptivity of this sort is built into moral claims. Given the popularity of the Humean Theory of Motivation, that's no small thing. Nevertheless Humean views about motivation are contentious. Some people are anti-Humeans and they will reject premise 2', premise 3', or both. So it is fortunate for the error theorist that the less controversial premises of the first shorter argument also lead to the same place, again assuming Mackie is right about the motivational that is allegedly "built in" to moral claims.

Of course, it isn't obvious that either of the strong indefeasible internalist claims expressed in premises 1 and 1' really are built into our ordinary moral judgements. And this is where the enemies of error theory will raise their most vigorous objections. It is precisely because it is pretty obvious that some people are not provided with "a direction and an overriding motive" by the moral judgements that the rest of the argument is plausible. So it makes sense to wonder how something so obviously false would be built into what we are thinking and saying when we make such judgements. (We'll come back to this later in the chapter.) The non-error-theoretic friends of motivational internalism seldom argue for indefeasible internalism of this sort. They usually suggest something weaker, for instance that moral properties such as rightness are necessarily accompanied by motivation *in those who are rational* (Korsgaard, 1986; Smith, 1994, 1995a). This kind of internalism could be built into or presupposed by moral judgements without obviously running afoul of Humean strictures, let alone the weaker constraints deployed in the first argument. All one would need to say is that people who lack the necessary independent states required to be motivated in line with one's moral beliefs are therefore irrational. So these people would present no problem for the claim that rational people must be motivated. There are even weaker internalist claims than that one, such as the claim that moral judgements must *normally* motivate people or rational people (Dreier, 1990). If that is all that is presupposed by morality, the fact that people may not be motivated by the moral judgements they accept would show nothing beyond the fact that conditions are not always normal.

Defenders of the queerness argument might thus wish to look for a different candidate for the queer-making feature of moral properties, one that cashes objective prescriptivity out in different terms. They can generate such a reading if they focus on reasons rather than motives. The basic idea is that moral judgements presuppose that moral properties are necessarily reason providing, even if they are not necessarily motivating. Mackie himself suggests that his denial of objective values is equivalent to denying that there can be objectively valid categorical imperatives. And categorical imperatives "would express a reason for acting which was unconditional in the sense of not being contingent upon the present desire of the agent to whose satisfaction the recommended action would contribute as a means" (p. 29). Taking a hint from these passages we might take the objective prescriptivity allegedly presupposed by morality to involve the claim that true moral judgements presuppose the existence of categorical imperatives. Or to put the point another way, objective prescriptivity requires a strong form of morals/reasons existence internalism.

From this starting point we can construct the following argument for error theory:

1*. A moral judgement to the effect that such-and-such is morally required predicates a property of that act-type that gives any agent in a position to do it a reason to do it, a reason that is not contingent on any desires that the agent might have or lack.
2*. All reasons to act depend on the desires of the agent for they are reasons.
3*. Thus the properties predicated by such moral judgements are not instantiated.
4*. And thus the judgements predicating these properties are false or suffer from presupposition failure.

The second premise of this argument is a version of the *Humean Theory of Reasons*, a view also often called *subjectivism*. The view is controversial but it is also popular among philosophers who think about such issues. Bernard Williams's argument against external reasons that we examined in some depth in chapter 4 is an argument for this kind of subjectivism. If Williams is right in making that argument, and if Mackie is right to think that moral judgements presuppose the existence of categorical imperatives, it looks like the argument for error theory is on a firm footing. This isn't to say that these premises are uncontroversial or that they should be. But the first premise of this argument seems less contentious than its counterparts in the previous ways of filling out Mackie's metaphysical queerness argument. So I think this version overall is somewhat stronger than the previous arguments. It poses a real challenge to realists.

This highlights the importance of the discussion of internalism in chapter 4. Not only is the first premise of the argument just a morals/reasons existence internalist claim, but also the subjectivist premise expressing a Humean view of Reasons is itself a species of indefeasible reasons/motives existence internalism. And if we want to bring in another variety of internalism we can just note that Williams argued for this from a defeasible version of reasons/motives existence internalism, as explained in chapter 4.

There may be a connection with the issues in chapter 2 as well. Olson (2014, §6.1) calls the present queerness argument "the argument from irreducible normativity" because he thinks it important to distinguish two senses of 'reason,' 'normativity,' 'favoring,' and so on, and to stress that it is a special irreducible sense of these terms that is at issue. His thought is that there is a reducible sense of each of these concepts that just has to do with following certain norms where these might just be codified rules without any further authoritative backing. (The rules of most games have this status.) Olson wishes to stress that the conceptual claim about reasons he thinks is built into moral notions is not merely like that. Rather genuinely normative reasons have an intrinsic bindingness or normativity that makes it a real mistake to ignore them. But the only way he has to express this thought is to use some other term that is itself normative and this term too might be interpreted in a not genuinely authoritative way. So the best we can do to say what we mean is to use some other normative word (like 'authoritative') to specify that we think there is a kind of action-guiding force required, one that can't be captured by nonnormative vocabulary. This thought sounds very close to Moore's conclusion, grounded in the Open Question Argument, though Olson never deploys that argument to defend the idea. Someone who thinks the Open Question Argument has the upshot that we can't capture the content of a moral judgement without relying on some non-natural normative language might well endorse Olson's normative irreducibility thesis on that basis. From there one might further conclude (as Olson does) that the nonexistence of irreducible normativity would be a reason to think morality (and all normative thought) deeply in error.[3]

Thus we see that Mackie and Olson's skeptical lines of thought arise quite naturally out of motivating ideas canvassed in chapters 2 and 4. As it turns out we can find further arguments grounded in the epistemic issues that form the focus of chapter 3.

5.1.2. An Epistemic Argument for Error Theory

The two interpretations of Mackie's metaphysical queerness arguments on which I focused each depended on attributing some constitutive metaphysical commitment to thought and talk about morality and then arguing that the content of the commitment was false. So for the arguments to work, we have to be in a position to know something about the essential content of moral claims. But not every argument for error theory requires such knowledge. Some arguments focus less on the content of moral judgements and more on the methods by which such judgements are reached. If it can be shown that our moral thinking is sufficiently unreliable, that in itself might be reason to think that morality is a big mistake. The mistake involved would be independent of the arguments we have examined so far, since one can mistakenly believe a truth when one lacks sufficient justification for believing it true. The mistake would consist in relying on epistemic methods that aren't trustworthy or trustworthy enough. Such arguments would be independent of the previous lines of argument and many of their most contentious premises. So they might survive criticisms rebutting the arguments relying on the alleged essential nature of moral properties. But these epistemic arguments are compatible with them and can buttress the upshot that we'd best withhold belief in moral claims of any substantial sort.

Mackie's own argument from relativity (discussed in chapter 2) is a version of this kind of argument; his explanation of moral disagreement there relied on mechanisms that (if actually present) should undermine our confidence that moral judgements are likely to be true. If we are in a position to know that our judgements about morality are unlikely to be true, we are likely unjustified when we continue to believe them. So that argument, if it works, does have the sort of skeptical upshot I am suggesting. But this is not Mackie's only epistemic argument for error theory. His queerness arguments (usually treated as distinct from the argument from relativity) include an *epistemic argument from queerness*. That is the argument I want to focus on here. I will fill it out by connecting it with more contemporary work, as well as with our brief discussion of intuitionism in chapter 3. In introducing this argument Mackie wrote:

> If there were objective values, . . . [and] if we were aware of them, it would have to be by some special faculty of moral perception or intuition, utterly different from our ordinary ways of knowing everything else. These points were recognized by Moore when he spoke of non-natural qualities, and by the intuitionists in their talk about a "faculty of moral intuition" . . . [T]he central thesis of intuitionism is one to which any objectivist view of values is in the end committed: intuitionism merely makes unpalatably plain what other forms of objectivism wrap up. Of course the suggestion that moral judgements are made or moral problems solved by just sitting down and having an ethical intuition is a travesty of actual moral thinking. But, however complex the real process, it will require (if it is to yield authoritatively prescriptive conclusions) some input or this distinctive sort, either premises or forms of argument or both. (1977, p. 38)

Mackie later tells us what intuition is needed for. It is necessary to supply information about the nature of the connection between the ordinary properties of actions, states of affairs or objects to be evaluated, and the evaluative moral properties that those actions, states of affairs or objects are supposed to have. Thus Mackie writes:

> What is the connection between the natural fact that an action is a piece of deliberate cruelty—say, causing pain just for fun—and the moral fact that it is wrong? It cannot be an entailment, a logical or semantic necessity. Yet it is not merely that the two features occur together. The wrongness must somehow be "consequential" or "supervenient"; it is wrong because it is a piece of deliberate cruelty . . . [H]ow do we know the relation that it signifies, if this is something more than such actions being socially condemned, and condemned by us too, perhaps through our having absorbed attitudes from our social environment? It is not even sufficient to postulate a faculty which 'sees' the wrongness; something must be postulated which can see at once the natural features that constitute the cruelty, and the wrongness, and the mysterious consequential link between the two. Alternatively, the intuition required might be the perception that the wrongness is a higher order property belonging to certain natural properties. (1977, p. 41)

The point here is related to our discussion of intuition in chapter 3. We need intuition to provide us with information about how the moral properties are linked to the ordinary nonmoral properties available to perception and ordinary empirical investigation. Mackie credits the intuitionists with seeing the need for some faculty to provide that "input." I noted in chapter 3 that talk of a "faculty of intuition" might be cashed out in terms of a reliable ability, one that doesn't need its own sense organ but that might be realized by a kind of judgemental capacity, one that allows us to judge the moral value of an action or outcome based on its empirically determinable properties. Mackie, as I read him, agrees. But he's skeptical that we have any such faculty. Our judgemental propensities are better explained as absorbed from our social environments than as the outputs of a genuinely recognitional ability.

We can bolster this skepticism by deploying a couple of lines of argument from more recent literature. Sharon Street's (2006) evolutionary debunking argument regarding moral knowledge undercuts the thought that our dispositions to make moral judgements are likely to get things right, at least if we think of the moral truth as independent of our dispositions to judge (as Mackie surely would). This argument is familiar from chapter 3 as well. We might present her view like this:

1. The moral claims we accept are largely determined by the psychological propensities we have evolved to manifest.

2. The selective processes that shaped our psychological propensities favored propensities that generate judgements that lead to reproductive success.
3. If the truth about morality is independent of our judgements about morality, the truth of such reproductive success enhancing judgements is not relevant to their promotion of reproductive success.
4. Therefore, any correlation between our propensities to judge one way or another and such judgement independent truth would be unlikely.
5. Unless our propensities to make moral judgements were generated by processes that favor true moral judgements over false moral judgements, we have no reason to think that our moral commitments are true rather than false.
6. We have no reason to believe that the moral judgements we are inclined to make are true or reliable if moral truth is independent of our judgements about morality.
7. Thus either moral truths depend on our propensities to judge, or we have no reason to think our moral beliefs are accurate.

Intuitionists will agree that the moral claims we accept are determined by our psychological propensities. For their faculty of intuition will be such a propensity. But they must see these propensities as reliable guides to the moral truth, and that is what Street's argument calls into question. Or at least it calls it into question for any view that does not make moral truths depend on our propensities to judge. *Response-dependent* theories, that is theories according to which the truths of morality are truths about our dispositions to respond to what we evaluate, escape the objection, and Street in fact deploys the argument to support such theories.[4] But those rival metaethical theorists who think moral truth is independent of our affective responses must oppose Street's argument more directly. If her argument goes through it calls into question the warrant for thinking of our response dispositions as the exercise of an actual epistemic faculty rather than as just the accidental upshots of selective pressure.

A second line of debunking argument traces its inspiration to a paper by Tamara Horowitz (1998). It too denies the reliability of any *a priori* element in moral judgement provided by intuition. Once again the argument aims to show that the propensities that seem from the inside to yield knowledge really don't because they track irrelevant rather than relevant features of actions. The argument proceeds by identifying ways in which irrelevant information tends to affect our moral judgements. If these influences are sufficiently common it can call into question the accuracy of our judgements, our propensities to make such judgements, and the accuracy of any putative faculty of intuition that might give us *a priori* insight into the moral truth. In pursuit of this idea Horowitz highlighted *framing effects*. Framing effects occur when features of the way a choice is presented affect the moral verdicts people tend to render about that choice. As it happens there is significant experimental evidence that such framing effects do influence our judgements about permissible courses of action. Kahneman and Tversky (1979) asked experimental subjects to choose between different policy responses to a dangerous disease that was sure to kill at least some people. Their subjects' answers varied depending on whether the identical course of action was presented to them in terms of saving people or instead in terms of allowing people to die. Petrinovich and O'Neill (1996) found similar results in their experiments. They asked subjects whether they should switch a train onto a side track in order to save a greater number of people. The subjects responses differed when the language of the possible answers was altered to talk about the lives that would be saved rather than the number of people who would die. Each of these experiments offered identical scenarios with identical outcomes, even when the words used to describe the options were different. Yet, every plausible moral theory agrees that the choice of terms is irrelevant in such cases, and in each experiment we have just one choice described two ways. Identical actions must have identical moral properties, so it is hard to avoid concluding that framing effects undermine the reliability of the dispositions that generate our moral judgements. These experiments thus put some concrete evidence behind the suspicion that our dispositions to come to moral verdicts do not constitute a genuine epistemic faculty. A faculty of the relevant sort must involve a reliable ability to track truths in the moral domain on the basis of nonmoral empirical evidence. If the dispositions to judge that allegedly constitute the faculty of turnout to be unreliable, the putative faculty won't be able to play this role and we'll be left without any way of determining the moral facts from those we have empirical access to. We should then conclude that we have no moral knowledge (Sinnott-Armstrong, 2006a, 2006b).

5.1.3. Other Arguments for Error Theory

While I think these are the strongest and most interesting arguments for error theory, they are not the only ones available. Many others exist in the literature, and like the ones we examined, they can be roughly divided into two groups, metaphysical and epistemic. The metaphysical arguments typically start from claims about what moral properties or facts would have to be like and go on to claim that nothing is or could be like that. So, for example, there are metaphysical arguments that take as premises claims that morality requires free will (Haji, 2002), or that moral properties must supervene on nonmoral properties, or that moral properties must be non-natural. They go on from there to cite problems for the existence of free will, with the supervenience relation, or for the possibility of nonnatural properties. Epistemic arguments, by contrast, aim to undercut the thought that we could have access to ethical truths if there were any. Since it is at least plausible that we should not believe in claims we have no evidence for, we should therefore not believe in moral facts. As Mackie recognized, these two sorts of argument can work together even when neither is strong enough on its own to ground skepticism about morality. But the contrast between epistemic and metaphysical challenges to morality is worth bearing in mind, insofar as each type of challenge is liable to different kinds of rebutting arguments.

5.2. Error Theory and "Nonnegotiable" Commitments

I began with an analogy: Error theorists about morality believe about the moral roughly what atheists believe about the divine. Just as atheists think it is mistaken to predicate being loved by God or gods of anything, error theorists think there is a mistake in predicating rightness or wrongness of any action, or moral goodness or badness of any thing.

The analogy can be extended. Some atheists are atheists because they think that the very idea of divinity contains some incoherence that makes it impossible for anything to instantiate properties that depend on God or gods. So, for example, some atheists think the problem of evil shows that there cannot be an all-powerful, all-knowing, and good being who created this world. Yet they think these attributes must be had by anything that qualifies as God. From this they conclude that there can be no God. Others think there is something incoherent in the very idea of omnipotence and reach similar conclusions. It is crucial to this mode of argument that the features mentioned be *essential* to godhood. If some being could be a genuine god without having those properties, incoherence in that set of properties would not show there to be no gods. The incoherence might instead show that gods have different properties than we thought. But those whose atheism stems from worries about these alleged incoherences think that the very features that generate the incoherence also must be features of anything worthy of the terms 'god' or 'God.' Hence they conclude no gods exist.

Typically error theorists about morality make similar claims about the nature of moral rightness or wrongness or goodness or badness. They claim that some set of features *must* be possessed by these properties themselves or anything that instantiates them. For example, they argue that the capacity to ground categorical imperatives is constitutive of morality. No action would qualify as morally right if it didn't give anyone suitably situated a reason to do that action. This just is (say such theorists) what it is to be right. Such error theorists then go on to argue about the impossibility of anything answering to those demands. Given that impossibility there can be nothing that is right. Each of the metaphysical arguments of which I am aware does something similar. Each rests on treating some feature or other of morality as "nonnegotiable" (Joyce, 2001; Olson, 2014) or "embedded in ordinary moral thought and language" to such an extent as to be constitutive of it (Mackie, 1977, p. 42).

In this section I want to focus on the status of these nonnegotiable claims. As I understand error theorists, they say that these commitments constitute necessary conditions for anything to qualify as a moral fact, a moral judgement, or a moral property. Each nonnegotiable claim is supposed to be rooted in the nature of morality or the nature of moral language or concepts. It is alleged to be in the nature of moral facts that they give reasons, that moral judgements motivate, that moral wrongness requires responsibility, and that moral properties supervene on natural or nonmoral properties. A non-reason-giving fact would not be a moral fact; a non-motivating judgement would not be a moral judgement; an action not freely chosen would not be wrong; and so on. These ideas are put forth as claims about the essential nature of morality. But there is something a bit puzzling about such claims when they are made by someone who denies that there are moral facts or properties. We find out the essential nature of many things by examining those things themselves. We learned that water was H_2O by examining water. We learned that whales are mammals by examining whales. And now that we know these facts we believe them to be essential truths about these things. A liquid would not be water unless it were H_2O. A creature would not be a whale unless it were a mammal. That is an essential truth about whales precisely because there are actual whales with a certain nature. We can't ground parallel claims about the nature of nonexistent things in the nature of the actual things, because there aren't actually any such things. Supposing that there is no Loch Ness monster, it would be odd to claim that being a reptile is essential to being the Loch Ness monster. We would only find that out if we caught or observed such a monster and found out by the usual empirical methods that it was a reptile. This method of securing claims to what is essential is ruled out when there is nothing to observe or examine. And the verdict extends also to the nature of morality if error theory is correct. We cannot determine the essential nature of moral reality by looking, if moral error theory is correct, because error theory entails that there is nothing to go look at.

The point doesn't extend to claims about the essential nature of moral judgements taken as attitudes. These judgements exist so long as people make them, whether they answer to any facts or not. So at least some claims about the nature of these judgements can be investigated empirically. For example some philosophers have investigated whether psychopaths make genuine moral judgements and whether they are motivated by such judgements if they make them (Aharoni et al., 2012). Often however, the error theorist's arguments for allegedly problematic internalist claims are more *a priori* than empirical. Many influential arguments are conceptual, drawing on people's responses to hypothetical scenarios to elicit their judgements about what would count as a genuine moral judgement. So, for example, Hare's (1952) Missionaries and Cannibals argument and Horgan and Timmons's (1991, 1992a, 1992b) Moral Twin-Earth argument rely on our willingness to classify a judgement as moral partly because of its connections with motivation.

This methodology suggests the central problematic commitments are thought of as conceptual truths secured by features of our conceptual schemes and not by the nature of things in the world independently of our way of picking them out in thought. A similar thought seems to lie behind error-theoretic claims about what moral facts and properties must be like. These essential features are not supposed to be discoverable by empirical investigation. They are *a priori* judgements made true by our conceptual schemes that (perhaps partly) settle what a thing has to be like to be what our terms designate. To go back to the example of the Loch Ness monster, we know that such a creature must be of the same species as a creature responsible for some of the reports of creatures glimpsed at Loch Ness. We know because our concept of the Loch Ness monster is the concept of the creature responsible for those sightings. We should note that this way of thinking of the underlying nonnegotiable claims is not completely uncontroversial, natural as it is. It is very much in the tradition of Fregean notions of the mind, according to which thought and language is mediated by descriptive senses that determine what a thing must be like to answer to our thoughts. I think it fair to say that most error theorists making arguments from nonnegotiable commitments or presuppositions are working consciously or unconsciously with this kind of picture.[5] Many of the scientific realists we'll encounter in chapters 11 and 12 are direct reference theorists who question this concept-mediated story about reference determination for moral terms. Theorists convinced by Quine's attacks on the analytic/synthetic distinction will also likely question this way of thinking about moral vocabulary, as it seems to insulate certain constitutive "analytic" truths from empirical or synthetic refutation.

5.3. A Worry About Charity and Some Replies

While Fregean conceptions of the mind, of words, and of concepts are controversial, they're not crazy or unpopular. And perhaps most philosophers remain unpersuaded by Quine's attacks on analyticity. So error theorists aren't biting any real bullets to rely on analyticity and meaning to ground their constitutive claims about morality. Still, error theorists have their work cut out for them when they wish to show that their nonnegotiable claims really are conceptual truths. This is for two somewhat related reasons. (1) When we attribute thoughts to ourselves and others, charity counsels us to interpret our subjects as making as few mistakes as possible consistent with our behavior and epistemic situation. And (2) some of the nonnegotiable claims made by the error theorist are also claims the error theorist later wishes to call into question, often on the grounds of an alleged conceptual incoherence. Since having conceptually incoherent thoughts is a kind of mistake one would often have easy access to, charity would counsel us to avoid attributing such thoughts to people if we could. I'll fill out this worry before going on to discuss how error theorists have typically tried to address it.

Suppose that a friend of yours is an error theorist about tables and chairs. They tell you that the concept of a table or a chair is of a unitary piece of furniture used for sitting. And 'unitary,' as those who wield the concept table and the concept chair use it, means that there can be no space between the parts of a single table or chair. But, your friend goes on to argue, tables and chairs are entirely composed of atoms consisting of electrons, protons, and neutrons with spaces between them. So there are no tables and chairs. Despite the fact that arguments of this sort have a respectable history in philosophy, you might be forgiven if you were unpersuaded. Even if ordinary users of table and chair talk *said* that tables and chairs must be continuous objects, you might think it uncharitable to take them to mean anything that excluded chairs and tables being composed of subatomic particles whirling around. After all, most of these people know subatomic theory. They're not stupid enough to mean to deny what it says about chairs. They just mean that in the ordinary ways that medium-sized objects may be continuous or not, chairs and tables are continuous. They might still be wrong. (In fact I'll bet you can come up with a counterexample to this condition on tables and chairs without too much work.) But they're not wrong because chairs are made of subatomic particles. The *principle of charity* counsels against attributing to people the contradictory thoughts that such furniture is absolutely without gaps and the thought that they are made of electrons, protons, and neutrons with space between them. And the principle seems very plausible in such cases.

Note that the case displays both of the features I suggested apply to most of the nonnegotiable claims underwriting error theories. Our friend's argument attributes a mistake to furniture theory, and it attributes one that evinces conceptual confusion, at least for people familiar with modern atomic theory. And that second attribution makes it more plausible that something has gone wrong with the argument. The very fact that the mistake is relatively simple and easy to see given normal background knowledge makes it somewhat implausible to attribute commitment to the relevant constitutive claim. Suppose instead the argument traded on the thought that chairs are normally for sitting, but then marshaled a surprising and clever argument that chairs were not for that purpose, an argument that no one could reasonably have been expected to come up with without much work. In that case it would be far less implausible to attribute the nonnegotiable constitutive claim to competent users of chair concepts. Given that it would take a difficult line of reasoning to show that chairs are not for sitting, it is not so implausible that ordinary people with ordinary background knowledge are committed to the claim that they are for sitting. I'm not saying one might not resist in this case as well. Philosophy is full of surprising arguments that we are wrong about the nature of our own thoughts and commitments. But it is easier to resist attribution of a constitutive commitment when the commitment is plainly and obviously false than when any problems are not manifest. And this is because it is more plausible to attribute a subtle error to people in general than it is to attribute errors of numbing grossness.

The error theorist has some responses available. One of them is just to point out that we have examples of putative entities about which we are now error theorists, given what we have found out. At one time scientists postulated ether as a medium for the propagation of radio waves, Vulcan as an allegedly undiscovered planet to explain anomalies in the orbit of Mercury, and phlogiston to explain combustion. But now we believe they were wrong and that there is no ether, no Vulcan, and no phlogiston. At one time people thought there were witches who cast spells and thus explained various kinds of misfortune, but now we think those who believed this were mistaken. There are no witches. So there are clearly cases where we come to see that some entity or kind we once thought there was does not exist at all. Our beliefs about them are in error and there are no such things.

This response is to the point as far as it goes. It clearly enough shows that we can reasonably accept error theories about some of the things people believe in. And some of these examples also seem to show that the relevant reasoning works like the envisioned reasoning of error theorists about morality. On the standard story, it was part and parcel of the idea of phlogiston that it was supposed to be released in combustion. Boyle discovered that some elements gained mass when they burned and this was inconsistent with the thought that burning substances gave up phlogiston unless phlogiston had negative mass. Still later, Lavoisier made the case that combustion was a process that required oxygen to combine with the substance burning or rusting. No particular element or substance was always released in such combustion. Thus, the story goes, nothing in fact plays the role constitutive of the nature of phlogiston according to phlogiston theory.[6] And therefore also, there is no phlogiston and phlogiston theory is in error. This version of the story does seem to fit the model on which falsification of a nonnegotiable constitutive commitment supports an error theory. And that model is the standard one adopted by moral error theorists.

Yet there are some differences between the phlogiston story and the story error theorists wish to tell. One is just that it took quite a bit of experimentation and empirical scientific work to falsify phlogiston theory. There was nothing conceptually confused in the postulation of phlogiston by earlier scientists. It made sense of phenomena with which they were familiar and was entirely coherent with what they then knew. It was only after experiments were conducted in which substances were weighed before and after combustion that troubles for the theory came to light. So there is an important disanalogy between the trouble with phlogiston theory and the alleged trouble for moral theory. In the former the reasons to deny the existence of phlogiston were not *a priori* available to the users of the term. It is thus not uncharitable to attribute to the advocates of phlogiston theory a commitment to the conception of phlogiston that in the end leads to falsification of the theory. The philosophical arguments for moral error theory rarely rely on previously undiscovered empirical evidence. Take the argument from objective prescriptivity, set out in steps 1*–4* earlier in this chapter. The main controversial premise is the Humean Theory of Reasons, captured by 2*. This claim is often treated as though it is *a priori*. It is also often a conclusion supported by reasons/motives internalism coupled with the Humean Theory of Motivation, and sometimes the latter is accepted on empirical considerations regarding weakness of will. This mode of argument for the Humean Theory of Reasons is thus empirical. But the empirical premise in the argument is not arcane. It relies on facts we all already recognize—that people sometimes don't do as they think they should. So if commitment to an anti-Humean theory of reasons is the error built into morality, it should have been easier to spot than the problems that undermined phlogiston theory. We would thus be less charitable to attribute that error to all users of moral language and moral concepts than we would to attribute similar errors in the phlogiston case.

That conclusion may be a little too hasty. Even if the premises of many error-theoretic arguments are *a priori*, they may not be *obviously* true, even to competent ethical thinkers. The premises of error-theoretic arguments are, in fact, almost all philosophically controversial. There are lively disputes about the Humean Theory of Motivation, about the Humean Theory of Rationality, about nonnaturalism, about the requirements for responsibility and about any number of other premises used to ground error-theoretic attacks on morality. Given that we know this, we also know whatever the truth is a number of our peers have missed it. If I have a view about who is right in these debates, consistency requires me to think that those on the other side get it wrong. Error theorists are as entitled as anyone else to say that those with whom they disagree have gotten it wrong, and this shows no lack of charity. So far then, charity doesn't decisively tip the scales against error-theoretic arguments from nonnegotiable constitutive claims about ethics.

It is important to step back and note the state of the debate here. Neither side has a knock-down argument. The opponents of error theory can point to historical examples where what seemed to be constitutive commitments of a discourse were given up in the face of evidence. People once thought atoms were indivisible and that this was essential to them. We no longer believe that. Yet we also have examples where evidence led scientists to conclude that entities postulated by a scientific theory do not exist and therefore that thought and talk presupposing that they do is false or otherwise inappropriate. For that is how things sit with ether, Vulcan, and phlogiston. Until we have an account of what separates these examples from one another, we won't easily be able to decide how things should go if we discover deep incoherence in people's most closely held moral convictions.

5.4. Epistemology and Reference

At this point it may be useful to bring in epistemic arguments for error theory. Such arguments don't rely on finding nonnegotiable commitments built into moral theorizing. They thus bypass objections to error theory that turn either on a lack of charity, or to rejection of analyticity, or to rejection of Fregean theories of reference for moral terms. The basic point of epistemic arguments for moral error is that we are not in fact in touch with anything about which our moral judgements reflect knowledge. That thought causes trouble for realism whatever your view of analyticity or your theory of reference.

It isn't all that surprising that an argument for the claim that we don't have knowledge about some domain will underwrite skepticism about that domain, at least in the sense that we have no reason to believe that what we think is true. But it is compatible with that thought that there are truths about the domain even while we don't know those truths. Perhaps we ought not assert, believe, or affirm anything about the domain, but there may be truths that remain hidden. As it turns out, however, arguments that undermine our claims to knowledge can in fact also be used to argue for something stronger, that the putative domain of which we purport to speak is in fact empty. There are no truths to be known and nothing for our claims to be true of. Let me explain.

We have already noted that some realists doubt the Fregean story of reference determination that the standard error-theoretic arguments often seem to assume. As we'll see, they can use that doubt to undermine standard error-theoretic arguments that proceed from allegedly problematic conceptual commitments built into moral claims. These realists think that moral terms are natural kind terms akin to scientific kind terms. And they think that natural kind terms get their referents not via a mediating description satisfied by their referents, but rather via causal interaction with their referents, interaction that gives those who refer to them knowledge about the referents. Well known proposals of this sort were popularized by Kripke and Putnam in the 1970s. The thought goes that we can speak of items outside our direct acquaintance because they are responsible for various observable phenomena that give us epistemic access to the referents via their effects. Richard Boyd's (1988) sketch of a semantics of moral terms develops the direct reference theory for moral terms. We'll examine it more closely in chapters 11 and 12 on scientific realism.

Here I want to emphasize a general feature of such accounts. Abstracting from most of the details, extant anti-Fregean, direct reference theories require the referent of a term to be among the causes of our beliefs about these very referents. And this requirement can be exploited by error theorists to argue that moral claims are not true in virtue because they lack a referent. Many of the arguments that undermine our claims to know anything about morality would, if true, show that we did not stand in the right sort of causal relation to properties that are candidates for rightness, wrongness, goodness, and so on. If causal theories of natural kind terms were correct this would show that such terms have no referent. Our sentences employing such thoughts would express no proposition and the thoughts most directly expressed by such sentences would be lacking in content.

Here's an example. Gil Harman's (1977) story about the hoodlums and the cat can be used to ground one such line of argument. As we saw in chapter 3, Harman argues that the best explanation of our moral observations (and hence our moral judgements based on those "observations") is our individual psychological profiles coupled with the ordinary descriptive phenomena that we see. And this explanation in no way depends on the truth of anything we believe about morality. If he's right that the best explanation of our moral attitudes in no way invokes moral properties or facts, a causal theory of reference won't be in a position to secure a referent for the terms used to express these attitudes. So Harman-inspired skepticism about moral knowledge leads directly to skepticism that moral claims are about anything at all, at least if causally mediated direct reference theories are correct. Sharon Street's (2006) and Richard Joyce's (2007) arguments about the evolutionary irrelevance of moral truth would have a similar upshot. On their views, any relation our beliefs about morality bear to independent moral truths would be a mere accident. Our moral beliefs are best explained by their adaptive consequences and not by truths they allegedly track. If these arguments work they can be deployed to counter realist uses of direct reference theory. Thus, if a causal account is the correct account of reference determination for moral predicates, it would open up an alternative rationale for the postulation of moral error. Rather than claiming that some unsatisfied descriptive condition must be satisfied by any property worthy of the name 'moral rightness,' error theorists could instead argue that moral terms are nonreferring expressions. The terms do not stand in the right causal reference determining relation to anything that might be their referent.

Such arguments will typically rely on some sort of inference to the best explanation as reason to exclude the candidate moral properties from causal relevance to the explanation of our moral beliefs. And such inferences typically are only warranted after considering all candidate explanations. So making the case would involve a lot of work. Still, such inferences provide error theorists with an additional strategy of argument, and one that is immune to many standard responses to the arguments that posit nonnegotiable commitments for morality.

5.5.   Error Theorists Owe Us a Theory of Error

In section 5.3 I suggested that error-theoretic arguments based on allegedly nonnegotiable moral commitments face a challenge in backing up the claim that these commitments are genuinely part and parcel of moral thinking. The more egregious the mistake in accepting such presuppositions, the less credible it is that our moral practices commit us to them. If these are genuine mistakes how could so many people been otherwise convinced? Error theorists have for the most part faced this challenge head-on by offering a theory to explain how it is that people come to make the error in question. The better their explanation, the more believable their overall position because such explanations make it more plausible that people are in fact guilty of the alleged error.

I can't canvass every theory of error an error theorist might propose to play this explanatory role. But I should at least provide an example. The one I have in mind owes a lot to David Hume (1888) but comes most directly from John Mackie (1977, p. 42ff.). The basic idea is that people are making a mistake when they judge that an action or thing has a moral property to which their reactions are an appropriate response. In reality the explanation goes the other way around. People are apt to have certain sorts of responses to certain sorts of things. When faced with things that trigger the responses, they project the causes of those responses into their objects, taking them to have some active property that causes them to respond in this way. But really the source of the responses lies within those who have the responses, in their dispositions and emotional propensities. They err in attributing their own responses to active powers in the objects they assess, powers that in some sense embody the responses in their natures. Theorists who like this kind of story accuse those who take morality at face value of making a "projective error," imputing to the objects of our judgements powers that really reside in us as we respond to these objects.

That's all very abstract. Let's get more concrete with an analogy. When one is nauseated by something it seems to us that the nausea-inducing phenomenon has a power over us and that we are reacting to a property in the target that manifests this power by causing our nausea. Suppose we are working in a daycare center and one child vomits. Almost immediately several other children follow suit. Nearly as immediately certain responses well up inside us as we observe the baby barf on the rug. We think about having to clean it up and we feel nauseated and we have to work to keep from adding to the mess with our own nauseating contributions. We take ourselves to be reacting to a property of the baby barf—that it is nauseating. The vile puddle seems to have a power over us in virtue of its nature. We are just responding to that power. It is objectively nauseating and all appropriately sensitive individuals would respond as we do.

But, the story goes, this is a mistake. Baby barf is not objectively nauseating. Instead we feel nausea and we attribute what we feel to a property of the object that triggers the feeling. We "spread our responses on the world" as Hume might say. If we think about this from the outside, we can come to realize that the real work is being done by ourselves, by our dispositions to respond to certain stimuli. Because our ancestors often shared food, it was adaptive to be nauseated by the vomit of one's compatriots. When we ate poison with our friends it might save our lives if we vomited at the first hint of trouble, the hint provided by their vomiting up what we both ate. So natural selection created creatures with our nausea responses, which include dispositions to vomit in sympathy. When we attribute our vomiting to a disposition of vomit itself we are making a kind of mistake in where we locate the causal powers. They are in us, not in the vomit. We make a projective error. Or so the story goes. Someone might well want to defend a dispositional account of the nauseating that would not entail that there's a mistake in thinking such things nauseating. But for the moment, let's go along with the story and concede that our judgement that baby barf is nauseating involves a mistake.

If this is a mistake, it is a very natural mistake. And that fact allows this story to explain how it could be that so many people could (allegedly falsely) think that baby vomit, or any vomit, was nauseating. They do so because they erroneously attribute a disposition to feel, actually located in themselves, to a special power in the objects that trigger this disposition. If the error theorist can make a parallel story plausible for moral beliefs—that they are mere artifacts of our mistaken disposition to conflate our psychological response dispositions with real powers of the objects to which they respond—the error theorist immunizes herself to the charge that her theory is implausibly uncharitable to those who make moral judgements. For it is the essence of charity to attribute common and easy-to-make mistakes to a person, rather than brute failures to ignore obvious truths. There may be other ways to construct a theory of error to pay the relevant explanatory debt, but this example should at least make clear how the debt could be paid.

5.6. Some Bookkeeping Matters: Error, Truth, Falsity, and Truth-Aptness

The exposition of error theory so far has sloughed over some issues about how best to describe the view. We've spoken of some sort of error central to continued use of moral words and ideas, but we've avoided saying that error theorists think that all moral judgements are false. Which moral judgements should be ruled false if error theory is to be accepted depends on some delicate matters of semantic bookkeeping. Most error theorists have argued for their theory by arguing that moral judgements presuppose or entail nonnegotiable but false commitments. And there are different views about how to treat presupposition and similar sorts of commitment when it comes to ruling sentences that involve them to be true or to be false. One view is that false presuppositions make a judgement false, whereas another is that they make the judgements that presuppose them unable to be either true or false. Let me explain via an example of Bertrand Russell's (1905). Take this sentence:

BALD KING: The present king of France is bald.

Russell suggests that this sentence really means that there is a unique individual who is presently the king of France and that person is bald. If that is what the sentence means, we should rule it false. A conjunction is false when either conjunct is false, so bald king is false. But another option is to think it presupposes but does not literally mean that there is a person who is presently king of France. On this view the sentence is not conjunctive in its content. Rather it has content on the assumption that there is a present king of France. And on that assumption it says of the person who is the French king that that individual is bald. Since there is no such individual, it doesn't predicate baldness of anyone and hence is neither true nor false. For all that, it is defective for relying on a false presupposition.

A parallel issue arises for error theorists who postulate nonnegotiable commitments standing behind moral discourse. If they treat these commitments as built into the meanings of moral sentences as an extra conjunct in what on the surface look like simple subject predicate sentences, they will have to rule them false. Suppose we analyze "Lying is wrong" as:

LYING: Lying has a property wrongness, and wrongness is necessarily motivating.

Error theorists who argue for their theory by denying the coherence of properties that necessarily motivate will think the second conjunct false. Hence they will think the whole conjunction false and be committed to ruling "Lying is wrong" false. Those who instead treat the problematic claim as presupposed will instead think that the sentence is not apt for truth or falsity.

There is a bit of discomfort in treating the problematic commitment as an extra conjunctive part of the sentence, insofar as "Lying is not wrong" also shares the problematic commitment "Lying is wrong" carries. It would say:

Lying does not have the property wrongness and wrongness is necessarily motivating.

This too is false if the error theorist is right. So, "Either lying is wrong or lying is not wrong" will be false as well. That follows from the fact that both are false and also from the assumption that all uses of the word 'wrong' will carry with it the extra conjunctive commitment. Whether that is a terrible view or not will depend on general considerations in the philosophy of language, and probably not on anything particular to metaethics. The same issues arise with 'ether,' 'Vulcan,' and 'phlogiston.' If the conjunctive view is implausible for those terms it will likely be the same for ethical terms as understood by error theorists. Such error theorists will then have available whatever view turns out to be correct about those terms. Treating the false claims as presuppositions that are not part of the truth conditional content of the relevant terms will likely be an available option.

These are interesting issues in their own right, but given that they must be faced in other domains, the error theorist can deploy the best general view and escape any deep difficulty.

5.7. Summary and a Moral

We began the chapter with several lines of argument to the effect that morality, by which we mean the things we currently think and believe about morality, involves an important error. These arguments developed ideas familiar from previous chapters into reasons for thinking that morality as a whole is unlikely to be correct or true. Some of these arguments were metaphysical whereas others were epistemic. Each of the metaphysical arguments treats some problematic claim as a nonnegotiable commitment of morality. The problematic nature of the nonnegotiable claim is allegedly inherited by our ordinary moral judgements so that they are themselves infected by the underlying error. If the problematic claims cannot be true, as error theorists allege, neither can the moral claims that presuppose them.

I suggested that the two main components of this strategy of argument were in some tension; reasons to think that an alleged commitment involves error are also reasons to think the commitment defeasible and negotiable. Furthermore, if the problem is obvious we have even less reason to think people have failed to notice the problem. And that in turn makes it less likely that they really did go on to build these claims into their moral concepts and commitments. I suggested that there were two ways error theorists might respond to reduce the tension. One is to put more weight on epistemic arguments that don't rely on privileging any particular controversial feature of our moral judgements as constitutive of morality. The other is to offer a theory of error to explain how people could come to build an allegedly false assumption into their moral practices at the ground floor.

We began our survey of comprehensive metaethical theories with error theory for a couple of related reasons. First, it highlights the seriousness of the puzzles we just recently surveyed; each error-theoretic argument suggests that one or another of these lines of thought makes it unlikely that we can give a vindicating account of morality and moral practices. Second, the possibility that this might be the correct conclusion to draw should add seriousness to our examination of alternatives. If you can't get yourself to believe that your moral views are all deeply wrong, you should be motivated to find an alternative view you can accept. And if you do find error theory plausible, you will want to survey the alternatives to assure yourself that there are no better metaethical options.

Questions

Comprehension

C1. Explain the parallel between moral error theory and atheism.

C2. Use an interpretation of objective prescriptivity to construct a simple argument for error theory.

C3. Give an example of an epistemic argument for error theory.

C4. Mackie agrees with Moore about moral epistemology in a particular respect. What epistemic claim is it that they agree on?

Extension

E1. Construct an argument for error theory that uses moral responsibility to argue for error.
E2. Construct an argument for error theory that uses convergence to argue for error theory.
E3. Is one or the other of these most plausibly thought of as requiring the central claims to be "nonnegotiable" or "built into" the meaning or essence of moral rightness, wrongness, goodness, etc.? Can the arguments do without making such claims about what is essential to the relevant moral properties?

Reading

Read along with: John Mackie (1977, chapter 1) and possibly Caroline West (2010).

Further reading: Brink (1984) and Shepski (2008) are critical responses to Mackie's arguments for error theory. Streumer (2011) provides an interesting response to some criticisms of it. Garner (1990) fills out a version of the queerness argument. Burgess (1998) is a reasonably approachable article-length defense of error theory. Joyce (2001) and Olson (2014) are book-length defenses. Finlay (2008) responds to Joyce. Street (2006) presses evolutionary challenges to realist metaethical theories, Wielenberg (2010) resists, and Vavova (2015) is a nice overview of the issues. I consider other experimental challenges to moral epistemology in van Roojen (2014). Strawson (1950) and Russell (1957) contain the Russell-Strawson debate about presupposition failure.

Notes

1   According to these latter two error-theoretic views, ethics still at least purports to be cognitive and representational, even if it fails to represent and the states of mind might fail to have genuine content. So I think it is still fair to say that even these versions of error theory endorse most of minimal realism. Presupposition failure will be part of all domains in one way or another without by itself calling into question the generally representational character of discourse in a domain that allows it.

2   Mackie's first chapter is a reworking of a much earlier journal article, Mackie (1946).

3   Whether we should treat this as a third metaphysical argument for error theory is probably not worth spending a lot of time on. Clearly an error theorist *could* argue that moral claims presuppose irreducible normativity and that there is no such thing, so moral claims are defective. And that would not be an argument explicitly about categorical imperatives or reasons. Olson himself is probably better interpreted as offering an alleged improvement on the argument from morals/reasons internalism that I offer as an interpretation of Mackie queerness argument in the main text.

4   Richard Joyce (2007) in fact uses his similar line of argument to support error theory.

5   I don't mean to say that all error-theorist must be Fregeans. For one thing you might
    think that there are ways of thinking of things that put conditions on what a thing has
    to be like but that fall short of anything capable of determining a unique referent. And,
    as I'll go on to argue, epistemic arguments can generate arguments for error theory that
    non-Fregeans can endorse.
6   Lavoisier (1777).

6   Simple Subjectivism

Standard *subjectivist* metaethical views define the content of moral judge-ments so that moral properties are about the subjective responses of moral appraisers and moral agents. Relevant subjective responses include desire and affective attitudes of many sorts depending on the particular theory. Subjectivism gets much of its impetus from the thought that there is some-thing especially practical about morality. This is the same idea that the internalists of chapter 4 are trying to capture. So it is no wonder that sub-jectivists are internalists. The simplest versions of subjectivism try to explain the practicality of morality by postulating an especially tight connection between the contents of moral judgements and the motives one might have for acting in accord with the judgement. In particular, the simplest subjec-tivisms make the contents of those judgements be *about* the very motives on which agents act when they do what is right or eschew what is wrong. One individualistic variant holds that the property of being right just is the property of being desired or approved of by the speaker or appraiser. Another adopts a similar view but says that the relevant motives must belong to the agent whose actions are being judged, not the speaker of the utterance. To enable discussion let's call views like the first variant *appraiser subjectivism* and those like the second *agent subjectivism*. (Appraiser subjectivism can also be called "speaker subjectivism," but since people can silently make moral judgements we'll try to stick with the former.) The individualized versions of each sort can be broadened by widening the group whose motivating attitudes is relevant. These versions will relativize their judgements to the motivating commitments of the speaker's or agent's society, to generate vari-ants we will call *appraiser group subjectivism* and *agent group subjectivism*. Since most of these views wind up relativist (in senses to be explained later) the very same views sometimes get called "speaker relativism," "speaker group relativism," "agent relativism," "agent group relativism," and so on in the literature. These views count as minimally realist insofar as they hold that the predicate 'morally right,' for example:

1.   Stands for a property, the property of being desired or approved of by the speaker (or agent or speaker's group).

2. The sentence 'X is morally right' represents X as having the property of being approved of by the speaker (or agent, or speaker or agent's group).
3. The content of 'X is right' is that X is approved of by the speaker (or agent, or speaker or agent's group).
4. An assertion of 'X is right' expresses the belief that X is approved of by the speaker (or agent, or speaker or agent's group).
5. The belief that X is right represents things to be just the way the sentence 'X is right' represents them to be; they both represent X as being approved of by the speaker (or agent, or speaker or agent's group).
6. The belief that X is right and the sentence 'X is right' are true when X in fact is approved of by the speaker (or agent, or speaker or agent's group).
7. At least some indicative sentences of the form 'X is right' do in fact represent the world correctly, and these sentences turn out to be true in virtue of correctly representing them as being desired by the speaker (or agent, or speaker or agent's group).

The view is cognitivist, inasmuch as both moral sentences and moral beliefs are interpreted representationally, it postulates real properties as the referents of moral predicates, and it classifies some moral judgements as true. So it is committed to central minimal realist ideas.

But keep in mind that minimal realism is my name for a view that involves these minimal features. Not everyone will understand what this name picks out, since I've chosen it as a name for a subset of features that realist views endorse. Most views people call "realist" go well beyond these features. Simple subjectivism of the sort we're talking about is far from robustly realist. For one thing, the property that is the referent of the target moral predicate is a subjective property, a property that depends on the subjective states of a speaker or agent. In fact individualistic speaker subjectivism is so far toward the subjectivist end of the spectrum that believing that an action is right comes close to making it so (at least if we can't be wrong about whether we desire something in the relevant way). Yet most metaethicists think it criterial for realism that the truth of a judgement not depend on its being made or even upon facts about the person making it. In expressing this view they suggest that realism requires "stance independence," "observer independence," or "response independence," as opposed to dependence. Group-oriented versions of subjectivism make them less dependent on the person making the judgement insofar as the truth of a moral claim depends on more than just the attitudes of that one person. Still they are dependent on the shared subjective responses of the group including the speaker or agent so they don't count as fully response independent.

Furthermore, these views tend toward relativism since different speakers, agents, and groups can approve of different things. Banning gestation crates will be right relative to the perspective of those individuals or groups that disapprove of animal cruelty, but not relative to those who think animal welfare has no moral relevance. The very same judgement will be true when made by members of one group but not by members of the other. We will focus some attention on several varieties of relativism later on. Here we should just note that this form of relativism is entailed by simple subjectivism along with the observation that people differ in their attitudes of approval and disapproval. Individual appraiser or speaker subjectivism will make the truth of moral claims relative to individual appraisers or speakers, and individual agent subjectivism will make it relative to individual agents, and group versions of these views will make such truth relative to larger groups. Insofar as most metaethicists class relativism as a version of irrealism, we have another reason to deny that the view is robustly realist.

6.1. What Simple Subjectivism Has Going for It

Simple subjectivism has one great virtue. It makes it easy to explain the action-guiding nature of morality and moral judgements. Or, more carefully, it makes it easy to explain some of the simplest and most direct versions of internalism that aim to capture the action-guiding nature of morality. The explanations are not exactly the same for each version of internalism, depending on whether the speaker, the agent, or a group is the main focus. But the explanations are related to one another. I won't discuss each and every internalist thesis aimed at capturing the practicality of morality, but we should look at several.

Recall that internalism postulates various necessary connections between moral judgements, reasons, and motives, and that we have adopted Darwall's slash-names to indicate what is necessarily connected with what. Morals/motives internalism holds that moral judgements necessarily involve a connection with motivation. Reasons/motives internalism postulates a similar connection between reasons and motives. And so on. Recall also that internalism could be a thesis about the facts about morality or reasons, or it could be a thesis about the psychological states that seem to have these facts as their contents. Judgement internalists think that the psychological state of believing one is morally obligated or believing that one has a reason is necessarily connected with motivation, whereas existence internalism claims that the fact that you have a moral obligation or have a reason is necessarily connected to some fact about motivation. And finally, recall that the nature of the allegedly necessary connection can vary. For example, it might be a very strong claim that true moral judgements about agents require actual motivation in the agent that they are about. Or it might be the much weaker claim that such judgements are true so long as the agent would be motivated if they were rational, had full information, and had time to think. The former claim is an indefeasible internalist thesis, whereas the latter is defeasible.

6.1.1. Simple Subjectivism Explains Morals/Motives Existence Internalism

Simple subjectivism entails the strongest versions of morals/motives existence internalism, for it says that moral facts just are facts about what an agent (or appraiser) desires to do (or have done). Since desires are a kind of motivational state, a true moral claim will entail that the agent (or appraiser) has a motive to do what the moral claim in question indicates is right. If, as simple appraiser subjectivism holds, the fact that giving to Oxfam is right just is the fact that giving to Oxfam is something I (the speaker, writer, or thinker making this judgement) desire to do, then necessarily if giving to Oxfam is right I will be motivated to do it. And if, as simple agent subjectivism holds, the fact that torture is wrong just is the fact that the agent for whom it is wrong has a desire that torturing would conflict with, then necessarily the agent will be motivated not to torture. The motives in question may or may not be strong enough to determine the speaker or agent's actions. Different versions of simple subjectivism might have different commitments about that. But they'd all have a very neat explanation for the truth of a strong version of existence internalism.

We've already noted that some writers use the term 'speaker subjectivism' as a rough synonym for 'appraiser subjectivism.' When a judgement is expressed vocally the relevant appraiser is the speaker who expresses it. This may call your attention to a pattern in the preceding examples. Just as we can distinguish versions of internalism that require motivation in *agents* from those that require the motivation in *speakers* (or writers or thinkers), we can construct versions of subjectivism that take the *agent's* motives as the subject and those that take the *speaker's* (or writer's or thinker's) motives as what make moral claims true. And once you notice that, it is just another small step to notice that agent subjectivism most directly explains agent internalism, while speaker or appraiser subjectivism most directly explains speaker or appraiser internalism. (Here we are using the terms 'agent' and ' appraiser' or to indicate whose desires and motives are the subject of the relevant subjectivist and internalist claims.)

Simple subjectivist explanations of these strong internalist claims are very direct, insofar as the content of the relevant moral judgement just is a claim about how an object or action connects with the motivations of an agent or appraiser. It is so direct you might wonder whether we have an explanation at all. Appraiser subjectivism entails appraiser internalism directly. It identifies the moral fact with a fact about the motivation of the person making the judgement. And agent subjectivism entails agent internalism in a parallel way, identifying the relevant moral fact with a fact about the agent's motivation. The directness of this explanation might lead to a puzzle. If the moral truth just is the same fact as the fact about motivation that it is supposed to be connected to, how can it explain that this fact obtains? For that would seem to be a fact explaining itself, and how could that be an explanation?

I think the thing to say here is that this isn't supposed to be a causal explanation. The subjectivist explanation of internalism is not trying to show that true moral judgements cause moral motivation (or vice versa), nor that the truth of subjectivism causes there to be a necessary connection between morals and motives. What subjectivists are trying to explain is why it is true that whenever a moral judgement is true, the agent about whom the judgement is made has a motive to do what the judgement indicates. They're trying to explain the necessity of this connection. And they explain that by postulating an identity between the things necessarily connected. When one thing just is a (seemingly) other thing, that will explain why we always find them together (so to speak). As it turns out they are just one and the same thing. That does offer an explanation of the connection. To use an analogy, suppose you notice that sisters always seem to have a sibling. And suppose you are told this is necessary and you go on to believe it. Still, you wonder why this is so. If you then find out that the property being female and having a sibling just is what it is to be a sister, you understand why it is necessary. What you formerly took to be two distinct properties turn out to be one and the same property, and that is why they necessarily co-occur.

6.1.2. Simple Subjectivism Can Explain Morals/Reasons Existence Internalism

Most simple agent subjectivists also accept morals/reasons existence internalism, often for reasons prior to their acceptance of subjectivism about morality. That is, many of them think that any reason to act must be based on motives for the action that the agent already has, and that such motives are constituted by the agent's actual desires. Views of this sort are often called "Humean" views about practical reasons. The name comes from David Hume who famously argued that "reason is and ought only to be a slave of the passions" (Hume, 1888, II. 3, §3). Bernard Williams's stronger internalist thesis (discussed in chapter 4) is a view of this sort. From this Humean point of view, it follows that morality can provide reasons for action only if it connects up with desires had by the agent who has the reasons. That seems to entail that moral considerations won't provide reasons to those without the requisite preexisting desires. The resulting view would seem to leave some large class of people—those lacking the relevant desires—with no reason to do what morality requires of them. What they do might be wrong, but they would still have no reason to avoid it.

   Agent subjectivists can resist this conclusion by trimming the demands of morality. On their view, moral judgements are true only when the agent has a motive that would be served by obeying morality's commands. For truths about morality just are truths about which actions serve a person's goals as given by their desires. The upshot will be that agents always have reason to do what morality requires of them. On one way of looking at things, this strengthens the authority of morality insofar as it guarantees that agents will have reason to do as morality demands. On another way of looking at things, it limits the authority of morality for it limits what morality can ask of any given person to fit their preexisting desires. Careful readers will notice that the view entails a kind of relativism. If morality only asks of people what they have reason to do, and if (as Humeans should believe) different people will have reasons to do different things in all domains, morality will ask different things of different people.

We'll come back to these issues later and eventually treat relativism in greater depth. For the moment I just want to note that the view under consideration is committed to morals/reasons existence internalism. So if you find such internalist claims plausible, simple agent subjectivism has that going for it.

6.1.3. With a Few Extra Assumptions, Simple Subjectivism Can Explain Morals/Motives Judgement Internalism

So there's a very tight connection between subjectivism and morals/motives existence internalism and also morals/reasons existence internalism. If moral truths just are truths about people's motivational states, it will not be a surprise that morality must motivate the people whose motivational states are the subject of these truths. Nor will it be a surprise that these people have reason to do what morality asks.

Do the entailments from subjectivism to internalism extend also to judgement internalism? Not quite. As long as people can be mistaken about what they have motives to do, a person might mistakenly think some action was right because approved of by herself, but be wrong about that. And in such cases the person making the judgement need not be motivated to do what they judge correct. Still, we don't need to make too many further assumptions to generate a judgement internalist upshot from most varieties of subjectivism. If we suppose that people are transparent to themselves, so that they know what they approve or disapprove of, they'll only make sincere moral judgements about themselves when they are in fact motivated to do what they judge morally required. This means that simple speaker subjectivism plus transparency entails that sincere moral judgements will of necessity motivate those who make them. Simple agent subjectivism will entail the same thing so long as a person is making a moral judgement about her own actions. But agent subjectivism won't give that verdict when the judgements are about the moral obligations of others. For, at least on the simplest versions, nothing guarantees that we will have the same motives as the agents about whom we make the judgements.

We've seen that even simple subjectivism comes in many varieties and that each of the varieties can explain at least some internalist theses. Thus someone who accepts one of these theses has some reason to accept the corresponding versions of subjectivism. Different internalist theses will support different versions of subjectivism because not every subjectivist view explains every kind of internalism. If you think the practical nature of morality demands that it motivate those to whom it applies, some version of agent subjectivism would offer an explanation of why this was so. Similarly, if you think that moral judgements must motivate those who make them, speaker subjectivism has a story to tell about why this is so, and that story might form part of an argument to the best explanation in favor of speaker subjectivism. And so on for various other internalist attempts to capture the practicality of morality. This way of thinking suggests that we might want to accept one or another version of subjectivism as the best explanation of a corresponding internalist thesis we take to be correct.

Of course good inferences to the best explanation depend not just on the ability of the favored view to explain some phenomenon or other. Their probative value depends also on how many things the favored view explains, how well it explains them, whether the resulting explanation has further implications that are false or implausible, and whether there are rival explanations that do at least as well as the favored view. It is fair to say that each version of subjectivism we've looked at has the ability to explain some version of internalism and also to explain all of the things entailed by any minimally realist view. Like other minimally realist views, it can explain why we call some moral judgements true and others false, why we use indicative sentences to make them, why the sentences that express them are true just when the beliefs they express are true, and so on. So each of these views explains several phenomena a metaethicist would like to explain. Deciding which one gives us the best explanation will involve among other things comparing their relative strengths and weaknesses and comparing them also to the strengths and weaknesses of views we have not yet considered in any detail. The next section will survey some of these weaknesses, while chapter 7 will survey responses to those weaknesses that generate more sophisticated subjectivist theories.

6.2. The Costs of the Simple Subjectivist View

6.2.1. *It May Entail Implausible Strong Versions of Internalism*

Even though these simple subjectivist theories offer explanations of internalism, there may be reasons to suspect the explanations on offer. One such reason might be that the *explanandum*—that is the thing to be explained—is not a genuine phenomenon. Just as explaining real phenomena counts in favor of a hypothesis or theory, explaining or entailing something that's false counts against them. You might think that all or most of the internalist claims we've canvassed are false or overstated. Since in many instances a given version of subjectivism *entail* the version of internalism it explains, this would be bad for that version of subjectivism. For example, simple agent subjectivism entails indefeasible morals/motives existence internalism. That's because according to this view, a moral judgement about an agent will be true only if the agent has some desire to do what the judgement indicates. But many people think that you can have a moral obligation to do something you have no inclination to do. If they're right, indefeasible versions of morals/motives existence agent internalism are false. And if that kind of internalism is false, any version of subjectivism that entails it also must be false. Similar implications hold for speaker subjectivism.

Because this kind of internalism is so strong, most morals/motives existence internalists accept weaker defeasible claims about the relationship between moral truths and motivations. They hold views that allow that some people could remain unmotivated even though there must be some connection between true moral judgements and motivation. One version of this weaker internalism postulates that true moral judgements must motivate only people who are rational. On this version, when a person is not motivated by a true moral judgement of which they are aware, they simply show themselves to be irrational. Theorists can adopt other strategies for generating a defeasible version of internalism. Many of those who go down this route think that indefeasible internalist claims are false precisely because they are so strong.

David Brink (1986, p. 30) suggests a class of examples in which people who are aware of moral obligations that they actually have and who nonetheless remain unmoved by those obligations. We looked briefly at his amoralist, for whom morality carries no weight in deliberation. Amoralists aren't immoralists—they're not trying to do what is immoral. Amoralists just don't care one way or the other about morality or immorality. Brink suggests that we can coherently imagine such amoralists in enough detail that we should think that they are genuinely possible. In fact he argues, some of the most interesting and realistic literature contains characters who are convincing amoralists. Plato's Thrasymachus, who thought that morality was a hoax foisted on the powerless by the powerful to secure their cooperation, is a good example. Given what Thrasymachus believed morality was about, it is perfectly understandable that he would not be moved by moral considerations. Insofar as we find it believable that there might be someone like that, we don't think amoralists are impossible. From examples such as this, Brink concludes that indefeasible internalism is false. Brink, in fact, wants to conclude something similar about defeasible internalism—that it too is shown false by such examples. But for now we can leave the issue aside. What matters to the debate over *simple* subjectivism is just that the example does call simple *indefeasible* internalism into question.

The simplest versions of subjectivism entail exactly these strong varieties of morals/motives internalism. That is a drawback if the strongest versions are too strong to be plausible. When a theory entails something false it is more than just a minor problem. And when a theory entails something probably false it isn't a whole lot better. So the possibility of someone like Thrasymachus is a problem for simple subjectivism. Of course, this is only the beginning of the story. Subjectivism can be made less simple, and much of the complication in the less simple versions is designed to help answer these sorts of objections. But before we add complication we should look at another problem for the view.

6.2.2. Simple Subjectivism Seems to Get Moral Epistemology Wrong

There is another set of worries that are independent of the worry that subjectivism entails too strong a version of internalism. We can highlight these worries by asking ourselves a hypothetical question: Suppose that subjectivism of some sort were true. What then should we be looking at in trying to determine whether a moral claim about an act-type, for example that lying to a relative is wrong, is true or false?

If either simple appraiser subjectivism or agent subjectivism is right, the truths of morality just are truths about psychology. According to simple appraiser subjectivism, to say that an action is right is just to say that the speaker or thinker has the appropriate emotional or subjective reaction toward that action. That is what the rightness of an action or act-type consists in. So all we need to know to determine whether an action is right is whether the speaker or thinker has the right attitude toward that action or action-type. And these psychological facts are, in the first instance, facts about the person doing the talking, writing, or thinking. So we should look at her or him to find out whether what she or he says is true. Things go similarly for agent subjectivism. If it is the desires, goals, and approving attitudes that the agent has toward the action in question that make it right or wrong, that rightness or wrongness consists in psychological facts about the agent. And if we want to know these facts, it is the agent toward whom we should be directing our attention.

This result makes it mysterious why we try to find out more about our options in order to decide what is right to do. For it is not obvious that I need to know much at all about an action itself in order to know that a particular person likes, dislikes, wants, approves of, or disapproves of that action. What I need information about is the person whose attitude is in question. So according to this theory the best evidence about morality is likely to come from psychological tests that ascertain what an agent approves of or disapproves of. Once we know that an agent likes an action and prefers it to any alternative we will know all we need to know to figure out whether that action is right or wrong, at least if as we're supposing simple agent subjectivism is correct. Thus it looks like such agent subjectivism makes moral knowledge too easy and directs our attention to the wrong place to find it. When we are trying to find out if an action is right or wrong, it looks like we want to know as much as we can about the action, not just whether the agent approves of it or not. Even if at some point we don't think we need to know more about the action than we do in order to decide whether it is right, it at least seems possible that more information about the action could cause us to rethink our verdict. And this possibility is open even when we know all there is to know about the agent's attitudes.

Things get even more problematic when we evaluate simple appraiser subjectivism. For on that view, our judgements are about our own psychological states. We're usually pretty good at tracking what we like and dislike. So appraiser subjectivism of this sort seems to make moral truths too easy to come by. It makes moral knowledge cheap. Know yourself well enough and you'll know what is right and what is wrong. Furthermore, in those cases where the theory doesn't make such knowledge easy to get, it still seems to direct us to the wrong place to find the answers we seek. In situations when our feelings are complex and we're not sure how we feel about an action we are contemplating, it isn't clear how finding out more about the *object* of our emotions will help with figuring out what we now are thinking. Finding out that some action will relieve unnecessary suffering might *make* me like it from now on, but it won't help me figure out whether I liked it before that.

6.2.3.   Simple Subjectivism Gets the Wrong Results When Applied to Vicious Agents

Simple subjectivism seems also to open itself up to the charge that it endorses the wrong moral verdicts whenever sufficiently bad agents have commitments relevant to morality. Take your favorite despot, or pretend that a villain from fiction is a real person. Among their other failings, such people tend to approve of much that is villainous as long as it is to their own benefit. Simple agent subjectivism will be committed to classifying the actions of such villains as right, so long as these villainous agents are sufficiently wholehearted. For these actions will meet with the approval of the agents who do them. Of course these same actions would not be right (according to agent subjectivism) if we ourselves (non-villains of course!) were to do them. At least they would not be right if we were to do them without a villainous change of heart. But that's not much comfort. We'd ordinarily like to be able to criticize villains for their villainy by calling their actions wrong.

Appraiser subjectivism seems, at first, to be in better shape. Since it allows us as appraisers to evaluate the villainous actions of others in light of our own attitudes of approval or disapproval, and since we disapprove of their actions, we can call their actions wrong. So far so good. But when Attila the Hun speaks proudly of his lack of mercy and his skill at mayhem he speaks truly. When he does that he's the appraiser and we have to look to his standards to tell whether what he calls wrong really is wrong. And of course Attila approves of cruelty, so it will be true that cruel actions are of the sort that Attila approves of. His attitudes did not include disapproval of his own cruelty and skill. Thus if all that it takes for an action to be morally right is that the appraiser approves of actions of that sort, Attila will speak truly when he praises his most vicious deeds as morally appropriate and admirable. That we will be right when we call those same actions vicious and wrong (that is disapproved of by *us*) will in no way call his seemingly conflicting judgements into question. And that leads us to the next objection.

6.2.4.   Simple Subjectivism Seems to Give the Wrong Verdicts in Certain Counterfactual Scenarios

Intuitively there are things that it would be wrong to do even if no one disapproved of them. Simple subjectivism, whether appraiser subjectivism or agent subjectivism, makes it hard to see how that could be so. If to be wrong is just to be disapproved of by some person (whether a thinker, a speaker, or an agent), nothing would be wrong in the absence of people who disapproved. Or to make a parallel point about language, if "Animal cruelty is wrong" just means what "I disapprove of animal cruelty" means, it will be true only when the latter sentence is true. And this entails that it won't be true when I don't disapprove of animal cruelty. So when I now consider whether it is or is not wrong, I should think it is wrong only in scenarios where I exist and continue to disapprove of such cruelty. But that typically is not what we think when we believe that such cruelty is wrong. We think it is actually wrong, but also that it would remain wrong were I to notice it or not and even if I did not exist to disapprove of it.

Philosophers often find it useful to talk about the modal status of a claim—about its status as necessarily true, merely contingently true, possibly true, or impossible. If the modal status of a claim is necessary it could not be otherwise. Philosophers often use a possible worlds metaphor to make the idea vivid. Necessary claims are true in all possible worlds. Merely contingent claims are not necessary. They may be true in the actual world, but they don't have to be. Things might have been otherwise and we can pretend there are other possible worlds in which they are otherwise to represent that fact. Other claims are impossible—they aren't actually true and they aren't possibly true. There is no possible world in which they are true.

Many of us think that at least some moral truths are necessary. It could not have been that murdering my parents out of sheer boredom would have been permissible. But simple subjectivism entails that all moral truths are contingent. Our psychological attitudes, including our attitudes of approval and disapproval, are merely contingent. I do in fact disapprove of parricide, but had I been brought up differently and perhaps abused I might not have disapproved of such cruelty. If the fact that such killing is wrong just is the fact that I disapprove of it, it must have the same modal status as that fact. For it just is identical to that fact. As Leibniz's Law reminds us, when we identify one thing with another we aren't actually talking about two different things; we are talking about one and the same thing. Any property the one fact has must then be one the (purportedly) other fact has. They're one and the same thing. The definitions of necessity and contingency ensure that a single fact can't be both necessary and contingent. For a fact to be necessary is for it to be impossible that it isn't true. And for a fact to be contingent is for it to be possible that it isn't true. So we might follow Mark Schroeder (2010, p. 67ff.) and call this the *modal problem* for simple subjectivism. It gives moral claims the wrong modal status. And this just means it makes the wrong judgement about certain sorts of counterfactual scenarios.

6.2.5. Simple Appraiser Subjectivism Seems Unable to Posit Disagreement Where We Think It Occurs

Common sense says that if I tell you that some particular action was wrong and you reply by saying that it was not wrong, we disagree. For example if

I tell you that Sam's sarcastic response to a comment of Sarah's in class yesterday was wrong in virtue of being insensitive, and you tell me that it wasn't wrong at all, we would be disagreeing with one another. We are talking about one and the same action, and I think it is wrong, whereas you don't. We may each have our reasons for what we think, and we may even each recognize that, but as long as one of us thinks the action wrong and the other thinks it not wrong, we disagree. Or at least it seems that way, and in the absence of some argument to the contrary that would be the verdict of common sense. Hare's Missionaries and Cannibals argument draws on this commonsense idea.

The simplest versions of appraiser subjectivism cannot deliver that verdict. According to such theories, we are each talking about our own attitudes toward the action in question. I am saying that it meets with my disapproval (or some such attitude) and you are denying that it is disapproved of by you. But those claims could both be true. It could be true that I disapprove of Sam's action and you don't. In fact, in most cases where I think something wrong and you don't, that is how it is likely to be. I disapprove and you don't. So the claim I assert (according to appraiser subjectivism) and the claim you deny (again according to appraiser subjectivism) are not the same claim. I assert something you don't deny and you deny something I don't assert. I am making a claim about my attitudes toward Sam's action and you are making a claim about your attitudes toward Sam's action. These claims do not disagree.

A fan of appraiser subjectivism might reply by admitting that the claims we make—the psychological claims about our attitudes toward Sam's actions—don't disagree. But still they might argue, our attitudes—the ones we are each talking about—do clash. That clash, they might argue, explains the sense in which our initial arguments disagree. Our judgements (which are about our attitudes toward Sam's action) disagree because the attitudes they attribute disagree. This reply has a certain amount of initial plausibility. Sometimes we do express disagreements by talking about our attitudes, as when I say, "I think the highway runs north-south," and you disagree with, "No, I'm pretty sure it doesn't. I think it runs east-west."

There's reason to be suspicious of this general strategy. On the most natural understanding of the subjectivist view, 'Sam's action was wrong' and 'Sam's action was not wrong' do not self-attribute conflicting attitudes. Rather the theory should say that one sentence self-attributes an attitude that the other self-attributes the absence of. For, on the most natural version of the theory, the negation of 'Sam's action was wrong' should be the negation of 'I disapprove of Sam's action.' And we negate 'I disapprove of Sam's action' with 'I don't disapprove of Sam's action.' Since 'Sam's action was not wrong' is the negation of 'Sam's action was wrong,' it should say the same thing. But then 'Sam's action was not wrong' doesn't attribute an attitude that conflicts with disapproval, it just denies the presence of the original attitude (in oneself). (You may need to reread this paragraph again to get the point that is simple enough once you grasp it.)

The highway example isn't like this. There you *disbelieve* what I believe; you don't merely lack a belief in what I believe. And that is crucial. You wouldn't express disagreement with me by saying, "I don't believe it runs north-south because I haven't yet made up my mind." It would take us deep into a discussion of semantics and pragmatics[1] to give a full story of how two people each talking *about* their own attitudes could express disagreement. I think the conclusion of that discussion would be that the speakers are making assertions about the direction of the highway indirectly by directly making claims about their attitudes. But my point here is just that when people do express disagreement by talking about their own attitudes there is reason to think that the attitudes themselves must really conflict. And simple appraiser subjectivism doesn't postulate attitudes of the right sort because disapproval doesn't disagree with the absence of disapproval.

Perhaps more importantly, even if we did self-attribute clashing attitudes when I assert and you deny that what Sam did was wrong, we would normally each be saying something true if we spoke sincerely. That would seem to make one of the most natural ways of expressing our disagreement inappropriate. "That's false!" is a natural way of disagreeing with what someone has said. And yet, if simple appraiser subjectivism were correct, it would be inappropriate because what it would say would be false. For someone who sincerely thinks an action wrong will normally, in fact, have the negative attitude they self-attribute according to appraiser subjectivism.

6.3. Taking Stock

To summarize the objections, these simple subjectivist theories make moral knowledge too easy to get, they make us look to the wrong kinds of evidence to get it, and in many cases they generate the wrong answers to substantive moral questions. And furthermore, appraiser subjectivism (but not agent subjectivism) has a problem positing disagreement where it seems to occur from a commonsense view of ethical discourse. Each of these objections will lead to some modifications of the simple theory to generate more complex relatives that do better at avoiding at least some of these problems. We'll be looking at several theories that are motivated in just that way shortly. But it will be worth our time to reflect a bit on how these simple theories fare with respect to one of the sets of puzzles with which I began the book. It should be no great surprise that this will take us back over much of what we've already said as we make the connections with the earlier chapters explicit.

In very broad strokes, the already familiar motivations for subjectivism have to do with explaining the practicality of morality, while the familiar difficulties have to do with the problem of giving an account of the subject matter that allows us to find moral disagreement where it intuitively seems to be, and with giving an account of moral epistemology that fits with how we actually figure out what is right and wrong. These difficulties are joined by a somewhat new one—that of avoiding implausible first order moral verdicts. Since this chapter took off from the internalist motivations of subjectivism, I won't revisit the connections with chapter 4 here. And since one of the main objections concerned the epistemic upshot of the simple subjectivist views I won't say more about those in this chapter. But it may be worthwhile to revisit some of the points we've made and to connect them to the arguments considered in chapter 2, in order to paint a more fine-grained picture of the connections between these two chapters.

Chapter 2 surveyed three important lines of argument with somewhat different putative upshots for accounts of the subject matter of morality. The first was the argument from disagreement, put forth by John Mackie. Mackie suggested that the range of different views about our moral obligations and prohibitions was such that we should not think that any moral judgements were in fact true. And this, he claimed, was because the diversity of views made it impossible to see people's moral beliefs as responses to a single subject matter, differing only in the accuracy of their representation. More plausibly, he thought, these views were a projection of people's affective attitudes (hopes, fears, likes, and dislikes) onto a world that contained nothing corresponding to the judgements they produced. Insofar as simple appraiser subjectivism generates a kind of relativism about the content of morality, it grants Mackie one of his premises—that the diversity of moral views is not to be explained by better and worse responses to a single domain of fact—but denies the conclusion, that it leaves morality without a true subject matter. Rather, simple appraiser subjectivism suggests, the moral judgements of different appraisers reflect similar but different subject matters for each appraiser—the affective responses of the appraiser making the judgement. So it looks like appraiser subjectivism has an answer to Mackie's argument from disagreement, though of course that's just the first move in a long argument.

As for difficulties for giving an analysis of the subject matter stemming from the Open Question Argument, the simplest versions of subjectivism are reductive naturalist theories. They identify the rightness or wrongness of a course of action with a property of that action, whether it meets or would meet with the approval of the appraiser or agent. So these theories are exactly the sort that the Open Question Argument was supposed to refute. I've already noted a couple of ways in which the Open Question Argument might be resisted. A further way to resist—one that will be favored by many reductionists—involves pointing out that if the OQA worked we could prove that the property of containing water is distinct from the property of containing H_2O. For we can easily imagine a time it was easy to be certain that ice was made of water while it remained open whether ice was made of H_2O. Of course it would be more convincing yet to have a diagnosis of where Open Question Arguments goes wrong. But the example on its own is quite telling and gives us reason to be suspicious of the Open

Question Argument as a reason to deny reductionism. So far then, the theory is doing rather well in answering the concerns raised in chapter 2.

Unfortunately for simple appraiser subjectivism, its strength in resisting Mackie's argument from disagreement becomes a weakness in answering the challenge posed by Hare (and the related argument by Horgan and Timmons rehearsed in chapter 11), that is the challenge of finding genuine disagreement where common sense tells us there is such disagreement. For the theory eluded the confidence-eroding character of moral diversity by suggesting that we could deny that it was disagreement about a single subject matter without thereby denying that each party to a seeming disagreement was giving a relatively accurate characterization of some subject matter or other. We should interpret each party to such seeming disputes instead to be talking about themselves and their reactions to the action or option in question. But that just is to say that there is no common subject matter about which they are disagreeing. And that's just one of the objections to appraiser subjectivism, that it finds no disagreement where common sense suggests there is genuine disagreement. When you and a friend argue about the permissibility of gestation crates there surely seems to be something you disagree about. But if one of you is saying that she or he disapproves of using such crates, while the other is saying that she herself or he himself does not disapprove, there seems to be no disagreement between you. So simple speaker subjectivism doesn't do so well preserving the commonsense thought that you two disagree, despite doing rather well with the first two challenges discussed in chapter 2.

Contrast this with the one we get with a version of simple agent subjectivism, in the guise of the view that some action is wrong just in case the agent who might do the action does or would disapprove of the action. That view has no problem with disagreement in such debates. When I say that it is wrong for a farmer or all farmers to use such crates I am saying that they do or would disapprove of actions of that sort, and when you deny that it is wrong, you are saying of those very same farmers that they don't and won't experience any such disapproval. That's a straightforward disagreement about the psychology of the farmers in question. But now, if Mackie's argument from disagreement gets any grip, this kind of simple subjectivist can't avail herself of the answer the simple appraiser subjectivist gave to elude the argument from disagreement. This kind of subjectivist does have to defend the thought that both parties to the dispute are talking about one and the same thing and that their disagreement arises because one tracks the facts better than the other. And that last bit is just what Mackie wants to use the ubiquity of disagreement to call into question.

If that's right, it may suggest that Mackie's argument from disagreement, and argument that metaethical theories must agree with common sense about where people genuinely disagree about morality, are more difficult to elude when they are taken together than when they are addressed individually. That's something to keep in mind as we look at more complex versions of subjectivism and also other metaethical proposals. And it seems to be an instance of a very general phenomenon throughout philosophical theorizing—theoretical innovations designed to handle one sort of puzzle or objection may well create new problems or exacerbate old ones. The present dilemma for subjectivisms—go appraiser relative and avoid Mackie's argument from disagreement, or go agent relative and avoid problems about disagreement—won't be the only instance of this kind of thing we'll look at. But it is also, I think, part of the fun of doing philosophy quite generally. It is somewhat surprising that intelligent people should continue to engage versions of many of the same issues that the smartest philosophers have been working on for centuries. But progress in handling one problem can be regress with respect to another, and this can motivate those of us genuinely puzzled to want to revisit the original motivations for considering the helpful and yet counterproductive innovation in the first place. So even as we find new things to say, we have reason to revisit what we have already said and come to believe.

Questions

Comprehension

C1. How would an appraiser subjectivist explain morals/motives judgement internalism?

C2. Why is agent subjectivism better able than appraiser subjectivism to capture genuine disagreement between two speakers?

C3. What circumstances would falsify the claim that murder was wrong if you were the speaker and appraiser subjectivism were true?

C4. What does the answer to question C3 tell us about the modal status of the claim that murder is wrong?

Extension

E1. Go back to the first formalization of the Open Question Argument in chapter 2 and substitute 'water' and 'H_2O' for the property terms in that argument. Do you get a convincing argument that water is not H_2O or that being made of water is not being made of H_2O?

E2. Is there a way to combine speaker or appraiser relativism with agent relativism? Would that leave us able to evaluate (that is label as right or wrong) all the actions we would want to?

Reading

Read along with: Gilbert Harman (1975) or Harman (1978) and Dreier (1990). All of these are not as simple as the views in this chapter.

Note

1   Very roughly, pragmatics is a theory about how a person can communicate information (including information that goes beyond what the sentence literally means) by using a sentence. See Grice (1991) and Bach (2011).

7   The Cognitivist Heirs of Simple Subjectivism

Ideal Observers and Ideal Agents

The previous chapter explained how simple subjectivist views aspire to capture the practicality of morality within the constraints of minimal realism. The resulting views were *only minimally* realist. They placed only a small distance between true moral thoughts and the phenomena that make them true. For example, on one simple view, the fact that a moral appraiser disapproves of an action is all that is required for it to be wrong. While disapproval of an action and the belief that the action is wrong will still be distinct according to the theory, these are closely related states of mind. So the facts that make that judgement (the judgement that the action is wrong) correct are very closely related to the psychological state of accepting the judgement itself. And that kind of dependence of moral truth on moral attitudes is thought by many to be a hallmark of anti-realism. So, once again, minimal realism is very minimal. And it is minimal enough that some consider it no sort of realism at all.

It is no surprise then that more robust realism-friendly philosophers find the view unsatisfying. And it should be no more surprising that they, among others, have directed various objections at simple subjectivism. The objections, which we canvassed in the previous chapter, included the following: (1) simple subjectivism entails false epistemic conclusions; (2) simple subjectivism entails implausibly strong internalist theses; (3) simple subjectivism must endorse unpalatable moral conclusions; (4) simple subjectivism grants some moral claims the wrong modal status; and finally, (5) in its appraiser-oriented versions, simple subjectivism eliminates the possibility of certain sorts of real disagreement. In fairness to subjectivism, it is very hard to find any metaethical theorist who defends subjectivism in its simplest versions, though philosophers are not always fair to subjectivism. Introductory philosophy classes and texts sometimes include readings from nonphilosophers defending very simple relativist theories that are versions of the simplest kind of subjectivism, usually as targets for refutation. This may be a fair move insofar as some students taking the class may accept these views. But it would be unfair to take these arguments as refutations of either subjectivism or relativism as a general approach. Subjectivism-friendly philosophers have long been aware of these objections, even while they stood by their subjectivist commitments. In fact many of these objections come from subjectivists who themselves already saw them as reasons to go beyond the simple view. So most of the subjectivist and relativist theories that people actually accept turn out to be much more sophisticated and subtle than the simple versions of those in the last chapter.

The objections we have canvassed are among the main motivations leading subjectivists to complicate their views. For those subjectivists who are also cognitivists, the complications generally include one or more of the following additions to the basic subjectivist idea: (a) enlarging the set of subjects whose attitudes are incorporated in the truth or appropriateness conditions for the relevant moral claims; (b) idealizing the conditions in which these subject's responses matter, (c) varying the nature of the subjective attitudes that are incorporated in the analysis, and (d) specifying ideal conditions normatively rather than purely nonnormatively. Other subjectivists have instead abandoned cognitivism and adopted some version of noncognitivism such as emotivism, prescriptivism, or expressivism. They diverge from subjectivism proper insofar as they deny that moral judgements are *about* the subjective responses of human subjects, though they do think they express the subjective responses of those who make them. Such noncognitivist theories will be the subject of the next chapter. Here we consider the innovations adopted by subjectivists who have remained cognitivists.

7.1. Enlarging the Relevant Group of Subjects Whose Attitudes Matter

One obvious way to modify the simplest versions of both appraiser and agent subjectivism is to expand the scope of the group whose subjective responses are the truth-makers for moral claims. And these modifications to some extent ameliorate the features of the pure simple versions that ground the objections canvassed earlier. For example, a subjectivist might suggest that a moral judgement to the effect that an action is wrong would be true just in case most members of the speaker's or thinker's society would disapprove of an action of that kind. This would bring back the possibility of real disagreement between speakers so long as they were members of the same society. If by saying that perjury is wrong I am saying something to the effect that most people in my society disapprove of perjury and you (also a member of my society) say it is not wrong and thereby deny that the majority of this same society disapprove, we are in fact disagreeing. I am saying something that will be true only if what you say is not true. So this modification makes some progress in answering the disagreement objection to appraiser subjectivism.

Does it also help keep this species of subjectivism from endorsing reprehensible moral verdicts when they are made by sufficiently reprehensible people? It does somewhat. Bad people who approve of cruel things won't be speaking truly when they label their own cruel actions "right"—so long as a majority of their group don't have the same bad attitudes. So not every such judgement will count as true. However, there are groups the majority of which still approve of very cruel things. And appraiser group subjectivism is committed to using the responses of the group as the standard by which rightness or wrongness is judged. Attila the Hun's peers were pretty blood-thirsty. They would have approved of most of his actions, including many of those we find reprehensible. So moving to the group won't save the theory from accepting seemingly depraved moral judgements when those judgements are made by members of depraved groups.

Just as we can move from simple speaker subjectivism to get speaker group subjectivism, we can move from simple agent subjectivism to some version of agent group subjectivism. And this will give us similar results with respect to avoiding the unwanted commitments of simple subjectivism. Enlarging the relevant group allows us to call the actions or inactions of problematically motivated agents "wrong" when their motivational profile is not typical of the group whose motives are relevant. John Wayne Gacy's many kidnappings were disapproved of by the members of most groups of which he was a part. So the theory allows us to avoid commitment to the thought that those kidnappings were right or even just not wrong. The overwhelming majority of Gacy's fellow contractors, fellow clowns, or fellow Illinois residents disapprove of kidnap and murder, so these activities will be classified as wrong by any version of subjectivism that takes the actual attitudes of the average contractor, clown, or Illinois resident as the standard of evaluation. So far so good.

But this is only a partial fix. Adolf Hitler's actions were at least as monstrous as Gacy's, yet many of the groups of which he was a member seemed to find them acceptable and even admirable. Perhaps there were groups of which he was a member that did not so approve. (Vegetarians for the most part did not share his views and yet he was a vegetarian.) But relative to the attitudes of many of the most natural groups to look toward when agent group subjectivism is made precise, Hitler's actions meet with little disregard. The average Nazi and probably the average adult German during the 1930s seemed to have been on board with much of what he was up to. And this fact commits this kind of agent group relativism to an uncomfortable verdict where such popular villains are concerned. This is not a point in favor of such group subjectivism.

There are further moves that subjectivists can make by carefully selecting the relevant group. One possibility is to go hybrid by coupling individual or group versions of appraiser subjectivism with agent subjectivism or agent group subjectivism (Harman, 1975). One of the more plausible might be a view such as the following: A moral judgement that such and such an action is right says that the action is of a type approved of by the smallest social group including all of (1) the agent, (2) the speaker or appraiser, and (3) the intended audience (if there is one). This would let us, that is you and me, avoid endorsing Hitler's choices. There's no group that includes all of us and Hitler as well that share the relevant attitudes. I won't raise any objections to the strategy here, but you might want to think about whether this view can handle all of the problems we have raised for the less complicated versions of subjectivism.

7.2. The Strategy of Idealization

The subjectivist theories we have surveyed so far all let the truth or falsity of a moral judgement depend on the *actual* motivations of some person or group. No doubt there is some idealization in talking about the average member of a group, or even what most of the members approve of, but still these views pretty much take the relevant group of people as they come and ask whether they approve of the action as they are. The subjectivist theories we will now examine idealize to a much greater extent. That is, they are interested in what a person or group *would* approve of *in conditions that may not obtain* but that idealize away various features of the people in question. A very simple version of this idea would be to equate what is right with what an observer would approve of in the presence of full nonmoral information. It might be right for me to avoid backing the car out of my driveway because if I knew that there was a small child behind me I would approve of staying parked. It can be true that I *would* approve of that if I was fully factually informed even while I now, in my ignorance, approve of backing out of the driveway. This proposal is still broadly subjectivist insofar as the rightness of an action is still supposed to be a fact about my subjective responses. But it is different from the theories we've considered so far in that the subjective fact that constitutes the rightness of the action is subjunctive or counterfactual. My responses don't have to actually happen so long as they *would happen* in the specified conditions. Such theories are often called *ideal observer theories* because they make rightness a function of the subjective reactions of suitably ideal appraisers or observers, as opposed to actual observers. (From here on I sometimes abbreviate ideal observer theory as 'IOT.')

The sense in which I use the term 'idealized' is not a moral or normative sense of the term. At least for most of the theories in question we aren't *saying* that if you were morally better you would approve of the right action. What we're using 'idealize' to indicate is that we are abstracting away some contingent features of the subject to try to figure out what would happen in some set of special circumstances that may or may not be actual. It is the sense in which a perfect plane described in geometry is an idealization of real physical planes in the world. Or, to take an example from the physical sciences, someone might predict that something would happen in a perfect vacuum at sea level, without committing themselves to the existence of any such vacuums. They would be saying something about what would happen *were there to be* a perfect vacuum at sea level, even if all real world vacuums only approximate true emptiness and are not therefore perfect in the intended sense.

There are ideal observer theories that do invoke a normative idealization, and they're important. A theorist who thinks that the property of rightness is the property of being such that a morally good observer would approve of it would be offering such a theory. I will have more to say about these theories later on. But I'm leaving them aside for the moment to focus on those that are consistent with reductive naturalism, that is those who think we can define moral properties in terms of nonmoral and nonnormative properties without circularity. That kind of Ideal Observer Theory will be careful to leave moral terms out of their candidate reduction. For example, if they say that the relevant circumstances in which an observer's responses matter include full information, they will be careful to qualify that to say full *nonmoral* information. So for now my discussion will be of theories that idealize in a nonnormative manner. I'll reintroduce normative idealizations to the discussion partly in response to objections to theories that idealize only in nonnormative or nonmoral ways.

Ideal *observer* theories develop relatively naturally out of appraiser subjectivism and are often designed to explain the alleged truth of some version of appraiser internalism. In fact the idea of an appraiser is just a slightly more general category of which an observer is an instance. So this should not be a surprise. You could, however, develop agent subjectivism in similar ways to construct an *ideal agent theory*. And ideal agent theories would be best placed, in the first instance, to explain the alleged truth of agent internalism. It seems to me that ideal observer theories have historically been more common than ideal agent theories. So my discussion of theories of this general sort will begin by focusing on ideal observer theories. Once we have surveyed a number of the main issues faced by such theories, we'll return to a discussion of ideal agent theories, noting parallels and differences.

7.2.1. Designing Ideal Conditions So That the Analysis Captures Moral Epistemology

There are many features of an appraiser or agent that you could idealize. We have already mentioned that we can idealize what they know, but you can see already that there are lots of others. Rather than discuss all of the options, I will focus on some salient combinations of features that a metaethical theory might idealize. And I'll focus on those by discussing a famous example of the Ideal Observer Theory introduced by Roderick Firth (1952). One way to think of Firth's idea is as a further development of the simple subjectivist model. His hope is to retain the advantages of subjectivism in explaining internalism and in explaining how moral judgements can be true or false, while avoiding the problems discussed earlier. In particular, Firth designed his version of the Ideal Observer Theory to handle the worry that simple subjectivism can't make sense of the ways in which we figure out what is right or wrong. That worry, as you'll recall, was that simple appraiser subjectivism would suggest that our attention focus on ourselves when we're trying to figure out what's right. And this made it very hard to see how the sorts of deliberation and evidence that people go through to figure out what is right or wrong could be relevant to that issue. If what matters to the rightness of an action is that I approve of it, why would I need more information about the action in question to decide? Wouldn't I just need more information about me? And if all that matters to the rightness or wrongness of an action is the disapproval of some group, why am I not just asking for survey evidence about members of that group, rather than trying to find out what the effects of the action on global warming (or whatever) really are?

Firth suggested that we look more closely at our actual practices of trying to figure out what is right and what is wrong, and reason backwards from there to find our subject matter. If people deliberating as well as they can about a moral issue want to know the effects of certain actions, then moral subject matter should be such as to make it relevant to have that information when we are thinking about what to do or endorse. If we notice that people often try to figure out what a certain course of action is like for all parties affected before they render a verdict on its rightness, we should take such imaginative acquaintance with these perspectives to be relevant to the determination of whether the action is right or wrong. If we think the best moral judges are impartial as between the interests of the parties to a dispute, we should develop an account of the subject matter that explains why this is so. And so on.

Firth sought to explain how these features of excellent moral thinking help us get at the truth about morality by suggesting that the subject matter of morality was about what ideal observers (with full imagination, impartiality, and various other features besides) would approve of with full relevant nonmoral information. His idea was that when we deliberate we try to approximate the conditions of such idealized observers. If we succeed, our own attitudes of approval and disapproval will be the same attitudes a fully ideal observer would have. And our having this approval would be good evidence that an ideal observer would approve or disapprove of the action in the relevant conditions (on the assumption that we get close enough to the ideal). It would still be a further step to our conclusion that the action was right or wrong, but we could use our positive or negative attitudes as a reliable guide in making such judgements. The resulting Ideal Observer Theory would explain why attending to the things we take to be relevant to good moral thinking actually are a way of tracking the subject matter of morality—the responses of ideal observers in specified conditions.

The conditions mentioned so far are probably not a fully adequate list. Firth himself thought we should also include a certain coolness of emotional response, consistency, and perspectival understanding (omnipercipience) into the idealization. Other theorists might propose additions or deletions, and in keeping with Firth's strategy, we might look to actual moral practice to determine what is needed by way of emendation. But the basic picture is relatively clear. An action will be right, as defined by the theory, if a person who satisfies the conditions built into the analysis would approve of doing the action when they contemplated the issue. So, on the assumption that there is something that a person like that in those conditions would do, this is a factual matter and often we will be in a position to make judgements about it. We thus have Firth endorsing a subjunctive claim of the following form:

> *Firth**: An action is right iff it is disposed to elicit approval from an observer who was fully nonmorally informed, impartial, disinterested, omnipercipient, consistent, and otherwise normal in normal conditions.

7.2.2.   The IOT, Dispositional Analyses, and Morals/Motives Existence Internalism

Firth meant his analysis to be a version of what is sometimes called a *dispositional analysis* of moral properties or concepts. At a very abstract level a dispositional analysis can be schematized like this:

Dispositional Schema: x is F iff x is disposed to elicit response R from O in conditions C.

On Firth's way of filling out the idea, it is:

> *Firth***: An action is right iff it is disposed to elicit approval from an observer who was fully nonmorally informed, impartial, disinterested, omnipercipient, consistent, and otherwise normal, in normal conditions.

It would, I think, be just a variation of the same idea if we changed the analysis to attribute the disposition to the observer rather than to the action triggering the response.

The dispositional variants of ideal observer and response-dependent theories in general are worth noting for several reasons. One reason is that many of our everyday terms and thoughts are dispositional. Thoughts about solubility are one example. Salt is soluble because it would dissolve if put in water of a certain temperature in conditions where the water is not already at its saturation point. And this brings out an important related point. Dispositional analyses can trade on the fact that a disposition can remain present even when its triggering conditions don't occur. Just as salt is soluble even when there is no water around, an action can be wrong though unobserved by anyone—let alone by a disinterested and fully informed observer. It looks like an action could have the relevant disposition even if there aren't any such observers anywhere in the universe. All that needs to remain true is that if there were such observers they would respond or be disposed to respond in the way specified.[1]

This feature of dispositional analyses comes in handy. Recall our earlier worries about the strength of the internalism entailed by the simplest subjectivist theories. On the simplest versions, the truth of a moral judgement required actual motivation from actual appraisers. And examples of actual amoralists, perhaps not the fictional Thrasymachus, but flesh and blood people with similar views about morality, make that requirement seem pretty implausible. Could it really be that no one could think an action right without approving of it? As we've noted, Firth's ideal observers are an idealized version of simple appraiser subjectivism's appraisers. But the idealization helps the theory elude the current objection because the counterfactual or dispositional nature of Firth's more complicated theory protects it from amoralist counterexamples. It is open to an ideal observer theorist to argue that people like Thrasymachus aren't fully informed and that this explains their lack of motivation. If Thrasymachus didn't falsely believe that morality was just a plot by the strong to take advantage of the weak, Thrasymachus might not remain unmoved. And if he had full information about the nature of correct actions, as well as the other features that go into the idealization, it may be plausible to think he would be motivated. If we cash out the Ideal Observer Theory in dispositional terms, we get even further resources to work with. Dispositions can be retained even while unmanifested in specified ideal conditions, so long as they are masked by some countervailing disposition. Salt remains soluble even when sitting undissolved in water as individual chunks coated in thin shellac. It retains its disposition to dissolve, but that disposition is blocked by the shellac coating that prevents it from getting wet. Similarly, amoralists might be disposed to approve of right action when they are in ideal conditions, even though something is keeping that disposition from manifesting in those conditions. This means that an idealized dispositional theory such as the Ideal Observer Theory can handle the amoralist objection better than simpler versions of subjectivism can.

To put these points more positively, the Ideal Observer Theory yields a defeasible morals/motives existence internalism. Roughly it entails that necessarily if an action is right, an ideal observer in suitable conditions would be motivated or disposed to be motivated. This is a version of existence internalism because it is the truth of the judgement to which this matters. And it is defeasible because it contains clauses about suitable conditions that therefore allow the motivation to be absent in unsuitable conditions. Furthermore, in versions of the theory that require only the presence of a disposition, we have an additional condition under which the motivation could be absent, namely when the disposition to be motivated is blocked or masked.

7.2.3.   Ideal Observers and Judgement Internalism

We've been discussing the way in which ideal observer theories can be used to ground a defeasible existence internalism. What about judgement internalism? Do ideal observer theories explain a similar defeasible kind of judgement internalism? With some further assumptions they can. The required assumptions are parallel to those that simple appraiser subjectivism used to generate an indefeasible judgement internalism. One of the needed extra assumptions is that the appraiser is self-aware. Another is that the relevant appraiser accepts the analysis. Self-aware appraisers who accept the analysis will only judge an action right in ideal conditions when they approve of the action that they appraise or believe that they are disposed so to approve.

But of course few of us are ever in totally ideal conditions. So we might be interested in knowing whether we get any stronger connection with motivation, one that might license the expectation that people in the real world will be for the most part motivated by their moral judgements. That idea extends beyond the domain of true moral judgements because people can sometimes falsely believe that some action is right. Most internalists think that even false moral judgements will be accompanied by the requisite motivation, at least in rational people. In general it seems possible to think that you would be motivated to do what your moral judgement recommends if you were in different circumstances than your actual circumstances, and yet not be motivated in your actual circumstances. And it remains possible for someone who is completely self-aware. What is it about the ideal conditions that makes it the case that one could not be unmotivated while thinking that you would be motivated in those conditions?

What of a different defeasible internalist idea, one that makes the defeasibility itself a normative matter? Christine Korsgaard (1986) and Michael Smith (1994) suggest that the right understanding of the internalist requirement is normative—an agent will be motivated by what she judges to be right *if she is rational*. But this idea also seems hard for the standard IOT to explain. Even if I come to know that if I were fully informed and otherwise as the ideal specifies I would approve of some action, that knowledge doesn't entail that I *should now* approve of it. Perhaps one or the other of the conditions that are stipulated to characterize ideal observers is what makes it the case that I would so desire in those conditions. Supposing that I'm not in those conditions, this does not show that I have any reason to desire as I would under such conditions. So the analysis doesn't show that I am now irrational if I don't desire what I would desire under the specified ideal conditions.

This is one reason why some theorists who see some merit in ideal observer and ideal agent theories want to characterize the ideal conditions in fully or partly normative terms. If you would desire to help the poor if you were *rational* (a normative claim), that does suggest there's something wrong with you if you don't. And it also suggests that if you *think that* you'd want to help the poor if you were rational, but you don't currently want to help the poor, you would then have good reason for judging yourself rationally inadequate and therefore reason to get yourself to be so motivated. Such normatively loaded specifications of ideal conditions do seem to secure the counterpart normativized internalist claim. But they also block the resulting theories from being fully reductive. They reduce one normative property (moral rightness) to another normative property (rational correctness), but unless they go on to define rationality in nonnormative terms, we have not reduced something normative to something specifiable in nonnormative terms. The normatively loaded ideal observer theories won't then (at least by themselves) vindicate naturalism. And many subjectivists like it precisely because it fits so well into a naturalistic worldview.

7.2.4. The "So What" Objection to Ideal Observer Theories

This brings us to a closely related objection to ideal observer theories. *Rationalism* suggests roughly that the requirements of morality are part of the requirements of rationality or good reason. That makes it a species of morals/reasons existence internalism. If doing what is morally right is part of being rational or part of doing what you have most reason to do, it follows directly that you will have a reason to do the right thing. The Korsgaard-Smith version of judgement internalism just discussed falls relatively naturally out of this picture. The analysis makes it true that right actions are those you would do if you were rational. Suppose you knew this and you judged some action to be right. Then, you'd also think that you would do that action if you were rational. And, it is plausible to suppose, this would also lead you to intend to do it intentionally. These are the underlying ideas behind this kind of normatively specified morals/motives internalism.

Many people find the underlying rationalist thought quite plausible. Some find it plausible because they think that it is always a justification for acting that the action in question is right. And they have a hard time seeing how this could be a justification if it did not also show the action in question to be supported by the balance of reasons or if the course of action was less rational than some alternative. There is more to say here both for and against this line of thought. Here I want to connect it up to a popular objection to ideal observer analyses of moral rightness and obligation. For the upshot of this objection is that such analyses are unable to capture the ideas that make rationalism attractive.

If you think that rationalism is the right view of ethics, you would expect an analysis of the content of moral judgements to explain it. In other words, you would want your theory to explain why an agent would always have a reason to do what is right for her. If your analysis of 'right' involves specifying what property moral sentences and thoughts predicate of actions, you would want that property either itself to be one that every person had a reason to go in for, or to be such as to ensure that some related reason-giving property was always present. The former strategy is probably the more straightforward.

To deploy a somewhat fanciful example, imagine that everyone necessarily desires chocolate. An analysis that equated the rightness of an action with the property of getting chocolate for the agent doing the action would be well placed to meet this goal. If you think that wanting chocolate is reason to do things that will bring you chocolate, you'll think that this analysis ensures that agents will have reason to do what's right. Of course, this fanciful example is not very plausible as an analysis of moral rightness. There's good reason to think that many right actions don't bring chocolate to those who perform them, so the analysis fails to capture the intuitive extension of 'right.' But the theory would do a good job explaining morals/reasons internalism. What those who like this morals/reasons internalism are hoping for is a non-fanciful analysis that can display how it could be that we necessarily have reason to do what morality asks of us.

The *"So what?" objection* is meant to show that ideal observer theories don't adequately capture the rationalist thought. The objection asks us to suppose that the ideal observer approves of an action, and then asks, "So what? Is there any reason to care about that?" (Johnston, 1989). Those who press this objection think the answer is that there is no reason to care. I now—in my actual conditions—may well have no reason to care what observers in the conditions specified in the analysis would approve of. I'm not in those conditions. And there may be nothing wrong with me insofar as I'm not in those conditions. (So far we repeat the argument that the view doesn't vindicate Korsgaard-Smith style normative internalist claim.) If there is nothing wrong with me, it is hard to see how I could have failed to respond to a reason I have. And so it looks like the IOT has failed to secure a reason for me to care about the objects of an ideal observer's desires.

This may be hard to see if you forget for a minute that 'ideal' in "ideal observer" means just what it does in "ideal vacuum." But recall that standard ideal observer theorists don't use 'ideal' in "ideal observer" to indicate that ideal observers are better than nonideal observers. The use of 'ideal' merely indicates that the target subject fully meets the conditions specified in the idealization. Just as you can be perfectly happy to have a ball that is near enough spherical, even though it isn't an ideal sphere, you might be perfectly satisfied not being a fully ideal observer. Many people who press the "So what?" objection accept the underlying rationalist thought. They think it is a condition of adequacy on any analysis of normative properties such as rightness that those analyses explain why a person should go in for actions that are right and eschew actions that are not right but wrong. The intelligibility of the "So what?" response indicates that there aren't reasons to choose the right and avoid the wrong as specified by the theory.

Advocates of the Ideal Observer Theory may at this point deploy a strategy they already use to counter the Open Question Argument. They can argue that the "So what?" objection depends on our finding it an open question that moral rightness is the property specified in an ideal observer analysis. But if the analysis is correct, rightness just is the property of being disposed to cause the relevant response in suitably described ideal observers. This is consistent with even competent speakers not being able to recognize that property as reason-giving when specified as it is in the analysis. Once we come to believe that there is only a single property here we will see that there is reason to care about the dispositional property because it just is the property of being right, and we have reason to care about rightness.

7.3.   Response Dispositional Theories and the Color Analogy

We noted in section 7.2.2 that an Ideal Observer Theory could be stated subjunctively in the form of a counterfactual or dispositionally, and that the resulting theories were very similar in most respects. We might think of rightness as the property that actions have when suitably described observers would respond with a certain affective reaction. Or we might think of rightness as the property that is disposed to trigger certain affective responses in observers of a certain sort. While these are not quite equivalent ways of specifying rightness they are very similar views. And there can be other similar theories that differ in somewhat further ways, while still remaining in the same broad family of such views. Philosophers have come up with various labels for the family of similar views. They've been called *response-dependent theories* (Johnston, 1989), *response dependence theories* (Enoch, 2011), *response dispositional theories* (Levin, 2000), and *moral sense theories* (Broad, 1944). I will sometimes slide rather easily between talk of ideal observer theories and response dependent, response dependence, and response dispositional theories because most of what I say is true of all members of the family in virtue of their similarities. Ideal observer theories are probably the most well-known specific instance of this more general kind of theory, and I'll sometimes make the relevant points about this sort of theory. Unless I note otherwise, the points I make in the following section apply to the entire family of theories.

Partisans of this sort of theory have often deployed an analogy with color to support and explain the kind of view they have in mind. One of the points of the analogy is to clarify the sense in which a response-dependent theory can be subjective (in depending on subjective responses) while yet being objective at least in the sense that response-dependent claims don't make themselves true (McDowell, 1988). The fact that the claim is about will be a fact over and above the fact that an agent does make or accept that claim. Even competent responders can make mistakes in using their response-dependent concepts, and when they do what they say may well be false. The analogy is also deployed to argue that adequate analyses of moral terms, properties, and concepts must display the way these terms, properties, and concepts have a constitutive connection to the response invoked in the analyses.

Here's how some defenders of the analogy put it to use. They begin by noting a broad divide among the sorts of properties we think that ordinary objects in our world have and share. One group, often called *primary* properties, are non-relational and intrinsic. On some tellings, primary qualities are basic and thus a proper subset of the non-relational intrinsic properties of things. Their alleged basicness consists in the way they explain the presence of the other properties things have. Primary qualities (using the term philosophers in the seventeenth century originally coined) are properties such as mass, density, shape, velocity, and so on. (It is lucky for us that this is not the important side of the contrast to pay attention to, since how exactly to characterize the relevant primary properties is a highly contentious matter.) Secondary properties, by contrast, are relational. They include colors, scents, tonal properties, various tactile properties, tastes, and so on. One way of dividing these from other properties, whether primary or otherwise, is that they all seem to be the proper objects of only one sense. That is, our most direct access to them is via one or another of our five senses, sight, sound, touch, taste, and smell. Contrast this with paradigm primary properties such as shape and mass. We can see shapes directly, but we can also feel them. Our access to mass is not especially linked to any particular sense modality. We can feel it when we are in a gravitational field but we can also observe mass via the effect one mass has on another. There are differences with respect to our access to putative primary properties, but since the point of the analogy comes from the similarity of *secondary* qualities to normative or value properties, we need not work out the details.

It is partly because each secondary property is directly accessed by just one sense modality, that one might think an adequate account of any secondary property should invoke that relation. Our most fundamental grasp of redness is via our visual sense apparatus. Any account of redness inconsistent with that fundamental fact would be very hard to accept. It would undermine our reasons for thinking that there is anything to talk about at all. Many philosophers have thought that this is good reason to build that connection into any adequate account of color concepts or properties. They do this by specifying the nature of the property, say redness, via its link to perceptions of it. One such analysis goes like this:

> *Red 1*: Redness is the unique property an object has if and only if it is disposed to look red to normal perceivers in normal lighting conditions.

Another similar idea is to formulate the truth conditions of redness predications in a manner along the following lines.

> *Red 2*: An object is red iff it is disposed to look red to normal perceivers in normal lighting conditions.

What advocates of these analyses think they have going for them is that they display the connection of the color redness with the way red things normally look to normal human beings, namely red. Partisans of these analyses think that is something you have to know to know what redness is, and some of them go so far as to argue that those who don't know the condition stated on the right-hand side of each analysis don't really have the concept red. These analyses are thus good candidates for getting at the essence of redness, or so think the advocates of such accounts.

At a certain level of abstraction the parallel with subjectivist dispositional analyses of moral terms should be quite obvious. That something looks red to you is a fact about your psychology, just as whether you desire something is a fact about your psychology. Similarly, just as an object's disposition to cause you to see it as red in a certain set of conditions is a disposition to affect your psychology, the disposition of a certain kind of action to trigger a desire, motive, or other affective response in you is also a disposition to affect your psychology. To bring out the parallel let's construct parallels to *Red 1* and *Red 2* earlier:

> *Right 1*: Rightness is the unique property an action has if and only if it is disposed to elicit positive affective attitudes in fully nonmorally informed, impartial, disinterested, omnipercipient, consistent, and otherwise normal observers in normal conditions.
> *Right 2*: An action is right iff it is disposed to elicit approval from an observer who was fully nonmorally informed, impartial, disinterested, omnipercipient, consistent, and otherwise normal in normal conditions.

Right 2 should be familiar since it is just what we got when we filled out the dispositional schema to generate *Firth***, our way of giving the truth conditions for claims about rightness consistent with Firth's dispositional analysis of morality. *Right 2* = *Firth***.

Thus, if subjectivists who employ such a dispositional theory are right, there is a parallel with secondary quality accounts of color. Is there any interesting moral that can be gleaned from the parallel? Partisans of response-dependent moral metaethical theories often think so. In fact, there are at least two ways they think we should find the parallel enlightening. The first has to do with the compatibility of subjectivism and objectivity and the ability to count certain judgements as incorrect. And this issue connects up with the worry that subjectivists must endorse reprehensible moral judgements. The parallel also allows a response to worries about the modality of moral judgements if subjectivism is correct. I'll discuss these in order.

7.3.1. Idealization, Objectivity, and the Worry About Reprehensible Moral Views

Critics of subjectivism often complain that such theories undermine the objective status of morality. Sometimes this criticism is put in the following way: Subjectivists don't think that we disapprove of an action because it is wrong, but rather they think that it is wrong because we disapprove of it. That criticism seems fair as against the simplest versions of subjectivism. But response-dependent theorists can employ the parallel with color terms, concepts, and properties to resist the claim when it is applied to their views.

Take first your or my everyday judgement that a particular sign is red. Is it red because you or I or both of us think it is red, or even experience it as red? Normally we'd want to say 'no,' and the dispositional analysis of color agrees with that answer. The sign would have been red whether we saw it or not. And if we saw it and decided that it looked blue to us, it would still be red. For when we don't look at the sign, it remains disposed to look red to normal observers in normal conditions. And when we decide that it looks blue, it can still be disposed to look red to us in normal conditions. Perhaps it looks blue to us because the light is bad and hence abnormal. Or perhaps someone has slipped a hallucinogen into our food and drink so that it looks blue to us. Still for all that, it is disposed to look red to normal observers in counterfactual normal conditions of good light and no hallucinogens.

The parallel treatment is available to a response dependence theorist of rightness. A given person's judgements of rightness may or may not track the judgements and/or attitudes that would be felt by someone who is fully nonmorally informed, impartial, disinterested, and so on in normal conditions. Thus it is open to a response dependence theorist to treat certain actual attitudes as irrelevant to the rightness of an action in virtue of their not tracking what a suitably idealized observer would feel. A person's thinking something right and approving of it because she thinks so won't make that very judgement true. This line of thought offers response dependence theorists a way to resist endorsing morally unpalatable views. Hitler's positive moral attitudes and judgements that tracked many heinous things were a result of a twisted psychology that arguably would not survive in ideal conditions. Whether that's so will depend on the conditions of idealization the theorists builds into the view, but the fact that most real people are not ideal gives the theorist some room to explain away troubling attitudes as not tracking the ideal dispositions.

How far this strategy can be taken and whether it allows us to keep the resulting view from endorsing reprehensible actions will be the subject of some controversy. It will help me to explain how if I begin with a clarification. So far I've been a bit loose about the target property of rightness. Philosophers disagree about whether our term 'right' picks out the property of being required or the property of being merely permissible. If it means the former it will be wrong not to perform a right action, whereas if 'right' merely indicates permissibility, it is compatible with that reading that any number of incompatible actions would be right to do. Thus it would not be wrong to fail to do a given right action, for one may permissibly have done another. I don't want to take a stand on the meaning of the English word. I'm just going to stipulate a usage for purposes of discussion. In the rest of this section I will take 'right' to mean required and 'wrong' to mean forbidden. That stipulation will leave it open that some actions may be neither right nor wrong. Such actions will be permitted but not required. This way of using the terms entails that we can't assume that an action that isn't right is wrong. It might be neither one—permissible but not required.

If the Ideal Observer Theory proceeds in this way, it will have to offer an analysis of wrongness that doesn't just equate it with the property an action has when suitably ideal observers would not approve of it. Nor should this kind of IOT define wrongness as the property of not being such as to dispose ideal observers to approve of it. Those would be good definitions of the property of not being morally required, but wrong actions are not just not required; they are forbidden. One option that might work is to work with the idea that actions are wrong iff suitably defined ideal observers would disapprove of the action in question. On the assumption that an observer will never both approve and disapprove of one and the same action, this analysis would explain why one and the same action cannot be both right and wrong, without defining the one property as the absence of the other. So let's adopt that ideal observer analysis for wrongness.

It seems disputable whether the conditions of idealization would eliminate all diversity of response in the relevant ideal observers when confronted with various courses of action. If disagreement remains in ideal conditions, there seem to be two options for treating those courses of action toward which ideal observers respond in divergent ways. An IO theorist could choose absolutism or relativism. Each option generates some worries about the treatment of some seemingly reprehensible actions. An ideal observer theorist could endorse Firth's absolutism and classify such actions as neither right nor wrong. When members of a group respond differently to the same stimuli, subjunctive claims about how they all would respond come out false. There is no single way members of a group like this would respond. So in the imagined case it isn't true that suitably ideal observers either *would approve* or *would disapprove* of the actions in question. Neither would it be correct to attribute a single disposition to respond to the members of the group of ideal observers. They have diverse dispositions with respect to these cases.

If the actions that don't get a uniform response are inconsequential enough there's no trouble for the theory. It is plausible that many actions are neither right nor wrong because there's no important reason to choose to do or to refrain with respect to actions of that sort. But if some of the actions toward which ideal observers have no uniform response are actions we think heinous, the ideal observer theorist is in an awkward spot. To hang onto the meta-ethical analysis, the theorist will have to bite the bullet and conclude that these actions are not wrong after all. They won't have to believe that such actions are morally required, so things are bit better than they are for the simple subjectivist. But it is still bullet-biting to conclude that such actions aren't just simply wrong. So the absolutist ideal observer theorist will have to hope that suitably ideal observers do in fact respond negatively to such seemingly bad actions.

The relativist ideal observer theorist is not much better off. Presumably this theory will be relativized to kinds of observers, and this means that relative to at least some kinds of observers the actions that elicit differential responses will still be right and/or wrong. So it will be possible to classify a seemingly heinous action wrong (relative to one kind of observer) as long as some ideal observers disapprove. So far so good. A problem still remains if it turns out that all ideal observers don't have the same responses to actions of some seemingly morally heinous sort. Those actions will be wrong relative to those observers who disapprove, but right relative to those having the opposite response of approval. So while the relativist can count the judgements of some that these actions are wrong as true, they will also have to count the judgement by others that they are right as true as well. That's not much less of a bullet to bite.

Ideal observer theorists will be best off if they can be confident that the conditions of ideality are robust enough to ensure that ideal observers will never approve of actions that are plausibly thought to be heinous. Still, as long as these conditions aren't given a normative or otherwise circular reading, it looks like this is an empirical issue. And the upshot of empirical issues of this complex sort is hard to predict.

There is more to say on these points and we will focus on the choice between relativism and absolutism later in this chapter. For now I just want to make two points: (1) The color analogy brings out some resources available to idealized subjectivism to handle the accusation that subjectivism must endorse bad moral verdicts. At the very least these resources restrict the range of cases in which the objection would have its force. And (2) these resources don't entirely make the worries go away. Ingenious philosophers on either side of the debate will have more to say about the issues.

7.3.2. The Color Analogy and the Modal Status Objection

Just as the color analogy highlights a strategy of response to the charge that subjectivists can't avoid endorsing heinous actions, the analogy also suggests some responses to the modal status objection. The very same resource can be used to avoid the conclusion that moral judgements are contingent on our attitudes, at least in certain ways. Recall the problem that generates the objection. Simple subjectivism entails that murder would not be wrong if I did not disapprove of it. For simple subjectivism makes the rightness or wrongness of an act or act-type turn on our attitudes toward those acts or act-types. When we are asked to consider counterfactual situations in which our attitudes are different, we have to use our attitudes *in that situation* in assessing the rightness or wrongness of the actions in question. But idealized observer theories don't tie the rightness of an act or act-type to the actual attitudes of any person. Rather, such theories use a counterfactual standard, one set by the attitudes we would have in the counterfactual situation where we satisfy the conditions stipulated in the particular ideal embodied in the theory. I can truly say that an act-type would still be wrong even if I did not endorse it, so long as I *would* endorse it were I appropriately ideal.

This is exactly parallel to what we said about the red sign as we were filling out the color analogy. It would be red whether I saw it as red or not, so long as it has not undergone a change to the properties that dispose it to cause it to look red in normal viewing conditions. If someone puts a drug in my drink and I now see it as blue, it is still red. If someone manipulates lighting conditions to make it look brown, it is still red. If I've become color blind, it is still red. And so on. The response dependence theorist can say the same thing in analogous cases.

7.3.3. Dispositional Properties and Disagreement

The analogy also points a way forward in handling the disagreement problem for subjectivism. When Robert says that there is a red sign on a certain corner and I say it is not red but green, we are in disagreement, even though it looks red to Robert and green to me. We disagree because we're not talking about how it looks to us but about what color it actually is, and that is determined by how it would look to normal observers in normal viewing conditions. And there is a fact about how it would look to such perceivers, about which we disagree. As it happens, Robert knows he is color blind and will immediately defer to others about colors, so the disagreement does not long remain. But that makes no real difference to the main point, which is just that we did disagree until he changed his mind. So long as our topic is about the dispositions of the very same sign to affect what a certain sort of observer would see in suitable conditions, we are both talking about one and the same thing and saying incompatible things about that. Hence we can use the same word to express a disagreement about color.

The same thing holds true when we move from talk about colors to talk about moral properties, so long as our thought and talk of moral properties is in fact parallel to color thought and talk in the way that the analogy suggests. If the Ideal Observer Theory is correct, moral judgements will be about the dispositions certain acts or act-types have to affect suitably described observers. We will be talking about the same topic. And if what I say or think entails that such observers would approve while what you say or think entails that they would not, we disagree in our thoughts and assertions.

7.3.4. Recap of the Points Highlighted by the Color Analogy

It is in these ways that the proponents of such response-dependent theories often think the color analogy brings out the strengths of their basic idea. The analogy points to strategies for resisting three of the main problems that beset simple subjectivist theories, that (1) such theories are able to resist endorsing many unpalatable moral conclusions because they leave room for error; (2) the analogy allows moral judgements to be modally robust by specifying the conditions under which an appraiser's response dispositions determine the relevant moral verdict even when the verdict is about an action under some other conditions; and (3) they leave room for different appraisers to disagree about morality insofar as they both are talking about what the same sort of appraiser would be disposed to approve of in relevant conditions.

7.4.   Relativist Versus Absolutist Ideal Observer Theories

While the ideal observer and response-dependent theories generate avenues of response to the standard anti-subjectivist objections, the theories do give up hostages to empirical fortune. As we noted, if there are to be some actions that are right consistent with the analysis, there must be some substantial group of actions that all suitably specified ideal observers would respond to in the relevant way. If some such observers respond by approving a type of action, and some other such observers respond by disapproving, and yet other observers don't take up any attitude at all to the very same act-type, then there is no *way* that an ideal observer *would respond* to actions of that type. Nor would these actions be disposed to elicit approval from normal suitably idealized observers. And thus that kind of action will not be right if the analysis is correct. If the relevant normal observers would differ in their responses to all act-types then, according to the analysis given, nothing would be right. Also, as we noted, it is an empirical issue whether this is in fact so. That means that empirical sciences like psychology will have something to contribute to assessing the view, though commonsense psychology may also give us relevant information.

I'm not going to spend much time here assessing the prospects for either uniformity or diversity of response dispositions among suitably specified ideal observers. Instead I want to discuss one reasonable reaction to such diversity if we are convinced it was inevitable. To make the point I will suppose that there is substantial divergence in the response dispositions of ideal observers. To make the case concrete I will use an ongoing dispute in normative ethics to specify the divergence. Recall that Kantian and utilitarian moral theories often disagree about the rightness of certain actions; Kantians think that using a person against their will even for the greater good is wrong, whereas utilitarians think such actions can be right if they lead to more overall happiness. Let's suppose that people who begin with Kantian sympathies retain those sympathies as they gain information and become omniscient, gain full imaginative awareness, lose partiality, and so on. And let's suppose that those with more utilitarian impulses retain these impulses as they gain information, imagination, impartiality, and so on. To use an analogy, just as a person's love of a certain food is unlikely to disappear under such conditions, perhaps a person's propensities toward moral sentiment remain in the face of the same changes. This would mean that for an important range of cases, cases that both Kantians and utilitarians think of as highly morally important, there would be no response that all ideal observers would have or would be disposed to have. But it is theoretically unsatisfying to say of such actions that they are neither right nor wrong.

To say that we'd have to overturn the commitments of *both* Kantian and utilitarian theorists who disagree about just these examples.

Another option is to relativize moral judgements to kinds of observers, or more specifically, to relativize such judgements directly to appraisers (or perhaps agents) and indirectly to observers. We might then say that your moral judgement that some action is wrong is true iff ideal observers most *like you* would disapprove of it. And my judgement that the same action is not wrong is true iff ideal observers *like me* would not disapprove of it. This means that our seemingly conflicting judgements might both be true—ideal observers like you might well disapprove of an action while those like me don't disapprove. Relativizing to kinds of observers thus yields a theory on which seemingly conflicting judgements can both be true, a classic form of moral relativism.

You can see how this avoids generating an error theory in the face of ideal observers with conflicting response dispositions. Suppose we have 100 "otherwise normal" ideal observers. If they are disposed to respond differently to the same actions, that is likely because of some psychological differences between them. If we pick one out, for example by specifying that the relevant ideal observer be the one most like the appraiser or agent, we eliminate this psychological variation and wind up with just one observer with one set of response dispositions. Given that one sort of psychology, there will likely be some interesting range of act-types to which such an observer is disposed to respond with approval. Since the analysis just says that the action is right if such an observer would respond with approval, these actions will count as right. And similarly for the actions of which such observers disapprove—they will be wrong. Error theory no longer looms.

The relativist maneuver also allows ideal observer theories to remain true to the internalist motivation in the face of diverse motivational dispositions. As we saw, simple subjectivists were motivated by one or another version of internalism, either in the form of appraiser internalism or agent internalism. And this means that they wound up relativist, given that they tied rightness and wrongness to the actual motivations of either appraisers or agents, and the plain fact that people differ in their actual motivating attitudes. Ideal observer theorists don't tie the rightness or wrongness to actual attitudes in this way, and that is one reason Firth thought the view could be absolutist. Yet if it turns out that appraisers and agents don't in fact converge in their important affective dispositions under ideal conditions as we contemplated earlier, it looks like the tie with motivation might disappear. Just knowing that some ideal observer or other approves of something will give me no reason to think that I would be motivated in those same conditions, given that other such observers remain unmotivated. That's why it is natural for relativist ideal observer theorists to analyze the judgements of appraisers or truth about agents in terms of the observers most like them. For given that the relevant observers are now stipulated to be as similar to the appraiser (or agent) as an ideal observer can be, it will follow that this agent would be motivated if similarly ideal. This is of course compatible with any nonideal person not being so motivated, even while they believed the action to be right. But that is true of all defeasible ideal observer views, and many consider that an advantage.

7.5.   Which Attitudes?

Any actual concrete ideal observer analysis will need to tell us the exact nature of the attitudes that the analysis invokes. Are they conative states such as desires, preferences, intentions, approvals? Might they be beliefs? Typically, ideal observer/response dispositional theorists have gone for attitudes in the first group. And they have shared the Humean assumption that there is a division of mental states into two kinds of attitudes, conative and cognitive, and that the kinds don't overlap. Some theorists friendly to such views have bucked the trend. Sharon Street (2008), who probably doesn't think of herself as falling squarely in this camp, has suggested that the relevant attitude is one of believing right.[2] And anti-Humeans, who believe that cognitive states such as beliefs can sometimes motivate action without aid from independent desire, could easily enough adopt a view in this ballpark, while maintaining the internalist theses at the core of subjectivism. Such views would be somewhat parallel to John McDowell's (1988) development of the color analogy, according to which red objects are disposed to "look red" to the relevant ideal perceivers. The parallel would come in deploying what seems to be the concept under analysis to give the analysis itself. As we noted, this would seem to make the view nonreductive. (See chapter 13 for further discussion of this kind of view.)

Even for views that stick firmly to deploying noncognitive attitudes, the choice will have import. It was useful in discussing the worry about diverse ideal observer responses for me to suggest that rightness/requirement might be analyzed in terms of approval, and wrongness/forbiddenness might be analyzed in terms of disapproval. If we cash these attitudes out in terms of preference so that approval just means most preferred of the available alternative courses of action and disapproval just means least preferred, we would have a nice explanation of why there is an incoherence in thinking that an action is both required and forbidden. But not every pro or con attitude is like that. I might admire cleverness and simplemindedness. So if admiration were the attitude, we won't get such a nice explanation of the incoherence that we seem to find. There's more to say here, and thinking about what it might be can lead to further insights.

7.6.   Ideal Agent Theories[3]

It should be relatively clear that *appraiser* subjectivism has the least difficulty explaining *appraiser* internalism (of either judgement internalist or existence internalist sorts), while *agent* subjectivism has little difficulty explaining *agent* internalism. Recall that appraiser internalism requires a connection with the actual or hypothetical motivating attitudes of those making moral judgements whereas agent internalism requires such attitudes of the agents doing the actions up for assessment. It should thus be no surprise that the former falls out of a theory that makes the attitudes of appraisers the truth-makers for moral judgements. Nor will it be a surprise that the latter falls out of a theory that makes the attitudes of agents the truth-makers for moral claims. While the nature of the required necessary connection becomes more complicated as we complicate subjectivist theories to handle various objections, each kind of theory still seems well placed to capture one or another internalist idea.

Ideal *observer* theories are the descendants of simple appraiser subjectivism. So they will offer relatively natural explanations for appraiser internalist presuppositions. However, if the Ideal Observer Theory is absolutist, the theory is committed to the claim that all observers in the appropriate conditions would agree in their responses to a right action or to a wrong action. That means it won't be much harder for such theories to explain agent internalism than to explain appraiser internalism. After all, agents and appraisers are people and in fact every agent is sometimes an appraiser and every appraiser is sometimes an agent. Someone who thinks that every appraiser will respond in the same way in certain conditions should also think that every agent will respond in just that way in those conditions. So whether your original attraction to subjectivism was for appraiser internalist or agent internalist reasons, the absolutist versions of ideal observer or response dispositional views are in a position to capture those motivating ideas.

Things change somewhat if the response dispositional theory is relativist. Different people will retain at least some of their different dispositions to approve and disapprove of morally appraisable actions, even as they become ideal. So theories that tie the truth or falsity of a moral judgement about a given action to the appraiser's perspective cannot be assured that the agent doing the action will have the same ideal dispositions as the person doing the appraising. That means that an appraiser-oriented dispositional theory—one that says that it is the ideal responses of an appraiser that matters for the truth of the judgement—won't ensure that there is a necessary connection to the motivations of the agent, even when the agent is in ideal conditions. This means that ideal observer/appraiser theories won't latch on as nicely to certain sorts of internalist motivations as ideal agent theories will. For example, if your goal in adopting subjectivism was to capture the rationalist thought that agents must have reason to do what is right while also holding to the Humean line that reasons must depend on existing desires, ideal agent theories will do better to capture those motivating ideas. Those motivations connect moral judgements to the reasons and motives of *the agents* who are obliged to do the morally right actions. So we might ask whether we can develop a more sophisticated version of agent subjectivism along the lines of those deployed in Ideal Observer Theory to handle objections that plague the simplest versions of agent subjectivism. And once we have that thought it is obvious enough that we should be able to construct several varieties of ideal agent theory that are in many ways parallel to corresponding varieties of Ideal Observer Theory.

7.7. Recap

In this chapter we have seen how one family of metaethical theories—ideal observer, ideal agent, and response-dependent views generally—develops out of simple subjectivist ideas and in response to worries about such simple theories. I'm hoping that many of the connections with the puzzles I rehearsed in the first several chapters will be relatively clear. In particular, the narrative emphasized the internalist motivations that make subjectivism, both simple and complex, attractive. And it grounded the move to more complex subjectivist theories in the goal of making room for the possibility of actual moral disagreement where simple subjectivism had trouble allowing such disagreement. The narrative also emphasized the role of moral epistemological concerns in generating the description of ideality employed by prominent ideal observer theories like Firth. This doesn't mean that every single puzzle discussed in the early chapters are as important as the ones I highlight here. Nor has every puzzle, or even each of the highlighted puzzles, been put definitively to rest. But I hope the chapter makes clearer how puzzles from each of the loosely related families have had a role to play in generating these more sophisticated subjectivist theories. In the next chapter we will see a different strategy for developing subjectivist ideas to handle some of these same concerns. It will involve giving up on even minimal realism and accepting some version of noncognitivism instead.

Questions

Comprehension

C1. What should the hybrid subjectivist at the end of section 7.1 say about the rightness or wrongness of an action when the speaker, agent, and audience do not share a moral outlook and when their individual outlooks have them take conflicting attitudes toward that action?

C2. Think of one phenomenon that agent subjectivism better explains than a similar version of appraiser subjectivism. List one phenomenon that appraiser subjectivism better explains than a similar version of agent relativism.

C3. How would a response dispositional secondary quality account answer the old clichéd philosophy question, "Does a tree falling in a forest with no one to hear it makes a sound?"

C4. What are the main virtues of a response-dependent analysis that models itself on analyses of secondary qualities like the colors?

Extension

E1. If you were coming up with a version of Ideal Agent or Ideal Observer Theory, what attitude would you use as the one that matters in ideal conditions? Is it the same for both agent and observer versions of idealized-response theory?

E2. In section 6.2.2, I suggested that simple subjectivism has trouble explaining features of moral epistemology. For example, the view has trouble explaining why we often try to get more information about actions before we decide whether they are right or wrong. And in this chapter I explained how Firth's version of the Ideal Observer Theory was designed to explain the relevance of information gathering, impartiality, and so on in figuring out what is right or wrong. Can Firth's Ideal Observer Theory explain all of the features of moral epistemology that give simple subjectivism trouble? Hint: Think about what we should be focused on as we decide such questions and what the theory seems to predict we should focus on. (This may be a hard question as the worry here is pretty subtle.)

E3. The rationalist thought behind the "So what?" objection seems like a reason to prefer ideal *agent* theories to ideal *observer* theories insofar as the idea is that moral judgements give *agents* reason to do what is right. Does moving to an ideal agent version of the theory rather than an ideal appraiser version completely answer the objection? Hint: Does it matter that "Ideal" in "Ideal Agent Theory" is normative or nonnormative?

Reading

Read along with: Roderick Firth (1952). And maybe one of David Lewis (1989), Gilbert Harman (1978), or John McDowell (1988).

Further reading: Westermarck (1932) is an early defense of a relativist version of Ideal Observer Theory that contrasts with Firth's Absolutist version. Harman (1978) offers a relativist subjectivist analysis of rightness that isn't quite an ideal agent or Ideal Observer Theory but makes the connections with internalism relatively clear. Lewis (1989) offers a dispositional analysis of value where the idealization clearly gets a nonnormative specification. Johnson (1999) raises a problem for ideal agent views. Thomson and Harman (1996) offers a good debate on relativism. McDowell (1988) is a difficult but rewarding paper that deploys the secondary quality analogy and also exemplifies a normative idealization. Johnston (1989) deploys the "So what?" objection against nonnormative versions of response dispositional theories. It isn't written for undergraduates, but you can get something out of it nonetheless. Street (2008) extends subjectivism beyond ethics to all normative domains.

Notes

1   I've come close to saying that the ideal observer theory is a dispositional analysis of moral terms. I should introduce a small note of caution. Not every dispositional claim can be analyzed counterfactually, so an ideal observer theory stated as a subjunctive may not be exactly equivalent to the very closely related claim you'd make in giving a parallel dispositional analysis. The following discussion that employs masked or blocked dispositions to handle the amoralist objection brings out some advantages of a dispositional treatment of ideal observers (Lewis, 1997; Bird, 1998).

2   At least her constructivism seems to yield the conclusion that normative judgements are true when the relevant subjects would converge on that very judgement in suitably ideal conditions.

3   The terminology here is a bit artificial, since an agent also observes what she does. Here I'm just using the terms 'ideal agent' in contrast with 'ideal observer' and 'ideal appraiser' to indicate whether we are idealizing the agent's psychology or a bystander's.

8 Noncognitivist Heirs of Simple Subjectivism

Noncognitivists agree with subjectivists that moral judgements are rooted in emotions in a deep way, and they accept the naturalistic metaphysical picture shared by both simple and complex subjectivists. But they reject the idea that moral judgements are *about* such emotions or attitudes, whether actual or hypothetical. Noncognitivists think moral judgements *express* these attitudes without talking about them. Noncognitivism, thus, develops the underlying motivations for simple subjectivism in a radically different direction. The complex subjectivists of the previous chapter responded to problems for simple subjectivism by complicating the contents of moral judgements while retaining a basically representational picture of that content. In other words they treated the judgements as still *about* the attitudes of relevant individuals, just as simple subjectivism does. Noncognitivists, by contrast, react to the same problems by rejecting the representational picture shared by both simple and complex subjectivist theories. In rejecting that picture they reject minimal realism. The crucial part of the noncognitivist view is thus double-barreled and negative: (1) Moral sentences don't represent the world in the way other sentences in the indicative mood normally do, and (2) moral "beliefs" don't represent the world in the way that genuine beliefs do.

8.1. Two Negative Claims

Noncognitivists deny that moral judgements—that is the psychological states we attribute when we say someone believes (for example) that lying is wrong, and the kinds of states that would normally be expressed by assertions of indicative sentences such as "Lying is wrong,"—are *cognitive* states. Hence, one reason for the label *noncognitivism*. Noncognitivists think moral judgements are *not* cognitive. On a standard division of the mental, *cognitive* states are states of mind that represent the world, in contrast with various *conative* states such as desires, emotions, and the like—states that are allegedly directed at the world but nonrepresentational. Standard noncognitivists typically also endorse a second negative claim about the meanings of sentences that employ moral terms. They deny that these sentences represent the world in the same way other indicative sentences typically do. In the literature you will often see this idea expressed as the claim that moral judgements are not "descriptive." We might give each of these negative claims a name as follows:

1. *Psychological noncognitivism*: The state of mind that constitutes accepting a moral claim is not really a cognitive state (where cognitive states are states that represent the world as being some way or other).
2. *Semantic nonrepresentationalism*: Indicative moral sentences don't function (primarily) to represent or describe the world in the same way that other indicative sentences do. Their meaning is not representational (at least in the first instance).

Since these are negative claims, they immediately raise two questions: (1) What kinds of mental state are the states we call "moral beliefs"? And (2) what then is the function of moral sentences and what do they mean? These questions demand positive answers.

8.1.1. Some Varieties of Noncognitivism

Different varieties of noncognitivism divide on the positive answers they give. Many of the familiar names for specific noncognitivist views taxonomize them according to their answers to these questions. Not all varieties treat the two questions as equally important. Some treat the semantic issues in more detail whereas others focus more on the psychology. Still each view does commit to some rough views about the relevant meanings and about the state of mind involved in accepting a moral claim. *Emotivists* suggested that moral terms are conventional devices for expressing emotion and encouraging others to share in it. One way of understanding this idea is to think of moral terms as linguistic devices for performing a certain sort of speech act, one that the audience would understand as expressing a pro or con attitude and also as exhorting the audience to share it. That answer to the question about language would then make it natural to identify the state of mind of accepting a moral judgement with the attitude expressed by the sentence involved. Early emotivist views are the ancestors of more contemporary *expressivist* views, and expressivists (as we'll see later) have answered both of the questions in much more detail—saying more about the attitudes involved and saying more about *how* these attitudes are expressed. *Prescriptivists* start from claims about language, likening moral sentences to imperatives apt for speech acts of prescribing. On the simplest versions of the view, 'Killing is wrong' just means the same thing as 'Do not kill.' On R. M. Hare's more complex view, *Universal Prescriptivism* (Hare, 1952), moral claims were generalized imperatives not translatable in other terms. These imperatives prescribed and proscribed the actions they targeted along with any relevantly similar actions done in appropriately similar circumstances.

So (very roughly) 'X is right' would mean something similar to, 'You all do X and any relevantly similar actions in similar circumstances.' The 'universal' in "universal prescriptivism" expresses the idea that these prescriptions apply to anyone in a sufficiently similar situation, including the agent of the action, the audience, and the maker of the judgement. It is more difficult to jump directly from this idea to a commitment about the nature of moral beliefs than it is to make the analogous jump from emotivist accounts of moral language to an account of moral belief and acceptance. That's because it isn't obvious that someone has to be in any particular state of mind either to issue a command or to accept it. Still, Hare did suggest that accepting an imperative involves a commitment to following through on the action it recommends.

Contemporary expressivist theories are the heirs of emotivism. They tie the meanings of moral terms somewhat more tightly to the particular states of mind expressed by the sentences containing them than their emotivist ancestors. In particular, the most systematic expressivists tie each sentence containing a moral or normative term to a corresponding mental state that it expresses as a matter of meaning. And they are typically more forthcoming about the nature of the expression relation. For example they might suggest that being in the state of mind expressed by the sentence is an appropriateness condition for its assertive use.[1]

8.2.   Noncognitivism as Heir to Subjectivism

It is in giving positive answers to the questions raised by the two constitutive negative noncognitivist claims that typical versions of noncognitivism show their subjectivist roots. Most noncognitivist views will try to elucidate the meanings of moral sentences by connecting them with the attitudes that make them appropriate to use. And the psychological question—"What is it to believe a moral claim?"—itself asks about the nature of a certain state of mind. Noncognitivists give these a subjectivist-inspired answer. The relevant states of mind are noncognitive subjective states, perhaps even the very same states that the simple subjectivists of chapter 6 thought moral judgements *are about*. And the sentences' meanings will make them fit linguistic devices for *expressing* these very subjective attitudes *without talking about or reporting them*. Here we have a second reason for using the label 'noncognitivism.' Noncognitivists make *noncognitive states of mind* central to the explanation of both what moral judgements are and what moral terms are fit to do. The judgements are such noncognitive states of mind and the meanings of moral terms make them apt for the expression of just these states.

It is hard, though, to overemphasize the way in which the view departs from ordinary subjectivism. Noncognitivists make a big deal out of the contrast between self-ascribing an attitude and expressing the attitude. They are not old-fashioned subjectivists precisely because they deny that moral judgements are about the subjective states that are the attitudes expressed by moral judgements. So we should get a better handle on the contrast between merely expressing a state of mind and talking about or self-ascribing it. Luckily we have some help. Noncognitivists point to various other forms of speech to serve as models for what they have in mind. One model is provided by 'hurrah!' and 'boo!' and other expressive terms that as a matter of meaning express positive and negative attitudes. If you wanted to explain the meanings of these terms to someone, it would be very natural to point to the attitudes they conventionally express and to note that they are conventional devices for expressing these attitudes. At the same time, it would be important to note that these terms are not used to self-ascribe these attitudes. They aren't used to report that the speaker has the attitude. They are not synonymous with "I approve," "I dislike that," or the like. The 'hurrah'/'boo' example thus models exactly what emotivists have in mind when they distinguish expression from self-ascription.[2]

Expressivists think we make a parallel distinction even for genuinely cognitive judgements between reporting or talking about and expressing these judgements. The distinction can be used to explain how noncognitivists think descriptivist subjectivism goes wrong. It is commonplace that simple indicative sentences express beliefs. "My car is in the shop," when sincerely asserted, expresses the *belief* one's car is in the shop. Even when insincerely asserted, there's a sense in which "My car is in the shop," expresses that same belief; it gives the audience some (possibly defeasible) reason to attribute the belief to the speaker. The meaning of the sentence makes it apt for expressing the belief in this way. But though it expresses the belief, it isn't about the belief. (By contrast, "I believe my car is in the shop," is about the belief.) If you use "My car is in the shop," I can disagree with what you say without denying that you have the belief. I need only deny your car is in the shop. That I can do this is some evidence that what you say is not about your state of mind, but rather about the car and the shop and their relative locations. So here, even in the realm of the descriptive, we have a model for what expressivists want—sentences that express a state of mind without talking about it.

Suppose we want to employ this model to construct an expressivist and noncognitivist account of how moral terms work. We'll want to say that moral sentences stand to the noncognitive mental states they express in just the same relation sentences of the form 'X is G' stand to the belief that X is G. When sincere they will express these mental states in a straightforward sense. And even when used insincerely, such sentences will express these states in a weaker sense—non-ironic use of the sentence will give the audience a reason to believe the speaker is in the state expressed. This is parallel to the sense in which an utterance of "thank you" expresses gratitude whether it is sincerely used.

Furthermore, we'll want the sentence 'X is not G' to express a state of mind that disagrees with the state expressed by 'X is G,' one that contradicts the state expressed by 'X is G.' At the same time we won't want 'You don't believe that X is G' to express that state of mind. Instead we want that sentence to contradict, 'I believe that X is G,' a sentence that talks about the state of mind of "believing" or accepting that X is G, not about whether X is G. Working out all of the details is actually more difficult than it looks, but for now the important point is we have a cognitivist model to show that there is a coherent notion of expression that can play the role noncognitivists want expression to play. Ordinary assertions of indicative sentences allow for the expression of an attitude without talking about it. And the assertion of a sentence negating a sentence expresses disagreement with the state of mind that that sentence expresses without *talking about* the attitude with which we disagree. Noncognitivists extend this model to noncognitive motivational or conative states.

To reemphasize the point we've already noted, this allows noncognitivists to claim the mantle of rightful heirs to simple subjectivism. They think simple subjectivists were right about something and wrong about something. Subjectivists were right to treat certain attitudes and their expression as central and even essential to the correct account of moral terms. But they were wrong about the way in which they were central. And they were wrong about the way in which moral judgements expressed those attitudes. The subjectivists, as noncognitivists view them, mistakenly focused on the kind of expression in play when one talks about or reports what one thinks or feels, whereas there is a more direct kind of expression that they should have been working with. This more direct expression does not report the attitude one expresses. It directly expresses the attitude by giving voice to it.

I said that noncognitivists think the attitudes in question are conative as opposed to cognitive. This can make it seem problematic when noncognitivists use "moral beliefs" or "moral judgements" to refer to these attitudes. But there is nothing all that tricky going on. Noncognitivists acknowledge that we ordinarily call the relevant moral attitudes "beliefs" and "judgements" and they often speak that way themselves. They need find no mistake in such usage. But they will insist that using "belief" in this way doesn't track the deepest distinctions between kinds of mental states. At the deepest level, what we call beliefs should be viewed as of two distinct kinds. Cognitive representational states and noncognitive conative mental states that we might more colloquially call desires. In other words, noncognitivists are Humeans about moral psychology and motivation. They think that states of mind can be divided into two fundamentally different kinds of states with different characteristic functions. One sort, beliefs or cognitive states, are representational—they tell us how things are, aim at truth, and are true when they represent the world as it is. The other sort, desires or noncognitive states, motivate us to act. If they represent anything at all, they represent goals, and there is nothing wrong if these states represent goals that don't match how things are. The mismatch will, in the right circumstances, get us to try to change the world to satisfy the goal. But if we can't do it the state is not therefore defective or untrue. It is an important part of this Humean picture that there is no overlap between these two categories, and that a map of the deep structure of the mental will make this distinction between kinds of states. Any tendency of ordinary English to classify some motivating states as beliefs just reflects a sloppiness in ordinary talk. Such talk fails to cut the mind at its most important joints. Or so say noncognitivists who endorse the Humean picture.

8.3. Moral Disagreement

When I say my house is gray and you say it is not gray, we disagree. And when you say lying is always wrong and I say it is not always wrong, we also seem to disagree. Non-relativist *descriptivists* have an easy explanation of why this is true in both cases. In each case I assert something has a certain property and you assert it does not have that very property. Since a thing cannot both have and lack one and the same property, what we each say is not compatible with what the other says. The claims we make cannot both be true. The contents of our claims are logically incompatible, and so when I assert what you deny we disagree. Simple subjectivist relativists can't just adopt this explanation without modification, insofar as their view is that the same moral predicate in the mouths of two different people can predicate two different properties. And if that happens in a case of seeming disagreement, it can mean that the contents of their utterances won't conflict. One says that a particular action is "right," and the other says it is "not right." But if the term 'right' picks out different properties in each of their mouths, neither asserts something that the other denies.

Noncognitivists often seize on this problem as a point in favor of their view, at least as compared with descriptivist relativist subjectivism. Their thought is that descriptivist subjectivism is put at this disadvantage because they treat indicative moral sentences as claims about an (actual or possible) attitude, and sentences about attitudes don't just inherit their logical properties from the attitudes they're about. (We noted this already in the previous section.) If I point out that two of my own judgements are logically inconsistent, that claim itself isn't inconsistent. If there is an inconsistency in the neighborhood, it resides in the attitudes that are the subject of my higher-order claim. Similarly, if I rightly point out that one of my attitudes conflicts with yours, the conflict is not between what I point out and your attitude, rather it is between the two attitudes I'm talking about. If that is the correct diagnosis of the problem with simple subjectivism, it points naturally to expressivism as a solution. If my attitude A conflicts with your attitude B, it is natural to think that the sentences that directly express these attitudes also conflict with one another. So as long as we pick attitudes that can conflict in the right way, the sentences that express them will as well.

Take the simple 'boo!'/'hurrah!' model. An expressivist can think that 'boo!' conflicts with 'hurrah!' when directed at the same target because the attitudes they express themselves conflict. So now we can stipulate that 'Lying is wrong' means just what 'Boo lying!' means, and that 'Lying is right' means just what 'Hurrah lying!' means. That is, each of these indicative sentences expresses just the attitude the corresponding 'boo'/'hurrah' sentence does. If the fact that the underlying attitudes conflict explains why the 'boo'/'hurrah' sentences conflict it can also explain why the two indicative sentences conflict. These sentences inherit their conflict properties from the attitudes they express. Now 'Such-and-such is right' will conflict with 'such-and-such is wrong' in the way that 'Hurrah! Bears' conflicts with 'Boo! Bears.' So far so good.

Still this only goes so far. It is nice to have the theory explain why there seems to be a conflict between predications of right and wrong. But I can think that some action is not right without thinking that it is wrong. And if I say that something is not right, while you say that it is, we also disagree. And the 'boo!'/'hurrah!' model doesn't yet explain that. Noncognitivists will thus need to extend what they've said so far to tell us what the negation of an indicative moral sentence means and they have to do that in a particular way. We need a story about what 'not' does to the meaning of a moral sentence and we need that story to explain why the negation of a moral sentence conflicts with the original sentence. And the story should explain why a person who accepts what that sentence expresses disagrees with a person who accepts what the first expresses.

8.4. Systematically Extending the Basic Account (the Frege-Geach Problem)

It isn't just negated moral predicates or sentences that we need to know more about. Like other predicates, moral predicates get used in all sorts of more complex constructions, and not all are in the indicative mood. For example:

Is cheating always wrong?
It is possible that cheating is always wrong.
If cheating is wrong, then so is tax fraud.
Both lying and cheating are wrong.
If tax fraud is wrong, then Sarah won't countenance it.
Either it was wrong to do that, or Harry lied to me.
It is true that Morton's callous response was wrong.
Imagine that helping others was always wrong.
Monica believes that cruelty is almost always wrong.
Dishonesty would be wrong even if no one noticed it.

I have listed only a handful of the many constructions we might run into. Very likely even this short list contains a sentence or two you have not previously considered. And yet you probably had some idea of what each of these sentences meant. That phenomenon, that we are able to understand novel sentences of this and even greater complexity, puts some constraints on how noncognitivists should fill out the account to handle such constructions. The meanings of these sentences must be compositional, by which we mean that the meanings of more complex sentences should be a predictable function of the meanings of the terms they contain.

Cognitivists have an easy time meeting this constraint when they tell us what complex sentences mean. Predicates in general, including moral predicates, represent properties. Simple indicative sentences of the form '**X** is **F**,' predicate the property picked out by the predicate in the **F**-position of the referent of '**X**.' They represent the proposition that the **X** is **F**. The sentence is true when the proposition is, and it is true when the referent of '**X**' has that property, false if it does not. More complex sentences employing connectives such as 'and,' 'or,' and '. . . if . . . then' express propositions whose truth is a function of the truth-values of the sentences they embed. A sentence that embeds two sentences flanking 'and' will express the proposition that is true only when both of the embedded claims are true. A sentence embedding two sentences flanking 'or' will be true when either one or both embedded sentences are true. And so on. As long as we understand the connectives and know what the predicates in the atomic sentences mean, it should be relatively easy to figure out what such more complex sentences mean. And we can explain the ability of ordinary speakers to understand new sentences as reflecting their knowledge of the meanings of the connectives and the embedded sentences. 'Is true,' 'is false,' and 'not' aren't connectives strictly speaking, but cognitivists can do something similar to explicate the meanings of these terms. '**X** is true' where '**X**' is replaced with an indicative sentence means just what '**X**' does, and it is true just when '**X**' is. 'Not **X**,' negates what '**X**' represents, and it will be true just when '**X**' is false.

This kind of story makes it no mystery how speakers can understand novel constructions and use them to think thoughts they might not previously have entertained. The story employs the compositionality of our language—the fact that the meanings of complex sentences are a function of the meanings of the parts—to explain an ability we obviously have. It would be handy if noncognitivists could offer a parallel story. For they too owe us an account of the meanings of more complex sentences and one that explains how we can be competent with such sentences given our knowledge of their components. Compositional theories typically require the meanings of embedded expressions to retain a constant meaning even while embedded so that this meaning can contribute to the meaning of the whole. That is why ordinary speakers are able to compute the meanings of complex sentences once they know the meanings of the parts. The meanings of the complex sentences are a function of the constant meanings of their parts.

Typical noncognitivist proposals for simple indicative sentences complicate the task of producing a compositional semantics for a language containing moral terms. One problem is just that moral predicates don't retain the features used by many noncognitivists to indicate their meanings when they are embedded in more complex constructions. Emotivists tell us that moral terms function as expressives to express pro or con attitudes toward the items of which they are predicated. And that is not implausible when such predications are employed in freestanding indicative sentences. 'Cursing is wrong,' when used to make an assertion does plausibly express a negative attitude toward cursing. But when someone says, "If cursing is wrong, then frankness is too," it isn't obvious that they express any negativity toward cursing. It doesn't seem that here the moral predicate's meaning is well-explicated by talking about its attitude-expressing function. Here it is doing something else.

Peter Geach (1960, 1965) argued that we could see the inadequacy of the emotivist proposal as an account of the meaning of moral terms if we put such sentences together in a valid argument. His example was:

P1. If tormenting the cat is bad, getting your little brother to do it is bad.
P2. Tormenting the cat is bad.
Ergo, getting your little brother to torment the cat is bad.

For the argument not to commit a fallacy of equivocation, 'is bad' must retain its same meaning in each step. But 'is bad' doesn't function to express disapproval in each step because moral terms in the antecedents of conditionals don't necessarily express disapproval. So the meaning of the term can't *just be* that it expresses disapproval. Geach attributed the point about meaning constancy under embedding to Frege. (He called it "the Frege point.") And as a result, the problem of extending moral semantics to cover more complex constructions is often called the "*Frege-Geach problem.*" It is also often called "the embedding problem" because it involves figuring out the meanings of complex sentences embedding simpler moral sentences within them.

Geach's example shows that noncognitivists should want a semantics for moral terms that enables the meaning of moral sentences to stay constant whether freestanding or embedded. Nothing in noncognitivism rules out meeting this goal. One can consistently hold that moral terms are apt for the expression of attitudes when unembedded and that they are not apt for such expression when embedded, so long as one doesn't go on to *identify* the meanings of the terms with their unembedded use. Noncognitivists should look for a meaning that the terms retain across all contexts of use. That meaning should make the terms apt for expressing noncognitive attitudes when unembedded, and apt for embedded uses that don't involve expressing these same attitudes. Given that noncognitivists deny the representational account of moral predicates, this account can't be the same as that available to cognitivists—one that commits itself to moral properties, propositions, and so on. But noncognitivists have some resources available, and various sophisticated expressivists and prescriptivists have tried to develop just such accounts.

Unfortunately, most of the promising accounts get quite technical quite quickly. A book of this sort is not the right venue to pursue every approach and to assess all (or even most) of the main problems. But many readers will want some idea of how noncognitivists have grappled with the problem and perhaps also of some of the difficulties encountered for these attempts. So the rest of this section will be a selective tour of some main approaches. Readers who find the details difficult can probably get by without understanding much of the next section. Others may find it whets their appetites for solving philosophical puzzles.

8.4.1.   Prescriptivism and Imperative Logic

Even before Geach pressed his challenge to noncognitivism, R. M. Hare was at work trying to explain the validity of certain patterns of inference. Hare was a prescriptivist. He thought that moral sentences were a species of imperative apt for a special kind of prescription, similar to the way an imperative sentence like "Close the door" is apt to give prescriptions in the form of advice or even some sort of command. Thus his basic idea was that moral terms in a sentence function like mood to indicate the nature of the speech act the sentence is being used to perform. As Hare thought of mood (as in the imperative mood of 'Close the door'), it serves as something like a force indicator—that is as a syntactic signal that the speaker is likely performing a certain sort of speech act. A sentence in the indicative mood creates a presumption that the speaker intends to assert the content of the sentence, interrogatives create a similar presumption of asking a question, and imperatives create the presumption that the speaker is giving advice or commanding something. Moral terms, Hare thought, served as similar mood indicators.[3] The use of such terms indicated that the speaker was issuing a special kind of command—one that was addressed to everyone and that applied to all actions of a certain sort. A sentence such as 'It is right to confess,' when uttered in a particular context, recommends confessing in those particular circumstances, but also to anyone else in similar circumstances. (Hence the name *universal prescriptivism* for Hare's view.) It is this universalized feature that makes moral prescriptions special according to Hare.

Of course we need to know more than the mood or the speech act type of an utterance to know what a sentence means. Hare thought that we could think of most sentences as having a content—a content that then interacted with the mood to assert something specific, or ask some particular question, or recommend a particular sort of thing. Those contents might be thought of as propositions or states of affairs—ways that the world might be. Two sentences could share this content despite being in different moods. 'Shut the door' and 'The door is shut' have the same content and represent the same proposition, though the former recommends bringing it about and the latter asserts that that is how things are. His name for these common contents was the "*phrastic*" and his term for the force indicating part of the meaning of a sentence was the "*neustic*."[4]

To use a crude analogy, Hare thought of speech acts somewhat like this: Imagine that language users were given a stock of sentences that could describe the world in as much detail as needed. These could be combined in various ways to create more or less detailed descriptions, in much the way that truth conditional semantics deals with indicative sentences. Suppose further that speakers have a magic chalkboard on which they can write such sentences in as much detail as they like. No matter how much they write it magically fits on the chalkboard. Now imagine that the chalk comes in different colors. Each color represents a different kind of speech act one might perform in writing down the descriptions. If one uses red one asks a question. "Jones washed the floor" when written in red asks the question, did Jones wash the floor? Yellow chalk is analogous to the indicative mood. If you write "Jones washes the floor" in yellow your audience will take you to have asserted that Jones washes the floor. Purple chalk indicates a speech act employing the imperative mood. "Jones washes the floor" in purple recommends to the audience that they make it the case that Jones washes the floor. Green chalk (representing universal prescription) does the same thing but furthermore extends the recommendation to anyone anywhere in an analogous position.

This model is a very simple compositional language apt for performing certain sorts of speech acts. We can predict what we are to understand from the meanings of the individual words and the color of the chalk. The words written on the board represent a way the world might be. They are the analogues of Hare's phrastics. The color of the chalk then tells us how we are to take this representation. Do we take it to describe reality, suggest a goal to us, or ask us whether it is true? The color of the chalk gives us our answer, the function of Hare's neustics. The green chalk is used for moral claims. Hare's idea then is that a moral term indicates the force with which the content of a sentence is being used in just the way the green chalk would indicate the same force in this model.

We should note how this story can explain why certain parallel forms of inference make sense even across different moods (or colors of chalk). In Table 8.1 we have a set of three arguments displayed in the left column. All of them seem perfectly straightforward and to support their conclusions. It doesn't take much rumination on the three to notice that they have something in common and that their status as decent arguments depends in part on what they have in common. Hare thinks that representing what they say via his neustics and phrastics can be used to illustrate what they have in common to explain their validity as arguments. They all share the same phrastics and Hare seemed to think that there were certain patterns of phrastic premises that validly led to certain phrastics as conclusions. The

Table 8.1. Hare's Logical Model

Original Argument	Formalization	
	Phrastic	*Neustic*
Assertoric		
All the balls are put away.	The balls all being put away.	Is true.
This is a ball.	This being a ball.	Is true.
Therefore, this is put away.	This being put away.	Is true.
Prescriptive		
Put all the balls away.	The balls all being put away.	Bring this about.
This is a ball.	This being a ball.	Is true.
Therefore, put this away.	This being put away.	Bring this about.
Moral		
The balls should be put away.	The balls all being put away.	Y'all[5] bring this about.
This is a ball.	This being a ball.	Is true.
Therefore, this should be put away.	This being put away.	Y'all bring this about.

three arguments above seem to instantiate one of them. If we add to this certain rules about how such arguments combine with neustics in certain patterns according to certain rules, Hare suggested we could predict when an argument would be valid and when it would not be valid.

This is far from a complete account of the logic of natural language. But it does seem to capture something important—that the three arguments share some formal features that are relevant to their common status as good arguments. So Hare thought he had grounds for optimism that with enough ingenuity the theory could be extended yet further.

I won't take the story much further but I do want to point out one difficulty for extending it to full generality. The logical connectives can be used to combine atomic sentences in different moods. We say things like, "If it is raining take an umbrella" and "If he's so smart, why did he get wet?" We embed moral sentences in similar ways. On the one hand that is more grounds for optimism. That we can embed moral claims and imperatives might be a reason to model the logic of moral utterances on the logic for imperatives as Hare is trying to do.

But this also makes things a bit more difficult in two ways. First of all, it adds complication—a full account can't just use standard truth conditional semantics to tell us the meanings of the phrastics and only afterwards apply rules that take the force indicating neustics into account. For what follows from what will depend on the mood of what's embedded. What follows from one sentence when coupled with another depends, among other things, upon whether one of them is a question or an indicative. You can see this for yourself if you go to the preceding chart. Change the second premise in each argument to a question and use "is this true" to represent the neustics for questions. Ask yourself whether the same conclusions follow.

Furthermore, there seems to be an important disanalogy between how we embed moral sentences and how we embed imperatives. Moral sentences go into the antecedents of 'if/then' conditionals whereas imperatives don't seem to. We say, "If it's the wrong thing to do, George will do it," but we don't say, "If do it, George will do it." If imperatives don't go into the antecedents of such conditionals, but moral sentences do, then moral statements are not imperatives.

These two complications do not doom this general strategy. Prescriptivists can complicate their account to deal with the first difficulty. And Hare was aware that syntactically imperative sentences don't embed in the antecedents of conditionals; he thought English includes other constructions that functioned semantically like embedded imperatives. But we'll leave prescriptivist solutions to Frege-Geach there. We're getting into pretty difficult and technical issues for a book like this.

8.4.2. Expressivism

Most recent work on the Frege-Geach problem has been a development of the expressivist program in the stricter more ambitious sense noted in section 8.2. Such strict expressivism aims to explain the semantics of every moral sentence by tying it to a particular state of mind it is especially apt for expressing. Since any full noncognitivist story necessarily has to explain what it is to "believe" a moral claim, this project has the virtue of doing what anyway needs to be done. And, since beliefs stand in logical relations to one another just as much as sentences do, it provides a new strategy for explaining the meanings of sentences in such a way as to make sense of the logical relations between them. The general idea is this: First develop an account of the states of mind expressed by certain sentences that explains how states of mind can stand in logical relations to one another. That account should explain (for example) how the belief that lying is wrong, and the belief that to deny climate change is to lie, combine to entail the conclusion that to deny climate change is wrong, and so on. Once we have the account we can say that sentences inherit their logical relations to one another from the logical relations of the states of mind they express. So the sentences, "Lying is wrong," and "To deny climate change is to lie" together entail "To deny climate change is wrong" because the states of mind those sentences express entail the state of mind expressed by the conclusion.

As part of this overall project, expressivists will have to tell us which states of mind are to be assigned to conditionals. And they then must make the case that these states of mind do stand in the right logical relations to the states expressed by the simple sentences they embed. They need to do this in order to explain the role of conditionals in valid inferences. One popular strategy has been to match conditionals with higher-order attitudes toward the attitudes expressed by their parts (Blackburn, 1984, chapter 6). Take for example, the meaning of 'If lying is wrong, then so is diplomacy.' A higher-order-attitude theory might say it expresses an attitude of disapproval toward disapproving of lying without also disapproving of diplomacy. Holding that higher-order disapproval to a combination of attitudes one in fact has will involve one in a certain sort of internal incoherence that one might resolve by giving up some part of the combination. In the example at hand one could give up one's disapproval of lying and thereby giving up the "belief" that lying is wrong. Or one could instead come to disapprove of diplomacy and thereby coming to accept the "belief" that diplomacy is wrong. The idea is that the incoherence we cite among these noncognitive attitudes is the very same incoherence we cite when we say it is incoherent to believe both that lying is wrong and that if lying is wrong diplomacy is wrong while not going on to believe that diplomacy is wrong. For these attitudes just are what this kind of expressivist says those beliefs are.

There are ways to pursue the expressivist program that do not employ this higher-order-attitude strategy. And it has drawn some critical scrutiny. But it presents a reasonably understandable picture of how expressivists might explain the logical relations among moral and nonmoral sentences in a reasonably systematic way.

8.4.3.   Hybrid Theories

Recently hybrid theories of moral sentences and the attitudes they express have gained some prominence. One motivation for going hybrid has been that such theories offer to help meet the Frege-Geach desiderata. The basic hybrid idea is that moral sentences have ordinary representational meaning, while also expressing (either semantically or pragmatically) additional non-cognitive content. The representational part of the semantics allows the hybrid theorist to take advantage of many of the resources of truth conditional semantics to generate a compositional account of the semantics insofar as it is representational. This account can then be supplemented with some additional principles to govern any expressive semantic content. To treat the expressive content as semantic would be to treat it as conventionally encoded in the meanings of the terms used. This would be analogous to the way the non-hybrid emotivist thinks of the expressive component in moral semantics. It just is a matter of convention that these words convey these attitudes. The hybrid theorist who goes this route only adds that the terms also have a representational semantic component. For example, a hybrid theorist could think that a term like 'morally right' meaning which makes it apt both for picking out some natural property such as promoting human health and for at the same time expressing a positive attitude toward that property.

On this model, when someone sincerely says, "Expanding Medicaid is morally right," they would be saying something that both conveys the information that expanding Medicaid would promote human health, and expresses their approval of promoting human health. A rough translation might then be, "Expanding Medicare would promote human health and Hurrah for promoting human health!"[6]

This would allow us to explain many of the logical relations that hold among moral sentences and other sentences. For example, we might look at a simple *modus ponens* argument like:

PREMISE 1:   If expanding Medicaid is right, then raising taxes is right.
PREMISE 2:   Expanding Medicaid is right.
CONCLUSION: Therefore, raising taxes is right.

The argument is valid. Now here is a hybrid-expressivist translation of it:

PREMISE 1:   If expanding Medicaid promotes human health, then raising taxes promotes human health, and Hurrah for promoting human health.
PREMISE 2:   Expanding Medicaid promotes human health and Hurrah for promoting human health!
CONCLUSION: Therefore, raising taxes promotes human health and Hurrah for promoting human health.

This looks pretty good as an explanation of the validity of the argument. The representational/descriptive part of the conclusion follows from the premises by modus ponens, and the expressive part follows from either of the two premises. One would want to fill out the view and check it against other examples of logical implication (and non-implication) to see how it fares overall before adopting a view of this sort.

This is just an example and one that leaves a number of theoretically important details unspecified. One is how the descriptive property—promoting human health—comes to be semantically expressed by the predicate 'morally right.' One way it might go would be if the descriptive content worked just like any other descriptive content for non-indexical expressions. It could be the words just are conventionally used to represent that property. And if the theory is filled out in this way, it will mean that these words mean that property whenever someone in the relevant speech community uses them. This will make the theory a version of reductive naturalism with an expressivist twist. And advocates of this sort of hybrid will have to defend it by employing many of the same resources deployed by nonsubjectivist naturalism. People who like this approach often use an analogy with slurs and epithets to fill out their idea. One might think that 'bully' is normally used both to describe a person and to express a negative attitude toward the characteristics ascribed. Hybrid expressivists who like this model will say moral terms work in roughly the same way. 'Morally right,' on this model, functions to ascribe a descriptive property to an act-type and to express approval of that property. On this model, the property ascribed by 'morally right' remains constant across different occasions of use of the term, even when the term is used by different speakers.

Another option is instead to let the representational/descriptive content be determined by the relevant moral attitudes of the speaker, so that in each person's mouth it predicates the property that the particular speaker approves of in the relevant moral way. This view would generate a sort of relativism since different speakers may approve morally of different properties. And this tactic would also require telling a more detailed meta-semantic story of how it is that the terms come to represent the speaker's attitudes. One option would be to model the semantics on that of indexicals like 'I' and 'here.' Moral terms might then have a character-like rule associated with them to tell us how to determine the property predicated from facts about the context of utterance (such as that so-and-so is the speaker). The rule might tell us to use the property that the speaker in the context morally approves of.[7] The resulting view looks very much like speaker-relativism of the sort proposed by indexical relativists such as Dreier (1990). The only difference is that on this semantically hybrid theory it is also part of the *semantics* that we express approval of the property while we predicate it.

On either way of developing such hybrid views, the resulting theories don't really accept either of the two negative constitutive noncognitivist claims. Predicative moral sentences do (among other things) predicate properties. And moral attitudes are (partly) cognitive states. So one might wonder why hybrid theorists see themselves as developing noncognitivism. Not all do. But those that do will likely point to the fact that on their theory moral sentences do function to express noncognitive attitudes and that moral beliefs involve these same noncognitive attitudes. And, their defenders argue, we won't call such sentences true just when the descriptive claims are correct, for to call them true would be to agree with all of their content, even the expressive content. So while moral terms will predicate properties, their truth conditions involve more than just descriptive accuracy. Much more can be said both to develop and support the hybrid strategy, and also to criticize it. But I'll just mention one further view in the ballpark. Our examples of hybrid views so far made the expressive content part of the semantics, that is part of the conventional meaning of the target expressions. One could develop the idea differently if one treated the expressive component as explained by the pragmatics of using moral terms, as something more like implication than what one strictly and literally says. Different strategies of developing such views will have different strengths and weaknesses (Barker, 2000; Fletcher, 2015).

As you can see, the Frege-Geach problem takes a good bit of work to get around. That work will be worth it only if noncognitivism has advantages over cognitivist alternatives. So we should look at some of the reasons many metaethicists favor noncognitivism.

8.5.   Noncognitivism and the Open Question Argument

One reason to favor noncognitivism is that it provides a neat diagnosis of the plausibility of the Open Question Argument. Recall that Moore argued in the following way: For any proposed definition of the target moral property competent speakers and thinkers can ask of something that has the property so described, whether it is good. When we do that we're not simply asking all over again whether it has the property we just used to define goodness. For if that were the case the answer would be a trivial "yes." We are instead asking a different question. That shows that the proposed definition does not represent what our terms 'good' or 'goodness' represent. That is the reason why it is coherent to accept the thought that something has the naturalistic property while wondering, doubting, or denying that it has goodness. One way the conclusion—that 'good' doesn't mean what the definition says it does—could be true would be if 'good' and 'goodness' meaning in whole or in part goes beyond the meanings of the terms used in the proposed definition.

Now suppose the noncognitivist is correct. The upshot of the Open Question Argument and some of the conclusions drawn along the way will fall relatively immediately out of the view. If the function of a moral term in an indicative sentence is not to describe the world and if the semantics of such sentences are nonrepresentational, it would be a mistake to say that some representational phrase captures what the moral term or terms mean. And similarly, if moral "beliefs" should have the same contents as the sentences that express them, the content of such beliefs cannot be precisely the same as that of any thought aptly captured and expressed by a purely descriptive sentence. Furthermore, expressivist noncognitivists will have something to point to when asked what of the moral content is missing from the descriptive analysis. They can point precisely to the expressive meaning of moral terms—their aptness for use to express noncognitive attitudes as a matter of their meaning. The description in the analysis will lack that. On this picture it would be no surprise that ordinary speakers might have doubts whether the characteristics codified in a candidate descriptive analysis would be sufficient to warrant calling that action right.

There are other responses available to the Open Question Argument. Many of them could be employed by the advocates of reductionist subjectivist views. Most of those responses deny that we can easily reach conclusions about the meanings of predicates and about the nature of the properties picked out by those predicates from tests such as the Open Question Argument. In general these responses deny that speakers are in a position to rule out claims about these issues just on the basis of their linguistic knowledge. What is interesting with respect to the present noncognitivist deployment of the Open Question Argument is that it generally agrees with Moore about the main argument. The present noncognitivist appropriation of the OQA accepts the idea that competent speakers are in a position to recognize a correct analysis when they see it and to eliminate doubt about its accuracy just in virtue of their competence with the relevant terms. So these noncognitivists accept most of the presuppositions that made the OQA hard to resist for much of the twentieth century. Since these noncognitivists shared Moore's main assumptions, the ability to provide this diagnosis—that any descriptive analysis of moral terms leaves out a noncognitive component their meaning—seemed a strong reason to favor noncognitivism over subjectivism. In fact, A. J. Ayer, the leading British advocate of emotivism, simply employed the Open Question Argument to argue for his theory via an argument by elimination. Since it was not a contradiction to deny any descriptive analysis, the only remaining contenders for metaethical plausibility were emotivism and Moorean nonnaturalism (Ayer, 1946, chapter 6). Or so he argued. Present-day noncognitivists are somewhat more careful, because they recognize the possibility of other ways to explain the ability of competent speakers to doubt even a correct analysis. Yet they often still point to the plausibility of the argument as at least weak evidence that descriptive analyses leave something out, something that noncognitivist expressivists capture.

8.6. Naturalism

Another attractive component of noncognitivism is that it doesn't require us to postulate any entities or properties beyond those we are committed to as a result of trying to explain the natural world. The metaphysical commitments of noncognitivism commits it to no more and no less than the metaphysics of subjectivism. There are the ordinary natural entities in the world that perception and so on give us access to, and there are our subjective reactions to them. There seems to be no difference between descriptive subjectivism and noncognitivism on that score. The differences between the views are semantic—one makes moral judgements about the moral attitudes whereas the other says they express those attitudes without being about them. But both theories are committed to the existence of such subjective states. Not that this is a very bold commitment. Almost everyone thinks that there are subjective states roughly of the sort the theories both postulate.

We noted earlier that it is hard to say anything substantive about what makes an object or property natural. As we noted, different naturalists emphasize different criteria as demarcating the category. But if we think of naturalists as united in taking their ontological commitments from science and scientific methodology, noncognitivism fits nicely with the view. Noncognitivism needs no properties or objects beyond those science already gives us reason to accept in order to make sense either of morality or our use of moral language. Thus noncognitivism gets much of its attraction for naturalistically inclined philosophers from its ontologically conservative stance.

This is not to say that supernaturalists or even theorists who thought there were nonnatural but not supernatural properties could not accept noncognitivism. If there are properties and objects beyond those permitted by naturalism, we could express our approval and disapproval of them, at least so long as we had epistemic access to them. But in general, non-naturalists in a broad sense will not be noncognitivists. For the paradigmatic candidates for nonnatural properties seem to be normative and especially moral properties as we'll see in coming chapters.

8.7. Morals/Motives Judgement Internalism as Motivating Noncognitivism

Noncognitivism is in a position to explain the same species of internalism that motivate speaker/appraiser subjectivism. For on standard expressivist noncognitivist views the state of mind of believing that some action is right just is that of holding a certain pro-attitude toward that action. And the state of mind of thinking some action wrong just is some sort of con-attitude toward the target action. It will thus be no wonder that people who believe an action right will be motivated to do it, nor will it be any surprise when those who believe it wrong are motivated to avoid it. Judgement internalism falls out of these simple claims. If a putative belief state just is a noncognitive motivating attitude, then it can't but be necessary that such beliefs motivate a person to act just as those attitudes motivate people to act.

In fact, given the Humean philosophy of mind that most noncognitivists accept, noncognitivist expressivism will be especially well-placed to explain certain very strong morals/motives judgement internalist claims. Recall that subjectivists had to invoke theses about the transparency of mind to explain why moral judgement was necessarily or reliably correlated with motivation. The basic idea in its simplest version involved the thought that a self-aware person would not make a judgement to the effect that such-and-such was wrong unless she disapproved of such-and-such. For, given that that judgement simply self-ascribed a certain con-attitude toward such-and-such, and given her reliable access to her own attitudes, she would be unlikely to make the mistake of thinking a moral judgement true unless she had that attitude. Thus simple cognitivist subjectivist explanations of morals/motives judgement internalism explained the necessary connection by suggesting that moral judgements tracked the relevant motivating attitudes.

Someone might want to object that this kind of explanation gets things backwards. Common sense expects our motivating attitudes to track changes in moral beliefs. When you convince me that it is wrong to eat beef due to the effects on climate, we expect my motivating attitude to change to fit the belief, so that I come to desire not to eat beef. We either expect the changes to happen at the same time or the desires to change in light of the changes in moral thinking. We don't expect the desires to change and the beliefs to change only after the desiderative change has occurred. A fan of this objection might fill it out by citing the role of moral arguments in attempting to change the minds of others. Insofar as many of these arguments work by exploiting the inferential and coherence relations between these judgements and other commitments, the epistemology of moral judgements (the process of using reason and argument to come to new moral beliefs) seems to favor thinking of these processes justifying the judgements directly and not via a more indirect process of checking what one desires before reaching a moral conclusion. In other words, our deliberation does not seem from the inside to involve an *inference* from our desires to our moral views.

Noncognitivist theories, it might thus be argued, are more consistent with this view of the phenomenology of moral deliberation. If the moral judgements just are the noncognitive attitude states that such views say they are, there is no need for a further inference from those states to a moral conclusion. They *are* the moral conclusions. To believe that lying is wrong, just is to have the appropriate con-attitude toward lying, so once a line of reasoning results in our coming to have that attitude we will thereby believe that lying is wrong. The considerations and arguments that led us to that state of mind will require nothing further to have their effect on our moral views. And that is how moral deliberation seems to us when we engage in it.

So in one respect noncognitivist expressivism is ideally placed to explain appraiser oriented versions of morals/motives internalism. The connection between moral judgements and motives is as tight as a necessary connection can be—identity. So you can't fail to have the one without the other. But this can also be a liability. Philippa Foot was already resisting strong internalism during the heyday of noncognitivism in the 1950s in such a way as to put pressure on the noncognitivist view. Noncognitivism seems to entail that it is impossible to accept a moral judgement and yet to remain unmotivated (in the sense of having some actual motive) by it. So objections to judgement internalism that warrant choosing defeasible over indefeasible varieties of internalism will also be reasons also to deny noncognitivism. Recall the argument by David Brink (rehearsed in chapters 4 and 6) that thoroughgoing amoralists like Thrasymachus and Uriah Heep are possible and likely actual. If such people are possible then it must be possible for someone to think an action right without having any motivation to do it. And that seems ruled out if we identify the judgement with the motive itself. Noncognitivists will try to respond, perhaps by arguing that even these putative examples of genuine amoralism must be reinterpreted to attribute some motivation, however hidden; or by arguing that the judgements of such amoralists are not genuine moral judgements. People differ as to the persuasiveness of these responses. But it will hard for noncognitivists to find real comfort in the continuing plausibility of defeasible variants of morals/motives judgement internalism. Identity is not a defeasible relation.

A different strategy might be to somehow resist identifying the noncognitive attitudes with the moral beliefs while hanging onto the idea that moral claims express such attitudes. Perhaps some versions of prescriptivism can be thought of as doing that. You might think that imperatives normally are used only when we want their targets to comply, but that one can issue an imperative even while hoping it will be ignored. So you might think that imperatives weakly express pro- or con-attitudes, not as a matter of meaning but just insofar as our ordinary uses of them mostly result from these attitudes. This is no longer a version of expressivism in the strong sense. And perhaps it isn't even expressivist in any very interesting weaker sense if the advocates of this approach work out an account of prescriptions that doesn't explicate them via a connection with noncognitive attitudes. But dropping the most straightforward connection with motivating attitudes has another cost. The resulting theory then needs an independent account of the states of mind involved in believing some action right or wrong. Somehow these will have to be both noncognitive and not essentially motivating or their indefeasibly motivating nature will once again cause problems. It really isn't obvious how this is to be worked out.

8.8.   Agent Internalism, Quasi-realism, and Reprehensible Judgements

Noncognitivism doesn't generate obvious commitments to agent internalism of any sort. Expressivist and related views bring with them a speaker orientation. I can express my attitudes, but it isn't nearly as clear that I can express yours, at least as long as I don't share them. And that makes it hard to see where an agent oriented constraint would come from. What about attitude expression would ensure that there is congruence between the attitudes I express and the attitudes of an agent whose actions are the subject? It seems I am free to disapprove of those who don't share my attitudes and also to express that disapproval. What could keep me from doing that? On a broadly Humean conception of the mind, desires and noncognitive states generally are not subject to rational criticism except insofar as they make the agent who has them incoherent. Noncognitivists who generally accept this kind of view don't think the world itself demands noncognitive attitudes of us because these attitudes don't aim to represent the world. The fact that the agent about whom I am thinking has or lacks certain attitudes does not constrain me to fit my moral attitudes to the perspective of that agent.

This won't be a problem if agent internalism has nothing going for it. No theory needs to explain something that's not true. And noncognitivists will argue that this very feature allows them to avoid endorsing reprehensible moral views where descriptivist subjectivism cannot. Recall the problem simple subjectivism had about endorsing reprehensible moral views. It arose because moral judgements were about some person or other's motivational attitudes, and these judgements so interpreted will be true whenever the relevant person has the attitudes attributed. Agent subjectivism postulates that the subject attitudes are the agent's, while appraiser subjectivism holds that the relevant attitudes are those of the person making the judgement.

Having said that, the theory is committed to finding a moral judgement true whenever these attitudes bear the right relationship to the target of assessment. For example, agent subjectivism rules a moral judgement to the effect that some action is right to be true just in case the agent has the right positive attitudes bearing on that action. Similarly, appraiser subjectivism must count the judgements of an appraiser true when they track her motivating attitudes in a similar way. The problem for these sorts of subjectivism arose when we considered judgements made about reprehensible agents or made by evil appraisers. Their attitudes of approval might reliably track actions of a very rotten sort. When the relevant agents are like that agent subjectivism must call these actions right. Appraiser subjectivism doesn't have exactly the same problem with rotten appraisers—we won't have to say what they say when they call some heinous action right. For our judgements will be made relative to our motivating attitudes, and given that we don't approve of the heinous we would be speaking falsely if we called such actions right. Still, for all that, it would seem we'd have to admit that what they say when they call the actions right—that those actions fit with their attitudes of approval or whatever—is true. That's not a whole lot better.

Since noncognitivism is more like appraiser subjectivism than agent subjectivism insofar as the attitudes that make moral utterances appropriate belong to the person making the utterance, it seems to inherit the advantages of appraiser subjectivism when dealing with this issue. There is no pressure to invoke the attitudes of agents in assessing the appropriateness of a given moral judgement or utterance. But many noncognitivists think that they are better placed to deal with the problem than even appraiser subjectivism. The general idea is this: Moral judgements are *not about* anybody's attitudes, even the attitudes of those whose judgements they express. Since they're not about such attitudes, those attitudes aren't truth-makers for moral judgements. Since the attitudes aren't truth-makers we can resist dignifying the judgements of the reprehensible as true even when they track the attitudes of the reprehensible people who make them. The issue is a bit delicate. In the next section, I'll rehearse a line of argument in favor of the conclusion and note a worry about it.

8.8.1.   Quasi-realism, Truth-Deflationism, and Endorsement

Noncognitivists, at least present day noncognitivists who want their theory to make sense of most moral discourse, will want to offer an analysis of talk using the word 'true' that makes sense of our counting moral utterances true or false. To be sure, early generation noncognitivists like Ayer made their point about the difference between moral talk and the rest of our discourse by denying that moral judgements could be true or false. But Ayer and many of his fellow travelers were less concerned with making sense of moral discourse than they were with removing a counter-example to the verificationist theory of meaning. That theory held that meaningful judgements must be subject to empirical test, so that some bit of evidence or other would in principle be able to decide the truth of any meaningful claim. But moral judgements seem to be meaningful and yet, if Moore was right, no judgement about nonmoral matters, including empirical evidence, could conclusively refute or confirm such judgements because no such judgements would entail a moral conclusion. So emotivism for Ayer was mostly a way of showing how moral judgements could seem to be meaningful—by having a different kind of meaning than that covered by the verification test—without being a counter-example to that test.

Stevenson (1944) and Hare (1952) had no such motivations. They thought that an adequate account of morality must explain its practical upshot and they thought their own noncognitivist theories did that better than competitors. And that orientation led to their trying much harder to accommodate features of moral practice that at first don't seem consistent with denying that moral judgements can be correct or true. More recently, Simon Blackburn (1984) has done even more to tame the realist seeming features of moral discourse, including our use of terms such as 'true' and 'false.' Blackburn has even coined a name for this explanatory project, "*quasi-realism.*" The idea is that a resourceful noncognitivist can make sense of the realist seeming features of moral discourse and practice all while hewing to the denial of cognitivism. Noncognitivists with quasi-realist sympathies notice right away that we use 'true' and 'false' just as easily with moral discourse as other areas of dispute. When I disagree with you about various policies, it is very natural to say that it isn't true that they are the right ones to adopt.

A serious quasi-realist will try to give such talk a noncognitivist underpinning. And here they can get some help from so-called *minimalist* or *deflationist* theories of truth. Minimalism about truth is usually put forth as a view about truth in general, not just in moral discourse. It is usually contrasted with robust or inflationist conceptions of truth. Robust theories of truth tell us what truth is by giving a relatively *substantial* account of the nature of truth. For example, correspondence theories of truth normally count as robust because they treat truth as a property of sentences or propositions, one that sentences/propositions have when they correspond to how things are. That is a substantial claim insofar as it presupposes both that sentences apt for truth must be representational and that all true sentences have something in common—the property of representing things as they are. The exact location of the line between robust and minimal is a little murky. Not everyone thinks that all forms of correspondence are nonminimal. And not all minimalists agree on how minimal an account of truth should be. What matters to us is that minimalists believe that there is some line to be drawn and that they can provide an adequate account of truth without crossing onto the robust side of that line.

One such account develops the idea that calling a claim true is a way of endorsing it. That endorsement is the same as the endorsement one gives a claim when one asserts it. If that's right, then I might be able to teach you what 'true' means in the following way. Suppose you know the meanings of most simple English predicative sentences such as 'Roses are red' and 'Sugar is sweet.' I now tell you that 'Roses are red is true' means just what 'Roses are red' means. And 'Sugar is sweet is true' means just what 'Sugar is sweet' means. And so on for all the indicative sentences of English. Furthermore, speech acts asserting claims of the form 'Such-and-such is true' where 'Such-and-such' is replaced by an indicative sentence perform just the same speech act as the one that would be performed by asserting just the embedded indicative sentence. We can capture this idea by saying that utterances of 'is true' sentences of that sort endorse just what the freestanding occurrences of the embedded sentence would endorse. Then I tell you that 'is true' lets us endorse sentences we aren't in a position to list, in just the way that the aforementioned uses of 'is true' endorsed the claims they were linked to. I can say, "Whatever Sally says is true" and thereby endorse and agree with what Sally says, even if I can't recall all she said. This story is minimal because 'is true' doesn't add anything to the content of the claims it is predicated of. But it allows us to agree with those claims, and to do it even when we can't ourselves rehearse them one by one.

Noncognitivists can employ this kind of minimal theory of truth to explicate what people do when they call a moral judgement true. Nothing we said in the course of telling the minimal story about truth in the previous paragraph turned on claims about the meanings of the embedded sentences. The story simply said that whatever that meaning is, we get the same meaning when we couple it with 'is true.' Similarly, nothing we said about the speech acts involved really turned on the nature of those speech acts. We just said that the speech act of assertion that employs a sentence coupled with 'is true' is the same speech act as would normally be performed if we asserted the embedded sentence without the 'is true' clause. Thus as long as noncognitivists have some way of accounting for moral assertions, they can employ this minimalist story to explicate the meaning of 'is true' constructions embedding moral sentences. Thus, for example, 'It's true that donating to Oxfam is right' will say the same thing as 'Donating to Oxfam is right.' It will normally be appropriate to say it whenever the latter is appropriate. If I want to say just what Jill said about some moral issue, I can use 'is true' to avoid repeating all of what she said and say, "Everything Jill said is true." In doing so I endorse just what she endorsed in making her various claims, and go very little if at all beyond what she said. Thus coupling minimalism with noncognitivism entails that moral 'is true' constructions express the same attitudes that the sentences they embed would express.

If this is the right account of truth, a person should not call some claim true unless she endorses it. She should refuse to call any judgement with which she disagrees true. And this should apply just as much to moral claims as nonmoral claims. So when a noncognitivist runs into another person whose attitudes she finds reprehensible and who expresses those reprehensible attitudes by calling heinous actions right and appropriate actions wrong, she should label those judgements as true only if she would make them herself. For her judgement that they are true would express just what the judgement "those actions are right" would express in her mouth—approval of those heinous actions. We're talking about heinous actions here and saying that already commits us to not approving of them. So a morally upright non-cognitivist should deny that these claims are true. To put it a different way, the minimal account says that 'is true' is a device for agreeing with another person and endorsing what they say. But our noncognitivist doesn't agree with the judgements of the reprobate moral assessor. She disagrees. So she should not call those judgements true and she is within her rights to call them false, just as she would be in her rights to express the same thought without the 'is true' locution.

In raising the problem for subjectivism of reprehensible judgements I'm not saying that the noncognitivist can only avoid it if she also takes on board truth minimalism. Since noncognitivism isn't ordinary subjectivism of the sort that assimilates moral judgements to attitude reports they've already avoided the problem. A moral judgement isn't acceptable (by our lights) just in virtue of being sincere. A noncognitivist can legitimately disagree with the sincere moral judgements of others. But I am saying that truth minimalism allows the noncognitivist a further way of expressing her disagreement with those judgements. She can say that they are not true, but false instead. That's a nice thing to be able to do.

It could turn out that truth is more robust than the minimalist account allows, and that might undermine the preceding line of argument by depriving noncognitivists of minimalist resources. But you can see how the minimalist response licenses a refusal to count the conflicting judgements of other agents as true. The same minimalist idea can also be employed by noncognitivists who insist that their view does not entail relativism (Horgan and Timmons, 2006). Noncognitivists who adopt minimalism will want to avoid calling each of two conflicting moral views true, for it would be incoherent to do so. If two moral verdicts conflict, they won't stop conflicting just in virtue of our restating the view using 'is true.' The more complex constructions will be just as much in conflict as the first order conflicting judgements they embed. If the minimalists are right, noncognitivists can coherently endorse at most one of the conflicting views.

Perhaps then, noncognitivists have the advantage over their cognitivist subjectivist cousins. Everyone agrees that it is a mark against a theory if its commitments force it to count reprehensible moral judgements as true. If truth minimalism enables noncognitivism to avoid endorsing that verdict, so much the better for the combined view. It is not as obvious that it is important to rule out all relativism. It may be possible to be a relativist and yet think that certain kinds of moral verdict are ruled out relative to every standpoint. And if that is so, some people may find the idea of truth relative to a perspective an attractive option. Still, many people deplore relativism, and for them it may be a bonus if truth minimalism rules it out in the course of eluding the problem posed for subjectivists by the judgements of those with reprehensible views.

But there remains some unease about the underlying challenge to subjectivism that is posed by the consistent judgements of rotten people. There seems to be so much in common between cognitivist subjectivism and noncognitivist subjectivism, that problems for the former likely have analogs that are problems for the latter. Both views seem to hold that the assessment of ends can only be done relative to an optional set of commitments. If we don't share in the commitments of the depraved we can avoid endorsing their actions and goals. Yet both views seem unable to show that the depraved have made a mistake in choosing their ends in some more objective sense.

8.9. Responding to the Modal Objection to Subjectivism

Chapter 6 canvassed a range of objections to simple subjectivism, objections that descendants of that theory hope to avoid. We've just revisited how the noncognitivist avoids endorsing reprehensible views where a simple subjectivist has difficulty. In this section I'll explain how the noncognitivist can avoid the modal objection to simple subjectivism. Recall that simple subjectivism seemed to make moral judgements contingent upon facts that seem irrelevant. For instance, we think that the moral status of many actions depend on facts about the actions in question and their effects and not on facts about what we approve of. Thus it is very natural to claim that:

TORTURE: Torture would still be wrong even if no one approved of it and even if everyone did not disapprove of it.

Simple appraiser subjectivist theories have trouble making that claim come out true. Such theories identify the property of being wrong with the property of being disapproved of by some person or persons. Given that identification, an action that is not so disapproved of won't be wrong. So were no one to disapprove of torture, it would not be wrong. That's just what _TORTURE_ denies.

Noncognitivists have a way out of the problem. Unlike subjectivists, they don't identify wrongness with being disapproved of by anyone, even in ideal conditions. Thus the absence of such disapproval won't entail that an action is not wrong. What gets identified with the disapproval or a similar noncognitive attitude is _judging_ something wrong. To call an action wrong is to express one's disapproval of it, and to judge it wrong is to disapprove of it. But I can disapprove of what would happen even in a circumstance where I don't disapprove. For instance, I may think it possible that I'll change my mind about certain moral matters as I get older, not for good reason. Perhaps I'll stop disapproving of warrantless wiretaps out of apathy occasioned by a feeling of impotence to change the relevant policies. Perhaps I'll go so far as to approve of such wiretaps out of unwarranted political loyalty to public figures I admire and who themselves approve of such practices. Still, for all that, I can here and now think the resulting attitudes mistaken. And I can express my current disapproval of warrantless wiretaps even when I know I'll change my mind later on. I can do that by saying, "Warrantless wiretaps are wrong!" And I can go on to indicate that my future attitudes are irrelevant to the matter, saying, "And they will be wrong in the future, even if I change my mind about the matter!" TORTURE can be read as expressing a similar thought about the attitudes of everyone. It both expresses my thought that torture is wrong (that is my negative attitude toward it) and makes clear that even undisapproved of torture is the object of my negative attitude.

8.10. Moral Epistemology

8.10.1. Avoiding the Explanatory Burden

Chapter 3 introduced the idea that every metaethical theory to some extent or other tries to make sense of moral epistemology. It also suggested that the seeming under-determination of moral theory by evidence can raise worries about the adequacy of some proposals regarding the subject matter. The earliest noncognitivists saw it as a virtue of their view that it did not have to explain how we got access to a distinctive moral subject matter that morality told us about. For in some sense these theorists denied that there was any distinctive subject matter for moral talk to represent and for moral claims to be true of. This is somewhat startling for those most familiar with more recent, quasi-realist, varieties of noncognitivism. But early proponents saw it as a virtue of their view that it in effect eliminated the need for much moral epistemology. In this spirit we have Carnap saying:

> But actually a value statement is nothing else than a command in a misleading grammatical form. It may have effects upon the actions of men, and these effects may either be in accordance with our wishes or not; but it is neither true nor false. It does not assert anything and can neither be proved nor disproved. (Carnap, 1935/1962, pp. 24–25)

Ayer was only somewhat more accommodating:

> . . . we hold that one really never does dispute about questions of value.
>   This may seem at first sight, to be a very paradoxical assertion. For we certainly do engage in disputes which are ordinarily regarded as disputes about questions of value. But in all such cases, we find, if we consider the matter closely, that the dispute is not really about a question of value, but about a question of fact. When someone disagrees with us about the moral value of a certain action or type of action, we do admittedly resort to argument in order to win him over to our way

of thinking. But we do not attempt to show by our arguments that he has the "wrong" ethical feeling towards a situation whose nature he has correctly apprehended. What we attempt to show is that he is mistaken about the facts of the case. . . . But if our opponent happens to have undergone a different process of moral "conditioning" than ourselves, so that, even when he acknowledges all the facts, he still disagrees with us about the moral value of the actions under discussion, then we abandon the attempt to convince him by argument. (Ayer, 1946, pp. 110–111)

Clearly both Carnap and Ayer's views on moral epistemology denied that there was any such thing. There might be perfectly ordinary epistemology for everyday moral facts that would be made morally relevant by the evaluative outlook of someone with a moral view. But there was, they supposed, nothing further to learn because that outlook could not be justified or undermined by evidence or argument.

As a description of actual moral arguments, Ayer's claims seem to miss the mark by a good bit. Disagreements between those who campaign against animal cruelty and their opponents, between consequentialists and non-consequentialists, and between those who favor legal abortion and those who don't, clearly involve some controversial and yet evaluative element that both sides of these disputes recognize and try to settle with evidence and argument. So probably the best interpretation of Ayer's idea is not as claiming that this is how people actually argue, but as suggesting that they should dispute in this more limited way once they become convinced of the truth of the emotivist view. But even interpreted in that way, the claim departs from the contemporary expressivist approach, which wants to preserve as many of the objectivist seeming features of moral discourse as it can. Among those features is the fact that in our everyday lives we sometimes make epistemic judgements about morality and people's views on morality. We say that Heather has reliably good moral judgement, that Ahmad knows what he should do, and that our moral thinking is better when we are calm. We profess uncertainty about the right thing to do, and worry that we may be wrong. We say that Aaron's opinions on sexual morality are better justified than Barry's. And we engage in many of the practices highlighted by Firth in arguing for the ideal observer theory, putatively in order to get at the truth about moral matters.

8.10.2.   Quasi-Realist Accommodation

Contemporary quasi-realist noncognitivists want to take these phenomena seriously. And if they're successful they will argue that the phenomena that the early noncognitivists tried to sweep under the rug actually support taking quasi-realist versions seriously. We won't be able to delve too deeply into very much of this, but we should look at some examples.

The reliability of a person's judgement on the most straightforward interpretation involves the likelihood of their getting at the truth. We've already noted noncognitivist appropriations of minimalism to underwrite truth ascriptions consistent with noncognitivism. Such judgements in effect just express agreement with the first order judgements they target and hence represent the very same thing as these judgements. If noncognitivists have done an adequate job explicating the first order judgements, the second order judgement that these first order judgements are true will be just as acceptable. Or so the minimalist story goes. It is a bit tricky to see exactly how to couple that analysis with the idea that judgements about the reliability of a person's judgement are about the likelihood that that person's judgement will be true. It can't be a judgement that their judgements track one's own, since one can think Heather has good judgement even where one hasn't yet got an opinion of one's own. Nor can one's judgement that Heather is reliable be the judgement that one would agree if one thought about it, since one can think that she is more likely to get moral matters right than one will oneself even after much thought. Perhaps the noncognitivist can say that one is prospectively endorsing her advice and endorsing giving it great weight in deliberation. But endorsement is a speech act and we also want an account of the mental state that it expresses. We should be told what it is to believe that Heather's judgements about morality are reliable. Perhaps the best thing to say is that the relevant state of mind is a kind of trust directed toward Heather's advice, both past and future. That's the kind of affective state of mind that noncognitivists cite when elucidating moral attitudes, and so the account seems fully compatible with the overall view.

What of justification and knowledge? Judgements about each of these seem to involve evaluating more than just the truth and reliability of the judgements that are justified and/or known. They seem to involve also a normative claim about whether the subject is responding appropriately to his or her evidence. How can a noncognitivist explain what it is to accept claims of that sort?

These attitudes are perhaps best pursued by thinking first of our first-personal judgements about ourselves. An agent may have pro- and con-attitudes about her own attitudes as well as about the actions of herself and other agents. She might approve of her own attitudes of approval and disapproval when they meet certain standards she accepts for coming to have such attitudes. She may have noticed that putatively moral attitudes formed under certain conditions were not stable when formed in the heat of passion, or under the influence of partiality, or without enough information or imagination. She might find these difficult to use as a basis for coordinated action over time as a result of their evanescent nature. And so she might come to approve of forming attitudes in conditions where they would be more likely to persist and underwrite coherent plans for action. She might then endorse making moral judgements in moments of cool reflection, rather than when influenced by passion or interest. She might endorse making such judgements in conditions of full imaginative acquaintance with all of the alternatives and after due reflection on the interests of all affected. Perhaps she might come to use words like 'justified' and 'warranted' to express her approval of judgements that meet her standards. And she might use these words to commend certain standards as correct when she meets and disagrees with another person who subscribes to different standards. There is much more to say about whether this or anything similar is an adequate analysis of these terms and of how and why we use them. But this brief discussion exemplifies the kind of thing a systematic noncognitivist is going to try to come up with to explain our epistemic judgements where morals are involved.

8.10.3.   A Small but Important Detour: Noncognitivist Expansion Beyond Morality

I should note that these maneuvers highlight the tendency of noncognitivism about moral judgements to spread to other normative judgements, such as judgements about justification and warrant. And these judgements seem to apply without homonymy to our nonmoral beliefs and credences as much as they do to our moral judgements. Once a theorist finds noncognitivism attractive for the moral domain, there is pressure to offer a similar analysis for all normative claims.

This makes it worth asking whether the main philosophical motivations for noncognitivism about the moral domain extend to these other normative domains. Is there something analogous to an internalist constraint for justification and warrant? Can an Open Question Argument be formulated using these as our target terms? It seems that the answer is a qualified yes to the first and a less qualified yes to the second. Let's consider the first question first. People do seem motivated by a judgement that a judgement of their own is unjustified or unwarranted either to suspend the target judgement, or to find some further grounds to bolster it. But it is hard to say if what we mean by "motivate" in this case is the same as what we mean when we talk of the motive for an action. That's the qualification. As for the second question, it would be just as hard to produce an indubitable analysis of 'justification' or 'warrant' or 'knowledge' as it is to produce an indubitable analysis of 'right' or 'good.' More than a few decades of the literature in epistemology attests to that. So if the Open Question Argument is a good reason to accept noncognitivism about ethics it is also a good reason to accept parallel views about fundamental epistemic concepts.

It should thus not be any great surprise to find that the most systematic attempt to develop the noncognitivist program, Alan Gibbard's norm- and plan-expressivist projects[8] start by first analyzing a very general normative notion of rationality (or the "thing to do") in noncognitive terms and then use it to analyze more specific kinds of normative claims such as moral rightness (Gibbard, 1992, 2003). Gibbard's theory is too complicated to explain in any detail here, so I will just note one of its general features that ties back into some points earlier on in this chapter. By working with one basic normative notion, that of rationality or the thing to do, he simplifies the project of constructing a compositional and systematic account of moral and normative language in general. For many other normative domains reveal parallel constructions to those with which we make claims about morality. Just as some action can be morally right, permitted, obligatory, and forbidden, a judgement might be rationally right, permitted, obligatory, and forbidden. Furthermore, most people think that as a matter of the meanings of these terms, the morally required excludes the morally forbidden and so too with the rationally required and rationally forbidden. You would thus expect the explanations to be parallel, and for any theory of meaning that explained the one phenomenon for it also to be part of the explanation of the other. Gibbard's account, if it is otherwise successful, would yield that result because of the way normative terms are all analyzed in terms of rationality as the basic notion, one that itself gets a noncognitivist analysis.

There's one more point to get out of all this. The general strategy of offering an account of one basic normative concept and then defining the rest in terms of that concept is not just for noncognitivists. Subjectivists, non-naturalists, reductive naturalists, and various others can deploy the same strategy: Offer an analysis of some core concept that would make it adequate to explain some of the puzzling features of morality, define morality in terms of that core concept, and thereby explain those puzzling features. If those features are also shared by other normative domains (as was suggested earlier), use the same strategy to account for those features in those domains. The greater explanatory success and power of the generalized strategy will be a selling point for any meta-normative theory that pulls something like this off.

8.10.4. Back to the Main Thread: Moral Epistemic Phenomenology

Noncognitivists who like the story in section 8.10.2 about what it is to think a moral judgement justified and about why and how we might come to care about that kind of thing might even go on the offensive against response-dispositional views such as ideal observer theories. Recall that Firth designed his ideal observer theory to explain many of the features of actual moral epistemology. These features included the fact that we try to get full relevant information before reaching a moral verdict, that we think imaginative acquaintance and engagement with the perspectives of those deciding and those affected is epistemically important, that we try to isolate ourselves from the wrong sorts of interest in the outcomes of the actions we evaluate, and so on. These are the very same features quasi-realists want to explain using ideas like those outlined in section 8.10.2. And noncognitivists can argue that they do these features more justice than ideal observer theorists do; ideal observer theorists must treat our actual responses under the relevantly ideal conditions as providing only evidence for the judgements in which they issue whereas noncognitivists can say something more direct. Noncognitivists can say that these judgements in those circumstances are themselves more likely to be correct because they are themselves made in those circumstances.

The point here is related to the now familiar (from section 8.2) idea that the belief that grass is green stands to 'grass is green' as the judgement that lying is wrong stands to 'lying is wrong.' Neither of those sentences (nor the states they express) is *about* the attitudes that are expressed by the relevant judgements, yet those judgements are expressed by those sentences. Noncognitivists think that descriptive subjectivists make the mistake of construing ethics as reporting moral attitudes rather than issuing from such attitudes. And they can argue that this is also reflected in the moral epistemology of ideal observer theories. Such theories make the subject matter the ideal judgements of agents, so that our reactions in ideal conditions are just evidence for the truth of the judgements, evidence from which a further inference is needed to get to the content of a genuine moral judgement. We are to reason as follows:

1. I am in nearly ideal conditions and I disapprove of lying to Keith.
2. If a normal person in nearly ideal conditions disapproves of an act-type it is likely that normal ideal observers would approve of the act-type as well.
3. Therefore, normal ideal observers would (probably) approve of lying to Keith.
4. What it would be for lying to Keith to be wrong is for such observers to disapprove of it, so lying to Keith is probably wrong.

This, it will seem to noncognitivists (and many cognitivists), adds an extra and superfluous step to our reasoning about what's morally right or wrong or whatever. We're not trying to make our moral judgements in ideal conditions because they best simulate the reactions whose presence in those conditions are the truth-makers for the judgement. We're trying to make judgements in nearly ideal epistemic conditions because we think those judgements themselves will be most justifiable and reliable if we make them in those conditions. (This point relates to one of the questions at the end of chapter 7.)

8.11. A Brief Look Back

As we've seen, noncognitivism starts by denying two claims constitutive of minimal realism: (1) That moral thought represents the world in the manner that cognitive states like belief represent the world. And (2) that indicative moral sentences represent purported facts about the way the world is—the very same facts as captured in the thoughts these sentences normally express.

It thus immediately takes on the dual burdens of explaining what moral thought does do, and of explaining what moral sentences do mean. Different varieties of noncognitivism give somewhat different answers to these questions, but the main extant versions explain the meanings of the words and the function of the thoughts in terms of some connection with action-guiding attitudes of a noncognitive sort. Prescriptivism begins with the sentences and then moves on to say something about the states of mind. It analyzes the meanings of freestanding moral predicative sentences as imperatival in mood, directing those in its scope to act in some way or other. The connection with action-guiding attitudes, according to prescriptivism, is just that accepting an imperative commits one to act as it directs. Emotivists and expressivists work from the other direction and make the connection more directly. Moral thoughts are themselves a species of practical motivating attitude. The meanings of freestanding moral predications are then explicated as expressive devices with which speakers express these action-guiding attitudes.

Quasi-realist noncognitivists, that is those who wish to give a largely vindicating account of moral practice on this basis, must then work to extend the theory to more complex constructions embedding such simple moral sentences, and also to the states of mind accepted by those who "believe" these more complex sentences. Because of compositionality constraints on the meanings of complex sentences this can be a lot of work. But it also gives noncognitivists resources to answer many of the standard objections to simple and even complex subjectivism. If all goes according to plan, noncognitivists hope to be able to explain the modal stability of moral claims, explicate the point of calling some moral claims true, improve upon subjectivist accounts of moral epistemology, and resist relativism. In each of these ways they hope to improve on their subjectivists forebears.

Noncognitivists also think their innovations give them an advantage in addressing issues that all metaethical positions must confront. They think their nondescriptivism frees them from onerous ontological commitments. They can accept pleonastic characterizations of what ethics is about, which use the very predicates up for analysis to say what the subject is. These will be seen as harmless and even useful artifacts of the linguistic forms that we use to express the moral attitudes this language is fit to express. But noncognitivists will resist ontologically committing claims made from a more disengaged higher-order perspective. Thus they will attempt to avoid what they see as a drawback for more realist approaches to metaethics, that of finding some property or properties that can serve as the referent or designee of moral predicates. They can avoid commitment to metaphysically suspect nonnatural properties without falling into reductionism about moral properties. This even allows them to endorse the Open Question Argument, since they won't deny its anti-reductionist upshot.

Most noncognitivists also believe they have the advantage over rival views in providing a plausible moral psychology that explains morals/motives judgement internalism. They can adhere to the Humean party line that belief alone is incapable of motivating action, while continuing to claim that moral judgements do motivate. For, despite the cognitive veneer provided by the predicative language in which they find expression, these judgements are really just conative attitudes in a misleading guise.

Much of the innovation in noncognitivist theorizing over the past 30 years has come from two interrelated projects, that of extending the quasi-realist program to yet further objectivist seeming features of moral discourse and practice, and in developing a compositional semantics for moral language adequate to the constraints of the Frege-Geach problem. Because the issues surrounding the latter are rather technical, I have stuck with a pretty schematic explication of the latter project. Nothing I've said is any reason to think that an adequate overall account is not to be had. But it is probably fair to say that a good deal of work must be done to produce it. Advocates of competing metaethical research programs hope to provide alternative proposals that obviate the need for making that effort.

Questions

Comprehension

C1. What is the difference between prescriptivism and emotivism?
C2. What is the difference between expressing a belief without reporting it and reporting a belief?
C3. In what sense does the expressivist think that moral beliefs are not really beliefs?

Extension

E1. In 8.4.2 I suggest that I can only express my own attitudes. Can we learn something about this by looking at expressives like "jerk" when used in a belief report as in, "Fred believes that that jerk Barney left the keys in the car"?
E2. What would a minimalist treatment of 'false' look like within an expressivist framework?

Reading

Read along with: A. J. Ayer (1946, chapter 6), R. M. Hare (1952, chapters 1 and 10).

Further reading: Blackburn (1984, chapter 6) is a good statement of his quasi-realism. From there Mark Schroeder (2010) is a fabulous overview of all issues surrounding noncognitivism, including the Frege-Geach problem. Geach (1965) is his own most complete statement of the objection, though it moves quickly. Schroeder's (2008a) is a specially good pithy statement of the problem, and my (1996a) is a fairly high-level but still understandable paper in the genre. Dreier (1996) is subtle, important, and fun. Hybrid-expressivist theories are introduced in Barker (2000), Jackson (1999), Ridge (2006), Boisvert (2008), and Hay (2013). Schroeder (2009) gives a nice overview of issues for these views. Bar-On and Sias (2013) surveys the varieties of expressivism. Gibbard (1992) is a difficult but wonderful book; Gibbard (2003) develops the view; and Schroeder (2008b) is an ambitious attempt to extend the basic expressivist project in order to uncover its flaws.

Notes

1   Because I will attend a good bit to the nature of the states of mind involved in accepting a moral judgement, and because contemporary expressivists have paid more attention to that than Hare, I will be spending more time talking about expressivism than about prescriptivism. Some readers, aware of Hare's pioneering status in the history of noncognitivism, may find this emphasis disconcerting.

2   In the discussion that follows I often vary the particular noncognitive attitudes that I use in my illustrative examples, talking about approval, disapproval, liking, disliking, preferring, and so on. No single theorist would be likely to use all of these attitudes, and using too many would make some tasks harder. I'm switching between attitudes to illustrate the range of attitudes an expressivist might choose to work with, and also because certain ways of filling out noncognitivism are most easily explicated if I use the particular attitude I pick.

3   Moods include the indicative mood, the subjunctive mood, the interrogative mood, the imperative mood, and so on. Some languages contain moods not available in other languages.

4   Hare (1952, p. 18). This might be a little confusing given that I have presented noncognitivism as first and foremost a nonrepresentational view and yet here I say it would be OK to think of neustics as propositional and as contents. That's why I have tried to be careful to say "not representational in the way that ordinary indicative discourse is representational," wherever I could. If prescriptions have propositional contents they aren't representing how things are with them, whereas ordinary indicative sentences represent the world to be accurately represented by their propositional content.

5   Y'all here is supposed to be a term of universal prescription addressed to everyone including the speaker and also addressed to agents in all similar situations even across all of time.

6   The model here is akin to the models proposed in Boisvert (2008) and Hay (2013) and in a more extended way with the model of Barker (2000). Ridge (2006) has a more complicated hybrid account. There are also models that let the expressive meaning be conveyed pragmatically, explored in Fletcher (2015).

7   Ridge (2006, 2007) and subsequent papers develop this idea in a more sophisticated way.

8   Roughly Gibbard's current idea is that normative judgements express the acceptance of a contingency plan for various circumstances. His similar older view was that they expressed acceptance of norms or rules for conduct. The details don't matter for the point in this text.

9 Fictionalism

If you were convinced that error theory was correct—that current ethical discourse is too infected with error to be successfully making true claims about reality—you would be faced with a practical issue: what to do from now on where ethics is concerned. Our everyday lives are filled with situations in which we are asked to render judgements about the rightness of some way of acting, about the moral status of some policy, or about the morally appropriate response to various difficult decisions. Sometimes it is our situation that poses such questions. We see someone being humiliated and have to decide whether we should speak up. At other times it is other people, our friends, employers, coworkers, or strangers in a cab who pose the questions. In the first sort of case we may be able to act without rendering a verdict about how we should act. In the latter there is at least some social pressure to say something. We could proclaim our current skepticism about all moral notions and make clear we think the question ill-formed, or that the only answer is that nothing is right or just or morally required. Or we could go on as though morality was all in order and give an answer as though we have no doubts. That is, we could pretend to accept morality and continue to make moral evaluations, all while not really believing what we say and seem to affirm. Perhaps we could pretend even to ourselves, acting and deliberating as if moral judgements were sometimes true, despite our reservations. It might be easier than the alternatives.

Many error theorists think this is the way to go. They think there are advantages to continuing on as if nothing was wrong, withholding one's actual assent from what one appears to endorse but acting as if ordinary moral claims were true. Some of these theorists even write books propounding the error theory. Still they recommend that we act as though morality is in fine shape once we close the book or exit the philosophical seminar. Those who follow this advice are *reforming* or *revolutionary fictionalists*. They are making a proposal. They suggest we speak of morality in the way that many parents speak of Santa Claus or the Easter Bunny around their young children. Those parents pretend to believe in these fictional creatures—at least while the kids are around. They act like they believe but they don't. And revolutionary fictionalists propose we do the same with ethics.

Revolutionary moral fictionalists think the revolution is still in the future. They think of themselves as the vanguard of a movement, or as somewhat lonely figures who have grasped a little-recognized truth about the nature of morality. Over time that truth may be recognized. But at present, revolutionary moral fictionalists take themselves to be unusual and uncommon. For the moment their proposal is aimed at those in the know. Should error theory come to be more widely accepted, their proposal would extend to the wider audience of converts to error theory. Error theorists should speak and act as though they believe in the myth of morality.

Hermeneutic moral fictionalists, by contrast, think that the revolution has already happened. They think that people already engage in pretense where morality is concerned. They see no need for revolution because they think everybody already treats morality as a useful fiction. They think current moral thought and talk is all in order because people need not and do not actually believe what they say. Instead of using moral language to express our sincere beliefs, we are acting out more complex attitudes. We're using the language fictively, as part of a pretense. Those who realize that understand the nature of moral judgement and moral practice as it already exists. So, hermeneutic fictionalists disagree with error theorists and revolutionary fictionalists about the status of current moral practice. Everything is OK because we're not committed to the errors that error theorists take morality to involve.

Still, we can see revolutionary fictionalists as proposing that we make hermeneutic fictionalism true going forward. Once we realize the truth of error theory they think we should think and act as the hermeneutic fictionalists think we already do. Thus it makes sense to begin our examination of hermeneutic fictionalism.

9.1. Hermeneutic Fictionalism and Error Theory

Hermeneutic fictionalism and error theory have much in common. The theories agree that moral terms are semantically representational. Moral terms represent properties as a matter of their meaning and indicative moral sentences semantically represent propositions apt for truth or falsity. Fictionalism and error theory also agree that the moral propositions semantically represented by these sentences are strictly and literally false. The reasons why they think this can vary from theorist to theorist; our discussion of error theory in chapter 5 should have introduced you to some of the range. Any reason an error theorist has for her skeptical conclusions can be adapted to support fictionalism, since fictionalism agrees with error theory about the falsity of most moral assertions.

Though hermeneutic fictionalists and error theorists agree that moral semantics is representational, they disagree with one another about how people *use* representational moral language. Error theorists think we use the language in a realist fashion, to describe reality and to express beliefs about the world, beliefs that will be true if the sentences that express them are true and false if those sentences are false. And that means they think that moral sentences express false beliefs as we actually use them. Fictionalists about our discourse disagree with this way of interpreting our use of moral language. They think we use it to express something other than belief in the contents of the moral sentences we employ in our discourse. The most prominent version of this idea suggests that we employ our semantically representational language to express conative states akin to those postulated by standard noncognitivists. We express these attitudes but not by uttering sentences that represent them (Kalderon, 2005).

To make this idea fly, hermeneutic fictionalists have to sharply distinguish semantics and pragmatics. Roughly, semantics concerns what gets built into the meaning of a term by the conventions that govern its competent use. These conventions associate meanings with words or phrases. Whole sentences then get their meanings in a compositional manner from the meanings of the terms they contain. Semantic meaning is thus a property of word, phrase, and sentence *types*. Pragmatics, by contrast, is about what a speaker is doing with a bit of language when she uses it on a particular occasion or set of occasions. It is thus highly concerned with the *speech acts* we perform using words and sentences. Pragmatics tells us what a speaker communicates when using a token sentence in a particular context, and about how the sentence serves to communicate what it does. In general, an indicative sentence is used to communicate acceptance by the speaker of its semantic content; but it need not always be used in that way. For example, when I'm sarcastic I might communicate that I accept the exact opposite of what my sentence means, as when I say "That was smart!" in response to a mistake by another. What I communicate is that the action *was not smart*. The fictionalist thesis is that in ordinary contexts indicative moral sentences are not being used to convey belief in the contents they conventionally mean (that is what they semantically express). Something else is going on instead, and the fictionalist will have to explain what that is. To do this they will have to tell us about the point of using these sentences fictively.

9.2. Why Accept Hermeneutic Fictionalism?

9.2.1. Fictionalists Hope to Elude Much of the Semantic Burden of Noncognitivism

In chapter 8, I suggested that standard versions of noncognitivism endorse two negative claims about moral thought and moral language:

1. *Psychological noncognitivism*: The state of mind of accepting a moral claim is not really a cognitive representational state.
2. *Semantic nonrepresentationalism*: Indicative moral sentences don't function (primarily) to represent or describe the world in the same way that

other indicative sentences do. Their meaning is not representational (at least in the first instance).

Because these claims are negative, they create a need for positive proposals about the nature of moral thought and language. You haven't told us much about ethics if you tell us only what's not going on when people accept moral judgements and what sentences containing moral terms don't do. So anyone, or at least any metaethical theorist, who accepts these negative claims shoulders a certain burden. The burden lies in supplementing these claims with a positive story that makes sense of moral thought and moral talk consistent with denying cognitivism and semantic representationalism.

Hermeneutic moral fictionalism holds out the prospect of cutting this burden roughly in half. It suggests that the two negative claims are logically separable, and in particular that the first negative claim does not entail the second. It might thus make sense to accept the first while denying the second. Perhaps "moral beliefs"—the states expressed by indicative moral sentences in everyday use—are not belief in the propositions expressed by the sentences when so used. And yet the sentences themselves might still semantically express propositions. This could be so even when the sentences are not normally used by speakers to express belief in those propositions. A simple model is metaphor or even better, worn metaphor. "The fog was thick as pea soup," almost never gets used to assert its literal meaning. Yet it communicates something. Here we can deploy the semantics/pragmatics distinction to describe what is going on. The sentence's meaning (its semantic value) just is the proposition that the fog was thick as pea soup. But the speakers who use it most often pragmatically communicate belief in something else—that the fog was very thick.

This combination of views—psychological noncognitivism without semantic nonrepresentationalism—saves someone who doesn't believe in moral properties but who does think moral discourse has a communicative purpose some work. They can avoid having to posit and fill out a nonrepresentational semantics for moral terms. Moral terms can mean exactly what they mean according to ordinary cognitivism and we already know what that theory says. Thus simple indicative sentences can be assigned truth conditions of a standard sort[1] and more complex sentences embedding such simple sentences can get their content specified in a relatively standard compositional truth conditional semantics. The ingenuity that old-fashioned noncognitivists have put to work responding to the Frege-Geach problem can be diverted to other kinds of theory development. Or so anyway think fictionalists; the point is controversial. We'll examine its viability more closely shortly. For now the idea helps us to understand why someone might find fictionalism attractive. If the fictionalists who endorse it are correct, they can get many of the main theoretical benefits of noncognitivism without having to explain quite as much in new and distinctive ways.

9.2.2. The Hermeneutic Fictionalists' Claim That Moral Attitudes Are Not Beliefs Commits Them Only to a Sparse Moral Metaphysics

Hermeneutic fictionalists hope to retain several of the advantages of standard noncognitivism. One central advantage, upon which several others depend, is that fictionalists need not commit to the actual existence of the facts, properties, and entities that seem to be discussed in moral discourse. Though moral sentences have descriptive claims as their semantic content, fictionalists deny that correct use of these sentences commits speakers to the truth of these sentences. Speech acts that employ the sentences are not straightforward acts of assertion. So they do not commit the speaker to the content of the sentence used. Neither will the states of mind expressed in such speech acts commit the speaker to belief in the propositions that are the semantic values of the sentences. "Moral beliefs" are not beliefs in the propositions semantically expressed.

As a consequence, fictionalists are under little pressure themselves to regard these propositions as true. If the people whose use of moral language in everyday life we are trying to understand aren't themselves committed to any such truth, there is little reason to invoke such truths to explain what they are up to. Fictionalists motivated by the same metaphysical worries that bother noncognitivists and error theorists will see this is a benefit. For example, take those fictionalists who deny the truth of many moral claims out of a commitment to naturalism. Such fictionalists think science tells us what properties and relations there really are, and that moral properties are not among them. This conclusion will be no bar to accepting representational semantics for moral sentences on the model of fiction, provided we can both explain how moral predicates have the representational meanings they do and provided we can make sense of continuing to use these sentences to express something other than belief in their literally false content. We'll come back to these two provisos later on.

It isn't only naturalism that makes theorists wary of postulating real properties of rightness, wrongness, moral requirement, and so on. As we saw, error theorists such as John Mackie and Richard Joyce have thought that moral properties would have to be such as to generate a very strong and indefeasible internalism. And since they can make no sense of properties actually satisfying that requirement, they go on to deny that there are any moral properties. Once again, fictionalists need not worry about that conclusion. Whatever problem one finds with the putative ontological commitments of seemingly realist moral discourse, the fictionalist can accept the underlying objection. She thinks we can sensibly pretend to speak of such impossible properties. And she thinks that is what most people in fact are doing. So the problematic commitment is not really a commitment of those who use the discourse as they do. Even when the sentences really contain those commitments among their truth conditions, those who use them are only making believe or acting as if they are true. They do not really accept them as they would if they believed them. Hermeneutic fictionalist ontological commitments are thus no more extensive than those of noncognitivism and error theory.

9.2.3. Fictionalists Use Their Psychological Noncognitivism to Explain Internalism

Many fictionalists think they can endorse something like the standard positive noncognitivist psychological claim that the state of mind of accepting a moral judgement is conative rather than cognitive. If they're successful they are in just as good a position to explain morals/motives judgement internalism as noncognitivists. They will explain internalism just as the noncognitivist does. Moral judgements are motivating attitudes and that is why those who accept a moral judgement will be motivated to act as it recommends.

9.2.4. But They Must Depart From Noncognitivism in Their Treatment of the OQA

It also looks like fictionalists can accept the Open Question Argument as a reason to deny reductionism about moral terms, if not moral properties. But it doesn't seem that they *must* accept the argument, nor does it seem that they can explain its upshot in the same way as noncognitivists typically do. Recall that noncognitivists agree with Moore that no moral predicate has the same meaning as any nonmoral predicate. They think this is true because moral predicates perform a different semantic function as a matter of their meaning. But a fictionalist does not say this. As far as the meanings of the terms go, fictionalists agree with cognitivists. That's just what it means to deny semantic nonrepresentationalism. So they cannot just adopt the standard noncognitivist explanation of the plausibility of the open question hypothesis. Those who like ordinary noncognitivism will think this is a reason to prefer it to fictionalism, but fictionalists will likely think the advantages of avoiding the Frege-Geach problem are well worth this cost.

9.3. Turning the Abstract Strategy Into a Flesh and Bones Model

Whatever the benefits of fictionalism in general, hermeneutic moral fictionalism is only a contender if we can explain the human point of using representational but false moral language and if we can explain how that point is served by continuing to use language in this way. So we need at least two things filled out. We need a conception of the overall purpose that is supposed to be served by speaking fictively about morality. And we need an explanation of the speech acts involved. On the assumption that these are communicative speech acts, that explanation would tell us what speech acts of fictive moral utterance communicate. And it would at least sketch how those speech acts communicate that information. Each part of the story would constrain the other as would the fact that as fictionalists we have committed to a representational moral semantics. The information communicated would have to be such as to fit the larger purpose of using moral discourse. If it turns out I'm expressing an attitude with my utterance we would want the expression of that attitude to further the overall point of using moral language according to the theory. We would also need the attitude to be one that fictive utterances could convey to the intended audience. And, for hermeneutic fictionalism to be plausible we'd need one more thing. We'd need at least a sketch of how people could wind up using language in this way.

Here I have an expository problem because there are a number of options for a fictionalist to choose. In particular, there are a variety of roles that fictions play in our lives and a variety of ways we might use fiction to communicate something. If I go through all of the possibilities we'll get lost in the details. So what I'm going to do instead is discuss a kind of discourse that has been given a fictionalist interpretation by some philosophers. I will explain how according to that interpretation what appear to be assertions and sincere expressions of belief in the semantic content instead become a different kind of speech act. Having explained the model I will adapt it to moral discourse, highlighting certain similarities but de-emphasizing others. Before I'm done I will have to tie the speech acts postulated to purposes that people might have, and to explain how such speech acts might serve those purposes.

9.3.1. A Nonmoral Fictionalist Model: Constructive Empiricism

Constructive empiricist views of scientific theorizing provide our model.[2] Roughly according to constructive empiricism, scientific theories are correct when they are empirically adequate. A scientific theory is empirically adequate if its use to make predictions about and to describe patterns in observable phenomena tracks the actual observable phenomena. So the scientific theory that postulates atoms made of electrons, protons, and neutrons is correct if it accurately predicts observations about objects large enough to see and what we observe when we use scientific equipment, such as microscopes, cloud chambers, and so forth. According to such empiricists, the best we can do to justify acceptance of subatomic theory is to show that it is fully empirically adequate. Supposing it were we would be justified in accepting it. Now comes the fictionalist wrinkle: Acceptance does not entail belief. So a scientist may justifiably accept the subatomic theory based on evidence of its empirical accuracy and yet not believe it, and not believe that it is true. The constructive empiricists we are discussing think there is no rational requirement to believe the theories we are fully justified in accepting. For the empirical adequacy of the theory does not entail its truth.

Constructive empiricists argue for their views in many ways. One mode of argument points out that scientists often slide from using one theory to another, even where the contents of the theories seem to be incompatible. So long as two theories are empirically adequate, as some such conflicting theories might both be, there is a point to using each. Suppose you believed that both theories could not be correct characterizations of ultimate reality, due to the nature of the entities they each postulate. On ordinary understandings of waves and particles the claim that light is a wave and the claim that light is a particle would seem to be of this sort. Yet there can be reason in a particular context for the same scientist to use this theory for one purpose and that one for another. The scientist accepts the theories for those purposes without believing them true. When someone thinks in this way they are not contradicting themselves or behaving irrationally. While belief in the theory would entail empirical adequacy, the entailment does not run in the other direction. So there is no contradiction involved in acceptance without belief.

We should extend the sketch to cover scientific discourse. According to our constructive empiricists, scientists who make claims about unobservable particles, such as "A proton just went through the cloud chamber," should not be assumed to believe that there was a proton in the cloud chamber. For the scientist's utterance of that sentence might instead express the weaker attitude, that the content of that sentence (together with some relevant background theory) would adequately guide our thought about observable phenomena. So if the theory predicts that protons in cloud chambers leave streaks, the claim that there is a proton will be adequate only if there is a streak. In a context where everyone knows that many scientists hold this kind of instrumentalist view, such sentences would communicate different information than the same sentences would in a community of scientific realists who do believe the theory is true. If a constructive empiricist says "A proton just went through the cloud chamber," I won't take her to be expressing her belief in protons or this one proton. I will instead take her to be expressing acceptance of the claim. And accepting that claim in that context comes to believing it empirically adequate.

When we are talking about what speech acts express we're normally interested in a particular kind of expression, communicative expression. This has to do with what a speaker intends her audience to take away from the conversation, given reasonable background assumptions. In a world of constructive empiricists an audience should take scientists to express acceptance of the claim that there is a proton in the cloud chamber, but not belief that there is a proton in the cloud chamber when they say, "There's a proton in the cloud chamber." For that is all a scientific speaker could expect people to infer from the use of that sentence given that the audience knows she is likely an instrumentalist, hesitant to believe anything about unobservable matters. So the speech act of making an assertion with our target sentence does not express belief in a proton, only a belief in the adequacy of the claim given the theory. Or so anyway says the constructive empiricist I'm describing; scientific discourse about subatomic particles is a kind of fiction, good for predicting and describing patterns in observable reality, but not necessarily the correct story about the ultimate nature of reality.

9.3.2. Adapting the Model to Morality

The feature of the constructive empiricist model that we would like to copy is that it has people systematically using sentences with one content, not to assert that content or to express belief in it, but instead to express a different attitude toward that content. The scientific instrumentalist story construed the attitude as a belief but a belief in a different content than the content of the sentence that expressed it. It was the belief that the content of the sentence uttered would be empirically adequate if used to guide to further research and prediction. Yet you might have said something very similar if you described it as a kind of confidence or trust that predictions and plans made while acting as if that content were true would generate accurate predictions and fruitful further research. Or, to push the attitude even more toward the noncognitive, it might be a kind of trust that acting as if what your sentences represented were true would serve your purposes better than not acting that way.

Are there attitudes in the neighborhood of practical deliberation and action with others that we might want to communicate? And might they be communicated by similarly fictive moral discourse? The hermeneutic fictionalist who sees her work as a development of noncognitivism will say there are. These will be practically committing attitudes that determine our future actions and also structure our emotional responses to the actions of others. Here a fictionalist might try to piggyback on the work of Simon Blackburn (1984) and Allan Gibbard (1990, 2003) as they develop their quasi-realist version of expressivism. Each of them in different ways offers an account of practically committing attitudes that is constructed to suggest that human beings might get great benefit out of having and communicating such attitudes. These attitudes facilitate pursuing one's own goals over time, and expressing these attitudes coordinates one's actions with others. It also allows one to reason together with other similarly situated people about common practical problems, both for individuals and for groups. Supposing this is right we could see how expressing such attitudes would serve a common purpose human beings like us could plausibly have.

Now we need to show how attitudes such as these could be communicated through the utterance of false indicative sentences whose meanings are representational. To do that we need moral language to already be in place and to be used consistently as realist cognitivists think it is used.

So let's suppose there were already an ongoing practice of moralizing on the model of minimal realism. People really did take themselves to be making judgements about the natures of actions when they called them right.

That is they took themselves to be predicating some property of those actions and they took themselves also to be in disagreement with others about an action when those others denied that the same action was right. Suppose it were part of that practice to judge as though the property of rightness supervened on the other properties of actions, so that people regarded it as a mistake to evaluate two actions differently with respect to rightness without being able to point to some nonmoral difference. There are also other moral predicates in play and those predicates interact with the predicate for 'right' and 'wrong' in interesting ways. In particular, the goodness of an item or outcome is treated as relevant to the rightness or wrongness of actions leading to those items or outcomes. There might, we will suppose, be a lot of agreement about which actions are right and wrong, but there is also a good deal of controversy. These controversies were treated as important because of the practical upshot of judgements of rightness and wrongness.

The people involved in this practice took their judgements of right and wrong, good and bad, and so on to legitimate certain practical attitudes, including plans and intentions. They expected people to do what they believe right and to avoid doing what they believe wrong. And they treated the rightness of an action as a reason for anyone to do it. When people failed to do what is right others treated it as appropriate to blame them and criticize them. And so on. I could go on, but I suspect you can fill in the rest as well as I can. This going practice generates expectations about how people will behave given what they say. And it allows participants to expect certain affective patterns from people who profess views about morality. In particular they expect people to do what they affirm to be morally required and to blame those who do what they think is wrong.

Suppose now that you and I are in such a society. But we have come to regard the beliefs of our compatriots as mistaken. For whatever reason, we think there is no property of rightness, nor of goodness, nor of wrongness. We don't think that reality vindicates the notions of moral requirement, moral prohibition, and so on. Yet we still have many of the affective responses we used to have. We disapprove of murder, plan not to live with what we used to think of as injustice, and get indignant at the cruel actions of others. We know that we are disposed thusly and we endorse that in ourselves and others. We also think that some ways of living make more sense and others make less sense in light of those dispositions.

Given the common linguistic background, fictive moral claims might be used to express these noncognitive attitudes and commitments, highlighting the structure of dependence and relative strength of these attitudes. If we each recognize our common skepticism about the prevalent metaphysics that postulates moral properties and use moral terms to predicate them, we can communicate the noncognitive attitudes without communicating the beliefs that normally go with them. We've already seen that it is possible to communicate one thought by using a sentence whose literal content is another claim. "The fog was as thick as pea soup" or "She is sharp as a tack" are rarely used to express belief in their semantic content—that is in the proposition encoded in those words in virtue of our conventions and linguistic practices. Rather these sentences are used to communicate something related to that content. In both cases it helps that both speaker and audience know that they *could not* be literally true and they each agree the other knows this. Given that common background the speaker can expect the audience to look for a nonliteral use. That same mechanism would be at work when people with mutual knowledge of their skepticism use moral sentences. If I know that you think there is no such property as wrongness, and you say "That's really wrong," I'm going to look for an interpretation of what you intend to tell me that has you intending to tell me something other than that some action is literally wrong. One salient possibility is that you would be trying to tell me that you have the attitudes that would be appropriate if the going practice were veridical and the thing in question were really wrong.

Much more detail would need to be filled in to rule out interpretations of your speech act on which you intend to communicate something else, and we do need to rule out many of those to get a correct fix on what you are saying. Different ways of filling out speech act theory will postulate somewhat different explanations about how such things work. But the basic picture is one on which speakers use common background and foreground knowledge, and common default assumptions about communication, to allow sentences to communicate their thoughts to an audience. Knowing what you believe, knowing what you take me to believe, knowing what things are salient to people like us play a role. These same mechanisms are in play even with literal communication. I have to take you to be trying to communicate something to me that I can grasp given what you said even to interpret you as asserting the contents of a sentence you utter. And such mechanisms play a large role also when you use a sentence without intending to assert its semantic content but something else instead. You have to pay attention to what is salient to me and what I know to pick a sentence that will make your intention clear to me. And I have to pay attention to what you know about me to figure out what you could reasonably have expected me to take away from the sentence you are using.

Anyway, that's a sketch of how an utterance by one skeptic could communicate to another skeptic affective attitudes other than belief in the content of the sentence uttered. We could imagine a group of such skeptics using moral sentences generally in this way. When all know that none really believe the content of moral sentences, they will naturally look for some nonassertoric interpretation of what a speaker is up to when he or she uses indicative moral sentences. And given the usefulness of the corresponding affective attitudes in thinking as a group (if the quasi-realists are right), communicating these attitudes will be high on the list of viable interpretations of potential speaker purposes whenever such a sentence is used.

It will be important that such a pretense could develop out of an initial moral practice of a more committed sort. It is plausible to think that people at some point in time took their noncognitive attitudes toward actions they regard as wrong or right to be fitting responses to real features of their objects. Natural sympathy, reciprocity, and fellow feeling may have caused them to respond to the features of various courses of action with approval and disapproval. They might, suggests a certain kind of anti-realist, have projected these responses onto the actions to which the attitudes are directed and come to see them as meriting these attitudes. As a result, they come to find them praiseworthy or worthy of criticism and think of these terms as naming real properties of the actions and objects we apply them to. A suggestive analogy is with the nauseating; though nausea is an attitude of ours directed at certain targets, we can come to see these targets as having a real property, that of being nauseating. We see our nausea as an apt response to these targets, one that reflects their nauseating nature. In this way we take a response of ours and think of it as a feature of the things to which we respond. In the same way, suggests this anti-realist, people take their attitudes of approval and disapproval and project them onto the actions and objects that they now take to warrant those responses in virtue of those features. The phenomenology can be of something objective even while the origin of the responses comes from within.

Suppose one is a participant in such a practice. At the start one takes these judgements at face value. When one says an action is praiseworthy, one takes oneself to predicate a real property of the action, one that exists whether we recognize it or not and that warrants the judgement and the noncognitive attitudes that go with the judgement. But over time, let's suppose, one comes to have doubts about the picture. One still feels the admiration and approval, but one comes to wonder about the order of explanation and about the thought that these actions are really objectively praiseworthy. Even so, one can go on as before, calling such actions praiseworthy and admirable as a way of expressing the attitudes that one previously took to be responses to a real property picked out by terms like 'praiseworthy,' 'admirable,' and 'right.' Now, however, one's seeming assertions no longer express belief in the semantic content of the sentence one utters. Rather, one expresses an attitude short of belief in these contents, the expression of which serves also to express the noncognitive attitudes that one previously took to be justified by a belief in that content. One has the attitude and is perfectly happy to express it, without actually committing to the contents of one's utterance.

Given that those around one are still part of a community of believers, they will recognize that you have these attitudes when uttering the sentence. But at least initially they will come to that conclusion only after first concluding that you intended to express a belief in the proposition that the sentence encodes as its meaning. But now suppose over time more and more people come to have their doubts. More and more of them come to think that the metaphysical commitments of their language—that moral terms represent genuine properties and relations—are strictly and literally false. In reflective moments they admit those doubts and even defend them. Over time people won't any longer reasonably attribute belief in the content of a moral sentence on the basis of a moral utterance. Any given speaker *could* be using it that way, but they *could* instead be using the sentence to let their audience know their noncognitive disposition. So now the audience would be most reasonable not to attribute an intention to express a belief that the speaker has. And if the situation becomes clear to everyone it might become most reasonable to recognize an intention to communicate the noncognitive attitude in all such speech acts and to do it directly, not via the expression of the belief that used to go with it.[3] After a while speakers might intend that their audience recognize that intention. The situation would then be very much like van Fraassen's conception of how scientists speak when they speak about unobservable entities. When a scientist tells us a proton was involved in such and such a process we can reasonably infer that the scientist thinks that hypothesis is empirically adequate—that she thinks we can make predictions on the basis of that claim together with some theory. She might also actually believe there is a proton there. But, if van Fraassen is right she might not. If it is widely known that this is how scientists think, we should no longer take scientists to assert that a proton is involved even though that is the content encoded in the sentences they use. Rather we should take them to be expressing an attitude it would be reasonable for a scientific speaker to expect us to recognize—her or his confidence that this hypothesis will be empirically adequate.

This process could happen without anyone ever intentionally spinning a fiction. And it could happen even while not everyone recognizes that skepticism about the status of morality is widespread. Doubts could creep in slowly over time, so that words that originally expressed belief now express a less committed attitude, perhaps even just the attitude of finding certain noncognitive responses appropriate. Mark Kalderon (2005) suggests that something like this has in fact happened to our moral convictions. He thinks that the way in which we now pursue moral disagreements with peers shows that we do not treat either their or our own moral judgements as having the status of belief. Where belief is concerned we should take peer disagreement seriously, allowing the judgements of others to affect our own certainty or uncertainty and spur us to think further to settle which view is more correct. Kalderon thinks we don't do this when our disagreements are over moral matters and he concludes that for most of us we don't really believe what we say. Thus we should not assume that what seem to be moral assertions really are such. Perhaps they are quasi-assertions, a kind of pretense that one performs as a way of expressing attitudes other than belief in what one says. In conversing about morality with one another, we would then often not know which direct speech act an interlocutor is performing. She may be asserting what she says or merely quasi-asserting it. Even so, speakers and listeners with differing views about the objectivity of morality could successfully use indicative moral sentences to communicate noncognitive attitudes via an indirect expressive speech act. An addressee who heard a speaker call an action wrong would not need to know whether the speaker meant to assert that it was wrong, or merely to express the judgement that acting as if it were wrong (with all its attendant noncognitive upshot) was appropriate. In either case the speaker has given the addressee a reason to think that she has the noncognitive attitudes that would be appropriate to believing the action objectively wrong. So communication of the noncognitive attitudes is successful even while the audience might be in doubt about the speaker's beliefs about morality.

This is similar in some ways to how the constructive empiricist sees indicative utterances about microscopic particles according to the first model for fictionalism that we looked at earlier. If the constructive empiricist is correct we don't need to know whether a scientist looking through a lens and uttering, "There are protons traveling through that chamber," believes in protons or merely thinks that the theory of protons yields correct predictions about observable matters. Since both full belief and mere commitment to the empirical adequacy of the theory entail empirical adequacy, we can learn that the scientist observed phenomena that according to the theory would be caused by protons. We don't need to know whether the scientist in question accepts subatomic theory merely as empirically adequate or as an objectively true account of subatomic reality. In either case she would say what she does only if her observations were consistent with the presence of a proton. The analogy is not perfect because constructive empiricism suggests that the point of postulating unobservable phenomena in science has to do with making predictions regarding observable phenomena and not forming conative attitudes. But the point is that in some circumstances an indirect speech act can serve to express an attitude in nearly the same way whether or not the underlying speech act is an assertion, quasi-assertion, or pretend assertion.

This is but a suggestive sketch.

9.3.3. Hermeneutic Fictionalism Would Be More Plausible If More People Believed It

Before moving on I should raise a problem. The main difficulty for hermeneutic fictionalism is that most people don't recognize it as accurate. Communicative acts of conveying one thing by saying another depend on mutual knowledge of the intention not to speak literally. In the story about scientific instrumentalism we built in that most scientists knew that many other scientists were instrumentalists. Thus it would be reasonable for a scientist to infer that a speaker believed in the empirical adequacy of what she seemed to assert, whether she strictly believed what she said or not. It was thus that acceptance of the empirical adequacy was able to be communicated while belief was not. If it isn't widely known or believed that most people don't really believe in the truth of moral claims, it won't be reasonable for speakers to expect their listeners to figure out that they don't believe what they say. And it won't then be reasonable for them to expect the listeners to pick up on the main expressive point of their saying what they do. This, it seems to me, is the main issue confronting hermeneutic fictionalism even if one agrees with the basically anti-realist picture of morality. I suspect it explains why hermeneutic fictionalism has fewer adherents than revolutionary fictionalism.

I won't offer a defense on behalf of the hermeneutic fictionalist here and that might be less than fair to this form of fictionalism. My exposition of the position is already little more than a suggestive sketch. I have not really filled in how the expression of such attitudes could serve to coordinate action. Nor have I sketched how fictive discourse could help us reason together about common problems we find when we engage in deliberation. I have just waved my hands in the direction of the arguments of the quasi-realists that attitudes of the sort described can play that role when expressed. The preceding discussion is also sketchy in another respect; I have essentially just picked one possible kind of fictive practice and run with it. For all I've said here other ways of using fiction might have worked better as a model for hermeneutic moral fictionalism. And perhaps they would not have been as susceptible to the worry that the theory is unbelievable because so few people believe it. Hermeneutic fictionalism is one of the less explored metaethical options and readers might come up with new ways to develop the view. That's a pleasant thought.

9.4. Revolutionary Moral Fictionalism

Revolutionary moral fictionalism is a proposal for how to go on to use moral discourse in the future given that something is problematic about extant moral discourse. Most revolutionary moral fictionalists are error theorists. They think that all or most of moral discourse is an error. Many error theorists think that the fatal error, whatever it is, comes close enough to the heart of morality to make moral sentences literally false. That in turn would make assertion of those moral claims similarly false. All error theorists think something like this. But only some go on to be revolutionary fictionalists. Revolutionary fictionalists are error theorists who propose that we continue to use moral sentences, even though what they semantically represent is by and large or wholly false. They propose we use moral language fictionally, much as the hermeneutic fictionalist thinks we already use it.[4]

Revolutionary fictionalists must think there would be a point to acting as if morality were true or talking about a moral fiction even if it is false or mistaken. They are, after all, putting forward their proposal as a sensible plan given the considerations that call the truth of morality into question or show it to be false. Usually the purposes are practical in some sense. One such practical purpose might be coordination with other people. An error theorist about morality, as opposed to about normativity and reasons altogether, can think that we have reasons to act together in various ways. Such error theorists will deny that there are any distinctively moral reasons for action or that any moral claims are strictly true. But she can allow that we have reasons to cooperate with one another in pursuit of common goals. She might also think that the tenets of an overlapping or even common morality, subscribed to by most people in the society around her, are a useful guide to cooperative action in service of these common goals. She'll think that the claims of morality aren't true, but that they are useful in coordinating human interactions. The common morality might be a useful collection of rules of thumb, helpful in allowing most people to live together with others in ways that further their ends, but not grounded in any categorical reasons for action that all the members of society must recognize or share in.

Someone who takes this view and who has many of the goals shared by her fellow citizens may well find it convenient to continue to use the rules of thumb to coordinate with others. Where she knows that others in her community will generally take the rightness of a course of action as reason to choose it, asserting that some option is correct will remain a convenient and effective way to organize cooperative action of that sort. And choosing to do an action that some other person has called right will make sense too, on the assumption that their cooperation in acting on that judgement serves common ends. There may thus be a definite cost to giving up on using moral language, at least unless a replacement for these coordinating functions is available. Even if one is available there may be little to recommend it over the current way of speaking and communicating given the costs of switching over. As Daniel Nolan, Greg Restall, and Caroline West put it:

> This eliminitivist price has seemed to many too great a price to pay. Moral discourse is extraordinarily useful. Morality plays an important social role in coordinating attitudes and in regulating interpersonal relations. Giving up moral talks would force large-scale changes to the way we talk, think, and feel and would be extremely difficult to make. We have, then incentive for finding some way in which to retain our realist discourse without its accompanying undesirable commitments . . . (Nolan, Restall, and West, 2005, p. 307)

When one becomes convinced that moral thinking is or presupposes some sort of error, one may be the only one so convinced or one may be part of a large mass of the disillusioned. Suppose you are one of only a few error theorists. In that case it is unlikely that people will in general give up using moral claims to propose common effort in pursuit of common goals, and it will then be highly difficult for the few error theorists to participate in coordinated action without at least using the moral vocabulary. Rather than drop out of common activities or spending a lot of time explaining what you really believe, you may find it more expedient to continue speaking as before. You can make it known if you like that you don't mean to assert what your sentences literally say, but you need not do that. So long as your fellows expect you to act as if what your sentences mean is true, cooperative action on the basis of what you pretend to assert or make as if to assert can go on as before.

Suppose instead that you are not alone; error theory becomes popular—everyone believes that moral judgements are generally false. Suppose the common verdict is that morality presupposes categorical demands of reason such that any agent, no matter what her prior commitments, has an over-riding reason to do what morality suggests. Suppose further that it is because the presupposition is false that everyone comes to believe morality in error. Sentences that formerly were used to assert judgements about the categorical reasons of morality can be retained now to express weaker claims with a similar practical upshot. People affirming a moral judgement could be expressing a commitment to acting as if the judgements are true. And they will find it natural to do that whenever they and their compatriots have overlapping noncategorical reasons to promote moral ends. That commitment would give them reason to act in much the same way as if they thought these ends were categorical demands of reason. Once again, moral thought and talk serves a useful coordinating function, at least so long as people still endorse the common ends that they previously thought were unconditional demands of reason. Even absent categorical moral demands speaking as if certain actions are categorically right and others wrong can still help coordinate action to promote what we used to think morality demanded.

A simple analogy might make the point. Suppose a community in which people thought that traffic laws were the universal commands of categorical reason. Their judgements of legality might encode that idea as a kind of presupposition. (Maybe there is a preamble that talks about the laws having been made clear by the divine light of reason.) Someone studying the group might conclude that calling something a moving violation predicated a certain property of an action, one that it had only if the natural laws of traffic rationality commanded obedience. Driving on the left was thought to be wrong because a universal law of reason forbade driving on the left. Suppose this is built into the very meaning of the words 'moving violation.' Now suppose that a stranger comes on the scene and tells of faraway lands where people drive on the left. At first the news is met with skepticism. How could that be if steering wheels are on the left side of a car? The stranger explains that cars in these lands have their steering wheels on the right. Over time people come to believe the stranger and come also to believe that no extraordinary harms befall those who drive on the left in these distant places. They come to consider the hypothesis that it doesn't really matter whether one drives on the left or right. Traffic laws are largely creatures of conventional choice, and there is no categorical reason not to do what would be a moving violation absent a desire to coordinate with others. These newly enlightened folk would have no very good reason to give up talking about moving violations. They might find it convenient to go on speaking as before, but no longer to assert what their words mean. They could put them forth as adequate for purposes of coordination and the like. Even if everyone knew this was what was going on there would be no reason to drop this way of speaking.

We may worry that the talk would wind up no longer expressing what it used to. Perhaps over time the words 'moving violation' would lose their meaning and no longer commit speakers to categorical traffic reasons. This is a real worry about how words presuppose the claims that according to error theorists make them false. (See section 9.5 for an elaboration of this worry.) But supposing that words do presuppose such claims in such a way as to make the judgements false, there would seem to be no reason in this story to give up on using the terms. And since we have stipulated that people no longer believe those presuppositions, this means that they have reason to utter sentences that they take to be false, as a means of pursuing common purposes. It is this idea that can ground one line of argument in support of revolutionary fictionalism.

There can be other reasons why error theorists will want to retain moral discourse in much its current form, even while believing that most of it is false and rife with error. Richard Joyce (2007, chapters 7 and 8) suggests that moral pretense will help our practical judgements retain motivational efficacy and hence give us more resources to combat weakness of will. Retaining moral discourse will thus be a useful strategy to achieve what we care about in the face of our own weakness. This idea and the previous one can be used to argue that we have good pragmatic reason to retain moral talk and to continue on much as before, even once we have become convinced of the falseness of moral discourse in general. Depending on why a theorist accepts error theory there may be further reasons as well.

This may be a good place to highlight something that is already implied. Revolutionary fictionalism seems to have to be about some limited domain of normative thought and talk. For the revolutionary suggestion is itself a kind of normative claim or demand—that it makes sense for us to go on speaking as before. And the revolutionary fictionalist error theorist doesn't think this proposal itself is mistaken or in error. At least there would be worries about the coherence of the overall position if the claim was itself thought to be in error. One upshot is that the error theoretic arguments that this kind of fictionalist takes on board should be limited in scope so that they don't spread to all normative claims in general. Many arguments for metaethical positions regarding the moral or the ethical do generalize to normative claims of all sorts. For example, if one's metaethical commitments are rooted in Humean doubts about the motivational powers of moral beliefs, beliefs about rationality and prudence are just as much beliefs as these. So one should treat these domains on a par with the ethical. That's no problem for many metaethical positions because they don't *undermine* themselves when generalized. But error theory says that all claims in the target domain are *erroneous*. If that claim generalizes to any normative claim whatsoever, the error theorist would be making a mistake to go on to assert such further claims in proposing revolutionary fictionalism. I'm not saying that revolutionary fictionalism has to fall into this trap. Not every reason to think morality erroneous is a reason to think all normative claims erroneous. For instance, many people think that moral claims presuppose categoricity but claims of rationality or prudence do not. If doubts about categorical demands underlie one's moral error theory, these doubts won't spread beyond the moral. We should thus expect fictionalism about moral discourse to be local to morality and ethics and not to extend to all normative or practical thought. Anti-realist arguments that must be global don't support fictionalism as a revolutionary goal.

9.5. Objections to Moral Fictionalism

9.5.1. An Objection From the Relation of Meaning to Use

It is very plausible that at some level words mean what they do because of how we use them. Exactly how this works is tricky and of some controversy. On one picture of how this might work, sentences get their meanings by being regularly used to communicate certain thoughts. Words in turn have the meanings they do in part because they contribute in systematic ways to the sentence whose meanings are composed of the meanings of the words they contain. Any concrete proposal about the precise nature of the dependence relations here will be controversial. Still, at least this much is plausible: If we normally used the word 'cat' to express thoughts about both cats and dogs in the way we now use it to express thoughts about cats, it would over time come to designate both cats and dogs as a matter of the term's conventional meaning and not just as a function of speaker intentions to use it to refer to both on a particular occasion.

One might worry that this casts doubt on fictionalism both as an accurate account of our current use of moral terms, and also as a viable long-term revolutionary response to deep moral error. If we regularly predicate the term 'morally right' of actions that it is useful to predicate the term fictively, even when these actions are not really morally right, that term might come to designate a new property. The new property would not be moral rightness as we antecedently thought of it, but the property actions have when it is useful, given our fictive practices, to call them "morally right." Call this property "f-moral rightness." As this objection goes, over time our terms 'morally right' would come to designate not moral rightness but f-moral rightness. Our utterances would now, as a matter of their semantic content, predicate f-moral rightness of the actions we characterize using the term 'morally right.'

We can be more concrete. One reason metaethicists become fictionalists, whether hermeneutic or revolutionary, is skepticism about metaphysical commitments they believe are built into words such as 'morally right.' To use a familiar example, they may think that our semantics presuppose the existence of a property that requires categorical requirements of reason. Wishing to eschew such commitments, they think we should use these terms only in ways that hold such commitments in abeyance; we should rather use the predicate only fictively to communicate that it is relevantly as though things are right, and as though there are such categorical requirements. If everybody were to talk this way over the course of many years, how would the words retain their unwanted metaphysical connotations? New speakers entering the community would not easily learn that these terms presupposed the existence of categorical rational requirements. Their mentors and teachers would never in fact adjust their seeming predications of rightness to be sensitive to the presence or absence of categorical requirements. They would go right ahead to label actions as morally right even absent support from categorical reasons. They would confidently make what seem to be judgements of right and wrong in the absence of such requirements. Any novice would come to think that those terms carried no commitment to the allegedly suspect metaphysics. And before long the conventionally underwritten semantic contents of the terms would no longer encode the commitment to such requirements. Perhaps something like this happened with the word 'charm.' At one time it was used to speak to a kind of supernatural magnetism that manifested itself in making the person who had it seem attractive. Then, as people lost their belief in this kind of magic, the word was retained now just to refer to the qualities that underlie the personal attractiveness.

If this is a good objection to revolutionary moral fictionalism it would also be a good objection to hermeneutic fictionalism. For one way to think about hermeneutic fictionalism is as the view that at some time in the past our linguistic predecessors were successful revolutionary fictionalists who revolted against the old way of speaking and successfully got people to adopt fictionalist practices going forward. If that's right, a hermeneutic fictionalist should suspect that our words may already have lost their objectionable commitments, as people no longer use them to express worrisome ancillary thoughts. Speaking fictively would no longer be needed, since all that would be encoded in the semantics would be the unobjectionable commitments that people regularly expressed when using the terms fictively.

There is something to think about in this objection. When people regularly use words to say certain things, these things can be taken up into the meanings of the words. You might think that the fact that many fictions are centuries old tells against the worry. But the claim is not that fictive use of language must cause words to change their meanings. The claim is that regularly using language to convey something other than the information semantically encoded will change the meanings of these words. At least it will if they are not ever used to convey what they conventionally mean. We may have an example of just this kind of thing when we think about generalized conversational implicatures. Perhaps when someone first asked, "Can you pass the salt?" the audience had to work out that the speaker wanted him or her to pass the salt by thinking about the relevance of asking that question. These days, though, no one has to work it out in that way. That form of words has become something of an idiom whose use to request the salt can be read right off of the sentence without any reasoning about relevance. To defuse the worry, we need examples where such nonliteral use doesn't lead to a change of meaning. Perhaps this is one. People can say, "Zeus must be angry," to remark on stormy weather. Perhaps it is among the more common uses of 'Zeus.' Yet we haven't so far made 'Zeus' designate thunderstorms rather than a fictive ancient deity.

9.5.2.   Can Fictionalism Really Bypass the Frege-Geach Problem?

If you think the Frege-Geach problem has to do with the relations of implication between the semantic contents of sentences, then it seems that fictionalism solves it neatly. Insofar as fictionalists affirm just what old-fashioned cognitivists affirm about the meanings of moral terms (that the predicates represent properties in all occurrences, etc.), they are on firm ground. But old-fashioned noncognitivists may reasonably suggest that the Frege-Geach problem goes beyond semantics. They may suggest that the attitudes expressed in putting forth a valid argument must stand in relations parallel to the logical relations among the semantic contents of the sentences used to express these arguments. Otherwise the underlying genuine arguments—the arguments people make by using sentences fictively—won't have any force. To put the point too starkly, suppose that 'Lying is wrong,' as used by a speaker in making an argument, expressed the attitude of disapproval toward lying. And suppose that 'If lying is wrong, Jason will surely do it' is used to express an attitude of dislike toward Jason. It won't be obvious that those two attitudes together would rationalize a state of mind a speaker could easily express with 'Jason is sure to lie.' Suppose the attitude expressed just is a state of belief, a belief in the prediction that Jason will lie. That surely isn't rationalized by jointly accepting an attitude of disapproval toward lying and dislike of Jason. And it is hard to think of an attitude that a speaker might express with 'Jason is sure to lie' that follows from those attitudes. The obvious way to fix the problem is to have the hypothetical sentence express a more structured attitude than mere dislike of Jason, perhaps a high credence for Jason's doing an action conditional on one's disapproval of the action. And that is the kind of attitude that quasi-realist noncognitivists invoke when they try to use a logic of attitudes to handle the Frege-Geach problem.

A noncognitivist critic of fictionalism might thus suggest that the fictionalist leaves all sorts of work yet to be done, in fact just the work that old-fashioned noncognitivists have toiled to accomplish when they constructed a logic of attitudes to correspond to the logic of the sentences that express moral or normative attitudes (Eklund, 2009, 2011). Their thought might be that fictionalists have to ensure that the logical relations between sentences mirror the logical relations between the attitudes they express in order for the logic of the sentences to be consistent with the way we use these sentences to make arguments. There is definitely something to this point as the earlier example of Jason-judgements illustrates. But it might be putting the upshot too strongly to conclude that the logical relations among the sentences must strictly parallel the logical relations among the judgements they express (Kalderon, 2008). For it is compatible with using a fiction that is useful precisely because of parallels between the fictional subject matter and what that subject matter analogically represents that there be some disanalogies present as well. A clever speaker can deploy parallels between the fiction and the subject indirectly represented by the fiction without committing to every parallel that is present.

Here's an example to make the point. It turns out that thinking about electricity like plumbing works pretty well for a number of practical purposes. You can think of voltage as water pressure, resistance as friction, current as current, generators as pumps. And there are other parallels as well. Just as raising the pressure in a pipe will raise the rate of current flow past a constriction in the pipe, raising the voltage will raise the amperage of the current through a resistor. You can thus use reasoning about water to guide you in designing an electric circuit. At least you can if you don't take the analogy too literally. You should not draw every inference that follows from thinking of electricity as a fluid in a pipe. There are important disanalogies. When you sever a pipe, the water in the pipe pours out into the environment. Generally the pressure in the pipe leading to a break will drop as the pressure is relieved by the easier passage of water out of the pipe. When you cut a wire with electricity flowing in it the opposite happens. The electrical current stops flowing. Voltage on the supply side of the break tends to go up, as no voltage is used to push current through the circuit. Anyone working with electricity would be a fool to ignore this disanalogy. The cost might be high in lives and electrical parts. That said, this does not detract from the usefulness of the plumbing model for thinking about electricity. So long as one refuses to draw certain inferences that would seem to be licensed by the fiction while freely drawing the rest, one does just fine. We seem fully capable of doing this kind of thinking. And if we can, not every feature of good moral thought will need to parallel the relations of implication between the sentences that are used to express that thought.

That is so far just a point about the instrumental use of models to represent features of reality. And that is not quite what the fictionalist who uses language to express noncognitive attitudes is doing. But the story is suggestive. It allows the fictionalist at least some room to claim an advantage over old-fashioned noncognitivism. The old-fashioned noncognitivist attempts to explain the logical relationships between sentences by treating them as reflections of the logical relationships between the attitudes they express. Thus you would expect the logical relations of the sentences to neatly mirror the logical relations between the attitudes given that view. But fictionalism doesn't treat the logical relations of the sentences as stemming from the relationships between the attitudes. Nor does it require the logical relations between the attitudes to be explained by the relations between the sentences pragmatically used to express them. The attitudes have certain commitments built into them on their own, and so do the sentences. As it happens, there are many parallels between the relations among the one sort and the relations among the other sort. This makes the sentences convenient tools with which to express the attitudes with the parallel structure. But not every feature of the semantic content of the sentence needs to be exploited for it to be a good tool, and in fact it may be a better tool if the user is careful not to use one of its features to represent the attitudes of interest. That's how it is with electrical theory and sentences that describe hydraulic relations. Some similar relation could hold between the things we want to express with moral sentences and the literal content of those sentences.

9.6. Summary

It looks as though revolutionary fictionalism will have to address many of the same worries that hermeneutic fictionalists must also answer. In particular both kinds of fictionalist have reason to worry about self-conscious fictionalist practice changing the meanings of the sentences that are used fictively to express whatever it is the fictionalist thinks they do or should. And if non-cognitivist critics are right to suggest that the hermeneutic fictionalist cannot shirk the task of grappling with the Frege-Geach problem, revolutionary fictionalists too might find themselves unable to use moral language in all the ways they want in order to accomplish the practical purposes for which they wish to retain it.

At the same time, revolutionary fictionalists aren't trying to explain anything with their proposal. Hermeneutic fictionalists are. Therefore, hermeneutic fictionalists have to worry about the explanatory adequacy of the theory they offer, whereas revolutionary fictionalists won't. We briefly raised a worry about this when we noted the difficulty of squaring the alleged fictive use of moral language with widespread doubt about such use. Hermeneutic fictionalists will also have to check how well their hypothesis explains plausible versions of internalism, and how well it fits with the other motivations that lead old-fashioned noncognitivists to adopt their rival view. If the fictionalist can make it plausible that moral talk expresses the very same attitudes that old-fashioned noncognitivists say it does (albeit in a different way) then the prospects for such explanations look pretty good, or at least no worse than rival noncognitivist views. If the fictionalist instead tries to be more original, coming up with a different story about the purposes of moral thought and talk and about the attitudes they express, we'll have to evaluate that package when it arrives.

Questions

Comprehension

C1. Distinguish hermeneutic fictionalism from revolutionary fictionalism.
C2. List several points of agreement between error theorists and hermeneutic fictionalists.
C3. On what do they disagree?
C4. Why do hermeneutic fictionalists have an explanatory burden that revolutionary fictionalists don't need to worry about?
C5. The chapter should have brought out that many of the motivations for hermeneutic fictionalism are parallel to those motivating regular noncognitivism. Does the fictionalist have any way to use the Open Question Argument to motivate her view that is parallel to noncognitivist appropriation of the OQA?

Extension

E1. Sometimes we talk about a fiction without pretending that it is true. Give an example. Can you think of some way that we could model moral fictionalism on this way of talking?
E2. What purposes do you think could be served by fictive use of moral terms? Are there other ways of fulfilling those purposes without using fiction?

Reading

Read along with: Daniel Nolan, Greg Restall, and Caroline West (2005).

Further reading: Kalderon (2005) is a thought-provoking book because it makes more suggestions than can be fit into one consistent version of fictionalism, and it is short. It is the main inspiration for the sketch of hermeneutic fictionalism in the text. Unfortunately there isn't a short paper by him to assign along with this chapter. Joyce (2007, chapter 7) proposes revolutionary fictionalism as a way of bolstering our will in the face of weakness. Chapter 9 of Sainsbury (2009) offers a short critical discussion of both Kalderon and Joyce. Bach (2011) is good at explaining how we can work out what a speaker means to convey from what a speaker says.

Notes

1   For the most part. Names and directly referring expressions complicate matters a bit.
2   This sketch is very roughly modeled on Bas van Fraassen's (1980) conception of scientific discourse to be found in *The Scientific Image*. I'm not trying very hard to capture any nuance in the original view.
3   For those of you who know some theory, I'm trying to describe how conveying the affective attitude could evolve over time from a perlocutionary intention accomplished via an illocutionary act with communicative upshot to become an illocutionary act on its own. In other words, something that originally is communicated as an intended effect of communicating something else (via a mutually recognized intention to communicate that something else) comes to be something one communicates via a mutually recognized intention to communicate that very thing.
4   It is in principle possible to be a revolutionary fictionalist without being an error theorist. One might, for example, be an agnostic about the truth of moral claims in general or of some proper subset of them, but propose that we go on speaking as if they are true, whether they are or not. Still the main proponents of revolutionary moral fictionalism, Richard Joyce (2007) and Nolan et al. (2005), seem to think that morality as we presently conceive of it is false and not merely unestablished.

10 Externalist Backlash

The two chapters that follow this one survey two varieties of naturalist metaethical theory in much the fashion the five previous chapters examined error theoretic, subjectivist, noncognitivist, and fictionalist theories. This chapter serves as a short lead up to the coming chapters on naturalism. It is narrower in focus than the chapters that surround it because it will not present a full metaethical theory. Rather it gives a brief overview of influential arguments against morals/motives and morals/reasons internalism. I proceed in this fashion in order to place the theories of the next two chapters in an appropriate context. One important variety of scientific naturalism is externalist, and it will be the subject of the next chapter. But externalist realism precedes that variety of naturalism. Philippa Foot already defended externalist realism beginning in the 1950s, when noncognitivist theories held sway. Her papers pose powerful challenges to internalism and to antirealist views rooted in internalism. It is thus helpful to see the externalist arguments of later scientific realists such as David Brink as developments of ideas already there in Foot's work. It is also helpful to contrast Foot's realism, which did not extend to offering an analysis or account of moral properties, with those of subsequent naturalists who do propose theories of a more committal sort. The popularity of Moore's Open Question Argument may have been part of the explanation. Even today some philosophers remain eager to accuse those who offer analyses of committing the "naturalistic fallacy." It took important work in philosophy of language and mind to make room for substantive accounts of moral properties.

The standard story about ethics and metaethics from the 1930s to 1960s has it that most ethical philosophy was metaethics and that metaethics was dominated by noncognitivist views such as Ayer and Stevenson's emotivism and Hare's universal prescriptivism. I'm not old enough to vouch for the accuracy of that story. I rather suspect that different views were dominant in different places. Judith Jarvis Thomson tells me that graduate students at Columbia University in the 1950s and 1960s paid Hare and noncognitivism in general little mind. She certainly would know. So we should be careful not to overemphasize the extent to which noncognitivism dominated ethics and metaethics during this period. Noncognitivism was, in any case, one of the leading views and many of those who dissented from it still thought that naturalism about moral properties had been rendered implausible by the Open Question Argument. Many philosophers thought that no noncircular descriptive conditions could be put on the appropriate use of moral predicates, and this in part explained the popularity of noncognitivism.

10.1. Philippa Foot's Challenges to Noncognitivism and Internalism

Working mostly at Oxford in the 1950s and 1960s, where Hare and Ayer also taught, Philippa Foot made it her work to question this prevailing idea. This in turn led her to challenge internalism of various sorts and to argue that there might be perfectly ordinary descriptive constraints on the appropriate use of moral terms. While she never really seemed to be a *reductive* or *scientific* naturalist, she opened up the possibility of a version of moral cognitivism that was neither nonnaturalist nor subjectivist. She hoped to show that the extension of properties such as goodness and rightness was constrained and was not up to the arbitrary whim of the speaker.[1] In this moral properties were not so different from other familiar properties. Her related arguments against internalism were taken up by later naturalists, including the "Cornell Realists" who constructed metaethical theories inspired by science and skeptical of subjectivism. They extended her ideas even while taking them in a more scientistic direction. This makes Foot's work of the late 1950s into the 1970s a good starting point for understanding subsequent naturalistic realist theories.

One strand in Foot's work argued against the idea that there are motivational constraints on the appropriate use of moral language but not descriptive constraints on such use. The target view seemed to be one that might fall very naturally out of noncognitivism: Using a moral term when not in the appropriate noncognitive state of mind is a misuse of language, whereas applying the relevant moral term ('good,' 'bad,' 'right,' 'wrong,' 'ought,' etc.) to any object of the right category (states of affairs and other objects for 'good' and 'bad'; actions or act-types for 'right,' 'wrong,' and 'ought') does not manifest any lack of competence with the relevant expressions and the thoughts they express. Against these ideas, Foot marshaled arguments to the contrary. She argued that, absent special background conditions, we would not know what someone meant if they argued that (for example) clasping and unclasping one's hands was morally good or right. The qualification about background conditions was necessary to rule out cases where background conditions made clasping and unclasping one's hands a way of doing something else intrinsically good or right, such as saving a life. She suggested that activities that could be thought of as morally good or right should have some at least arguable connection with recognizable human goods and bads. If an action could not have an impact on anyone's well-being, or well-functioning, it is very hard to make sense of the idea that it has moral value or disvalue (Foot, 1958a, 1958b, 1961).

The specific descriptive background conditions Foot suggested are of a sort that might be used to explain the plausibility of internalism without vindicating it. For, as a matter of arguably contingent fact, people do care a good bit about their own well-being and the well-being of others. This makes it no surprise that people are reliably motivated to favor properties with important connections to well-being and human good. If it turns out that moral concepts are such as to ensure a connection between moral rightness and such goods and between moral wrongness and various bads, we would be in a position to explain why people are regularly motivated to favor what is right and disfavor what is wrong. All of this could be true without that result being necessary. For the underlying desires that ground the regularity will still be contingent.

Foot followed up on these arguments with her influential paper "Morality as a System of Hypothetical Imperatives" (1972). In it she set her sights on the morals/reasons existence internalist (and Kantian) idea that correct moral judgements must favor actions that everyone suitably situated would have reason to do, no matter what their current desires or attitudes. The paper is, I think, best read as a challenge to such internalism, rather than as a direct argument against it. Foot highlights etiquette as a system of practical rules, imperatives, or principles that are meant to be action-guiding. These rules are "grammatically" categorical[2]—we don't withdraw judgements of etiquette upon learning that the person of whose actions we speak doesn't care a bit about the possibly arbitrary rules of polite society. They are thus categorical in the sense that their appropriate deployment is entirely independent of facts about the motivational states of the agent of whom they are predicated. One is violating etiquette when one replies in the first person to an invitation written in the third person, even when one just doesn't care about these rules and wants to signify one's sincere delight by saying, "I'd love to." One has not done the polite thing, even if one was responding sincerely and perhaps even kindly. The rules of etiquette are conventional and laid out in books by Emily Post (1960) and others; they don't change with our current interests, even if they might change over time because of our interests.

For all that, and perhaps because of that, etiquette is not categorical in Kant's favored sense. It does not provide interest or desire-independent reasons to those whose conduct it assesses. A person who violates etiquette may have no reason to comply with its dictates. That person might have noticed that some of etiquette's arcane rules divide society into the polite and the not so polite in such a way as to reinforce class distinctions. Perhaps they therefore conclude they should flout its dictums wherever possible, as an act of righteous rebellion. Perhaps instead the person flouting the relevant rule is merely in a bad mood and just wants to offend. The demands of etiquette don't yield to such challenges, but one's reasons to act "properly" may. So it plausibly is with etiquette.[3] And Foot then uses this to challenge morals/reasons internalists: Why can't it be this way with morality as well?

As Foot saw it, the move from "grammatical" categoricity to Kantian reason-requiring categoricity is a conflation. We move from a fact about the appropriate use of a term to an alleged fact about rationality and moral psychology. But that is a mistake. The two propositions are distinct. One is about language and the other about the extension of a property relative to the extension of another. And it is hard to see how the rules about using a word could make it the case that people must have reason to do those things to which the word applies. Foot didn't only think that the inference was mistaken. She also thought that the conclusion was positively false. Morality doesn't give anyone and everyone a reason to do as it demands. The reasons that most of us have to do what morality requires have to do with our contingent motivations and motivational dispositions, and not with a categorical reason-giving power vested in morality itself.

Recall that Humean conceptions of reasons require roughly that reasons for acting must be based on desires for goals toward which one is already favorably disposed. On standard versions of the view beliefs and desires are distinct existences, so that the desire for the relevant goal is distinct from any belief about the goal, including the belief that it is good or desirable. Foot's argument is very much in this standard vein:

> . . . it is supposed that moral considerations necessarily give reasons for acting to any man. The difficulty is, of course, to defend this proposition which is more often repeated than explained. . . . [W]e must be told what it is that makes the moral 'should' relevantly different from the 'shoulds' appearing in normative statements of other kinds. Attempts have sometimes been made to show that some kind of irrationality is involved in ignoring the 'should' of morality: in saying 'Immoral—so what?' as one says 'Not *comme il faut*—so what?' But as far as I can see these have all rested on some illegitimate assumption . . . The fact that the man who rejects morality because he sees no reason to obey its rules can be convicted of villainy but not of inconsistency. Nor will the action necessarily be irrational. Irrational actions are those in which a man in some way defeats his own purposes, doing what is calculated to be disadvantageous or to frustrate his ends. Immorality does not *necessarily* involve any such thing. (Foot, 1972, pp. 161–162)

If we take reasons to be the kinds of things that make actions counter to them irrational, there is no necessity that morality and reason line up on the same side. Reasons for action are all hypothetical, depending on the agent's ends given by their own desires and goals. And thus no fact can offer categorical reasons in the Kantian sense.

It can be useful to think of Foot's challenge here as a response to Mackie's queerness argument. Foot and Mackie agree that it would be a queer thing if a fact of a certain sort could be necessarily reason-giving to anyone, no matter what their antecedent desires or interests. Mackie thinks that moral facts must be like that, and concludes that therefore there can be no moral facts. Foot's thinks that this is a mistake. We should instead give up on the thought that moral requirements must have this sort of connection with reasons. And her argument suggests a diagnosis of Mackie's error. He mistakes morality's "grammatical categoricity" for its offering genuinely categorical reasons. It is, Foot thinks, in some sense built into the meaning of moral claims that they are categorical in the sense that we don't withdraw such claims in the face of evidence that an agent is unmoved or otherwise has no reason to comply. That is what "grammatical categoricity" comes to. But it is not built into the meanings of moral claims that they must offer such people Kantian categorical reasons. Because Mackie mistakes the former for the latter he finds himself forced to deny the truth of moral claims. Or so Foot would suggest.

Foot's arguments on these matters all point in the direction of a cognitivist conception of moral judgements and a representational semantics for moral terms. But even while highlighting some descriptive constraints on intelligible moral judgements, she did not go on to propose any specific analysis of their content. This likely reflected Foot's suspicion of analyses and reductive projects, but it also likely reflected something general about the state of play in philosophy prior to the semantic innovations of the 1970s.

10.2. The Paradox of Analysis and the Open Question Argument

Moore's Open Question Argument exploits the fact that competent speakers can doubt any informative identity statement involving moral terms. In various asides throughout the book I have suggested that the argument proves too much. Competent speakers seem able to doubt any identity using different terms to define or describe the nature of the object or property under discussion. Even the simple claim that vixens are female foxes can be put under pressure by the realization that there are female fox kits that we aren't all that quick to identify as vixens.

By the mid-twentieth century philosophers were well aware of the *Paradox of Analysis*, which is itself closely related to the Open Question Argument. The "paradox" is this: Philosophers offer their analyses of various problematic ideas or words as an account of their content and meaning. Yet these analyses are usually surprising and controversial. How can that be if the analysis is just supposed to tell us what we already know when we understand what our words mean? This puzzle struck many as a paradox. Moore's Open Question Argument limited itself to moral terms, but seems to be an instance of the general phenomenon. What the paradox points out is that competent users of any term can just as easily doubt every interesting analysis of that term. So if there is a problem with 'good' and goodness, there is a parallel problem for the other terms and concepts philosophers hope to analyze. Once that idea sank in, it may have seemed a bit risky to keep analyzing troublesome philosophical concepts. This may partly explain Foot's caution about offering analyses herself. One can be a lot more confident about having identified a constitutive truth about the nature of an object or property than one might be about having constructed a fully adequate analysis of the same target.

The next two chapters suggest that a confident return to the project of informatively specifying the nature of moral properties required an explanation of the paradox of analysis and a diagnosis of where the Open Question goes wrong. And those two chapters explore two different naturalist strategies for developing such specifications in light of different explanations of the paradox, as well as competing diagnoses of the Open Question Argument. One of the strategies is most single-mindedly developed by a group of philosophers known as the Cornell Realists. These philosophers are best known for pursuing a naturalistic and externalist account of moral properties. We'll spend a whole chapter exploring their views about moral properties and how we come to refer to them. But first I want to spend some time in this chapter examining their arguments for externalism, as these are direct extensions of the work undertaken by Philippa Foot.

10.3. David Brink's Externalist Arguments

We have already briefly encountered David Brink's chief argument in favor of externalism in section 4.2 on the practicality of morality. It works by positing a figure who he calls "the amoralist" who is stipulated to be someone who sincerely assents to a moral judgement to the effect that some act-type is morally required, but who feels not the least bit of motivation to perform it. If such figures are possible, indefeasible morals/motives judgement internalism is refuted. And if such a figure is not irrational, one of the most popular versions of defeasible morals/motives judgement internalism is also refuted. Defeasible internalism of the relevant sort holds that people must be moved by the moral judgements they accept *unless they are irrational* (Korsgaard, 1986; Smith, 1994).

So far then we have an argument against two varieties of morals/motives judgement internalism. But, as Brink argues, the claim that the amoralist is not irrational also undercuts an attractive variety of morals/reasons existence internalism (Brink, 1989, 57ff.). The underlying thought is that reasons are things that make things rational. If you have a reason to get up tomorrow morning and no reason not to then it is more rational for you to get up than not. And if, having a good reason to get up, you for no reason decide to stay in bed, you are acting irrationally. So similarly, if an amoralist believes that it is morally required to give money to Oxfam[4] or similar groups, and yet does not give to any such organization despite having no compelling reason not to, there seem to be two options. It must either be irrational not to donate, or thinking that it was morally required supplied the amoralist with no good reason to donate. Brink claims that it is not irrational for the amoralist not to give the money. So that leaves the other alternative; believing that donating to Oxfam is morally required gives us no reason to donate to Oxfam.

There is some slop in this form of argument, at least as an argument for existence internalism, because it leaves room for our belief to be false. Perhaps giving to Oxfam is not morally required, even though we believe that it is. In that case, we have not falsified existence internalism because morals/reasons existence internalism connects true moral claims with reasons. But that gap seems relatively easy to close. As I write, thousands of people are dying of Ebola in countries where Oxfam is providing essential support. Furthermore, in many other places, thousands of others are being kept from a deeper poverty and acute threats of food insecurity through the efforts of Oxfam and similar organizations. Some of the threats to their security are caused by policies that we are responsible for (O'Neill, 1975). It sure seems as though we have an obligation to give to Oxfam or similar groups on most plausible theories of what morality requires.

There is also another bit of wiggle room for the morals/reasons existence internalist. Such an internalist could think it necessary that a person who has an obligation to φ also has sufficient reason to φ, but not think that rational agents must *know* this. Not all necessary claims are knowable *a priori* and this internalist thesis might be one that's not. In that case, someone who rightly came to believe she had a moral obligation to φ would not necessarily thereby learn she had a reason to φ. Brink, in effect, admits the point, but stipulates that internalism as he understands it must be a conceptual truth and knowable *a priori* (Brink, 1989, p. 62). Thus, according to the morals/reasons existence internalist he has in mind, it must be *a priori* knowable based on mastery of the concept of moral obligation that true judgements of obligation entail sufficient reasons to act. If, as Brink maintains, a rational person could coherently believe herself to be obligated and yet remain unmoved it would present a counter-example to the thesis. For such a person would immediately understand herself to have sufficient reason to act (in virtue of her competence with the concept of obligation). But then the assumption of rationality would require her to act on those reasons.

Internalists, of course, will want to question one or another premise in the argument. One response to the argument is to question whether we are right to think that the amoralists we are imagining are really possible. Perhaps we can't both sincerely accept a moral obligation and be genuinely unmoved, absent irrationality. Perhaps we only think it is possible because what we imagine is really something different than what we take it to be. Our brief discussion of amoralism in chapter 4 pointed out that internalists may think amoralists don't really believe that the actions in question are morally required. They may argue that amoralists accept the relevant moral judgements only in an "inverted commas sense." Rather than believing that the action is required they may only believe that they are "morally required," where the quotation marks indicate a certain distance from the judgements they are alleged to believe. Perhaps what they believe is that these actions are what people generally call "morally required." And we may mistake that thought for the genuine moral belief that the action is morally required.

Here, I think, Brink's efforts to point to believable amoralists from fiction strengthens the argument and makes the premises more plausible. If like Thrasymachus one thinks that morality is a scam foisted on the weaker by the stronger in order to make the weaker easier to control while serving the interests of the stronger, it really would make sense to think that moral rightness or requirement offers no reason to do what is right or what is required. And it really does seem possible to think this without thinking that conventional morality fails to track moral rightness or moral requirement.

There is much more to say on both sides of this debate. Some of what internalists would want to say was briefly rehearsed in chapter 4. And there is more to say on behalf of the externalist as well. I myself think that these issues are at the heart of much metaethical theorizing. That is in effect what I argued in chapter 4. Many philosophers line up on one side or the other of the debate over internalism and also over the Humean Theory of Reasons. So I think it is fair to say that the issues are still alive and that there is more work to be done. That's one of the reasons metaethics is worth our time. There's still much to figure out and important issues turn on it.

The point with which I want to conclude is simply that externalism, if true, opens up the range of properties that would be candidates for a reduction of moral properties to natural properties. If the properties that are candidates for the referent of terms like 'right,' 'wrong,' 'morally obligated,' and so on need not be properties that necessarily move rational agents, there will be a longer list of viable properties to which these properties can be reduced. Brink and the other naturalists who took up Foot's defense of externalism did so partly for this reason.

Questions

Comprehension

C1. Distinguish the two notions of categoricity that Foot thinks her opponents conflate.

C2. Explain why a rule of etiquette such as the one requiring that we respond to invitations written in the third person with a reply also in the third person are not necessarily reason-giving. Are they necessarily motivating? Why or why not? Would this be an argument for or against etiquette/motives internalism?

> *Extension*
>
> E1. Do you agree with Brink that people who make sincere moral judgements and yet are not moved to do what those judgements recommend are a genuine possibility? Do you think they are rational when they do so?
>
> E2. Often what's rational for people to believe depends on what they know about the things they have beliefs about. How does this fact affect debates about the rationality of amoralists?

Reading

Read along with: Philippa Foot (1972).

Further reading: Foot's papers developing her externalist views can be found in Foot (2002). It includes a reprinting of Foot (1972), in which she distances herself from her earlier Humean conception of reasons and thus distances herself from her position in that paper. David Brink (1986) contains his amoralist example. His book Brink (1989) rehearses his arguments for externalism in more detail and then develops a variety of the Cornell Realism that is the subject of the next chapter. Sigrún Svavarsdottir's (1999) paper develops the externalist side of the internalism-externalism debate in response to especially Michael Smith's (1994, 1995a, 1996) development of defeasible internalist theses. Nomy Arpaly (2000) also addresses Smith's view at length. Her discussion of Huck Finn (2003) offers us another realistic example of a possible amoralist. Van Roojen (2010) defends a morals/reasons internalist treatment of such cases.

The issues in this chapter are at least partly empirical. Adina Roskies (2003) looks at the data about sociopathy and argues for its relevance. Karen Jones (2006) suggests that one has to be careful about how one interprets empirical evidence. And Jeanette Kennett (2006) argues that the empirical evidence from psychopathy does not undermine rationalism. A good overview of much relevant empirical work is to be found in sections II and III of Valerie Tiberius's (2014) book on moral psychology.

Notes

1 Not that Hare would have disagreed about that.

2 Foot used this term in an unusual way, perhaps due to the influence of Wittgenstein. Think of grammar in this usage as supplying rules of correct speech that go beyond ordinary grammatical issues, the violation of which shows some lack of appropriate competence with the term.

3 If you don't think this is so of etiquette, Foot's discussion of arbitrary club rules such as, "Ladies must not be allowed in the smoking room," provides another convincing example.

4 A famine relief organization founded at Oxford. Philippa Foot was an early member and long served as a trustee. The group has grown to the point it now provides hundreds of millions of dollars in aid each year.

11 Scientific Naturalism I

Cornell Realism

'*Naturalism*' in metaethics is the view that moral properties are natural properties. Or, we might say, it is the view that there are no *nonnatural* properties.[1] Neither definition is very informative until we know what natural properties are or what the difference between natural and nonnatural properties is. G. E. Moore might have said that the natural properties were the nonmoral properties or at least the nonmoral nonsupernatural properties. But naturalists who think that moral properties are natural properties cannot agree with that definition. So we need some more informative way of dividing things up. One way might be to make a list of moral or normative terms, such as 'right,' 'good,' 'wrong,' 'rational,' 'forbidden,' and so on. Then we could say the natural properties are those we can talk about without using terms from the list (Jackson and Pettit, 1996). But there are tricks for talking about any property you like using a restricted vocabulary. For example, we could still talk about the property goodness by talking about Moore's favorite property. So we need a better handle on the natural.

I don't know any way to define the natural in a neutral way that captures what everyone who uses the term 'natural' is trying to get at. But I can gesture at one way of making a distinction that may be close enough to capture what most of the people in this chapter are after. An important kind of naturalism aims to assimilate moral properties to the properties studied by the natural sciences. Or to put it another way, this kind of naturalism is committed to the idea that the methods of the empirical sciences broadly conceived are adequate for understanding all of reality. The theories that I want to explore in this chapter and the next pursue that strategy by reducing moral properties to properties of the same sort as those scientific properties. When people use the term 'reductive naturalism' they are often getting at the same idea, but some people who I want to include here renounce that label. That renunciation has to do with disagreement about what a philosophical reduction involves. Some of the target theories *identify* moral properties with properties studied by these sciences or with complexes created out of those properties. Others suggest that moral properties are *constituted by* scientifically respectable base properties in much the way that biological properties might be constituted by physical properties, or economic properties by social, psychological, and physical properties, or psychological properties by biological and physical properties. Both of these relations between properties have often been called "reductions" but not everyone agrees on what reduction requires.

We need a new label, so I've chosen '*scientific naturalism*' as my name for the views I want to discuss in this chapter. These views accept all of the tenets of minimal realism set out in chapter 2, but they go somewhat further. They share the additional idea that moral terms and moral thoughts predicate properties that are in important ways just like the properties that are studied by perfectly familiar scientific enterprises, such as sociology, psychology, biology, neuroscience, and physics. Commitment to that idea comes along with the thought that we can have empirical access to the nature of these properties. And this allows many proponents to claim that the view is *methodologically* naturalistic as well as *metaphysically* naturalistic. The majority of theorists covered in this chapter and the next regard morality and natural science as largely continuous in subject matter and in methodology. So 'scientific naturalism' it is.

Examples of the view are not unfamiliar. We have already encountered versions of scientific naturalism in the guise of subjectivist theories that identify moral properties with psychological properties. If the rightness of an action just is its being what I'm disposed to desire under certain specifiable circumstances, that rightness will be a complex psychological disposition. We will have the same sort of epistemic access to facts about morality as we have to facts about such dispositions, and that access is largely empirical. So this kind of subjectivism assimilates moral matters to psychological and therefore empirically discoverable scientific matters. The subjectivist views we looked at all involved some relativity to the creatures whose psychological dispositions were incorporated into the analysis. And perhaps that will be a feature of most plausible versions of scientific realism about ethics. Still, as we'll see, most of the theorists who I discuss in this chapter minimize the effects of that relativity on the correctness of a given moral verdict. They tend not to be relativists of the sort who emphasize that two fully conflicting moral judgements can both be true. And they largely want to buffer the effects of a speaker or agent's actual desires on the truth or falsity of a moral claim made by or about such speakers or agents.

11.1. Cornell Realism

Starting in the 1980s a group of philosophers in the US took up the project of assimilating moral epistemology and moral metaphysics to the epistemology and metaphysics of the sciences. They also tried to infuse the resulting account with an updated conception of scientific kinds, the meanings of scientific words, and of scientific epistemology. These theorists were dubbed "*Cornell Realists*" because most of them had some connection to Cornell University, either as graduate students or as professors. Richard Boyd, David

Brink, and Nick Sturgeon are paradigm Cornell Realists, and Peter Railton's ideas make him a comfortable fit in this group.[2] These theorists share a perspective that makes it easy and useful to think of them as kindred spirits.

11.2.   Cornell Realism and Causal Moral Semantics

In section 10.2 I noted that Philippa Foot didn't herself offer a full analysis of rightness even while she was defending externalism.[3] I suggested that the paradox of analysis and certain examples put philosophers in a position to see that the Open Question Argument did not refute naturalism. But there remained an uneasiness about philosophical analysis. It may be that a general diagnosis of the flaw or flaws in the Open Question Argument was required before ethicists would once again confidently propose descriptive analyses of moral terms. An explanation of why the paradox of analysis is no bar to offering interesting and even surprising accounts of the nature of the subject matter would allow philosophers to more confidently propose descriptive analyses of moral terms. The naturalists of this chapter and the next each developed such diagnoses.

For Cornell Realists the diagnosis became possible upon the development of a new way of thinking about linguistic reference, one that was not mediated by a descriptive sense that must be satisfied for a term to pick out it's referent.[4] And that theory of unmediated reference was soon extended beyond language to thought content as well. Working in the 1960s to 1970s, Ruth Marcus (1963), Saul Kripke (1972), Hilary Putnam (1975), David Kaplan (1979), Ruth Millikan (1984), and Richard Boyd (1988) developed so-called *direct reference* theories, according to which terms contributed the items for which they stood directly to the contents of the sentences and thought they expressed. The "directly" here is meant to contrast with the indirect way the referent of a term is contributed to content according to standard Fregean theories, where the referent has to satisfy a descriptive sense, one which is according to these theories also part of the meaning they contribute. By the 1980s Cornell Realists had taken up these ideas as they worked to assimilate moral epistemology and moral metaphysics to the epistemology and metaphysics of the sciences.

Of special interest to us, given worries about the Open Question Argument and the Paradox of Analysis, are the semantic theories these realists proposed for moral terms. Richard Boyd's adaptation of direct reference theory allowed naturalists to claim a natural referent for moral terms, even while speakers lacked knowledge of the essential nature of that referent. The adaptation drew on work by Marcus, Putnam, Kripke, Kaplan, Millikan, and Boyd's own work in the philosophy of science. And direct reference theory itself harkens back to John Stuart Mill's view that the referent of a term *just was* the meaning of the term that named it. The obvious next question for proponents of such views concerns how a term comes to have the referent that it does. The various direct reference theorists mentioned above each provided various different but related proposals in answer to that question. Boyd's work in metaethics extended the theory of reference determination he had already proposed for scientific terms. To explain it I'll proceed by rehearsing a direct reference account of names, contrasting it with a simple Fregean account of the same. From there I will extend the theory to natural kind terms, including property terms. Finally I will explain how Boyd adapted the idea to ethics, offering a realist and directly referential semantics for moral terms.[5]

The big direct reference idea is that some terms refer to what they refer to *directly*, unmediated by anything else represented as part of the sentence or thought content. This is supposed to rule out a Fregean story according to which the meaning of a term includes a descriptive sense. According to orthodox Fregeans, the referent of a term gets to be the referent by satisfying the description provided by the sense. Direct reference theorists do without senses in constructing their theories of meaning. The simplest direct reference theory is offered as an account of ordinary proper names. The basic idea is that names are just labels or tags that contribute the person they name to the content of sentences or thoughts in which they appear. They do this directly without any help from a descriptive sense. This content is all that they contribute; any particular way of picking out the person is not part of the contributed content. Let me give an example of how names work according to this theory. Suppose you say or think "Hasheem Thabeet is fluent in French and Swahili." In doing so you may think of Hasheem Thabeet as the tallest active professional basketball player, but that isn't any part of the proposition expressed by 'Hasheem Thabeet is fluent in French and Swahili,' nor is it part of the content of the thought you would most naturally express using that sentence. The sentence just says, of a particular person (Hasheem Thabeet), that he is fluent in French and Swahili. Neither the sentence or the thought have anything about basketball or height as their content. These would be further thoughts expressed by different sentences.

Direct reference theories of names contrast with Fregean theories that postulate senses even for names. According to such theories the referent of a name is the object that satisfies some mediating description, often one that the speaker or most speakers use to think of the referent of the name. On one way of developing the idea, the sense of the name would be part of the proposition expressed by sentences employing the name and part of the contents of the thought expressed with sentences that use it. Our sentence about Hasheem Thabeet's fluency would then really be saying something like: the tallest currently active professional basketball player is fluent in French and Swahili. Or, more carefully, it would say: There is exactly one tallest active professional basketball player and she or he is fluent in French or Swahili. You can see this way of thinking of names is different than that proposed by the direct reference theory. The original sentence about Thabeet would (as direct reference theories interpret it) be true even were he to have retired long ago, or never played basketball, or been only 5 feet tall. But the Fregean translations that put senses into the contents of the sentences would not be true under those conditions. This is a point in favor of the direct reference (or Millian) theory of proper names, and one reason why even those who favor Fregean accounts of predicates often prefer to agree with direct reference theorists about names.

A complete account of names and referring expressions has to tell us not only what they stand for, but also how it is that they stand for what they do. That is what a *philosophical* or *metasemantic theory of referring* provides.[6] Standard Fregeans have a theory of this sort ready to hand in their two-part theory of meaning. They say the referent of a term just is the thing that satisfies the description offered by the sense of that term. And these together, the sense and the referent, constitute the meaning of that term as Fregeans see it. Non-Fregean direct reference theorists need to construct a theory of referring without invoking anything like a sense as part of the explanations, for fear of undercutting their idea that names are just tags. That story will make it the case that the meaning is the referent, but that story itself won't be part of the meaning of the term. It is metasemantic not semantic. The name is the semantic value of the term. The story is an account of how it gets that semantic value. The simplest such stories for names involve some event in the past where the name gets associated with a particular person. It might be a baptism or explicit dubbing but it may be something less formal. From there the use of the name to pick out that person gets passed down from one person to another through chains of overlapping use. Thabeet's parents give him the full name "Hasheem Thabeet." Another person picks up the name from the person who first uses it to refer to the subject, intending to use it in the same way. Another gets it from her, and so on. And on it goes until I pick it up from a use of the name on the internet. Each such use is causally connected to the previous ones stretching back in time to the first use. At the end of the chain I can use the name 'Hasheem Thabeet' to refer to the very same person as those who bestowed the name and yet know nothing about how they were thinking of little Hasheem at the time. And if I say, "Hasheem Thabeet is tall," it will be true just in case the person baptized with that name at the other end of the causal chain leading to my utterance is tall. This will be so even if I associate different or even false information with the referent of that name. Thabeet's parents probably didn't think of him as a basketball player when they named him. And I may falsely think he's from France. But as long as my use of his name is connected in the appropriate way to its original use to name Thabeet way back when, my use refers to Hasheem Thabeet.

This is a very natural way to think of names. It is perhaps less natural when extended to kind and property terms. Still there are direct reference theories of kind and property terms, including moral property terms like 'right,' 'wrong,' 'good,' 'evil,' and so on. Like the direct reference account of names, direct reference theories of kind and property terms hold that these terms refer directly, unmediated by a descriptive sense that must be satisfied in order for the term to pick out its target. On such theories, sentences or thoughts deploying a kind or property term contribute only the kind or property itself to the meanings and truth conditions of the sentences of which they are components and the thoughts that those sentences express. This means that they are treated semantically almost like names as the direct reference theory depicts them. Just as 'Hasheem Thabeet' contributed only Thabeet, the person himself, to the content of sentences using the name, 'right' contributes only rightness *the property* to sentences in which that term is used. To be sure, a particular speaker may think of rightness in a particular way, just as you or I may think of Thabeet in a particular way. But that way of thinking doesn't enter into *the content* of the sentence used, nor into *the content* of the thought that it directly expresses. The thought expressed by 'It is right to complain' directly predicates rightness of the act-type of complaining. Its content just is a proposition relating a property and an act-type. Ways of thinking of the kind or property do not enter in, either as part of the content, or as a set of conditions that must be met for the sentences or thoughts to have their contents.

Just as with names, direct reference theorists about kind and property terms owe an account of how these terms come to refer to the kinds and properties they pick out. And here the theory of reference can be parallel to the one they offer for names. We have some initial event or set of events in which a particular property comes to be associated with a particular term used to pick it out. This way of using the term gets passed down over time, with one person getting it from another intending to use it in the same way. My use of 'The car is red' predicates redness of the car in virtue of the existence of a causal chain of the right sort leading back to some initial use of 'red' to pick out a color property. It is easy enough to see now how the account might treat moral predicates. Predicates like 'right,' 'wrong,' 'good,' and so on are tags for properties that they contribute directly to the propositions expressed by sentences in which those terms occur. And the explanation of how they come to contribute those predicates is parallel to that for other predicates. There is some initial use of the term to pick out the relevant property that is then passed down through a chain of overlapping use. My use of 'is right' (for example) predicates rightness of the objects to which I apply the term because there is a causal chain of the correct sort leading back to some initial use of that term to pick out that property. And similarly for other moral predicates.

There is some additional complication to the account when we move from names to predicates. It is relatively easy to see how a word might first be used as a tag for a concrete object with which we are directly acquainted. So the simple dubbing or baptism story for names is not too implausible for many names, and where it isn't quite right we can see how something in the neighborhood of those simple stories might be available to ground the original use of the name. With many property terms and especially scientific property terms, things are not as simple. We causally interact with instances of a property in a particular time and place and this might be a kind of complex causal relation with the property itself. But at any given time and place we are causally interacting with a number of different but overlapping property instances. When I interact with an instance of blue I am also interacting with an instance of some particular shade of blue. How is it that the term 'blue' comes to stand for the more general kind rather than the more specific shade? It is in their somewhat different answers to this kind of question that different direct reference theorists distinguish their views from one another. Some employ speaker intentions, others follow Millikan in adopting a kind of natural selection story to narrow the referent down to a property the representation of which was selected for. There are several other ideas in play besides these and some of them can be combined. My main point is just that when we go from direct reference accounts of names to similar accounts for properties, we introduce complications into the reference determination account partly because of the nature of the difference between ordinary individuals like people or buildings and universals such as kinds and properties.

The most worked-out account of reference determination within the metaethics literature is the aforementioned theory of Richard Boyd. Working in the philosophy of science, Boyd proposed a *causal regulation* account of reference determination for natural kind terms. On this sort of account, a term refers to the property that causally explains how beliefs expressed using that term come to be more nearly true over time when construed as picking out that very property:

> *Roughly*, and for nondegenerate cases, a term *t* refers to a kind (property, relation, etc.) *k* just in case there exist causal mechanisms whose tendency is to bring it about, over time, that what is predicated of the term *t* will be approximately true of *k* (excuse the blurring of the use-mention distinction). Such mechanisms will typically include the existence of procedures which are approximately accurate for recognizing members or instances of *k* (at least for easy cases) and which relevantly govern the use of *t*, the social transmission of certain relevantly approximately true beliefs regarding *k*, formulated as claims about *t* (again excuse the slight to the use-mention distinction), a pattern of deference to experts on *k* with respect to the use of *t*, etc. . . . When relations of this sort obtain, we may think of the properties of *k* as regulating the use of *t* (via such causal relations), and we may think of what is said using *t* as providing us with socially coordinated *epistemic access* to *k*: *t* refers to *k* (in nondegenerate cases) just in case the socially coordinated use of *t* provides significant epistemic access to *k*, and not to other kinds (properties, etc.). (Boyd, 1988, p. 195)

This is a very complicated idea, and Boyd's entertaining writing style doesn't make it easier. The basic point is that properties are real things of which there are instances in the world with which we can interact, often in ways that are mediated by other things. If we're lucky we can wind up in a situation where our interaction with those properties gives us information about the property, information we might express using some predicate. If (1) we find out more about the property to which the term might refer as a result of the causal connection, and if (2) we revise our views purporting to be about that referent so that they are closer to true, and if (3) this is a regular process, the predicate used does in fact refer to the property that our beliefs come to more accurately represent. (There is some circularity in this way of putting it, though I think the circularity could be eliminated in a sentence too long to easily grasp.) This somewhat complicated story is introduced to explain how we can think and talk about properties that affect us in ways we only indirectly perceive. It allows us to have thoughts about gravity and momentum and radiation even when we aren't directly acquainted with those things. And it allows us to share those thoughts with earlier thinkers who had very different ideas about the referents of those terms. So long as we and they are in virtuous causal-epistemic feedback loops involving those properties, we can be talking about the same thing, and the words we deploy to express what we learn can mean the same thing. In this sense this theory is not what I have called "satisfactional" in the way Fregean theories are. The referent of a term need not *satisfy* some uniquely determining description understood by the speaker and codified in its sense. A speaker may even think that the referent of her term is essentially one kind of thing and not the kind of thing it in fact essentially is. For example, Dalton (a pioneering chemist) would have defined atoms as the smallest indivisible particles of stuff (Burge, 1986). But as we know, atoms can be divided. Boyd's account offers an explanation of why we nonetheless take him to be talking about what we are talking about when we talk of atoms. Both he and we are regulated by atoms so that our use of the term 'atom' is in an epistemically virtuous feedback loop with atoms, and that feedback loop is partly responsible for our having discovered that atoms are divisible.

It is worth noting that the postulated regulation seems to be social in nature. Any given individual's epistemic access to most kinds and properties will be mediated by the epistemic access of other members of her community. The process of correcting and expanding our beliefs expressed using a scientific kind term is a group project and when it works it is a social accomplishment. That much can be easily read off of the quote from Boyd. But it is also social in another way, if I understand Boyd correctly. The body of beliefs that become truer over time are those in common social currency. A given individual in a community might not come to know more about the referents of her terms. She may not pay attention to the relevant research while using the term with the same meaning as others in her community. She still counts as using that term with its ordinary meaning because she is related to others in her community who do improve their views in the appropriate way over time. Her use of the term is part of the network of use that makes feedback possible, even if she doesn't avail herself of it. So, as I understand Boyd's account, it is compatible with individual people not improving their views through causal feedback, as long as they are connected in the appropriate way with those who do.

Boyd's moral semantics take this account over from his work on scientific kinds. A given moral predicate refers to that natural property that regulates the beliefs we express using that predicate in such a way that our body of belief gets closer to the truth over time. As Boyd emphasizes, it is a contingent matter whether our terms do stand in that relation to a candidate for their referent. Some terms may not be so regulated, and when that's true those terms fail to refer. This seems to have been true with 'Vulcan,' a term introduced as the name of a planet that was thought to be needed to explain deviation in the orbits of other planets. If we are reasonably lucky, as Boyd believes we are, our use of 'good' and 'goodness' will be regulated in the appropriate way by a natural property that is instantiated at various places and times. That property will be the thing "tagged" by these words. It will be what they mean. It will be a constituent (along with unemployment insurance) in the proposition that makes, 'Unemployment insurance is good,' true. And so on. All this because it stands in the reference constituting relation to our use of these words.

11.2.1. Direct Reference and the Open Question Argument

An account like this is tailor-made to explain why there can be open questions about true identity statements even for the most competent speakers. Two terms can pick out the very same thing without a competent speaker of both having to know that they do. A person might know that groundhogs are a kind of marmot. And they might know that woodchucks are a kind of marmot. They might use 'groundhog' and 'woodchuck' to express these bits of knowledge. And yet they might not know that groundhogs are woodchucks.[7] Were we to ask such a person whether this rodent that they know to be a groundhog is a woodchuck, they might reply with, "I know it is a groundhog, but I don't know whether it is a woodchuck. That question is open for me." That they might say this shows us nothing about whether groundhogs and woodchucks are one and the same kind of creature. It shows us nothing about whether the property of being a groundhog is the same as the property of being a woodchuck. Direct reference theories like Boyd's offer an explanation of how this might be. A single speaker can be competent with two terms, each of which stands in the appropriate causal-epistemic feedback relation with the same referent. And that speaker can use terms standing in that kind of relation without knowing that the terms are related in that way to only one single kind of rodent. If the theory is right, the openness of the relevant question will not be probative with respect to the identity of woodchucks and groundhogs, nor will it be probative with respect to the meaning of 'woodchuck' and 'groundhog.' We can expand the moral a little further if we note that the same result falls out when only one of the two terms being identified is a directly referring expression. As long as the reference of one of the two terms is unmediated by any description the speaker has to know, that speaker can remain ignorant of the fact that their referents are one and the same thing.

Nothing changes when we switch from kind terms like 'woodchuck' and 'groundhog' to property terms like 'the property of being a woodchuck' and 'the property of being a groundhog.' Nor does it change when the properties get more complicated or the predicates less artificial, such as with 'is healthy' or 'is fit' or 'is wise and healthy.' At least nothing changes so long as these terms too get their referents in the way postulated by Boyd and other direct reference theorists. And all of this applies to moral predicates as well. If these predicates refer to whatever property stands in the appropriate regulation relation with use of the predicate by a community of speakers, they too might pick out a property that is also the referent of another term without speakers being in a position to tell that they are. Direct Reference theorists can thus reject the open question test as a test for sameness of meaning or for sameness of referent.

This is a happy result for scientific naturalists. The Open Question Argument won't block their claims that goodness, rightness, and so on are natural properties, even when that claim is made by identifying these properties with some property picked out in wholly nonmoral terms. Such a claim could be true without being deducible from the knowledge necessary for competent use of the relevant terms. The alleged openness of any question about the identity won't count against it.

11.2.2. Terminological and Metaphysical Interlude: Reductive Versus Nonreductive Naturalism

I want to come back to causal-epistemic regulation and its role in a naturalistic direct reference philosophical theory of reference. But we need to do a bit of metaphysics in order to set up that discussion, and the metaphysics is of interest in its own right. Several of the main Cornell Realists call themselves "nonreductive naturalists." This label contrasts with 'reductive naturalism.' But there are several possible contrasts a given person might be trying to highlight when using this label. 'Reduction' can mean a number of things in the mouths of philosophers. One such thing is identity. When we *identify* one thing with another we are really showing that they are one and the same thing and have thereby reduced the number of things we might have thought there are. If seemingly distinct things are really one and the same thing then (by Leibniz's law) the things that are identified with one another must share all of their features. If the Morning Star is to be identified with the Evening Star it must be one and the same thing as the Evening Star. And if so, everything that happens to the Morning Star must happen to the Evening Star. If the Morning Star has a certain temperature at a given time, then so must the Evening Star. Similarly also for properties.

If goodness just is pleasantness then everything true of goodness must be true of pleasantness. So, for example, every good thing must be pleasant, and increasing pleasure must increase goodness, and so on. Identity relations are symmetric. If goodness is pleasure then pleasure is goodness.

Sometimes people seem to think they have a reduction in hand when they can show one property necessarily supervenes on another. Supervenience is not symmetric. For example, the pictorial properties of a video screen supervene on the distribution of light on that screen. We could not change what was pictured without changing the illumination properties of the screen, and two screens that were alike with respect to their illumination properties would not differ in their pictorial properties. But we might be able to change the illumination properties without changing what's pictured. So the illumination properties do not supervene on the pictorial properties of video screens. The relationship is asymmetric. Still, any given set of properties supervenes on itself. So identity entails supervenience. And where we have an identity relation supervenience claims will go both ways. Identity entails supervenience, but not vice versa.

Constitution or *composition* relations are also asymmetric.[8] They hold when one thing is made up of a bunch of other things. If the soup is wholly constituted by or composed of vegetable broth, beans, and salt then it is entirely made up of vegetable broth, beans, and salt. Why would we want to say that the soup was constituted of vegetable broth, beans, and salt when we would not want to identify the soup with the broth, beans, and salt? Here might be one reason; we could have left out the salt and still had the soup. The soup would still exist had we failed to add salt, whereas the thing consisting of the broth, beans, and salt would not have existed if we had left out the salt. The two things mentioned, the soup and the collection of ingredients, have different existence conditions, so they don't share all of their properties. They have different existence and persistence conditions (on the assumption that salt is not essential to the soup).

Properties can be composed of or constituted by other properties. The property of being a sister is constituted by the properties of being a sibling and being female. When a property is wholly composed or constituted by a set of properties the distribution of that property supervenes on the distribution of properties of which it is composed or by which it is constituted. The relationship between constitution and identity is somewhat murkier than the relationship between identity and supervenience. While entities supervene on themselves, making it fine to say that being a man and being unmarried supervenes on bachelorhood, or vice versa, it is at least odd to claim that something is composed of or constituted by itself. And yet when we have a constitution relation there seem to be identities nearby. If the soup is constituted by broth, beans, and salt, the soup is the thing made of broth, beans, and salt. And vice versa.

Philosophers sometimes use the word 'reduction' to specify an identity relation and sometimes to refer to some sort of composition or constitution relation. Some even seem to use it for a supervenience relation, but I think they are best understood as using it for a composition or constitution relation that explains why supervenience holds. Still others use the term 'reduction' to pick out *a priori* knowable relations of these two sorts, identity or composition. A self-described "nonreductive naturalist" might be using 'reductive' in any of these senses. They might be denying that they take their position to have *a priori* status. Or they may be denying that we have any way of specifying in nonmoral terms the natural property that is identical with the moral property in question. Or they might be denying that they are identifying moral properties with nonmoral properties rather than postulating a constitution or composition relation.

Cornell Realists certainly do deny the first claim—that knowledge of identity or constitution relations in the moral realm are *a priori* accessible. As we've already seen they reject the picture of philosophical analysis on which philosophers find out about the nature of some interesting entity by reflection underwritten by the meanings of the terms they deploy. On one reading then, the point of calling oneself "nonreductive" would be semantic and methodological. It would not say anything immediately about the metaphysical nature of rightness, wrongness, and so on.

Still, a philosopher who calls herself a "nonreductive naturalist" for this reason is also committing herself to a metaphysical point about the nature of moral properties in virtue of calling herself a naturalist. Naturalists think that moral properties supervene on natural properties, in the sense that two possible actions can't differ in their rightness (for example) without also differing in their perfectly natural properties, at least in the world as it is.[9] This supervenience claim is already a metaphysical commitment; it tells you about the relations between two sets of properties. But it is one shared with many nonnaturalists who also think that moral properties supervene on natural properties. As noted earlier, supervenience relations are compatible with identifying properties at the supervening and subvening level. And supervenience relations are compatible with some stronger constitution, composition, or making relation holding between the sets of properties. That one makes either of these further claims beyond the supervenience claim would warrant calling oneself a naturalist. In the one case one would be a naturalist in virtue of identifying the moral with the natural; in the other one would be a naturalist in virtue of thinking that the moral is constituted by the natural.

Self-described nonreductive naturalists might, however, be trying to get at a *metaphysical* contrast when they use the label 'nonreductive.' They might be making the point that they are not *identifying* moral properties with any natural property constructed in this way. That is, they might think that the properties bear some looser relation to each other than identity, such as constitution or composition.

Some self-described nonreductive naturalists might mean something even stronger in their denial of reduction. They might think that there is no interesting relationship beyond supervenience on the natural that connects the moral properties with the natural properties. They would deny that any set of natural properties constitutes or composes moral properties, perhaps because of worries about possible but not actual supernatural worlds (van Roojen, 1996a; McPherson, 2013). Yet they might still think there is a point to calling themselves naturalists. That point would be that the relationship that holds between moral properties and the natural properties on which they supervene is just like the relationship between the economic, psychological, and biological properties and physical properties or even one another. It might turn out that we could not capture the extension of economic properties in physical terms without deploying infinite disjunctions of physical properties. The relations might be the same between psychological and physical properties or biological and physical properties. If you think infinitely disjunctive properties are not the stuff of genuine reductions you might want to be a nonreductive physicalist about these properties. You would think that economic, biological, and psychological properties were not identical to these disjunctive properties but that any instance of the one was constituted by one of the physical disjuncts. And yet you might consider yourself a naturalist just because there is nothing spooky going on at any level. If the psychological and the biological are natural and the relationship between the moral and the physical is just like the relationships between the psychological and the physical and the biological and the physical, why not call the position a form of naturalism? This seems to be part of Sturgeon's (2003) point when he notes that he thinks that the moral supervenes on the natural because the thinks moral properties are natural properties and that each property supervenes on itself.

Sturgeon's idea provides another way of characterizing the point of naturalism. The naturalist thinks that there is a set of properties that are similar to one another in some real respect. That respect is that they all count as natural and their being natural properties just comes to their sharing this similarity. Different naturalists may then go on to say more about the nature of the similarity in virtue of which they all count as natural. The previous discussion canvassed some of these proposals and there are others. Sturgeon himself suggests that being causally efficacious is what natural properties all share. But here I'm focusing on the abstract point that the natural properties are supposed to have something in common, whatever that turns out to be. In other words, naturalists think that the natural properties form a natural kind of properties, that is a kind all the instances of which share a real similarity with all the other properties in the kind. And they think that moral properties share this similarity and so are natural.

11.2.3.   Moral Kinds, Natural Kinds, and Reductive Strategies

Some philosophers, even of a naturalistic bent, think it inevitable that any specification of the morally right in terms of the natural sciences must be highly disjunctive. But it isn't obvious that it must be so. And if we have a nondisjunctive way of picking out a naturalism-friendly candidate for the referents of moral terms the prospects look better for reduction, whether in the form of an identity or constitution claim. How easy this would be to accomplish depends partly on the nature of the correct normative ethical theory. If consequentialism were correct it would greatly simplify providing a general reduction of all ethical properties. We could first define rightness as goodness-promotion or relative goodness-promotion. There are various ways to do this, but one way is just to say that an action is right if it is the action from amongst one's options that maximizes expected goodness, where expected goodness is a function of likelihood and value. This has the welcome result that we will be able to reduce rightness to a relatively simple relation involving one's options, probabilities and goodness. If we had a simple reduction of goodness as well we could have a noninfinite reduction of both properties. It is thus not all that surprising that many scientific realists are fans of consequentialism of one sort or another. It simplifies their work.

So what then are the prospects for getting a simple naturalistic account of goodness? Several theorists have toyed with reducing it to a quasi-biological property similar to healthiness or flourishing. I'll briefly sketch a couple of proposals. They are of interest both in their own right and as metaphysical proposals about the nature of goodness as a natural property. And having these proposals in mind will help when we return to epistemic issues and the theory of reference in sections that follow.

Once again, Boyd (1988) has the most worked-out story. He begins with the notion of a *homeostatic property cluster*. Sometimes a number of properties are instantiated together and sometimes they are commonly instantiated together, so that where you find some you are likely also to find the rest. There might, in turn, be an explanation of why these properties are often found together in a given environment. There might for example be causal relations between them such that several of them cause the rest. These causal relations might be intricately structured into positive feedback loops, so that once you have a certain number of the properties in the cluster they would interact to produce the rest. A simple model might be the presence of sea anemones and the presence of hermit crabs. Hermit crabs and anemones have a symbiotic relationship. Each does something that benefits the other, and each does things that increase the likelihood that the other will flourish. The crabs provide food for anemones that they allow to hitch rides on their backs. And the anemones help the crabs repel predators such as octopuses. Because of this relationship you are likely to find one where you find the other. And the two properties, there being an anemone nearby and there being a hermit crab nearby, tend to go together. They stand in a homeostatic relationship in which each promotes the presence of the other.

Boyd suggests that there can be more complex homeostatic property clusters and that the clusters themselves can be thought of as complex properties made up of the properties in the cluster. These properties can come in greater or lesser degrees depending on how many of the properties in the cluster are present and to what degree. Health is supposed to be an example. A healthy human is physically fit, well-nourished, concerned to provide for its own continued existence and fitness, active, intelligent, curious, social, and so on. Each of these traits helps preserve and even restore each of the others, at least in normal human conditions. Our social natures help us secure goods that nourish us and keep us mentally and physically fit, and these in turn help make us good company. Curiosity enables us to find out better ways to take care of ourselves. A somewhat more extended set of properties including health form a cluster of properties that is good for humans. And Boyd thinks that these properties stand in the same sort of homeostatic feedback relationship to one another as the various components in health. Presence of enough of the properties in the cluster fosters the rest. This cluster can be used to define moral goodness, so that actions, policies, and character traits can be considered good to the extent that they promote the instantiation of this cluster property (Boyd, 1988, p. 203).

It should be obvious how the view is continuous with Boyd's view of science. Boyd is offering a *real definition* of goodness. Real definitions are fixed nonconventionally, by the nature of the referent of our terms, whatever that nature turns out to be. Conventional definitions may help us get a fix on a referent, but such definitions do not determine the nature of the things to which we refer. We can get a fix on a referent via some accidental feature of the referent, one that isn't necessary to it. This feature may not be part of its nature. But Boyd thinks that there are genuine natures to be had where scientific properties are concerned. And he thinks that these natures are determined by the world, that is by the causal structure that makes it the case that certain features are instantiated together. These may or may not be transparent to us, and when they're not we may consider certain questions open even if in reality the nature of the referent determines an answer and closes the question. (Remember for example, that atoms have always been divisible, despite no one having known it for some time.) In Boyd's case it seems that he is making both a constitution and an identity claim, at least in rough outline. He thinks that goodness is composed of the various properties and relations in the homeostatic cluster. And he thinks that goodness is identical to the property that is composed by these properties when they are related to one another in the appropriate homeostatic way.

Peter Railton, another prominent Cornell Realist building on ideas of Richard Brandt's, suggests a strategy that is a kind of idealized subjectivism (Railton, 1986). We start with what a person wants for herself. These are her subjective interests. But these interests may be based on false information or misunderstanding of her situation, or perhaps a failure of imagination about what she wants. So we cleanse and supplement those desires by asking what she would want were she to be fully informed, to understand the situation well, and to fully exercise her imagination. If a present desire is based on false information it won't be relevant. And if new information would add some desire that she does not currently have, that will be relevant. What we're concerned about is what she would want herself to do in her actual circumstances if she were to think of herself in those circumstances from much more ideal conditions. We are asking a counterfactual question, often even about what she would want in circumstances she can't realistically expect to be in. But her desires in those unrealistic circumstances will *be about her actual circumstances*. The thought is that in ideal conditions she will care about what she would want to do and intend to do were she to be in less than ideal conditions. What she cares about in those circumstances will be her *"objectified subjective interests"* (Railton, 1986, pp. 173–174). And this agent's nonmoral good is identified by Railton with her objectified subjective interests.

From here Railton proposes to get to moral norms, such as norms constituting a kind of definition of moral rightness, in two big steps. First off he suggests that people have reasons to do what is in their individual objectified subjective interests. Thus we can evaluate actions in terms of how well they serve the agent's objectified subjective interests. And we can say that an agent is rational to do what best serves these interests. So we have a notion of individual rationality, one that requires a certain amount of trading off between individual objectified interests over time and the like, but one that we might imagine tracks what the agent would choose in ideal conditions. We can, Railton thinks, apply something like that notion to a different kind of problem, and that constitutes the second big step. The problem is that of weighing up the intrinsic interests of everyone in such a way that the interests of each count equally. And when we do that we are now concerned with social rationality. Outcomes will be morally good if they are socially rational. Actions, policies, and courses of action will be right if they are what it is socially rational to choose. Or, to say what is supposed to be the same thing, they are right when they promote the moral good (Railton, 1986, pp. 189–191).

There is an additional feature of Railton's account that is also taken over from Brandt. This feature is that he is offering his account as a *reforming definition* (Railton, 1986, p. 157; Brandt, 1979). Railton makes no claim to have captured the existing meanings of the terms he analyzes. Rather he proposes these as possible replacements for our current vocabulary. If we meant what he suggests by 'good' and 'right' we would be using terms that did all of the work worth doing now done by our moral terms with their actual meanings. This move is an analogue of the revolutionary fictionalist's proposal for what we should do when we find out that our existing terms don't quite capture reality. It is a proposal for the future, not an account of past usage. It isn't entirely clear when put to use in service of a realist proposal like the present one, that it must be incompatible with the causal semantics offered by Boyd. It could well be that all of the work worth doing now done by our moral terms is done because they are regulated by some complex property of the sort Railton suggests. If so, it might be that all along the term was regulated by that property, even if the term came to be associated with further commitments that speakers took themselves to express when they used moral terms. The proposal that we accept the reduction as a reforming definition might just come to a proposal that we get rid of those connotations that some speakers may have identified with the sense of the expressions, whether those really were senses of these terms or not. In any case, the idea of a reforming definition is a module. It need not be coupled with the rest of Railton's view about the referents of moral terms. And it can be coupled with any positive view about the meanings of moral terms as a proposal for the future.

The reductions of Boyd and Railton are but examples, one less subjective than the other, of the kinds of properties this sort of realist might specify as the referents of our moral terms. They both also illustrate a promising reductionist strategy for capturing all of the moral in a systematic way. They first define what is good and then define rightness in terms of goodness. This allows them to simplify their reductive tasks. As long as they can find a way to reduce the notion of goodness to naturalistically acceptable properties they can do the same for rightness. It might be possible to adopt a similar strategy working from a different base. It is an interesting question whether we could start with rightness and go from there to reduce goodness. Some subjectivism friendly realists have started instead with the idea of a reason and tried to work from there to notions of rightness, and so on (Schroeder, 2007).

11.3. Realist Moral Epistemology and Causal Efficacy

Both Boyd and Railton (1998) are at some pains to show that the properties to which they reduce goodness and rightness can be causally efficacious. They have several reasons to worry about this, some more pressing than others. Firstly, some metaphysicians are skeptical that there are genuine properties that are not causally efficacious (Kim, 1989). They think for reasons of simplicity that we should only accept properties necessary to explain our experience into a sane metaphysics. If one agrees with these theorists rightness, goodness, and so on will be genuine properties only if they can be causally efficacious. Secondly, and I think more importantly to a scientific realist, moral epistemology and therefore indirectly moral semantics depends on our being able to have epistemic access to these properties via their effects. Boyd's semantics for moral terms relied on causally realized feedback loops to give us better and better information about the properties that are the referents of our terms. We can only be regulated in our use of a term by the referent of that term if that referent can impinge in some way on our sensory apparatus.

Harman's challenge to moral explanations, canvassed in chapter 3, might be a real threat to realist epistemology and hence also to the theory of reference, depending on its upshot. Recall the general outline of the argument. Harman asks us to imagine some putative instance of moral observation, for instance when an observer "sees" the wrongness of torturing a cat. Recall also from the previous discussion that Harman has no problem with taking the belief that results—that something very wrong is happening—as an observation. His worry is about the explanation of that observation. The best explanation of the belief that something very wrong is going on need not invoke the wrongness of the action witnessed. All we need to explain the observation is facts about the event seen, a theory of vision, and some facts about the observer's psychology. If the observer is disposed to disapprove of animal torture, that plus the observable facts will explain her reaction. The worry then is that wrongness is in no way implicated in the explanation of the observation that something wrong is going on. The wrongness might be an explanatory idle wheel.

It should not be all that surprising then that we find Cornell Realists opposing Harman's challenge by insisting that moral properties can do real explanatory work. Nicholas Sturgeon offers several examples where a person's virtue or lack thereof is used to explain an important historical event. DeVoto's well-known account of the travails of the Donner party offers the fact that Midshipman Woodworth was "no damn good" as an explanation of his behavior and the debacle to which that behavior led (Sturgeon, 1985, p. 246). Another example involves the injustice of slavery that on some accounts led to its abolition (Sturgeon, 1985, p. 245). In each of these cases it is very natural to advert to moral properties in explaining why things went as they did. There's a good deal of literature that comes out of this debate, including further papers by Harman (1986) and Sturgeon (1986). Those arguing against the causal efficacy of moral properties claim that we get a fully adequate explanation of the events in question if we cite only the events on which the moral properties of Midshipman Woodworth and of slavery supervene. We might suppose nihilism true and yet still think that Woodman's selfishness and cowardice led to disaster. And similarly, the cruelty of slavery might have been enough to bring about its abolition even if there were no moral values or standards.

It is tempting to think that the parties are talking past one another at least a little bit. Harman originally posed his challenge as a problem for *nonreductionist* accounts of moral properties. If moral properties can be identified with natural properties, that is, if they are one and the same thing as some simple or complex sort of natural property, then they just have the causal powers that those natural properties or their instances do. Reductive naturalists who identify moral properties with such natural properties were not Harman's target and if their identity claims are correct they seem to elude the objection. What of nonreductive naturalists? Supposing that their allegiance to nonreductionism just comes to favoring composition over identity, they may plausibly argue that higher level properties inherit the causal powers of the properties that constitute them. Composition and constitution are not themselves identity claims. And we can have reasons to resist identity claims whenever we think the persistence conditions of the item composed are different from the persistence conditions of the items they are composed of. Yet it seems part of common sense about such composition that things inherit the causal powers of their constituents. I'll make the point using the example of a statue. We have reason to think that a malleable iron statue is distinct from the iron that makes it up because the iron could survive being pounded into a lump, whereas that pounding would destroy the statue. When what seem to be two items really are just one and the same thing, they must share all of their properties. Since the statue has a property the iron lacks they must be distinct. Despite appearances, we have two items in one place at one time, a statue and a hunk of iron. The statue supervenes on the hunk of iron and the iron composes the statue. Now suppose we drop the statue on one end of a teeter totter, thereby launching the occupant of the other end into a nearby pool. It seems that the statue hitting the teeter totter caused the person's launch into the pool. Were you to be called to testify under oath no case for perjury could be made out if you said that was so. And that remains true when we realize that it was the hunk of iron hitting the teeter totter that caused the launch. It looks like in this case we are comfortable citing either cause because the statue inherits the causal powers of the iron that makes it up. It isn't obvious that the same considerations shouldn't hold when we turn to property instances rather than concrete particulars, like statues and iron. If the cruelty of slavery (partly) constitutes its injustice and wrongness, common sense might allow the injustice and wrongness to be part of what led to its abolition.

At this point the nonreductive realist might point to the relations between the special sciences (biology, chemistry, genetics, psychology, physics, etc.). It is plausible that ideal physics would completely explain what happens in the universe. This would mean that physical properties and objects are themselves sufficient to cause whatever has been caused and will be caused. Even so, we have perfectly respectable sciences of chemistry, biology, genetics, and psychology that also posit causal relations. If these sciences posit causal explanations, and it seems that they do, we have companions in guilt. That is, the properties invoked in biological and psychological causal explanations supervene on the physical properties of the world. And yet these properties play the leading roles in causal explanations offered by the special sciences.

The nonreductive realist can go on to argue that these examples don't just provide companions in guilt. They also provide a rationale for hanging onto explanations that posit properties and objects at the higher level. The nonphysical special sciences highlight higher level unities that would be harder to capture in a simple way at the underlying physical level. Biology, for example, may have laws that are relatively simple to state at the level of gene frequencies in a population, but because genes could in principle be realized by any number of arrangements of atoms, stating those laws in purely physical terms will be so complicated as to hide generalities that can be expressed relatively simply using properties and objects (e.g. gene, population, frequency) at the higher level of description.

There is much more to be said here. My main point has been to emphasize the way that Cornell Realists require moral properties to be causally relevant both so as to sustain the favored analogy with science, but even more importantly to underwrite the theory of reference favored by these realists. This explains, I think, the amount of ink that has been spilt over the issue of moral explanations by fans of this kind of view.

11.4. Cornell Realism and Morals/Motives & Morals/Reasons Externalism

Earlier in this chapter I noted that Cornell Realists have adopted Foot's early resistance to internalism. That is, they mostly deny both that there is any necessary connection between moral truths and moral judgements on the one hand and reasons or motives to do what those judgements favor on the other. David Brink, whose arguments we canvassed in the previous chapter, is a paradigm case.

It is an interesting question whether Cornell Realists *must* be externalists, as most such realists seem to think. The issue is actually quite complicated and much seems to turn on the way in which the relevant sort of internalism is conceived. There is more to say about the compatibility of the amoralist story and internalism of various sorts, but I want to focus on a couple of issues in particular. I want to ask which features of Cornell Realism make externalism seem to follow from the view, and then to ask whether they in fact require an externalist response. It will turn out that certain sorts of internalism might be compatible with major components of the Cornell Realist view. There seem to be two ways that a commitment to even defeasible morals/motives and morals/reasons internalism might follow from a Cornell-style realist view. One just has to do with the nature of the moral properties identified with rightness, wrongness, goodness, and so on. If the property in question is not plausibly one that people inevitably desire or have reason to desire, even under ideal conditions, we should not think there is any necessary connection between moral rightness (or whatever) and reasons or motivation. The other has to do with the nature of the reference relation and with a specific way that many realist externalists formulate their externalism. I will discuss both issues, but begin with the former.

As a matter of fact the two most well worked-out accounts of moral rightness and moral goodness, offered by Boyd and Railton, identify these properties with complex properties of a sort that might just leave a person cold. I just might not care about the homeostatic cluster of properties including health that lies at the end of the causal regulatory chain that secures that property as the referent of my term good. Perhaps I've become convinced by Noir literature and biographies of my literary and musical heroes that a somewhat seedy life of cigarettes, strong drink, and cynical detachment is the life for me. I could have a life of health and vigor but I'd rather be elegantly wasted. That much seems at least possible, if not actual (Richards, 2010). Do I have reason to abandon that sort of life for another? Well, that's at least open to argument. What of the reduction of rightness? Boyd is an indirect consequentialist where rightness is concerned. Very roughly his view stands to goodness as defined by this homeostatic cluster as rule-utilitarianism stands to happiness. What is right to do is what would be required by a system of rules chosen on the basis of its ability to promote maximal expected goodness were it to be adopted and followed as a moral system by society as a whole. And here might come more room for reasonable alienation from morality. If one can reasonably think that a life alienated from goodness as Boyd defines it can be choiceworthy, why can't one also demur from that as a communal goal? And even if it is a communal goal, why should it be my goal? Given that conception of goodness, it looks open to remain aloof. Thus this conception of goodness doesn't ensure any necessary connection with motivation or reasons to promote the good and do what's right so-conceived. Railton's reduction of goodness is liable to similar arguments, modified to take into account that he is a direct consequentialist rather than an indirect consequentialist.

Given these conceptions of the subject matter of morality it seems possible that even reasonable people may not favor the good. People may not be moved by such conceptions first-personally—that is they might prefer a different sort of life. And even if they like them for themselves, they may remain unmotivated to provide them for others, as both direct and indirect consequentialists sometimes require. Whether alienation from the good of others is compatible with rationality may be up for dispute—perhaps there are rational requirements that we worry about the good of others in certain circumstances. And if there are such requirements of rationality there might be the beginnings of an argument for defeasible morals/reasons internalism. This might affect the notion of rightness even if internalism about goodness is less plausible. Still, showing even that much would require a long argument. Unsurprisingly, Boyd and Railton are skeptical. They pretty well accept the conception of rationality that Foot deployed to argue there are no categorical imperatives—that is requirements of rationality binding on people no matter what their underlying tastes and desires. Given that conception and given the good and the right as defined by these theorists, just about every version of internalism seems ruled out. We should note, however, that the underlying conception of rationality is controversial. A subsequent theorist might try to combine the Cornell-style theory of reference, an anti-Humean conception of rationality, and a somewhat different conception of the good to generate at least a defeasible morals/reasons and perhaps even morals/motives internalism. The plausibility of that combination is hard to assess in the abstract. Extant Cornell Realist views haven't gone that route and their conceptions of rightness and goodness are such as to make externalism most plausible.

But let's move on to the next way that externalism might fall out of a Cornell-style view. By deploying a theory of reference that makes the theory immune to open question arguments, Boyd-style theorists have made it difficult to vindicate any conceptual constraints on rightness or goodness. This is relevant to the internalism debate since many externalists have assumed or presupposed that internalism must be defended as a conceptual claim. Brink, for example, asserts that the central existence internalist claim—that moral facts must motivate—is *a priori* precisely because it is conceptually secured (Brink, 1989, pp. 39–43). The underlying picture being attributed to the existence internalist is Fregean, and that is probably fair to most such theorists. Concepts are senses that must be grasped by competent speakers of a language. These senses determine the referent of the speaker's terms in a satisfactional manner. If something doesn't satisfy the condition it cannot be the referent of the term. The term 'morally wrong' picks out the property wrongness because this property satisfies the condition specified—the condition that it motivate agents to avoid wrongness. Properties that don't meet that condition would not be candidates for the referent of 'moral wrongness.' If this is what internalism requires, any anti-Fregean account of reference will be incompatible with morals/motives or morals/reasons existence internalism. Suppose, as direct reference theories do, that moral predicates are just tags for moral properties. These tags directly contribute the property itself (however described) to the content of the sentence of which it is a part. The picking out is direct insofar as it is unmediated by any descriptive sense. In that case, there just won't be any conceptual truths of the required sort that speakers know just in virtue of knowing the meanings of their terms. There just won't be anything built into the meanings of the relevant expressions that requires the referents to be capable of motivating. There merely needs to be a causal chain leading from the referent of the expression to a speaker's meaningful use of that expression. The speaker need know little about what is at the other end of that chain in order for her term to refer. She just has to be so connected. If that is how reference works there can't be a conceptually guaranteed requirement that true moral claims be motivationally efficacious.[10]

This helps explain the Cornell Realist aversion to existence internalism of the morals/motives sort. A parallel argument might also be made about morals/reasons existence internalism, since the argument turns on there being no conceptual truths mediating the reference relation between moral terms and moral properties. In any case, these arguments work to the extent that they do, only against the claim that the necessities at issue are supposed to be conceptual and *a priori*. They don't show that there may not be metaphysical constraints on the properties themselves that require them to be motivationally efficacious that aren't conceptually grounded.

It is even harder to assess what these accounts should say about judgement internalism of various sorts. But the idea of a term as a tag for a property that refers to it directly seems to go with the idea that such a tag could enable one to think about the property. And it also seems to go with the idea that one could think that property applied to one of your options without having any idea that it might give you a reason to go in for it. For you could be competent with the term and use it as a tag for a reason-giving property and yet not know that the property was reason-giving. At least that would seem to be true if you think of terms as just tags. Perhaps then it is no surprise that Cornell Realists have by and large been externalists about every connection between morals, reasons, and motives. That is they've by and large insisted that the motivating and reason-giving potential of morality rests on contingent facts about our relations to it.

Still, they've often recognized that this saddles them with a certain explanatory burden. Railton's title "What the Noncognitivist Helps Us to See the Naturalist Must Help Us to Explain," suggests the basic idea (Railton, 1993). It is hard to avoid thinking that morality is practical in a way that most other subject matters are not. And this seems to involve a more direct tie to choice and action than most other domains of discourse. Externalist rationalists don't want to have to deny these suggestions. They want to explain them without overstating them, as they think internalists do. To do that it may be enough to explain why most people have some reason to go in for what's good and to do what's right most of the time. Both Boyd's and Railton's rough reductive accounts look to be in a good position to do that. A self-reinforcing property cluster including health will be good for most people, even if not for all. Other things equal they'll have reason to go in for it. Similarly, what you'd want if you knew all the facts is the kind of thing we'd expect to move you, if someone could just tell you what that was. These aren't necessary truths, but they are pretty robust. If I tell you that you'd really want to go to this movie if you only knew what I know about it, that is at least some reason to go to the movie. If you trust me you might even go. Now imagine Penelope is your ideal advisor and you know it. Given what your ideal advisor knows about you, you'd be even more likely to take Penelope's advice than to take mine. So we might get at least a reliable connection to intention and motivation from a view like that, even if it isn't a necessary connection.

11.5. The Moral Twin-Earth Objection

In chapter 2 I introduced Hare's Missionaries and Cannibals argument, whose upshot was supposed to be that no descriptive content could be the common meaning shared by general moral terms. I also mentioned the Moral Twin-Earth argument of Horgan and Timmons, claiming that it was an updated generalization of Hare's argument. I promised to come back to Moral Twin-Earth in the context of particular proposals about the reference of moral terms. Having introduced Boyd's causal regulation theory of reference, this is the place to keep that promise. Boyd's causal regulation semantics is the theory that the Moral Twin-Earth argument was designed to refute.

11.5.1.   Moral Twin-Earth and Causal Regulation Semantics

Horgan and Timmons (1991, 1992a, 1992b) ask us to imagine a planet much like Earth on which people speak a language just like English with a few small exceptions. In all *discernible* ways they use moral terms such as 'good,' 'right,' and 'wrong' in much the same way we do. People on this planet (Moral Twin-Earth) apply these terms to actions, institutions, and states of affairs; the inhabitants take "goodness" or "rightness" to be important, and they are normally disposed to do what they believe "right," to avoid doing what they believe "wrong," and to choose what they take to be "good." In other words, *on the surface* Earth and Moral Twin-Earth are indistinguishable. At the same time we are to imagine that the planets differ in causal structure. One natural property causally regulates our use of "right" and another "wrong" here on Earth, whereas different properties causally regulate the use of the same terms on Twin-Earth. The properties are similar enough to account for common ways the terms operate on the two planets, but they are still distinct. For vividness Horgan and Timmons suppose the properties on Earth are such as to make consequentialism of some sort true whereas the properties on Moral Twin-Earth are such as to make nonconsequentialism true. To allow the variation, a bare minimum of subtle but real differences in the psychologies of the relevant populations is allowed, so that somewhat different properties can play the same roles for the groups on each planet (Horgan and Timmons, 1992b, pp. 164–165).

Horgan and Timmons then ask us to decide whether we would translate the moral terms on Twin-Earth with our counterpart terms, or not. Does a speaker on Earth disagree with a speaker on Moral Twin-Earth when one asserts, "Lying is not wrong," and the other asserts "Lying is wrong"? Do I contradict what my counterpart on Moral Twin-Earth says if I deny that lying is wrong while he asserts it? These questions about disagreement and contradiction are relevant because genuine contradiction seems to require that one person denies precisely what the other says. For someone on Earth to use "is not wrong" to contradict what someone on Moral Twin-Earth says when they says that something "is wrong," 'wrong' must mean the same thing when each uses that term. Thus a verdict of yes to the question about contradiction presses us to translate our term 'wrong' into their term 'wrong.' And if the terms mean the same thing on each planet they should also designate the same natural properties, at least if they designate natural properties at all.

This verdict causes problems for Boyd's causal regulation semantics. Causal regulation semantics entails that the terms pick out different properties on Earth and Moral Twin-Earth. The thought experiment was set up so that different properties regulate speaker's use of the words 'right,' 'wrong,' and 'good' on the two planets. And Boyd's theory holds that terms designate whatever it is that causally regulates the use of the relevant term. So the theory entails that they designate different properties and mean different things on the two planets.

Many of us find it very plausible that we should translate the terms on Twin-Earth into their counterparts on Earth, and vice versa. We find it plausible that when an inhabitant of one planet says that lying is always "wrong," and the other responds by saying that lying is sometimes "not wrong but right" they disagree. And many people find it plausible that the disagreement is there in the *semantic content* of what they each assert when they say those things. If what they find plausible is actually correct, this is a problem for causal regulation semantics, at least where moral terms are concerned.

Horgan and Timmons themselves think the thought experiment favors a version of expressivism. They note that the feature our translations treat as crucial for sameness of meaning for moral terms is that they guide action. This is just the feature that Hare took to be crucial to translating missionary talk into cannibal talk even when the two groups approved of different things. If it is this shared feature that explains the (alleged) sameness of meaning for the terms on the two planets the terms cannot have a representational semantics, or so Horgan and Timmons argue. They thus join Hare in reject-ing minimal realism about morality for just the same reason. They reject a representational semantics on the basis of a translation argument. That rejec-tion on the basis of the Moral Twin-Earth argument commits them to thinking it works against all representational semantic accounts for moral terms. And this is in fact what they argue, as we'll see in the next chapter.

Direct reference naturalists may well just want to bite the bullet here. As Janice Dowell (2015) points out, it isn't obvious that we must regard our reactions to the thought experiment as providing reliable information about moral semantics. If the direct reference theories targeted by the experiment are correct, our responses may not be evidence about the referent of our terms. For it is part of direct reference theory that we can refer to something without knowing much about it. On the other hand, many of us find it hard to believe that there is not a genuine disagreement about morality dividing the disputants on Earth and Moral Twin-Earth. And it does seem hard to hang onto that thought without also thinking it due in part to the meanings of the terms in question. Externalist realists might resist that thought. For example, they can try to explain the persistent suspicion that the two do disagree using pragmatic mechanisms of communication. Or they might suggest there is some sort of shared presupposition in play when people use moral vocabulary and that the disagreement is generated by the conjunction of these commitments and what people in fact say when they use moral terms. For example, perhaps in both communities, people use moral terms only when they think moral claims relevant to practical delib-eration over what to do. If so, calling something 'right,' either on Earth or on Moral Twin-Earth, will carry with it a commitment to whatever it is that 'right' applies to, even when this is not part of the meaning/semantics of the term. Two people might then find themselves in practical conflict when one affirms and another denies that some action is "right." And that would remain true even if the term 'right' picks out a different property in each of their mouths.

If you didn't understand a word of the previous paragraph, that's OK. You can see how quickly these debates carry us into highly abstract and complicated issues in the philosophy of language and the nature of semantics and pragmatics. There is obviously more to say and more work to be done thinking about the options. Once again, there are a number of live issues that have important upshots for the nature of ethics.

Questions

Comprehension

C1. Give a rough characterization of what it means for a property to be natural. Remember that I could not give an uncontroversial answer to this question in the chapter, so be content if you can capture the idea less than precisely.

C2. Why would it be a problem for Boyd's theory of moral property terms if we could not have causal contact with moral properties or instances of them?

C3. Explain briefly why the Moral Twin-Earth thought experiment conflicts with what Boyd's theory entails for the meaning of moral terms.

Extension

E1. If there were ghosts and other supernatural entities it seems like they could act rightly and wrongly. Does this cause problems for naturalist reductions of moral properties? Why or why not?

Reading

Read along with: Richard Boyd (1988) or Railton (1986) or Sturgeon (2006) and perhaps Terrence Horgan and Mark Timmons (one of 1991, 1992a, 1992b).

Further reading: Nick Sturgeon (1985) engages Gil Harman in a debate about the explanatory role of moral properties, and the debate continues in Harman (1986) and Sturgeon (1986) in the same volume. Sturgeon (2006) is a nice overview article about naturalism. There is a huge literature on the Moral Twin-Earth argument. David Copp (2000) and Geoffrey Sayre-McCord (1997) offer partial responses on behalf of the realist. I've taken a crack at it myself in van Roojen (2006). Schroeter and Schroeter (2013) give a skeptical look and offer an alternative. In addition to Dowell (2015), Plunkett and Sundell (2013) offer another line of resistance.

Notes

1 That way we could include noncognitivists and error theorists among the naturalist in virtue of the fact that descriptive naturalists, noncognitivists, and error theorists commit themselves to nothing beyond the natural. If we add to this definition that there *are* moral properties we'd rule out those two anti-realist views but retain the descriptive or representational naturalists.

2 David Brink, Richard Boyd, and Nicholas Sturgeon, all spent significant time at Cornell. Peter Railton didn't, but somehow many of us think of him as a member of the club.

3 Foot did offer an account of moral evaluation in *Natural Goodness*, published in 2001, and it does go much further to tell us what ethics is about in a naturalistic way. But by then she had given up the externalism of her earlier work.

4 Once such theories were available, ingenious revisionary Fregean theories were able to do some of the same work.

5 If you find this material difficult, the first three chapters of Lycan (2008) is a wonderful road map through the ideas of importance here.

6 On this way of talking semantics tells us what the terms mean and metasemantics tells us how they come to mean what they mean. Some prefer "philosophical theory of referring" to 'metasemantics'.

7 I'm speaking loosely here. There are puzzles even for direct reference theory about the appropriate ways to describe what such people know and don't know.

8 It is controversial whether compositions (which involve parts and wholes) and constitution (which is less well defined) are the same, different, or one a species of the other (Johnston, 1992; Thomson, 1983; Baker, 2007). I'm treating them as at least very similar to one another and hope nothing here will turn on that.

9 There are many more things to say about how the distinction should be drawn, and I'm putting my head in the sand with respect to myriad issues by not saying them.

10 I should probably note that there are direct reference views that include conditions on competent use directly referring expressions. Since these further conditions don't seem to play a reference mediating role, reference is still direct. But such further conditions could underwrite conceptual truths including perhaps truths of the sort internalists favor without playing any role in fixing the referents of the terms.

12 Scientific Naturalism II

Moral Functionalism and Network Analyses

The Cornell Realists, and Boyd in particular, have a certain take on how the epistemology of science works, on how the special sciences relate to one another, and on how reference to scientific properties and kinds is secured. The package is well-suited to explain how the Paradox of Analysis and the Open Question Argument get off the ground, as a way of defanging them as obstacles to reduction. But it isn't the only such package. An alternative picture, drawing inspiration from the work on scientific terms by David Lewis, aims to vindicate philosophical analyses as a fruitful philosophical and scientific tool, while giving the Open Question Argument and the Paradox of Analysis their due. The approach, sometimes called *"Canberra Plan* reductionism,"* is associated most closely with Frank Jackson and Phillip Pettit, each of whom spent a good deal of time at the Australian National University in Canberra.

12.1. Unobvious Analyticity

While the Cornell Realists by and large backed away from *a priori* philosophical analyses as a legitimate methodology for reducing moral properties to natural properties, not everyone did. Some think there is a simpler response: Rather than give up on such analyses in the face of the paradox of analysis, we should just realize that *a priori* truths, including philosophical analyses, can be unobvious (Lewis, 1989). If we conceive of philosophical analyses as something a speaker or thinker explicitly deploys when thinking about the subject matter at hand, it can be hard to see how this is so. But we need not suppose speakers using the word 'right' explicitly think of rightness as satisfying the conditions laid out by a correct analysis of the term. They may just deploy a tacit concept that guides them to think, speak, and act with rightness in mind. Such speakers will have various inferential dispositions involving rightness, dispositions to judge that certain kinds of actions are right, dispositions to communicate such judgements and others related to them, and dispositions to act in various ways upon learning that something is right. The analysis of rightness might then just be a good way to systematize and summarize the tacit knowledge deployed by thinkers who use the word as they communicate, think, and act. The analysis will be adequate to these purposes just as long as the knowledge that users rely on in using that concept is derivable from the analysis and that nothing that is not part of that tacit knowledge is derivable. If that condition is met we can use the analysis to capture the sum total of that knowledge in a relatively simple way. This picture makes it less surprising that competent speakers who know what they mean might have doubts about a correct analysis. For it is not always obvious what best summarizes such a body of tacit knowledge, even when one is in possession of that whole body. And if the range of tacit knowledge that we're trying to capture is sufficiently complex, even the most competent users of the concept might be unsure whether any statement of it is actually complete. It could turn out that the best summary is just too long to take in all at once when made explicit.

A move like this is available to proponents of most *a priori* philosophical analyses of moral concepts and properties. It provides a rejoinder to the Open Question Argument consistent with an *a priori* metaethical methodology.

12.2.   Defining Theoretical Terms via a Network Analysis

If you were to follow people around so as to get a sense of the range of tacit knowledge that we would want an analysis of their moral concepts to capture, you would soon notice that many of the inferential and communicative dispositions connect moral judgements with other *moral* judgements. You might notice that when an outcome is judged to be better than alternative outcomes people are also more apt to think that actions leading to it rather than the alternatives are right. You might notice that fair procedures are more often considered right than unfair procedures. You might find people more apt to call an honest person good than to call a dishonest person good. And similarly a person who reliably does the right thing is judged to be virtuous and morally good. It thus looks like a lot of the tacit knowledge exhibited in these dispositions to infer, judge, and express connects one moral or normative judgement with another. An analysis that aimed to systematize and encapsulate this tacit knowledge would likely then analyze moral properties in terms of other moral properties. So it might seem that no naturalistic analysis could capture these connections. We'd need to analyze each moral property in terms of other moral properties. So we would never get an analysis with our target moral terms appearing only on one side of the identity claim and only nonmoral terms on the other. The analysis would be informative insofar as it told us something about the structure of the interrelations between our various moral concepts, but it would not yet help us to reduce them to nonmoral or natural terms.

This is where *Moral Functionalists* turn to a new idea taken over from a strategy for reducing facts about the mental to facts about the physical (Jackson and Pettit, 1995). They hope to use the fact that our moral terms and concepts are so interconnected to provide a *network analysis* of each. The basic idea is to interdefine roles for each of the moral properties of interest and then to reduce them to natural properties all together and at once. The model is functionalism about the mental, according to which particular kinds of mental states are defined by functional roles they play in our mental economy, where many of those roles are roles for interacting with other mental states. Each kind of state is defined by its role in the overall network. To use an overly simple example to get the idea across, the belief that I have a dollar in my pocket is a mental state that plays the following role: Together with the thought that I can buy lunch if I have a dollar, and the strong desire for lunch, it will cause me to buy lunch; and together with the belief that a dollar is a kind of money, it will cause me to believe that I have money in my pocket; and it will be caused by the knowledge that a dollar feels a certain way and getting that feeling when I stick my hand in my pocket; and so on. And each of the beliefs and desires mentioned in specifying the role of this belief will play complementary roles. The thought is that if we extend this story to include all of the ways that beliefs and desires interact with one another and build them into the relevant roles, we can identify a given belief with whatever it is that plays the role specified for that belief, even though that role will advert to other mental states defined in complementary ways. It might be a particular kind of physical state in the brain and nervous system, or it might be something else. But when we find the thing that plays the role we've found the belief. And if we find a physical state playing that role we've reduced the mental to the physical. Or so says one kind of functionalist about the mental (Lewis, 1972). The parallel moral functionalists hope to exploit is the networked nature of the target to be reduced in both the moral and the mental realm. If we can find a role for each moral term in our vocabulary we can fix the referent of that term via that role. In fact we can do more than that, we can say what it is to be right (for example) by specifying the role in this network a property must play to be rightness. That's why moral functionalist theories are also known as *network analyses* of moral properties.

Let me fill this out by explaining how we reach a specification of the relevant roles. In the course of developing the non-obviousness response to the Open Question Argument, I suggested that many theorists think analyses capture complex tacit knowledge. Most moral functionalists seem to think that the relevant knowledge is not only tacit. They think that we can come to have explicit awareness of the judgements the tacit knowledge underwrites. In fact they think we do have explicit awareness of many of the most important judgements that reflect these patterns. Thus there are certain "commonplaces" about moral life that the conceptually competent will endorse without much reflection. For example, right actions tend to make things better, that some procedure is fair generally makes it right, fairness is morally more important than politeness, virtuous people will be motivated to do right, and so on. Competent ordinary moral thinkers will be apt to endorse these claims and to find them platitudinous, at least for the most part. Jackson and Pettit (1996) call the body of commonplaces "*folk moral theory*" on an analogy with "folk psychology" in the philosophy of mind. Beginning from this folk theory we can gather a body of commonplaces about morality. Not every commonplace need be universally accepted, so long as those regarded as most competent by the rest of the folk regard them so. The commonplaces will include various relatively uncontroversial observations about goodness, rightness, fairness, virtue, honesty, wrongness, badness, and so on. The commonplaces won't just include claims about the interrelations between moral kinds and properties. They will also include connections to perfectly natural objects, properties, and relations. This will be all to the good.

Suppose now that we take this vast body of commonplaces and conjoin them all into one very long sentence. That sentence will now capture "folk moral theory" and its commitments. Now take this sentence and rewrite it so that properties occur not as adjectives but as named objects. If one of the sub-sentences says "Lying is usually wrong," we rewrite it to say, "Lying usually has the property of being wrong." "Right acts tend to help people" becomes "Actions that have the property of being right have a tendency also to help people." And so on. The point is to refer to the properties in such a way that we can talk about them as objects over which we can quantify. From there we take each moral expression and substitute a distinct variable for each type wherever it occurs. To be safe we should do the same for normative predicates that may not be strictly moral, such as "reason" and "the property of being rational." So we now have a long sentence with free variables wherever there formerly were moral or normative terms. As yet these variables are unbound by any quantifiers. So they need to be bound in order to generate a claim with content. And the content we want is a content that folk morality is committed to—*that there are things that play the roles* of each of the variables in our very long sentence. So we must bind each variable with an existential quantifier to let the formula represent the claim that there exists a thing that plays each role. That after all is what folk moral theory is committed to, at least according to our moral functionalists. Lewis called the long sentence the "*Ramsey sentence*" of the theory, after Frank Ramsey whose work Lewis was drawing on. But this is not all that folk moral theory is committed to. It is committed as well to there existing only one property to play each role, so we add a uniqueness clause for each variable to get the *modified Ramsey sentence* of the theory. It says for each role that there is one and only one thing that plays the role.

12.2.1. An Oversimplified Example

There is more to explain, but I should probably give a simple example to illustrate the basic idea. To do this clearly I will use an oversimplified folk moral theory. The example that follows treats the simplified folk moral theory as the moral functionalists suggest.

Suppose an overly simplified folk moral theory says this:

1. Rightness is a property of actions, institutions, and policies.
2. Goodness is a property of people, outcomes, states of affairs, facts, and constituents thereof.
3. Right actions always make things better than the alternative actions that could have been performed instead.
4. One outcome is better than another if it contains more moral goodness than the other.
5. Pleasure is usually morally good.
6. Fairness is morally good.
7. Politeness is morally good.
8. Fairness is more important than politeness.

When we conjoin these we get:

> Rightness is a property of actions, institutions, and policies, and goodness is a property of people, outcomes, states of affairs, facts, and constituents thereof, and right actions always make things better than the alternative actions that could have been performed instead, and one outcome is better than another if it contains more moral goodness than the other, and pleasure is usually morally good, and fairness is morally good, and politeness is morally good, and fairness is more important than politeness.

Rewriting that using property names for purposes of quantification we get:

> The property of rightness is a property of actions, and the property of goodness is a property of people, outcomes, states of affairs, facts, and constituents thereof, and actions that have the property of being right always make things better than the alternative actions that could have been performed instead, and one outcome is better than another if it contains more of the property moral goodness than the other, and pleasure usually has the property of morally goodness, and things that have the property of fairness have the property of moral goodness, and things that are polite have the property of moral goodness, and the property of fairness contributes more to a thing having the property of moral goodness than politeness does.

We can replace each *moral* term in that theory with a distinct variable like so:

> **r** is a property of actions, and **g** is a property of people, outcomes, states of affairs, facts, and constituents thereof, and actions that have **r** always

make things better than the alternative actions that could have been performed instead, and one outcome is better than another if it contains more of **g** than the other, and pleasure usually has **g**, and things that have **f** have **g**, and things that are polite have **g**, and **f** contributes more to a thing having **g** than politeness does.

Now we add quantifiers:

There exists an **r**, there exists a **g**, there exists an **f**, such that **r** is a property of actions, and **g** is a property of people, outcomes, states of affairs, facts, and constituents thereof, and actions that have **r** always make things better than the alternative actions that could have been performed instead, and one outcome is better than another if it contains more of **g** than the other, and pleasure usually has **g**, and things that have **f** have **g**, and things that are polite have **g**, and **f** contributes more to a thing having **g** than politeness does.

This is the Ramsey sentence of our overly simple folk moral theory. We might symbolize the previous paragraph thus:

∃**r** ∃**g** ∃**f** [M **r g f**)]. (The whole formula in brackets says what the words after the quantifier phrases said in the previous formulation.)

Now to get the modified Ramsey sentence of the theory we have to add that there is only one property that plays the role specified for each variable. The modified Ramsey sentence says that there is one and only one thing that plays each role specified by folk moral theory:

∃**r** ∃**g** ∃**f** [(M **r, g, f**) & ∀**x** ∀**y** ∀**z** M (**x y z**) ↔ (**x** = **r**, **y** = **g**, **z** = **f**)].

Or, in English:

There exists a unique **r**, there exists a unique **g**, and there exists a unique **f**, such that **r** is a property of actions, and **g** is a property of people, outcomes, states of affairs, facts, and constituents thereof, and actions that have **r** always make things better than the alternative actions that could have been performed instead, and one outcome is better than another if it contains more of **g** than the other, and pleasure usually has **g**, and things that have **f** have **g**, and things that are polite have **g**, and **f** contributes more to a thing having **g** than politeness does.

From here, depending on which moral property we are interested in, we can formulate an identity statement with the property term on the left hand side and an analysis exploiting the preceding formulation of the theory and containing no moral or even normative terms on the right hand side. So, to use rightness as an example:

The property of being right = the unique **r** such that, there exists a unique **g**, and there exists a unique **f**, and **r** is a property of actions, and **g** is a property of people, outcomes, states of affairs, facts, and constituents thereof, and actions that have **r** always make things better than the alternative actions that could have been performed instead, and one outcome is better than another if it contains more of **g** than the other, and pleasure usually has **g**, and things that have **f** have **g**, and things that are polite have **g**, and **f** contributes more to a thing having **g** than politeness does.

Or, once more in symbols:

The property of being right = the **r** such that $\exists$**g** $\exists$**f** [M **r**, **g**, **f**) & $\forall$**x** $\forall$**y** $\forall$**z** M (**x y z**) $\leftrightarrow$ (**x** = **r**, **y** = **g**, **z** = **f**)].

12.3. Internalism and Network Analyses

If you look at our original list summarizing the simple folk moral theory you can roughly divide it into (a) clauses specifying the relations of various moral properties to nonmoral properties that make for goodness, rightness, and so on, and (b) clauses specifying the interrelationships between moral properties and each other. I say roughly because (8) is a hybrid if we treat politeness as a nonmoral property as I have. Connecting this back to the psychological functionalism that is the inspiration for the view, we can think of the former set of clauses as analogous to the input clauses for mental states in the psychological theory. And we can think of the latter set as analogous to the internal role clauses that specify how mental states interact with one another according to psychological functionalism (Jackson, 1998, p. 130). For simplicity I left out anything analogous to the output clauses of a functionalist theory, which connect the various states to the behaviors they typically cause. But I could have added clauses that connected moral value and rightness to the kind of behavior and motivation we would expect from agents. The exact nature of these conditions would depend on which commonplaces about such connections are vindicated by the commonplaces of folk morality. If Hare's Missionaries and Cannibals example reveals what competent folks think about morality, we'll add a clause to the effect that judgements of rightness and value normally motivate people who accept them to act on those judgements in particular ways. If folk moralists agree on something stronger, we will add a stronger condition.

These clauses ensure that the properties playing the relevant roles meet the internalist constraints that common sense would vindicate. They put further constraints on candidates for the roles of rightness, goodness, fairness, and so on. And they put the theory in a strong position to meet any legitimate insistence that the theory explain this or that plausible internalist condition. For if the insistence is legitimate, there will presumably be some good reason to think it is a genuine constraint. And this reason will be given its due by competent folk moral theorists who will then include the upshot among the commonplaces they accept. And moral functionalist theorizing will then build the condition into the list of conditions that specify the relevant functional roles (Jackson and Pettit, 1996).

So far so good. Right now, however, folks seem divided about internalism. What do we say to that? One idea, proposed by Frank Jackson, is that we wait and see what happens with folk moral theory. We let people argue about these things until they settle them, and then build the resulting consensus into the theory to be incorporated into the role. If this answer works it can be deployed at other points on which there is no consensus. There are after all disagreements about many moral matters, including some that would seem central to any robust role we'd have to specify. Even our oversimplified theory has a clause that seems to endorse consequentialism, despite the going controversy over that view. And in fact Jackson means his suggestion to apply across a wide range of similar issues that are presently unsettled. (Jackson, 1998). There is lots more to say here.

12.4. From the Rightness Realizing Role to Metaethical Naturalism

Given the very few constraints offered by our overly simplified folk moral theory, the idea that there would be just one realizer for the rightness role is obviously a fantasy. But moral functionalists hope that given a more robust folk theory each role will be uniquely realized. Let's go along with this assumption for now. Moral functionalists go beyond that commitment to suggest that the unique realizer for all of the roles defined for each of the moral terms we started with will itself be a natural property. If one already knew that all properties were natural properties this would follow immediately. But in this context we can't just assume that all properties are natural. For one thing at least one party to the debate, the moral nonnaturalist, thinks that moral properties are nonnatural. And for all that has been said they need not deny that the moral property rightness, which they believe to be nonnatural, plays the rightness role specified by the moral functionalist, nor need they deny that it plays that role uniquely. They only need to deny the very last move in this chain of reasoning—that the role filler is a natural property as opposed to a nonnatural property.

Furthermore, even some naturalists think that naturalism is a contingent hypothesis. They think it is true that our universe is natural, but that it could have been otherwise, for instance if there were gods or ghosts (or perhaps if there were nonnatural moral properties). And if the universe could have had gods or ghosts in it, then there are supernatural properties that could have been instantiated but are not. It seems this sort of naturalist should think that there are properties besides the natural properties, though they should also think they are uninstantiated. So there seems to be no very quick argument that the role filler must be a natural property (van Roojen, 1996a).

On the other hand naturalism itself seems to place no special burden on the moral functionalist. By this I mean that independent arguments for the truth of naturalism might be available, and if they are correct and there is no problem with moral functionalism independent of any commitment to naturalism, the combination should be a viable position. This may seem both a bland thing to say and a mere assertion on my part. So far it is both. But we can back up the assertions with two points coming from opposite directions. (1) Moral functionalists have a way of loosening the restrictions set by the Ramsey sentence of folk moral theory so as to find a realizer even when strictly speaking there is no candidate that meets all the conditions. This can be exploited if adding naturalism as a constraint generates an analogous problem. And, (2) as the next section will argue, the most important worry for the functionalist is that there are too many candidates for each role, so that there may be no unique realizers of the role because uniqueness fails.

Suppose that the conjunction of conditions in the Ramsey sentence of folk moral theory was unsatisfiable, perhaps because it is contradictory. Or perhaps no properties in the actual world are related just as the theory specifies. Moral functionalists can suggest that the properties that come closest to meeting these roles be allowed to be the referents of the relevant property terms. Or more carefully, that the set of properties whose assignment to each of the roles in an appropriate way makes the theory closest to true is the correct one (Jackson and Pettit, 1996). This strategy was already part of David Lewis's proposal for defining theoretical terms and in particular mental terms. There is no guarantee that the folk theory of anything is fully correct and we should therefore expect the theory to be near enough true if there are items that come close to interacting in the way the theory specifies. It may of course be a difficult matter to decide which assignment of referents makes the folk story come as close as it can to the truth. But that, the functionalist can argue, is an epistemic issue and not metaphysically important. As long as one *is* in fact closest, all is OK. If allowing this sort of play is OK when the problem is generated by constraints from within folk moral theory, it should not be any worse if the problem arises between some part of folk moral theory and the commitment to naturalism, at least if the naturalism is itself well-motivated. So if conjoining naturalism with folk theory all by itself causes the theory that includes both to become unsatisfiable, the naturalist can say that we deal with this problem in the same way as we deal with internal incoherence in folk theory.

On the other hand, if the problem is that we have too many ways of assigning properties to the roles so that the theory comes out true, then an extra constraint may even come in handy. For it will rule out at least a few of the too many candidate assignments and so make the problem of choice more manageable. This is not to say that the too many candidates problem, or the "*Permutation Problem*," as Michael Smith (1994, 48ff.) has aptly named it, does not still have its own bite.

12.5. The Permutation Problem

The permutation problem is the problem of making sure that the network analysis yields just one candidate for each role. Smith gave it that name because he worried that we might be able to rearrange the referents of the variables in the Ramsey sentence and still wind up with a true description of each. And in fact we may be worried that for many finite sentences defining the relations of multiple variables there will be several ways of replacing the variables with names that make the description come out true. We want some reason to think that the same is not true for the Ramsey sentence that captures folk moral theory.

The problem is made somewhat more pressing by the nature of the theory as an analysis, as opposed to merely a reference fixing description. Sometimes it is easy to come up with a uniquely identifying description for some item, be it a physical object, a person, a kind, or a property. "The post box on the corner of 17th and Sumner in Lincoln," picks out a particular mail box. "The man at the bar of the St. Francis Hotel," might have picked out Dashiell Hammett, on a slow day in the 1920s. "Moore's favorite property" might uniquely pick out goodness. In these examples we pick out a thing using some contingent feature *only it actually has* and use that feature to uniquely identify it. And in each of these cases the contingent feature itself involves reference to a particular (Lincoln, the St. Francis, Moore), not itself obviously mediated by a uniquely identifying description. Our task would be much harder if we could at no point refer to particulars in this way to uniquely identify what we're after.

If we understand a network analysis as offering a reduction that tells us *what it is to be the thing reduced*, it looks like such an analysis must do without exploiting such contingent relations to particulars to which we can directly refer. For the idea is to treat the relevant properties as role properties. *What it is to be the property wrongness* (for example) is to be the property that fills the role spelled out for wrongness in the folk moral theory captured in the Ramsey sentence for folk morality. But what it is to be wrong cannot include in it any contingent particular whose nonexistence is compatible with something still being wrong. Here's an example. We should regard it a commonplace that antebellum slavery was morally wrong. But the existence of slavery in the United States was contingent. Had it not existed, wrongness the property would still be around. After all, in the absence of slavery there would have been plenty of other things that were wrong. The existence of the particular institution of American slavery is not essential to the property of wrongness, though it is essential to wrongness that anything that treated people the way slavery did would be wrong. That is a general property and it involves *a type* of institution. It is perfectly acceptable to build a relation to that property or that type of institution into our Ramsey sentence if we do it in the right way. But the relationship to the actual particular token institution is not essential to wrongness. So it should not be in the Ramsey sentence.

Because we're talking about abstract things, in particular properties, the point is hard to state concretely. But we can use analogies to illustrate its basic idea. If I wanted to tell you who Dashiell Hammett was, I might say "The man at the bar in the St. Francis Hotel," at least if Hammett was at the bar there when I said it and you could see him. I can use that description to introduce you to him and to show you who I mean by the name Dashiell Hammett. I would be allowing you to find out the referent of that name. And that is fine so long as reference fixing is my goal. But suppose I was trying to tell you about the nature of Hammett. It isn't part of Hammett's nature that he be at that bar at that time. He might never have gone into the St. Francis and yet still been Dashiell Hammett. There may be other features of Hammett's that were essential to him, and if there were, we might be able to talk about *what it is* to be Dashiell Hammett. But being at that bar would be no part of that story. Similarly, being Moore's favorite property is not essential to goodness. Moore might never have been born and goodness would still be around. So we should not build being favored by Moore into an account of the nature of goodness if we are offering this as an analysis of goodness. And so on for any contingent feature of any moral property.

Given that moral functionalists are aiming to provide an analysis of each moral property, they can't use such contingent features in specifying the goodness role or any of the other roles. And that strengthens the worry that we won't be able to narrow things down to one candidate property to play each role. In the current situation, without any actual analysis to evaluate, it is hard to be sure. Perhaps we *can* find a uniquely identifying description for rightness, wrongness, and the like that picks them out only by necessary features of a role that they play. Moral Functionalists recognize the worry. One reaction to it is Jackson's (1998) idea that we might wait for morality to mature so that there is greater convergence and hence a larger noncontroversial body of commonplaces to build into the analysis. These would constrain the assignment of properties to the variable more than what we currently regard as commonplace and so make it more likely that we find a unique referent for each variable. These issues warrant further attention.

12.6. Moral Twin-Earth and Network Analyses

The Moral Twin-Earth objection is in its most natural home when it is applied to dispute Boyd-style causal regulation accounts of moral semantics. But Horgan and Timmons (2009) claim it can be adapted to cause problems for any descriptivist or representational semantics for moral terms. They think it causes trouble for network analyses and they modify the original thought experiment to show this. (Go back and read section 11.5 if you need to refresh your memory.) The adaptation goes like this. Once again we have Earth and Moral Twin-Earth. Once again the surface phenomena are mostly the same: The use of moral terms supervenes on nonmoral differences, people normally are moved to favor what they believe right, there are disputes about what is right and wrong, people apply their terms to roughly the same things, and so on. But there are also differences though they are subtly distinct from those in the earlier Moral Twin-Earth scenario. According to the present adaptation, the differences aren't about what causally regulates the terms, but rather in the best systemization of folk morality. On Earth *the commonplaces of folk morality that give expression to their tacit knowledge of the role of rightness* fit better with consequentialism whereas on Moral Twin-Earth the best systemization of the commonplaces would be nonconsequentialist.[1] Horgan and Timmons once again expect us to find it plausible that people on Earth agree with the people on Moral Twin-Earth when they both say that lying is usually wrong, and that a denizen of Earth who holds that abortion ought morally to be available disagrees with a resident of Moral Twin-Earth who thinks that it ought not be available. As before, such agreement and disagreement would seem to require that the identical words mean the same thing in the mouths of the respective parties. The conclusion that the terms do mean the same thing, creates a *prima facie* objection to the moral functionalist analysis. For the moral functionalist analysis predicts that the speakers on the two planets would be using their phonologically and orthographically identical moral terms with a different meaning and a different referent on the two planets.

Horgan and Timmons go on to argue that we're not mistaken to think that the terms have the same meaning on the two planets. They argue that our judgements about the case reflect the actual semantic facts that we tacitly grasp. To bolster this last claim, which can be doubted, they invoke Putnam's original Twin-Earth scenario, which was used to show that 'water' is a directly referential term for a natural kind. I'll describe Putnam's example briefly. There is stipulated to be a planet, Twin-Earth, on which a substance indistinguishable in most ways from water is as abundant as it is here on Earth and it exists in all the same sorts of places. A visitor from Earth to Twin-Earth would immediately conclude that this substance was water. Still, a chemist who analyzed it would be able to determine that it is some other substance than H_2O; Putnam abbreviates the substance as 'XYZ.' Twin-Earth is divided into countries in the same way ours is, and corresponding regions of Twin-Earth contain speakers of what seem to be the same languages as there are in those regions on Earth. But, as it turns out, there is a small difference. The word 'water' as used by those on Twin-Earth refers to XYZ. Our word 'water,' Putnam suggests, would not pick out this substance on Twin-Earth. Nor, he argues, did that word extend to XYZ even before the advances of chemistry made it possible to tell water from XYZ. It meant H_2O then and it means H_2O now. Thus a speaker on Earth who says "Water is not XYZ" and one on Twin-Earth who says "Water is XYZ" do not disagree. For both speak truly in their similar but not identical languages (Putnam, 1973).

Putnam expects his audience to agree with all of this. Horgan and Timmons think that he's right to do so. And they think that he's right because the tacitly understood semantic rules of our language with respect to 'water' guide us in recognizing that XYZ is not water. Similarly, they think that if the moral functionalist were right our tacit knowledge of the semantic rules for moral terms would guide us to judge that those terms mean something different on Earth and Twin-Earth. But we don't. We judge there to be one word with one meaning. Horgan and Timmons conclude that the semantic rules for English rule out treating moral terms as having different meanings. And this goes against the interpretation of the relevant words that would be assigned if the network analysis for each term were correct.

12.7.   Stepping Back a Bit

It is fair to say that the Moral Twin-Earth argument is a significant challenge. But rather than go into more of the back and forth I want to pull back and pay attention to the overarching narrative with respect to moral semantics and the puzzles of chapter 2. That narrative starts with Moore and the Open Question Argument. Moore countenanced two basic modes by which we could talk and think about things and by which our words could come to designate them. One method was mediated by an identifying description known to the thinker. The other was via acquaintance.

When designation is secured via a mediating description, the terms we use pick out their referent in virtue of match between that description and the thing we designate. So this kind of thought is satisfactional, referents get to be referents by *satisfying* the mediating description. Furthermore it seems that the mediation must be conscious to the thinker and speaker. The description that determines the referent of my terms must be one that I consciously employ. The basic idea seems very much a version of Fregean notions that distinguish sense and reference and hold that sense determines reference. But Moore's version of the idea has some interesting further features. Moore also thought that the mediating description should involve the real nature of the thing to which we refer and about which we think. At the very least it should tell us something important about how it is composed. And it should be sufficiently informative about it that we could use the description to tell someone what we are talking about in such way that they could come to know it (Moore, 1903, pp. 7–8). It falls out of this pretty quickly that the mediating conception must be complex.

The Open Question Argument seems to close off this way of securing reference to moral properties in thought or talk. A competent thinker like Moore could at once think about a moral property and at the same time doubt any description of it. Given the assumption of transparency, that rules out every description as a candidate for the reference determining sense. By Moore's lights this left the other option, acquaintance, as the sole means by which we could come to talk about moral properties and know what we are talking about. To his way of thinking it also entailed that the nature of goodness was simple, for had it been complex some description would capture that nature. This last assumption is one of the things later direct reference theorists call into question. On one way of looking at it they also extend what acquaintance may come to include epistemic relations that have many links. But Moore seems to endorse a more demanding notion of acquaintance, one on which I myself need to be directly in contact with a simple referent in order for my terms and thoughts to really be about it (Moore, 1903, p. 7).

About half a century later Hare (1952) introduces the Missionaries and Cannibals story to put pressure on descriptive or representational analyses of moral terms. While his goal was to show that commendation was essential to the meanings of moral terms, the example can also be used to put pressure on Moore's acquaintance based theory of moral reference. Suppose that competence with some predicate consisted in being acquainted with it so that one gained a recognitional capacity—the ability across a range of circumstances to recognize it when you see it. This seems to be what Moore means by intuition, the capacity that allows us to have moral knowledge. If two people claim to have this capacity with respect to some property that they express with a certain predicate, we may come to wonder whether they are picking out the same property. Given that Moore's story rules out their telling us about its nature via some description, the best way to check would seem to be to figure out whether they think this property has the same extension. If, as with the Missionaries and Cannibals, they each apply the predicate to a very different set of things, we would seem to have to conclude that they have intuitive acquaintance with different properties but just happen to use the same word for these properties. But, Hare points out, that isn't what we want to say about the Missionaries and Cannibals when the word in question is a general term of commendation. We instead want to say they mean the same thing with that word. If the intuitive acquaintance model generates a different verdict, so much the worse for that model.

Then a few decades later, direct reference theory comes on the scene and in a certain way calls into question the picture that set up Moore's dilemma. One way of thinking of the direct reference proposal is as broadening the notion of the kind of acquaintance necessary to think and talk about a thing. One no longer has to have been personally introduced to it as it were. One just has to stand in some epistemically fruitful causally mediated relation to it. Direct acquaintance will give you that. But so will being in a position to use a name that has been passed on from those who had the right kind of acquaintance relations. And so will being in a causally mediated feedback loop that allows one to find out more about the very thing you are using your words to designate. This puts us in a position to think and talk about things with which we are not directly acquainted, while not having that ability mediated by some descriptive sense that the referents of our words must satisfy. On this way of thinking Moore has offered us a false dilemma. We don't have to choose between direct acquaintance or a Fregean sense that must fit the referent of our terms. Two further features of the Moorean picture are abandoned along the way. One is transparency to consciousness of the mechanism whereby we manage to refer. Once that mechanism can involve causal and social mediation outside the mind, there's no reason to think we have to be in a position to know all of what needs to be true for our terms to pick out the things they do. Secondly, we give up on Moore's assumption that the real nature of the things we think about can be known through *a priori* analysis. We can know very little about the things to which we refer, and what we know may be inessential to them. The access we have to their real natures may be empirical and mediated by exactly the same causal links that allow us to think of them.

Not too much later, Lewis's advocacy of the Ramsey method for defining theoretical terms opens up a different response to the Open Question Argument. The method by which our predicates come to stand for certain properties may be satisfactional, but the conditions that must be satisfied may not be obvious. On the one hand they may be quite complicated. And, through the deference of some speakers to the expertise of others, they may be socially mediated so that what matters is the best systemization of a group's criteria for the use of a term. Further complication is added by the fact that various moral terms all need to be defined at once because they are linked in various ways. So we get a different strategy for resisting the Open Question Argument. Predicates can pick out properties in a description-mediated way, but not via a description that every competent speaker must be in a position explicitly to know.

Then Horgan and Timmons come along and try to cause trouble for both of these strategies using a variety of similar Moral Twin-Earth scenarios. In the course of doing so they resist the idea that speakers and thinkers do not know conditions the referents of a given term must meet, at least tacitly. The knowledge they require of competent speakers is metasemantic, knowledge about how a thing gets to be the meaning or semantic value of the terms we use. They think that our responses to Twin-Earth scenarios reveal this tacit knowledge. When we refuse to let some feature of a Twin-Earth thought experiment cause us to assign different referents to two similar terms we are displaying our tacit metasemantic knowledge that that fact is not relevant to determining the semantics of that term. So Horgan and Timmons aim to reinstate the idea that there is some condition that a competent speaker must know that has to be satisfied, for that speaker to be able to use her term with the meaning it has. This is no longer a condition that says anything important about the real nature of the referent, but it is nonetheless something that has to be satisfied.

All of this is controversial, and all of it is still the subject of lively debate. As emphasized by Janice Dowell (2015), the conditions Horgan and Timmons build into linguistic competence are very demanding and controversial at best. Direct reference theorists will reject them. And even network theorists who think the nature of the network depends on the tacit knowledge of speakers need not think individual speakers are in a position to grasp all of that network. The knowledge involved might be knowledge possessed by the group but not every member of the group.

My point in stepping back is just to draw attention to the arc of the debate and the way certain ideas come back to motivate similar positions even in the face of vigorous opposition. Depending on one's orientation one might think this is a testament to the attractiveness of the ideas or to the difficulty of removing philosophical prejudice. But it sure is interesting on either view.

Questions

Comprehension

C1. What do Jackson and Pettit think it means to call a claim a "platitude" about morality? What does it tell us about our conception of morality as Jackson and Pettit conceive of it?

C2. Construct a network analysis of what it is to be a pawn or a knight in chess. Is there a permutation problem for this analysis? Why or why not? (This will be a bit of work because the number of different kinds of chess pieces will make the analysis long. But the question counts as a comprehension question because answering it doesn't really go beyond what the chapter explains.)

Extension

E1. In his 1998 book, written without Pettit, Frank Jackson adds a wrinkle to the analysis by suggesting that we should wait for folk morality to mature before we seek to systematize it and work out the functional roles from there. Do you think this makes the view more plausible or less plausible?

Reading

Read along with: Jackson and Pettit (1996).

Further reading: The last two chapters of Jackson (1998) are probably the fullest development of moral functionalism. Smith (1994) introduces the permutation problem as an objection to moral functionalism. Wedgwood (2001) develops a conceptual role semantics for moral terms that offers yet another approach.

Note

1   Horgan and Timmons's argument contains an extra wrinkle having to do with Jackson's (but not Pettit's) claim that it is mature folk morality that matters. I think the complication obscures the issues, but it also make it easier to react to the example in the way that Horgan and Timmons predict.

13 Nonnaturalism and Antireductionism

If the guiding thought of scientific naturalism is that moral properties are in all important ways like the properties studied by the natural sciences, the guiding thought for metaethical nonnaturalists is just the opposite: Moral properties are *just too different* from paradigm natural properties to be natural themselves. Or, to be a bit more careful, nonnaturalists think that normative properties including moral properties are different enough from the paradigmatic natural properties that it is a mistake to think of them as a kind of natural property. Most nonnaturalists extend their nonnaturalism to include reason-involving properties in general, nonmoral rightness, wrongness, goodness, badness, oughts including all-things-considered and prudential oughts, and the various properties that at least arguably are practical in the senses at issue in chapter 3.[1]

Nonnaturalists differ about what they are willing to say about the relations between the various normative properties. Some will take one or another normative property or relation as basic and then analyze the rest in terms of the basic notion. Moore (1903), for example, treated goodness as basic and then defined rightness as goodness promotion. And Scanlon (2014) takes the relation of being a reason for an action (by an agent in specified conditions) as basic. But nonnaturalists don't *have to* do that. They could treat one or all of them as undefinable in any terms, natural or otherwise. Apart from differences over what property (if any) is basic, nonnaturalists differ over the internal nature of the normative properties they target. Moore took the Open Question Argument to show that goodness was simple. Thus there would be nothing informative to be said to reveal the real nature of that property. You can point to it but you cannot tell someone what it is really like. Scanlon is willing to tell us more about what reasons are by telling us that it involves a four-place relation and by telling us what sorts of things go into those places. John McDowell (1988) tells us that value is the kind of thing that merits certain affective and motivational responses, and he thinks that when he does so he is telling us about the real nature of value. The view is nonreductive because merit is itself a normative term. We'll look into these differences later in the chapter.

Nonnaturalists are minimal realists, although they are more than minimal realists. They think that (1) there are properties or relations corresponding to moral predicates, that (2) moral sentences predicate these properties, and that (3) moral thoughts represent actions, people, or things as having these properties. They think that (4) some of these sentences and thoughts predicating moral properties are true and that (5) we believe the propositions they represent when we accept them. These are all part and parcel of minimal realism as I've sketched it. Nonnaturalists go beyond minimal realism in their substantive claims about the nature of the properties predicated—that these properties are sufficiently different from paradigm natural properties to be of another kind entirely. This way of putting it evinces a certain presupposition—that the natural properties form a natural or unified kind. Natural properties, relations, and kinds, as nonnaturalists (and many naturalists) think of them, share enough similarities with one another to count as a higher order kind (a kind of kinds). To say that a property is nonnatural, then, is to say that it does not belong to that higher order kind. Whatever it is that unifies this kind, even if it is only a certain sort of family resemblance, nonnatural properties lack that unifying trait. Nonnaturalists also deny supernaturalism, though they usually only make that commitment clear in passing. Either, (like thoroughgoing naturalists) they think there are no supernatural kinds, entities, relations, properties—thus they don't need to say anything further to divide the supernatural from the nonnatural. Or, they think the supernatural is a higher order kind of properties, relations, and kinds on a par with the natural. In that case their claim is just that the normative should not be classified as falling in either one of those two higher order kinds.

13.1. The Just Too Different Motivation

David Enoch (2011) identifies the underlying motivation for nonnaturalism as the "just too different intuition." He thinks that we find ourselves wanting to say that normative properties are just too different from other properties to be natural properties like the other properties of our acquaintance. And he thinks this is a pre-theoretical thought that we have before we start metaethical or metanormative theorizing. It is fair to ask *too different in what way*? Or, to break that question into two parts, to ask, (1) What distinctive feature do moral properties have? and (2) Why think natural properties cannot have them?

13.1.1.   Normativity, or What's Special About Moral Properties?

It isn't completely obvious that every nonnaturalist would point to the same feature as distinctive. Nor would those who agree on a common feature likely go on to fill out the nature of that feature in the same way. So the rest of this section describes one answer to the "what's so special" question, one that I think is relatively popular with nonnaturalists. In a word that answer is *normativity*. But the word by itself isn't much help. Nonnaturalists understand normativity in a particular way. They think that genuine normativity has a certain sort of authority. We can illustrate with Philippa Foot's (1972) example; sexist club rules that ban women from the smoking room are normative in the sense that they specify norms of behavior. But they don't give us any reason to follow them just because they have that form. In fact we have reason to flout them. They're not authorative in the sense that norms prescribing kindness or honesty might be. When nonnaturalists talk about normativity, they take normativity to have the kind of authority that the sexist club rules obviously lack.

This answer is connected with the practicality of the morality—the feature of moral thought that the various internalists of our third chapter were trying to give an account of. But it is more general. For judgements that aren't practical can have normative authority. When we're focused on morality we naturally think of it as governing choices between actions and so we find it natural to gesture at what we mean by practicality by saying that morality is action-guiding. And part of what we mean by this is that moral judgements can answer deliberative questions about what to do, at least in the absence of countervailing practical reasons. We can extend the basic idea of normativity beyond the practical if we extend our focus from actions to beliefs. Just as we can deliberate about what to do we can deliberate about what happened or about theoretical issues and about what to believe. Normative claims about what we ought to believe can answer to deliberative theoretical questions. There are reasons to reach theoretical conclusions just as there are to act one way rather than another and we can respond to these reasons well or badly. In roughly this way both sets of deliberative judgements (the practical and theoretical) are *reason-involving*, and insofar as there are norms for the appropriate response to reasons in these domains they are *choice-guiding*.

But that is not the whole story as nonnaturalists see it. There is more to being genuinely normative or having normative authority than just being choice-guiding. Judgements or attitudes can be choice-guiding but not genuinely normative. Desires can be choice-guiding, but nonnaturalists think their guidance is of the wrong sort to fill out the kind of normativity that distinguishes the ethical from the natural. Nonnaturalists typically think that authoritative guidance is categorically reason-giving. Guidance is authoritative only insofar as it is nonoptional and categorical reasons are nonoptional. The demands that genuinely normative reasons make do not depend on contingent features of individual psychology or on voluntarily undertaken commitments. For example, that it would be disrespectful to interrupt Siobhan is a reason not to interrupt, however I feel about it. That I really want to talk doesn't change that. It wouldn't change if I didn't like Siobhan. It just is not up to me that that fact counts against interrupting her. This, the nonnaturalist will think, is different from how it is with desires or even plans. That my plans disfavor interrupting is a contingent matter. I might have changed my plan or had a different plan entirely. If my reasons not to interrupt depended on my plans I would then have had no reason not to interrupt. But that disrespect of this sort counts against interrupting isn't contingent, at least on most nonnaturalist views (FitzPatrick, 2011, p. 23).

This way of cashing out normativity combines morals/reasons existence internalism[2] with a fundamentally anti-Humean conception of reasons for action. It says that fundamental normative properties are necessarily reason-giving even while it makes facts about what we have reason to do independent of our desires and goals. We can see the combination on display in Derek Parfit's antisubjectivist agony argument.

> Who could possibly deny that the nature of agony gives us reasons to want to avoid being in agony, and that the nature of happiness gives us reasons to want to be happy? (Parfit, 2011, I: 57)

> [Suppose] I have no desire to avoid . . . agony. Nor do I have any other desire or aim whose fulfilment would be prevented either by . . . agony . . . Since I have no such desire or aim, all subjective theories imply that I have no reason to want to avoid this agony, and no reason to try to avoid it if I can. (Parfit, 2011, I: 74)

Here Parfit is suggesting that at least some reasons must be non-Humean and that subjective theorists (who base reasons in pre-existing desires) cannot account for the fundamental reason-giving normative features of reality. Much of the rest of his difficult book is aimed at showing that naturalist theories in general cannot capture these features because they identify normative facts with nonnormative facts. The categorical reason-giving nature of normative facts is at the root of these arguments.

As we've seen, many metaethicists are skeptical of anti-Humean accounts of practical reason. Thus the commitment to categorical reason-giving authority as the distinguishing feature of genuinely normative phenomena is one source of skepticism about the view. As we saw, one argument for error theory starts by agreeing with nonnaturalists that morality requires such reasons, but then insists that there can be no such reasons. But nonnaturalists have some responses to such skeptical challenges. They can point to at least one other normative phenomenon that seems also to be categorical. We seem to find the same sort of normativity in the epistemic realm. That we have reason to believe, for example, that our global climate is changing does not depend on how we would like things to go, but rather on the evidence to which we have access. That greenhouse gas levels have been rising, that average temperatures have too, and that we already have good reason to believe that atmospheric gases regulate the temperature of a planet's surface all constitute good reasons to believe that worrisome changes are coming to pass. This evidence has a rational pull on us. It requires us to believe in the reality of climate change. When we don't respond to that requirement, we are making an objective mistake. The norms regarding theory choice on the basis of evidence exert categorical reason-giving force where epistemic attitudes are concerned. They don't depend on what we desire or even on whether we accept those epistemic norms. Failure to accept them is just a mistake and that is an expression of their normative authority over us. The nonnaturalist can argue that genuine normativity has this feature in both the theoretical and practical realms. To be sure, the responses required by the normative truths differ in the two realms. But in each case, the most fundamental norms do not depend on desires. That is the point of the analogy.

It would be an additional step to show that there were categorical *practical* norms. But there do seem to be plausible examples. Christine Korsgaard's (1986) justly well regarded paper "Skepticism About Practical Reason" argues that Humeans themselves should think that the instrumental norm has genuinely normative status. So Humeans should not, she thinks, object in principle to the extension of genuine normativity to practical matters. The fact that you make a mistake if you don't take the recognized necessary means to your ultimate ends does not depend on any desire. Failing to take such means is constitutive of rational failure. That doesn't depend on what you desire even though the status of an action as a means does depend on your goals and their causal relations to that action. So we have here, in the realm of the practical, genuine categorical normativity. Or so the nonnaturalist will want to argue.

13.1.2. Against Natural Normativity

By itself this view of normativity doesn't make one a nonnaturalist. For all that has been said so far, normative properties could be natural properties. Naturalists don't need to deny that there can be categorical reasons, although some do. They can instead say that the property of generating such reasons is itself a natural property partly because such reasons are natural entities. So the nonnaturalist needs to provide an argument against this sort of view in order to substantiate the "just too different" intuition. And this is where things get a little bit difficult. Some nonnaturalists seem to think that the intuition itself provides a defeasible reason to believe its content. But it isn't clear that we should trust intuitions about such things (McPherson, 2013). Caterpillars just seem too different from butterflies to be the same species and yet they're not. Are we really confident enough in our ability to tell when one property is enough unlike another property that they can't be of the same sort to rely on bare intuitive judgements here?

The OQA and the Autonomy of Ethics

Here we often find nonnaturalists falling back on the Open Question Argument or at least an adaptation of it. David Enoch (2011, pp. 80–81, 107–109) suggests that when one is deliberating and asking oneself what one should do, no purely naturalistic answer will provide an answer. Rather, he thinks, a naturalistic answer would change the subject from something normative to something else. Pointing out that one option for action satisfies all the interests involved won't be an answer unless one already thinks one should satisfy all the interests involved. Similarly for pointing out that it would be keeping a promise. Those purely naturalistic claims only help if one already thinks that one should satisfy all involved interests or keep promises. And these, Enoch believes, are normative nonnatural claims. The connection with the Open Question Argument is that Moore too thought that no such information definitively settled what he took to be the basic normative question, whether something is good. We could, he thought, know any naturalistic fact we like about something, and yet not have settled whether it is good. Both lines of argument move from facts about the state of mind of an agent, such as that the agent can be sure of one (naturalistic) fact and yet seemingly unsettled about a particular normative fact, to argue that they are distinct facts of distinctively different kinds.

Whether this should convince anyone presumably stands or falls with the soundness of the Open Question Argument. We saw in several earlier chapters that there are reasons to think it problematic—it isn't obvious we can go from facts about what people can think about a thing to claims about that thing's real nature. Those ignorant of the real nature of water may doubt that it is H_2O, without this showing that water is not H_2O. And people can doubt that temperature is mean molecular energy without that ruling that theory out as the appropriate scientific understanding of temperature. These kinds of examples sometimes give nonnaturalists pause, since they recognize that we should not use Open Question Arguments to undermine such scientific verdicts. They sometimes suggest that it is not the argument itself that gives us reason to accept the nonnaturalist verdict, but rather the fact that we are tempted by it that shows that naturalist reductions or identifications of normative properties with natural properties leave something out.

The Euthyphro or "So What?" Objection

A related line of argument comes out of Plato's *Euthyphro*. In that context it is an argument against supernaturalism rather than naturalism, but the upshot can be extended at least to subjectivist naturalism. Famously in that dialogue Socrates offers Euthyphro a dilemma in response to Euthyphro's proposal to identify piety with being loved by the gods. The dilemma is about what explains what. Is something pious because the gods love it or do the gods love it because it is pious? You can imagine a similar argument posed against naturalistic response-dependent accounts of normative properties such as rightness. Is the action right because I would choose it in conditions of full information and imaginative acquaintance, or do I choose it because it is right? The underlying thought seems to be that we want to say the latter but that a reduction of rightness to a property essentially about the ideal responses of observers or agents reverses that order of explanation. It is, I think, the same thought that motivates those who press the "So what?" objection to ideal observer theories (Johnston, 1989). They see it as a condition of adequacy on an account of rightness or value that it justify us in our pursuit of it. A reduction that doesn't explain why we have a reason to go in for these things does not satisfy.

This is very much related to Christine Korsgaard's (1996) demand that an account of normative domains answer "the normative question," which amounts to showing the agent who is faced with a choice that she *must* act as she has normative reason to act. This demand is, in effect, to require every analysis of a normative claim to transparently highlight a first personal justification for the claim that the agent has a reason to do what she has reason to do. And Korsgaard argues that any "realist" or voluntarist[3] answer cannot do that when the agent in question has no interest in the natural or supernatural property allegedly identical with being practically required. For example, if someone is not interested in what she would want in certain idealized conditions, an analysis of normative reasons or requirements and ideal observer or agent analysis would leave her cold. Telling her that she would want to do that if she were only in those conditions would not make clear why she must do what she is obliged to do.

Why do nonnaturalists think their own account avoids running afoul of the requirement while naturalist accounts don't?[4] I'm not sure. That they aren't in the business of offering reductions and the condition of adequacy is a condition of adequacy on reductions sounds good at first, but it really only pushes the question back. Why must reductions meet this requirement while nonreductive theories get a pass? There are at least two ways of looking at the matter that seem to put the views on a par. On one way of looking at it, *every* view needs to *explain* why the target normative property offers authoritative reasons. No one gets a pass if that is how we look at it. On another way of looking at it, both views can meet the requirement in the same way. Nonnaturalists start by saying that the most basic normative properties stand in a primitive favoring relation to the things they recommend, one that we all recognize. And given that, options that have this property will be those we have reason to go in for. But then naturalists can say almost the same thing. All they have to deny is that the favoring relation is primitive, if by primitive the nonnaturalist means irreducible. When reductive naturalists then go on to add that they think they can reduce the property to natural properties (whatever they mean by that) they are not taking back the claim that choosing actions that are right is favored.

Relatedly, naturalists will in any case want to repudiate Korsgaard's demand as a condition on adequate analyses of normative terms. They won't have to deny that one has a reason to do what's right, or whatever. But they will deny that reductions must *transparently* preserve the phenomenology of normative force. They will distinguish two kinds of why questions that can be asked with "Why do I have a reason to do this action?" The first kind of "why?" question asks for a justification for doing the action. Answers to this question will display the action as a reasonable choice to make in the circumstances. Such answers will cite substantive reasons, perhaps that the action is kind or fun or a means to get what one wants. Since this question is a normative question it gets answered by citing features of the option that give us normative reason to make that choice. But naturalists will want to distinguish that use of the "why?" question from a specifically metaethical use, one that asks *what it is* to have a reason to do something, or to be good, or whatever. This "why?" question demands a constitutive answer. Such answers won't generally satisfy Korsgaard's constraint. They won't help someone not already in the grip of reason to see the point of doing what they have reason to do or favoring what is good. This doesn't show that such people are not making a mistake when they remain unmoved—they are after all unmoved by reason. Thus the naturalist who gives this response should agree with nonnaturalists that failing to be moved by reason is a mistake. But a reductive account of what something is won't be the kind of thing that can cure failures to recognize reasons (Schroeder, 2005).

My exposition here is a little unsatisfying. I'd like to be able to do better to explain why some nonnaturalists think the "So what?" objection favors their views. And the fact that I don't may cause you to doubt that these ideas do underwrite some people's allegiance to nonnaturalism. To make matters worse, Korsgaard's own use of her "normative question" is deployed on behalf of a certain sort of constructivist account that doesn't seem naturalist to me, but also isn't clearly a version of nonnaturalism. So I shouldn't attribute the thought to naturalists on the basis that Korsgaard objects in this way. But Johnston's (1989) paper does deploy the "So what?" objection against subjectivist versions of naturalism views and Johnston's own view in that paper is anti-reductionist and nonnaturalist.[5] And, at one time I myself thought Johnston's objection a reason to favor nonnaturalism.

The Autonomy of Ethics

There might be an underlying motivation in the neighborhood of both the Euthyphro argument and the OQA, one that is independently attractive even if the OQA and Euthyphro argument fail. That motivation finds its start in *the autonomy of ethics*. "The Autonomy of Ethics" is sometimes used as a name for the thesis that you cannot derive an 'ought' from an 'is' (Jackson, 1974). That thesis, sometimes also called "Hume's Law," is itself hard to get precise about in the face of putative counterexamples and responses to them. Luckily we won't need to work through that problem. The motivating thought I am trying to explain here is related to Humean thesis, but it is both less specific and broader. It is about appropriate moral thinking and not just about logic or logical implication. The important thought is that good ethical thinking is unconstrained by conclusions that aren't themselves reached by normative theorizing. On this way of thinking, ethical reasoning is an autonomous domain, with its own standards, whose truths stand or fall depending on how well they meet those standards. On one understanding of it the thought might be cashed out by saying that no *basic* moral principle is a hostage to empirical fortune. The correctness or incorrectness of basic ethical facts can't be either supported or undermined by empirical results from another domain.

Adopting the autonomy thesis can seem to lead fairly immediately to nonnaturalism. For suppose we knew that moral rightness just was the property actions have when they promote overall happiness. Psychology might then tell us what best facilitates happiness, and various other empirical disciplines could tell us how to do those things, and we would be able to derive truths about ethics from premises in psychology and the natural sciences. Results from these empirical disciplines could be put together with work in other empirical fields to disprove various moral claims. All that work would need to show is that some action we thought was right did not in fact promote happiness. The most brilliant and convincing moral arguments to the contrary would not undermine these empirical claims provided we knew and continued to know the identity of rightness with that natural property. That is how it looks to the nonnaturalist. Naturalists can either deny that ethics is autonomous in the way described or argue that their metaphysical claims do not rule it out. I'll have a question about this at the end of the chapter designed to help the reader think about how a naturalist might do that.

An Instructive Parallel

It looks like arguments for the "just too different" verdict, and naturalist responses to them, lead to a standoff with each side offering a coherent response to the underlying suspicion of difference. It might help the non-naturalists to make their case if they point out that they are not all by themselves in concluding that moral properties are too different from natural properties to be a kind of natural property. They find allies with respect to these claims even among those who think that our world only contains natural stuff. Error theorists, who are naturalists as far as metaphysics is concerned, also think that normativity is just too different to be a natural property. In giving substance to the "just too different" or "normativity" motivation for nonnaturalism, I have tied it pretty closely to the idea that morality is supposed to be genuinely reason-giving and that these reasons should be objective and not up to us. Construed in this way, the objection finds resonance in one of the main arguments for error theory. When Mackie (1977, chapter 1) appeals to the objective prescriptivity of moral value to argue that there are no true positive moral claims, he is agreeing with the nonnaturalist about what moral values must be like and agreeing with them that natural properties could not be like that. The claim that this is one of the ways that moral properties are "queer" is just that combination of claims.

Nothing in the natural world is like what moral properties would have to be like if there were any. The error theorist goes on to conclude that there must thus not be any such properties. The nonnaturalist draws the conclusion that genuinely existing moral properties are unlike any others.

13.2. A Pessimistic Induction?

People sometimes find themselves drawn to nonnaturalism for a different reason. They reflect on the history of attempts to reduce moral or normative properties to natural properties and find a worrisome pattern. A theorist proposes a naturalistically acceptable identity claim involving goodness or rightness. Very quickly someone else comes along to argue that the reduction entails a moral falsehood or leaves some obvious moral truth with the wrong status. Parfit's agony argument was a response of this sort targeting all subjectivist reductions. If the objection is telling, those friendly to the original proposal then set about modifying it to get around the objection. In time they produce a new reductive view that is a close relative of the first. And the process starts over again. Someone who surveyed the history of such putative reductions and the responses to them might well conclude that there is little reason for optimism about the project. There seems to be no reason to think that future attempts will be any more successful than those already encountered.

This line of thought targets reductive naturalism proposing to identify moral properties with independently identified natural properties, and perhaps also those that aim to explain how normative properties are constituted by or composed of complex natural properties. It does not so much count against naturalists, such as Sturgeon (2003), who argue that these properties are natural but not in virtue of being constituted by a distinct thing that is natural, nor in virtue of being identical to some property for which we already possess nonnormative terms. Such theorists can think it a mistake to offer accounts that identify normative properties using only nonnormative vocabulary. And, even against its primary targets, our pessimistic induction may just tell us something about our ability to come up with the right account, not about the nature of reality. The history of philosophical analyses of almost anything is littered with defeat at the hands of those wielding clever counterexamples. Yet we would not want to conclude that nothing was constituted by anything or that we could not make true informative identity claims.

13.3. A General Worry About Nonnaturalist Explanation

Nonnaturalists are a diverse lot with a broad range of attitudes toward philosophical explanations and ontological commitment. On one end of the spectrum we have *quietists* who want to show that everything is in order with the ethical domain, even in the absence of any naturalistic reduction of ethical properties. Quietists hope to vindicate moral thought without undertaking any significant metaphysical commitments.[6] On the other end of the range we have nonnaturalists postulating robust moral properties existing in Platonic Heaven (Enoch, 2011). We also have a great deal of diversity in what nonnaturalists are willing to say about the nature of normative properties. Some nonnaturalists such as McDowell (1988), Johnston (1989), and Scanlon (2014) are happy to make substantial claims about the relations that structure the ethical realm so long as those are read nonreductively. Others, such as Moore (1903, chapter 1), seem to think that the simplicity of the basic normative notion, goodness in Moore's case, foreclose informative characterization of its real nature.

Nonnaturalists who accept this Moorean view will be at some disadvantage. Nonnaturalism is a version of minimal realism supplemented by the further commitment to the relevant properties being nonnatural. This means that every puzzle for minimal realism will be a puzzle for nonnaturalism. But the nonnaturalists key extra commitment, that moral properties are nonnatural, won't help with many of these puzzles. Merely postulating that the normative properties represented in moral thought are not like natural properties doesn't explain much. Nor does it explain much away. If you were worried about how moral talk latched onto the world in the face of widespread disagreement, you would likely still be worried after finding out that the properties to be latched onto were nonnatural. If you had worries about explaining internalism of some sort, you would probably still have those worries after Moore had said all he has to say about the nature of goodness. If you were worried about moral epistemology, in particular about how it was that we are reliable judges of at least some moral matters, you would still be worried about that. To be sure, Moore's suggestion that we have an intuitive faculty that allows us to make reliable judgements is fine as far as it goes, but for most faculties we have we can say something more about how they give us such access. So Moore's version of nonnaturalism leaves most philosophical puzzles about even minimally realist conceptions of morality unsolved.

It is thus a good thing that nonnaturalists need not follow Moore in concluding that the basic normative notion must be simple. If I were doing detailed Moore scholarship I would argue that his commitment to the simplicity of goodness had to do with his conception of philosophical analysis. Here I will just assert it. The important thing is that nonnaturalists need not share Moore's conception of what philosophers have to offer when they propose analyses. So nonnaturalists need not follow Moore in concluding that moral properties cannot have a complex real nature. And, I'll argue, nonnaturalists can and probably should deny that the real natures of normative properties and relations must be simple. For nonnatural properties might for all their nonnaturalness be composed of and/or be reducible to further nonnatural properties. It is thus consistent with anti-reductionist claims of the sort favored by nonnaturalists that there be structure to normative properties or relations. And, for all that has been said so far, they might even claim that it is part of the real nature of the nonnatural that they stand in certain relations to natural things.

Scanlon (2014) is one prominent example of a nonnaturalist who eschews simplicity. He suggests that reasons are the fundamental normative notion and that a fact gets to be a reason by participating in a four-place-favoring relation. Facts are reasons in virtue of standing in a primitive favoring relation to an act or attitude-type for a person in a set of circumstances. The account is nonreductive insofar as there are many four-place relations that might relate facts, act-types, people, and circumstances so we don't get sufficient conditions for standing in the favoring relation out of the claims made. Yet it tells us something about the nature of the relation, at least if Scanlon is right.

In the sections that follow I will introduce some complaints against non-naturalism that it cannot meet this or that explanatory desideratum with respect to some important phenomenon or other. I'll focus primarily on explaining supervenience and internalism as well as on moral epistemology. I'll introduce each issue and then suggest some things nonnaturalists can say and have said in responding to it. In each case, the availability of the responses depends on the nonnaturalist telling us more about the nature of moral properties.

13.4. Explaining Supervenience

Take some action in your past that you think was morally required of you. Maybe it was a situation where you were required to be honest with someone about a difficult matter. Perhaps you had to admit to doing something less than admirable to a person whose opinion matters to you. So you told the truth as you saw it, despite the difficulty. That action we'll suppose had the moral status of being right and even morally required. Now imagine a second situation just like that one in all the nonmoral details. You admit to doing the very same kind of less than admirable action to the very same person at the very same time in the very same way. The second action is just like the first in every nonmoral respect. Could it be wrong? I don't mean, could it be wrong if we changed some feature of the situation, for example if in the first case what you admit doesn't hurt the other person's feelings while in the second it does. The action in that situation is no longer exactly like the first nonmorally. What I am asking about is an action *exactly like* the first in all nonmoral respects. Could an exact nonmoral duplicate of the first have a different moral status than the first? Could the first be right and the second wrong?

I predict you are going to answer "no." Given that no nonmoral property is present in one and not in the other it is impossible that they have a different moral status. I think that is the right reaction to have. (Why wouldn't they be the same!?!) And most people, including people who do metaethics, have the very same reaction to cases of that sort. They think that two actions can't differ in their moral respects without also differing in their nonmoral respects. Those of us who agree on this thereby agree that the moral facts supervene on the nonmoral facts. We think that two actions, outcomes, or events can't differ in their moral properties without differing in their other nonmoral properties. Or at least we agree on something that comes to that, even if we might prefer to express it in different words. We think that the distribution of moral properties supervenes on the distribution of some set of the other properties. This thought seems very commonsensical. And yet despite being part of common sense it is hard to make it precise in an uncontroversial way.

This idea has played an important role in metaethical debates over naturalism and nonnaturalism. Most metaethicists think that there is an important necessary truth about morality in the neighborhood of:

> *Supervenience**: Two items (actions, objects, events) cannot differ in their moral status without differing in their base properties.

But not all metaethicists interpret this claim in the same way because different metaethicists will have differing ideas about the nature of the relevant base properties. So it's fairly difficult to say in a theory-neutral way exactly what most everyone agrees on here.[7] And yet many people think that some claim of this sort is not only necessary but also *a priori* knowable. Simon Blackburn (1988, 1998, 315ff.), for example, thinks that the claim is analytic and that anyone who doesn't accept the relevant supervenience claims is displaying incompetence with moral language.

Luckily we don't need to settle on a particular formulation to talk about the problem supervenience poses for nonnaturalism. Nonnaturalists too have the commonsense reaction to such cases that underwrites supervenience claims. Nonnaturalists agree with Moore that we can specify the base properties in *Supervenience** as nonmoral. They can agree that, so interpreted, *Supervenience** is true. And this commits them to thinking that we have necessary connections between two sets of properties, properties that if nonnaturalists are correct are distinct from one another. So the supervenience of the one set on the other is not a trivial consequence of the sort explained by properties supervening on themselves. The supervenience claim for nonnaturalists is thus fairly robustly metaphysical. It links the distribution of one set of real properties to the distribution of another set of distinct and also real properties. The distribution of any property in the first nonnatural set cannot vary between two scenarios (or possible worlds if you like) without a variation of properties in the other set across the same scenarios.

When we have links of this sort between two distinct sets of properties, it is fair to ask for an explanation. Even if the relationship weren't necessary, we would want an explanation when one property only varies with another property or set of properties. Take for example the claim that all species whose members have hearts are also species whose members have kidneys. If this is true, in our world, being a creature of a kind that normally has a heart supervenes on being a creature that normally has a kidney. And yet these are distinct properties. We may not know the explanation but it seems fair enough to think there must be one. It is very tempting to speculate that there must be some causal story involving natural selection that explains the correlation. And that is true even in this simple example, where the supervenience in question is contingent as opposed to necessary. In cases where we think a supervenience claim is necessary we should want even more of an explanation. We should want to know why things could not have been otherwise. So it is certainly fair to ask such a question in the moral case: Why is it necessary that moral properties supervene on nonmoral properties, given that they are sets of distinct properties?

Many contemporary metaphysicians are persuaded that Hume was right to think that there could not be necessary connection between distinct existences. We're already acquainted with *Hume's dictum*, as some call it, from the debate over the Humean Theory of Motivation, but it is relevant here as well. *Supervenience** postulates a necessary connection between moral properties on the one hand and nonmoral properties on the other. So it falls afoul of *Hume's dictum*.

It will be helpful to be a bit more careful about the nature of the problem because not every supervenience claim entails a necessary *connection*. Any set of necessary facts supervenes on whatever you like. For, if some fact is necessary it could not be otherwise. And if it could not be otherwise, it could not be otherwise without a change in any other set of facts you like. Similarly, if the extension of a property is necessary, then there can be no change or difference in what it applies to without a difference in anything else you like. I should illustrate with an example. The facts of pure mathematics are necessary. There can be no difference in those facts. So there can be no difference in those facts without a difference in some other facts. But this is not mysterious at all and requires no explanation beyond whatever explanation we give of the necessity of pure mathematics. We therefore don't need a connection between the facts of pure mathematics and the other facts to explain why mathematical facts don't change unless these other facts do. We just need claims about the nature of pure math.

But that isn't how it seems to work with ethical supervenience. We don't think that moral facts supervene on the nonmoral facts merely because the moral facts never change or differ. Nor do we think that the distribution of rightness or wrongness in the world supervenes on the distribution of other properties because we think these other properties irrelevant to determining what is right or wrong. We think supervenience holds because we think the nonmoral nature of an action or thing partly determines its moral nature. In our earlier discussion, confessing the nonadmirable fact was right because of the various other features that action had—that it involved speaking truly to a friend who expected certain things of you, and so on. The supervenience displayed in that case, the fact that the action could not but have been right given the same nonmoral facts about it, involved precisely *a connection* between those nonmoral facts and its rightness. So it looks like the non-naturalist must deny Hume's dictum. That may not be so bad. Hume was a clever man but many things that seemed obvious to him and even obvious to us when he said them turn out to have problematic implications. His dictum may have been one of these. In any case, nonnaturalists look to be up to their elbows in necessary connections between distinct properties.

All of this underlines the original demand for an explanation of the necessary connection. We have a relationship of covariation, where the explanation of the covariation is asymmetric. Differences of one sort require differences of the other sort, but not vice versa. And we want to know why they require them. A theorist like Moore, who takes the target moral property to be simple, seems to be at a disadvantage in trying to explain such things. What can such a theorist say?

Here is one kind of response that might be open. It is to suggest that it is ethical facts that secure the relations between the supervenient ethical properties and the base nonnormative properties (Kramer, 2009, pp. 352–353). So, for example, if utilitarianism turns out to be true, there won't be any difference in the rightness of two actions without a difference in their happiness-promoting properties (or something on that order depending on which utilitarian theory you buy).[8] But this is just to say that there is a necessary connection between the happiness-promoting facts and the rightness of an option. Here we have another necessary connection that you might want explained. I'm not sure that merely calling it a moral fact adds much to the explanation unless you go on to tell me more about the nature of moral facts and the properties they involve. And that is something Moore's simplicity claim seems to rule out.

So I think it will be helpful to the nonnaturalist to give up on simplicity. Giving up on simplicity at least lets the nonnaturalist say something about the internal structure of normative (including moral) properties. And that structure can then be used to at least say something that might look more like a kind of explanation. Let's look at Tim Scanlon's (2014) proposal, for an example. Scanlon is willing to say something about the structure of basic normative properties so he is not treating them as simple and unstructured. Scanlon thinks we can explain all other normative properties as reason-giving properties. An action will be morally wrong, on his view, if there is a certain kind of reason for not doing it. And an action will be permissible if it isn't wrong. It will be required if not doing it is wrong, and so on. So the supervenience of these moral properties on other properties will depend on the supervenience of reasons on these properties. Reasons, Scanlon further tells us, are facts that fill a certain place in a four-place relation:

> "is a reason for" is a four-place relation, $R(p, x, c, a)$, holding between a fact p, an agent x, a set of conditions c, and an action or attitude a. This is the relation that holds just in case p is a reason for a person x in situation c to do or hold a. (Scanlon, 2014, p. 31)

If the worry is about Hume's dictum, we haven't made any real progress since **R**, the reasons relation, is now a relation between four distinct existences, and Scanlon thinks that this relation holds of necessity. But if we're just worried about getting an explanation, it seems like we've made some progress. We've been told something that together with more information about the relation **R** might help us to understand why reasons supervene on other facts. There is already a little bit of help in the structure of the four-place relation insofar as the structure makes clear that whether a fact is a reason for a person or not depends on the conditions in which that fact occurs. And this helps to make clear that at least potentially the very same fact p, in a different context would not be a reason for even the very same agent. If the context is a set of natural facts, this structure helps highlight one kind of natural variation that would lead to a difference in which facts are reasons. It doesn't appear to be a full explanation yet, but it does seem to make the supervenience relation less opaque.

There is further work that the structure can do because it makes clear that the nature of the facts that might be reasons, the act or attitude-type they may be reasons for, and the conditions specified by **c** all work together to determine the reasons an agent has. The schema allows Scanlon to factor an explanation for the extension of the reasons relation in the actual world into two components: (1) A necessary truth about the extension of the **R**-relation across all the possible combinations of facts, agents, circumstances, and actions or attitudes. And (2) contingent facts about which of combinations are instantiated.[9] Since the truth of the first claim about the extension of the **R**-relation is necessary it supervenes on any other truths. There can be no change/difference in the truth of that claim without a change/difference in the truth of other claims because that fact doesn't change truth value no matter what. So there is no mystery about why that basic moral truth supervenes on the nonmoral truths. We also don't have contingent facts about the distribution of nonmoral properties playing any role in the status of this basic normative truth. So no mystery so far. Given the content of that necessary truth there is also no mystery about how changing the nature of the contingent nonmoral facts could change the facts about who has a reason to do what. The first necessary truth tells us precisely how that works. And that explanation ensures that nonbasic moral truths supervene on the relevant nonmoral truths.

I should make clear that I don't think we've got everything we could possibly want by way of an explanation. The first necessary component in our explanation does relate distinct existences so we haven't given an explanation that avoids running afoul of Hume's dictum. But we have at least pushed the explanatory demand back to explaining the principle or function that tells us the extension of the reasons relation.

There may be room for the nonnaturalist to say more, depending on what further she is willing to say about the **R**-relation. What we have is that the reasons relation relates agents, facts, and options for acting or attitudinizing in a context. We want to know why these facts are reasons for agents to do these acts (have these attitudes) in these contexts. Or to put it another way, why do these facts in this context constitute a reason for this agent to do this act (have this attitude)? Put that way it looks like it is asking a question about constitution or composition. And we have other domains in which constitution and composition occur, and other examples of constitution and composition relations. Perhaps it is possible to find some guidance there.

We have for example the relation of statues to the stuff that makes them up. A particular statue may be made of clay in a certain configuration. How is it that this clay can make up the statue? I'm not sure I know exactly what to say, but I'm pretty sure the explanation will have to involve facts about the nature of statues, that they are objects that must have a shape, that the shape must be discernible by people contemplating them, and so on. And then it will talk about how clay is able to fill the role of composing such a thing. It might even be the case that anything that fills the role in the way clay does (when certain further things are true of it) will compose a statue. (I'm going out on a limb here, but I'm doing it on behalf of the nonnaturalist.) If that were so, at least in this case, to have a good explanation we are going to have to treat being a statue as a certain sort of role property and then explain the constitution relation by showing how clay is capable of playing that role. Other things that don't constitute a statue will, we might argue, not be able to play that role.

Many philosophers think that in worlds with laws like ours psychological properties supervene on physical properties. And we can think of that as involving a constitution relation as well. These physical states constitute these mental states in such and such conditions. Philosophers have found it very natural to think of the mental properties as functional role properties. To believe that the carpet is red is to be in a state of mind that plays a certain role. That role has it interact with other states of mine in specified ways. Together with the desire to avoid red things it motivates a person to avoid the carpet. When paired with a the desire to sleep on something red it motivates a person to bed down on the carpet, and so on. We might then explain the constitution of this mental state by the relevant physical states by showing how the other properties of the physical states make those states apt for filling the roles definitive of that mental state. There are a couple of things to notice here. One is that we seem to be giving a nonreductive specification of the relevant role—we specify it by citing connections with other possible mental states and with actions. So this seems like a sort of thing a nonnaturalist might be willing to do with respect to normative relations such as the **R**-relation. Nothing so far violates nonnaturalist anti-reductive scruples. The other thing to notice is just that this involves being willing to say quite a bit about the nature of the psychological states and the roles they play. If the moral or normative nonnaturalist is willing to be as informative about the nature of the normative they have moved quite a ways from Moore's conclusion that the nonnatural must be simple. And thirdly, you should notice that I'm so far just dealing in analogies. I haven't said anything concrete about the nature of the reasons relation that we could use in applying this strategy to it. So maybe it won't pan out. Still I'm hoping that I've sketched the worry about explaining supervenience in a way that takes it seriously and also made some suggestion about how a nonnaturalist might try to answer it.

13.4.1.   Partners in Guilt Across the Great Divide?

The supervenience worry is an old one. It goes back as far as Mackie (1946, 1977) who used the claim that moral properties must supervene on non-moral properties as a premise in one of his arguments from queerness. Mackie aimed at all realist views, not just nonnaturalism and he didn't put the worry as an explanatory demand. Still he did talk of something like a making relation between the supervening facts and the moral facts and he did ask what we could possibly mean by 'because' when we say an action "is wrong because it is a piece of deliberate cruelty." I bring up Mackie here because he himself suggested one response to the supervenience worry. That was to find partners in guilt where we were pretty sure similar super-venience relations hold and then argue on that basis that supervenience is not so strange after all. That's not how I was deploying the supervenience of the psychological on the physical in the preceding section—I was using it as a source for suggestions about how one might try to explain super-venience. But plenty of realists have followed Mackie's suggestion. Often they cite the example of psychology supervening on the physical (Shafer-Landau, 2003, p. 88). There are several rejoinders on behalf of the naturalist, including that of citing differences between the cases, such as that the psychological necessity seems to depend on scientific laws whereas the supervenience of the moral on the nonmoral would survive a change of scientific laws.

My interest here however is with what we should think were the partners in guilt strategy to be successful. Suppose that we find a sufficient number of other perfectly ordinary or at least indubitable instances of such a super-venience relation elsewhere. So then we decide is isn't too strange to accept supervenience in the normative and moral realms. If all of the instances we find involve the supervenience of one set of natural properties on another set of natural properties we may have undermined the argument that nor-mative properties are "just too different" from nonnormative properties. Or, to put the same point in a somewhat friendlier way, maybe we will have discovered that there is just no bright line between naturalism and nonnatu-ralism. At least some naturalists had after all been busy arguing that the relationship of the normative to physics was not interestingly different from the relationship of other special science properties to physics. They suggested that there were no interesting identity relations between psychological and biological properties on the one hand, and physical properties on the other, even though the facts of psychology and biology supervene on the physical facts.

13.5. Moral Epistemology, Reliability, and the Because *Desideratum*

Chapter 3 laid out some epistemic worries about even minimally realist metaethical positions. The general thought was that any theory that says that some of our moral beliefs count as moral knowledge will have to explain how it is that we come to know them. The issue becomes more pressing whenever a view says that the relevant moral properties are properties over and above the ordinary natural properties belief in which is ultimately based in observation. Here I don't mean to limit the ordinary natural properties to directly observable properties, but also to include other physical, biological, and natural properties and facts, belief in which may be justified by ampliative inferences such as inference to the best explanation. The worry comes in once we are justified in believing whatever we know about those. How is it that we get from there to knowledge of the moral facts and to knowledge of the extension of moral rightness, wrongness, goodness, badness, and so on. To some extent the same issue falls out of nonreductive naturalist views. If you think that the moral properties are natural but still further properties over and above the natural properties on which they supervene, how do we find out which things have those moral properties? The fact that one theorist calls them natural and the other doesn't seems neither here nor there with respect to epistemic issues.

Moore and other nonnaturalists typically answer this challenge by positing a faculty of intuition. In fact that response is so typical that nonnaturalists are often just called *intuitionists*. I argued in chapter 3 that this faculty should not be thought of as coming with its own proprietary sense organ on the analogy of a third eye that could independently tell which things were right and which wrong. For that way of thinking of it would lead the supervenience of the moral on the descriptive to be a complete mystery. Why should we have any confidence that the output of this sixth sense organ would always treat descriptively similar items in the same way? Rather what the intuitionist needs is a reliable ability to go from facts about the nonmoral nature of things up for evaluation, to verdicts or defeasible judgements about whether things of that nonmoral sort were of a certain moral sort (right, good, or whatever). Given that this faculty should not be paired with a special sense organ, it is open to nonnaturalists (and nonreductive naturalists, for that matter) to think of it as a faculty of judgement that from the inside doesn't seem any different than other judgemental abilities that we have. In fact it doesn't have to be distinct in any way from our other judgemental abilities, except that it will deliver somewhat different contents than judgements about other things.

If it is to be capable of giving us knowledge we need it to be at least somewhat reliable. It had better at least be more likely to get things right than to get things wrong. And, intuitively, it seems we would also want it to yield the correct judgements because they are correct, or because matters are as we judge. Judgements that are correct but accidental don't count as knowledge (Gettier, 1963). Let me say a little bit more about each of these in turn, that is about reliability and nonaccidentality.

There are various issues in the literature in the neighborhood of reliability. On one way of understanding, rebutting the worry requires showing that it isn't just a massive coincidence that our beliefs about morality happen to be close to true, at least across a wide range. Sharon Street's (2006) evolutionary arguments push in that direction. She suggests that our actual moral judgements reflect our affective natures and dispositions and that these are the result of a process of evolution that we have no reason to think would have been sensitive to moral truths. Given that lack of sensitivity, it would be a massive coincidence that we are right.[10] For the dispositions we have will then be independent of the truth about morality. Various authors have responded to the charge of massive coincidence by, in effect, giving a kind of common cause argument:

1. The contents of morality is not a coincidence since moral truths are necessary.
2. The content of morality is substantially built around such and such moral truths.
3. Natural selection would select for creatures that cared about things closely related to such and such.

Different authors have filled in different values of such and such. Enoch (2011) suggests that the goodness of survival and reproductive success make up a good part of morality and pointed out that it is no surprise that evolution selected for caring about those. Skarsaune (2011) suggests that pleasure is good and that the evolutionary function of pleasure depends on our caring about it. My own favorite response would cite reciprocal limited altruism as both an important part of the content of morality and also as something you would expect to evolve in social creatures like us (Sober and Wilson, 1999).

Street herself suggests that her challenge is specifically to views that make moral truths facts that don't connect with us. If she is right about that, it once again looks like nonnaturalists who eschew simplicity are in a somewhat better place to respond to her than those who don't. If Scanlon is right reasons are essentially relational and agent-involving. One of the four places in the reasons relation must be filled by an agent or at least a kind of agent. And that at least helps him to respond to Street's challenge, if not answer it completely.

There is quite a lot more to say about Street's challenge. But it is also important to realize that we should not just be worried about evolution and any luck involved in the origin of our faculties. If I have a microscope that gives me access to things too small to see, you don't undermine my claims to knowledge by pointing out that I won it in a very chancy lottery. To be sure that shows that it is in one sense a massive coincidence that I know about the paramecium on the slide in front of me. But, because microscopes are reliable, I nonetheless know about the paramecium. The point cuts in two directions. Some sorts of coincidence are mitigated if we have reason to believe our current epistemic methods are reliable. That helps the nonnaturalist realist. But we should still be concerned about the reliability of our methods, even if we have gotten past worries about their origin. We should want to know whether the way we come to have beliefs about what is right, wrong, good, bad, and so on, is sufficiently reliable that we might credit ourselves with knowledge of moral matters. And this involves ruling out a different kind of brute luck than the evolutionary argument tends to focus us on. The most important question is about how our judgements, as a matter of fact, are likely to get things at least somewhat right, however they came to be.

In some good sense, the only resources we have to answer this question are our capacities of judgement that include the very ability we wish to believe is reliable. This can be a bracing thought, but it is in a way no different than how it is with any other capacity of judgement. We don't have a grip on the reliability of our five senses without using those very senses. Pointing this out is not yet to answer the question, but I think I'll leave issues about the bare correctness of our moral judgements here.

Reliability of the kind relevant to knowledge requires more than correctness. We also, it seems to me, want to know that we believe what we do about morality *because* we got things right. Whatever that means. What the 'because' is supposed to capture is the idea that when we know something we're not just lucky in the sense that people in Gettier (1963) cases are lucky. We don't really come to know that it is four o'clock by looking at a stopped clock, even if the stopped clock said it was and even if it is in fact four o'clock. This is not a case in which we believe it is four o'clock *because* it is four o'clock. More generally, we want the methods by which we come to believe the things we know to be *sensitive* to the evidence. With nonnecessary matters this can be cashed out in terms of certain counterfactuals. Roughly what we want to say is that if it weren't true we would not have believed it. And our believing that it is four o'clock on the basis of the stopped clock doesn't meet that test.

Here our problem is that while many moral claims are contingent some of the most important are not. That Pete did something wrong is contingent. That mistreating a loyal employee is wrong is not. For the contingent moral truths we can construct counterfactual tests of whether our beliefs are in fact sensitive to the truth. Perhaps, following Nozick (1981), we can say something like the following. I know that Pete did something wrong only if in the most similar situation where Pete did not do something wrong, my methods would not have led me to conclude that he did. But we can, if we wish, factor these contingent claims into two components, at least if nonnaturalism is correct. (1) That Pete did an action of such and such a type. And (2) that actions of such and such a type are intrinsically wrong. The specifically ethical worry about sensitivity for nonnaturalists is about whether we are sensitive in believing (2). And the problem is that the kinds of counterfactuals that intuitively get at sensitivity for contingent matters don't seem like the right way to test whether we believe what we do about which act-types are wrong *because* they are. All of those counterfactuals will have necessarily false antecedents. For there are no situations in which the act-type in question is not wrong, at least if we have focused on the most basic relevant act-type, those that are intrinsically wrong.

We might look to other domains in which the matters at issue are necessary. In such domains we seem to have the same problem. For example, we might see if we can get some help from math, whose truths are also necessary. What would it come to ask ourselves whether if two plus two had not been four, would we still have believed that it was four? We just don't really seem to know what we're asking in that case either. Perhaps it is helpful to move to thinking about kinds of truth rather than particular truths. We might then ask what would happen if we applied the same method to propositions of the same kind that are false. If I used this method of computation to compute whether a number was prime on a nonprime number would this method still lead me to conclude that it was prime? If the answer is no, we seem to have found some sense in which my getting the answer right reflects the sensitivity of the method. Whether this can be extended to methods of reaching moral conclusions is unclear. A lot seems to turn on what counts as a method of reaching moral verdicts and also on what sorts of moral propositions are treated as being of the same general sort.

13.6. Internalism

Nonnaturalists don't have to be morals/reasons or morals/motives internalists of any sort, whether it be judgement internalism or existence internalism. But there are very natural internalist positions that fall out of certain nonnaturalist positions. Take Scanlon's position once again. He's a nonnaturalist about morality precisely because he is a nonnaturalist about reasons, and he analyzes moral claims in terms of reason claims. So he starts out a morals/reasons existence internalist. Whether that should lead him also to be a morals/reasons judgement internalist of any sort is a delicate matter that I can't do justice here. What about morals/motives existence internalism? Here again the issue is tricky, but I want to look to a paper by John McDowell to answer it. McDowell is happy to call himself a naturalist, yet many nonnaturalists view him as a fellow traveler (Dancy, 2006). McDowell favors a secondary quality account of value (McDowell, 1988). But his favored version is nonreductive, insofar as he thinks the analyses roughly like the following are enlightening:

> Something is virtuous or valuable iff it is such as to merit certain motivational responses in creatures of our kind in appropriate conditions.

The right hand side contains two terms that are themselves normative, 'merit' and 'appropriate.' He thinks analyses such as this one are informative because they explain something about the nature of virtue and value. In any case, this analysis commits a theorist to morals/motives existence internalism. But it is of a defeasible kind insofar as the motivation is required only in appropriate conditions, and only those who respond appropriately to things that merit the response will have the motivational response. This thus isn't the kind of morals/motives internalism that generates a nonnormative test for value or virtue. Yet it is a kind of internalism nonetheless.

13.7.   Nonnaturalism, Antireductionism, and Quietism?

This leads me to a last issue of classification. I've already noted that it is hard to draw a bright line between nonreductive naturalists and nonnaturalists. And McDowell is an interesting figure in that regard. As noted many nonnaturalists consider him a fellow traveler even while he's happy to claim the 'naturalist' label (on his own understanding of naturalism). Many nonnaturalists have *quietist* tendencies. Quietists think that ethics is perfectly OK on its own, without worrying about connections it may have to metaphysical commitments of other disciplines or other domains. Scanlon, for example, thinks we can vindicate reasons talk from within. It is enough, he thinks, that the questions we ask when we have practical or normative concerns are sensible and that our methods of resolving them are adequate to the point and purposes of posing them. We don't need to find a way of specifying the place of reasons in the world from outside of the normative domain. McDowell too, thinks something like this. It is enough that we can explain the structure of moral thought from the inside. The nonreductive gloss on value and virtue given by the still fully normative biconditional tells us something, and is part of vindicating morality. But that vindication does not require explicating moral or ethical claims purely in terms of the natural or in terms that don't wear their normative nature on their sleeves. I take Scanlon to have a similar view. His quietist tendencies don't prevent him from saying much that is substantive about reasons and morals.

Some nonnaturalists take quietism further than that, for example Parfit with his talk of "nonontological" existence. The idea seems to be that nonnaturalism carries no ontological commitments with it. But that is a stronger claim than the claim that you can do ethics without worrying about how it fits with the ontology of other disciplines. And it sometimes feels like people who say this stronger thing are saying something and then taking it back.

That raises an issue about whether quietists really belong with nonnaturalists at all. It was part of the setup of the book that minimal realism committed to properties (and relations) corresponding to moral predicates. And on that way of thinking of things, nonnaturalists and naturalists alike are minimal realists. They agree that there are properties but disagree about their nature. For some of the theorists with quietist inclinations, I'm inclined to think they meet this condition, but couple it with a methodological claim—that you can vindicate morality without worrying about deep metaphysics. But insofar as Parfit would seem to deny any ontological commitment to properties, I don't know where to place him.

Questions

Comprehension

C1. What do many nonnaturalists think genuine normativity comes to?
C2. What other theorists besides nonnaturalists deny that natural properties can have this kind of normativity?
C3. Explain how Moore might have used the Open Question Argument to support his nonnaturalism. (You may want to look at the relevant sections of chapter 2 to help construct this answer.)

Extension

E1. Construct a nonreductive "account" of the sort that McDowell provides for wrongness. Can you think of a counter-example to it? If you can't, could you modify it to make it subject to counter-examples without losing its nonreductive character?
E2. Suppose that moral rightness was identical to the property of promoting overall happiness. What more would need to be true for that to constrain people's reasonable beliefs about which actions are right and which actions are wrong? What does the answer to that question tell us about the autonomy of ethics?
E3. What metasemantic theory should a nonnaturalist deploy to explain how moral terms come to pick out nonnatural properties?

Reading

Read along with: Russ Shafer-Landau (2006).

Further reading: Jonathan Dancy's (2006) chapter on nonnaturalism is a sympathetic overview of nonnaturalism. Cuneo and Shafer-Landau (2014) is an ambitious defense of nonnaturalism. Margaret Little (1994b) is another good source, and should be read with Little (1994a). On the autonomy of ethics, see McPherson (2008). Matt Bedke (2009) develops Sharon Street's (2006) worry about massive coincidence in a useful way that targets nonnaturalism. The last three chapters of Russ Shafer-Landau's (2003) book develop nonnaturalist moral epistemology in fruitful ways. Crisp (2002) is also useful. Chapter 7 of David Enoch's (2011) book defends a "pre-established harmony" account of moral epistemology, that rejects any sensitivity-like test for moral knowledge.

Notes

1   To be clear, supernaturalists are not nonnaturalists. Divine command theorists, who think that rightness just is the property of doing what God demands, don't identify rightness with a natural property. But they won't by the lights of nonnaturalists be members of the club just on that basis. The nonnaturalists who are the subjects of this chapter would be just as unhappy (and just as wrong) if we could identify normative properties with supernatural properties or complex combinations of natural and supernatural properties.

2   More precisely, it is normative-property/reasons existence internalism, of which morals/reasons existence internalism is a special case if morality is normative.

3   Voluntarists believe that ethics is determined by the will of God.

4   Another way to see the worry is just to ask yourself whether you could ask the "So what?" question upon being told that one action among a number of alternatives had a simple unanalyzable nonnatural property. Thanks to Tristram McPherson for pushing me on this.

5   Russ Shafer-Landau (2003, 42ff.), a prominent nonnaturalist, raises the Euthyphro objection against constructivist naturalism including views of the sort Johnston targets.

6   Here I have in mind Parfit's (2011, 2:486) claims about "non-ontologically" existent normative properties, and in a different way internal realism of the sort that Scanlon sometimes suggests (Scanlon, 2014, p. 52).

7   Moore (1922), for example, thought that moral properties supervene on all the other properties so he would have been happy to say that there can be no difference in an item's moral properties without a difference in the item's other properties. But now take Sturgeon (2003, 2009), who thinks that moral properties supervene on natural properties just because moral properties are natural properties and all properties supervene on themselves. He would therefore not agree with Moore's formulation, nor would he want to specify that the base properties are nonmoral. Yet other naturalists will like *Supervenience** just as well when we let the base properties be nonmoral. For they are naturalists precisely because they think that moral properties are composed of natural properties and that composition requires supervenience but not identity. There are also differences between metaethicists about which relational properties get into the base. Is the base limited to intrinsic properties or does it include relational properties? And if relational properties are in the base do we include all relational properties? If any relational property of a thing can affect the moral properties it has, we wind up with the fairly weak claim that two possible worlds cannot differ in the distribution of their moral properties without also differing in their base properties. Skarsaune (forthcoming).

8   I realize that Moore took goodness to be indefinable and was often happy to define rightness in terms of goodness, so it would be more true to the letter of Moore to work with goodness than rightness. But the point isn't about Moore, it is about simplicity. I'm considering a view on which rightness is among the basic nonnatural properties, coupled with Moore's claim that the nonnatural must be simple. Working with rightness allows

me to use ordinary examples of moral theories which differ in what they say about rightness even when they agree about goodness.

9 Here I borrow a point of Mark Schroeder's (2014) that he finds in Price (1769/1974).

10 Street's actual view is a bit more nuanced than this. She thinks it would be such a coincidence if the moral truths are sufficiently independent of us. Matt Bedke (2009) also emphasizes the worry about coincidence.

14 Odds, Ends, and Morals

Our overview of substantive metaethical positions has gone in a kind of circle. We started with error theory, a view that calls ethics into question based on some of the worries about even minimal realism raised in our introductory chapters. We then surveyed different systematic attempts to defuse many of these worries, either by supplementing the minimal realist commitments or by rejecting them. Subjectivism and scientific realism took the former path, whereas noncognitivism and fictionalism (to a lesser extent) took the latter. And then we came back around to examine a view popularized by Moore in the face of the Open Question Argument, nonnaturalism. It is just minimal realism paired with the claim that the properties represented in moral thought and language are *sui generis*. My hope is that the survey organizes the main metaethical positions in a useful way, displaying them as at least somewhat natural responses to various *desiderata*, importantly among them the ability to respond to at least some of the puzzles introduced in the early chapters.

While providing a reasonably digestible overview of a complex terrain, the discussion thus far leaves a few loose ends. There are certain important theses and developments that extend beyond the purview of any particular comprehensive metaethical view. And there are a few positions, or at least terms, that may seem to have been left out. More specifically, most readers will have heard the words "rationalism," "constructivism" and "divine command theory" in metaethical contexts and may be wondering why there are no chapters on these topics. The short story is that the first two of these labels apply to variants of several of the positions we have already surveyed, and the last, divine command theory, can be relatively well understood as a supernaturalist cousin of reductive naturalism. I'll discuss each of these in the following sections. But first I want to raise one general issue that takes us beyond any particular comprehensive metaethical theory and even in a sense beyond metaethics.

14.1. From Metaethics to Metanormativity

This book presents itself as a book about metaethics. I've motivated much of the discussion by surveying various puzzles that arise from the nature of ethics and morality. Many of the features that lead to these puzzles are shared by a somewhat larger domain of enquiry that includes ethics but goes beyond it. We might call this domain the *normative*. Very roughly, a domain is normative if it involves standards for guiding choices, such as choices between actions or beliefs. Typically when someone thinks some domain is genuinely normative they think that those standards should get a grip on the agent or chooser, so that he or she *should* choose as the standards commend. Philippa Foot's sexist club rules are not genuinely normative because there is no good reason to obey *those* standards. Since most people think there are normative standards that go beyond the norms of morality, we can think of morality as a proper subset of the normative. There are standards of prudence that may require you to take your own future into account when making a decision. These are genuinely normative insofar as you really do have reason to look out for your longer term interest. There are standards for good reasoning, which recommend certain inferences on the basis of various sorts of evidence and which disfavor other sorts of reasoning such as that involved in wishful thinking. You really should endorse the conclusion of a short argument whose premises you accept unless you suspend belief in the premises. That's what you have reason to do. At least so say standard views about these nonethical domains.

Because these domains have so much in common with the ethical, many of the concerns that get people interested in metaethics also motivate an interest in the parallel metanormative issues. And thinking about metanormativity often generates positions that parallel standard metaethical views. We've already seen this at various points along the way but it is worth emphasizing. Probably anyone who favors nonnaturalism in ethics will favor nonnaturalism about normativity in general. This is no real surprise given the kind of arguments nonnaturalists make for their contention that ethics is just too different from the natural to involve natural properties. The features of moral judgement that nonnaturalists point to are features shared by reason involving judgements quite generally. For example, it is as easy to find open questions about the nature of practical rightness in general (including nonmoral rightness) as it is to find such questions regarding moral rightness. Similarly, the kinds of internalism that motivate some theorists to become sophisticated subjectivists or response-dependence theorists about moral properties such as moral rightness, seem just as attractive when applied to judgements of prudential reasons and the right thing to do where one's self-interest is concerned.

The point extends beyond realist and descriptivist metaethical views. The most sophisticated forms of noncognitivism start with an analysis of a very general noncognitive normative attitude, and then distinguish different normative domains by subject matter or otherwise construct moral attitudes out of the more basic normative attitude (Gibbard, 1990, 2003). The obvious advantage is that it allows the noncognitivist to construct one overarching noncognitivist explanation of the target phenomena wherever they arise.

Differences between these domains are then explained by further features that they don't all share. So the move from metaethics to metanormativity is very natural and attractive. It allows a theorist to take a shot at providing a unified explanation of common phenomena where they occur.

We should note, however, that not all metaethical positions extend to the entire normative domain as smoothly as others do. It is harder to be an error theorist about normativity in general than about ethics in particular. For it is easier to deny the existence of specifically moral practical reasons than it is to deny the existence of practical reasons in general. Suppose for example, you think there are no generally applicable other-regarding reasons. You think that whether we have reason to help others depends on our contingent concerns for them. But you also think that morality essentially requires universally binding and reason-giving requirements to help others. This combination of views naturally leads to an error theory about morality. But it is consistent with thinking that there are good reasons to do all sorts of things, even including helping others. All you deny is that such reasons are generally binding and necessarily shared. You therefore think that there are some normative truths—truths about what people have reason to do. So you would not be an error theorist about normativity in general, just about moral reasons that you believe require altruistic categorical imperatives.

Still, even error theorists about morality pay some respect to the cross-domain similarities that underwrite the move to metanormative theorizing. When Mackie (1977, p. 39) suggests that realists can answer his queerness arguments by pointing to companions in guilt, he is in part noting that there are domains besides ethics that involve many of the same features that motivate his error theoretic approach to ethics. Some of these are reasons to be error theorists about the normative in general if they are reasons to be error theorists about morality. And conversely, if these shared features aren't reasons to be error theorists about normativity in general they are then also not strong reasons for adopting error theory in the moral domain.

14.2. Supernaturalism

Supernaturalism is the view that moral properties are properties or relations involving divine or supernatural entities. The most well-known supernaturalist view is probably *divine command theory*, the theory that (1) for an action to be morally required is for it to be commanded by God, or favored by his or her will, (2) for an action to be morally forbidden is for it to be ruled out by God's command or will, and (3) for an action to be permitted is for it not to be ruled out by God's commands, and so on. Depending on whether one thinks 'morally right' means morally required or just morally permitted, one will choose an appropriately related reduction for rightness. Further moral properties can be analyzed in a similar spirit.

This makes the view very like reductive naturalism, except that it expands the ontology to include supernatural entities, and uses these supernatural entities to provide a reduction base for moral properties and the contents of moral thought.[1] As a result the view faces many of the same burdens as ordinary naturalist views and has available many of the same resources to meet these burdens. This may seem surprising, but it isn't really all that startling. Moore thought that the Open Question Argument ruled out both naturalistic and supernaturalistic accounts of moral terms and properties. And the various explanatory burdens that naturalists must shoulder equally burden the supernaturalist. Just as naturalists need to provide a theory of reference for moral terms that explains how these terms latch on to the natural properties for which they stand, supernaturalists need to provide a theory of reference to explain how those terms latch on to supernatural properties. That the properties are natural or supernatural doesn't much change the problem. Perhaps a god's omnipotence might make the causal properties of supernatural referents more robust, and perhaps this could make it easier for such properties to stand in the right causal relation to be a referent according to a causal regulation theory like Boyd's, but the burden is still to vindicate that sort of theory as a theory of moral reference.

And similarly with epistemology, though with a twist. Perhaps in principle, a god could easily make it known which things he or she approves and disapproves of, and thereby simplify our deliberations about what is right and what is wrong. But in actual fact there seems to be no consensus about the exact contours of divine approval and disapproval where controversial moral claims are involved. Religious texts leave much undecided and yet people take themselves to know divine views on these matters. It often seems, people reason first about what they take to be right and wrong and adjust their views about divine approval accordingly. So adherents of divine command theory will have to have a story to tell about how we come to know what is right and what is wrong, just as naturalists must. One such story posits a faculty of rational intuition, implanted by a benevolent God, so as to help us figure out what is right and what is wrong. Rational intuition on this picture would give us insight into the properties of God's will, and this may fit well with *reliabilist* epistemology. Reliabilists think that many of our epistemic methods get their epistemic status in virtue of being reliable guides to their subject matter, even when we have no independent way to vindicate the methods in question. What distinguishes our five senses from intuition is that the former as a group are reliable guides to the things we come to know through their functioning, whereas intuition is not similarly reliable. On this view, if divinely implanted rational intuition gives us access to God's will, we are justified in believing what we do through its functioning. The strategy depends on reliabilism, but if reliabilism is correct we have a parallel both with reductive naturalism and with nonnaturalist intuitionism. The parallel with naturalism will be that our reliable empirical faculties give us knowledge of the natural properties with which rightness is identified. The parallel with nonnaturalist intuitionism will be even closer. Both theories will posit a reliable faculty of intuition giving us access to moral truths over and above any natural truths. But the nonnaturalist will say these truths are nonnatural whereas the divine command theorist will say they are supernatural.

Supernaturalism might have an advantage when it comes to explaining several varieties of internalism. A punitive god could give people plenty of self-interested reason to do what she or he approved of. And, the rightness of an action might motivate those who believe in such a god to act in accordance with that god's wishes. But we might worry that it generates the wrong kind of reason to do what is right. We would hope that people are kind to one another because kind actions are a fitting response to those who benefit from our treatment, not because we are afraid of being punished if we don't.

14.2.1. Euthyphro Worries

The most famous objection to divine command theory comes from Plato's Euthyphro and it seems to raise a related issue.[2] As we saw in chapter 13, that argument is posed as a dilemma. Socrates asks, do the gods love certain actions because they are pious, or are they pious because the gods love them. Nonnaturalists, as we saw, can adapt that question to challenge naturalist reductions of rightness to natural properties. A similar question can be put to divine command theories: Does God command certain actions because they are right, or are those actions right because God commands them? The question is thought to pose a challenge because it seems intuitive to think that God should be justified in commanding us to do what's right. And we don't want it to be the case that some actually heinous action might be right, if only God had commanded otherwise. Would not indiscriminate killing have been wrong even if no god had forbidden it? The divine command theorist who offers her theory as a reduction of rightness, must say no. She can make that answer easier to swallow by arguing that it is necessary to God's nature that s/he commands all and only those things s/he does. But that answer then requires further defense.

Supernaturalist might benefit from borrowing a naturalist response to similar unease about the normative status of reductively analyzed moral properties. This is appropriate as the original target of the unease was theological voluntarism of which divine command theory is a species. We noted the response as we were discussing nonnaturalist exploitation of the Euthyphro objection and Korsgaard's demands that a metaethical account answer "the normative question." Korsgaard (1996) suggests that any adequate account must show why an agent must do what an agent is normatively required to do. Answers to the Euthyphro that have God commanding right actions because they are good, at least gesture in the direction of such an answer since they imply that God had reason to command as he or she did. But they fail as reductions since the answer depends on God having choice-independent reasons to command as she or he does. Those choice-independent reasons remain unreduced. Offering the other answer, that the actions are right because God commands them, threatens to treat the choice as arbitrary and hence to leave the normative question unanswered.

Supernaturalists might follow a certain style of reductive naturalist (Schroeder, 2005, 2007) to distinguish two kinds of "why?" questions. Sometimes when we want to know why something is wrong we are asking a moral question, that is we are asking for the reasons why it is wrong. But at other times we are asking a metaethical question. In those cases we are asking after the nature of the property that actions have when they are wrong. Reductive naturalists think the answer will cite a natural property, whereas divine command theorists cite being forbidden by God. Both can respond that it is a mistake to take these answers as answers to the first kind of "why?" question. The question here is metaethical and gets a metaethical answer, whereas "why?" questions that ask for justifications are different questions altogether. We should not expect answers to this kind of metaethical question to answer justificatory questions. To put the point a different way, sometimes we explain why someone has a reason to do some action by showing that action to be a way of doing something we already think the person has a reason to do.[3] You have a reason to go to class and discuss the reading, for example, because you have a reason to understand metaethics, and going to class and discussing the reading is a way to come to understand metaethics. I have a reason to work on this book because that is the only way I will finish it, and I have lots of good reasons to finish the book. And so on. This kind of answer goes some way to answering Korsgaard's normative question because once we get the explanation we can see that the person has a reason of the sort we are trying to explain. But such explanations must run out. For we can as easily ask why I have a reason to finish the book or why you have a reason to understand metaethics. At some point we must find a reason that does not get explained as a way of doing something else we have reason to do. Any "why?" questions about it must get a different sort of answer. Or else we have a regress.

Reductive naturalist accounts of the ultimate nature of moral reasons or obligations are one sort of different answer. If they're correct they tell us why someone has a reason to do what they have reason to do, without reference to something else they have reason to do. To have a moral reason to Φ is for Φ to be a means to something you desire, or for Φ to be what your ideally rational self would want you to want, or for Φ to be what promotes the proper functioning of the agent in question, or whatever the reduction proposes. These claims are not meant as telling us about something other than Φ-ing that the agent has reason to do and that the agent can do by Φ-ing. They just tell us what it is for us to have a reason to Φ. Reductive supernaturalists can make the very same move. They might say to have a reason to Φ, is for Φ to be one of the actions commanded by God for those in one's circumstances. That, they might suggest, just is what it is to have a reason to do something. This looks like a formally adequate response for those who wish to answer the Euthyphro question by saying that the actions are right because God commands them. It is entirely on par with the similar answer given by a reductive naturalist when she offers an account of what it is to have a moral reason.

I suspect that most people drawn to divine command theories may find this response on their behalf unsettling. For I suspect most divine command theorists think that we have reason to do what God commands and that this is part of why divine command theory seems attractive to them. Most theists, I predict, will view their reasons to do what God commands as good answers to non-metaethical "why?" questions about our justifications for acting. We have reason not to expose unwanted children at birth because God commands us not to, and we have reason to do what God commands. But that kind of explanation assumes we have independent reason to do what God commands, perhaps due to his or her perfect nature or benevolence. And then we no longer have a general reductive supernatural account of moral reasons. For at least the reasons to do what God commands are treated as there already independent of those commands. So this way of viewing divine command theory no longer fully answers metaethical questions about why we have the moral reasons we do.

There may be one further move available to the divine command theorist who wishes to retain the attractive thought that we have reason to do what God commands, but also to reduce moral reasons to facts about God's commands. That is to distinguish moral reasons from the reasons we have to obey God's commands. Such a theorist could identify moral reasons with those reasons we have because of God's commands, but insist that we have independent nonmoral reason to do whatever God commands. That independent reason would not get a supernatural analysis as explained by God's commands. The notion of reason in general would either have to get another analysis, or remain unanalyzed. Such theorists will be in effect offering a reduction of the moral to a subspecies of the *normative* or reason-giving, but offering no reduction of the normative or reason-giving in general.

This won't be entirely metaethically or metanormatively satisfying, at least until these theorists say more about reasons and normativity in general. Many of the same issues that got us looking for an analysis of moral properties, including moral reasons, apply to reasons and normative properties in general, even outside of the normative domain. If the features that cause us to seek an account of moral stuff are features shared by normative stuff in general, we can't avoid wanting an account of normativity in general. That is what led to the developments highlighted in section 14.1. Partial divine command theories, by which I mean supernatural reductions of moral reasons that don't extend to reasons or normative entities and properties in general, stop short of offering an explanation of at least some of the things that puzzled us in the first place.

Before turning to other issues, I want to reemphasize the extent to which supernatural theories share the burdens of reductive naturalistic metaethical theories. This implies that one of the best ways to develop supernaturalism is to borrow resources from naturalist theories and deploy them in defending supernaturalist positions.

14.3. Constructivism and Contractualism

Very roughly, *constructivism* is the view that ethical truths are determined or constructed by the outputs of some sort of ideal procedure. So on one interpretation of this broad idea, response-dependence theories are constructivist; such theories equate moral truths with truths about how some sort of responder would respond under some set of conditions that define a procedure of sorts. Take Bernard Williams' characterization of reasons as an illustration. He suggests that we have a reason to do something if correct deliberation based on true facts, starting from our existing motivational set, would yield a motivation to do that thing. This is to specify what we have reason to do as the output of that deliberative procedure, and it is in that sense a constructivist account of reasons. A moral rationalist, who thinks that our moral obligations are a subset of the things we have a reason to do, might take this idea to apply constructivism about moral obligation and say:

> We have a moral obligation to do an action iff correct deliberation from our existing motivational set and based on true facts would wind up motivating us to do that action.

This is in one good sense a constructivist view about morality. It suggests that what we have moral obligations to do what we would have motivations to do after a certain sort of procedure.[4]

These claims make the view *somewhat* reductionist in that it reduces facts about morality into a different kind of fact, facts about correct deliberation. But it is only *partly* reductionist. It reduces one kind of normative thing (morality) to another kind of normative thing (correct deliberation). But as it stands it stops short of reductive *naturalism*. For all that has been said so far the rationalist constructivist could think no further reduction was possible or she could go on to offer a further reduction of deliberative correctness in naturalistic terms. So rationalism of this sort is compatible with both naturalism and nonnaturalism. And, insofar as this sort of rationalism is constructivist about moral obligations, constructivism too is compatible with either view. We can use a helpful distinction introduced by Sharon Street (2008). Some kinds of constructivism are *restricted*, limiting themselves to a part of the overall normative domain. Others are *thoroughgoing*—they countenance no limits and cover normative matters in general. The view just sketched would be restricted if we don't say anything more about the nature of correct deliberation, but it would become thoroughgoing if we went on to give a constructive analysis of such deliberation without invoking any further unreduced normative concepts or properties.

What of realism/antirealism? Many authors treat constructivism as an antirealist view because they think realism and response dependence are incompatible. The basic thought seems to be that such views allow the responses of those in the procedure to determine what is right or obligatory, and that such determination makes moral status too dependent on us to be realist. Once again, the issue may turn on how the limited constructivism is supplemented with further commitments. For all we've said, the relevant procedure might involve substantive constraints on correct deliberation. The wayward judgements of those who find cruelty permissible might run afoul of these substantive criteria for correctness. And now the view doesn't leave the content of morality up to us in the way it would without such constraints.[5] (The discussion of response dependent theories in section 7.3.1, makes essentially the same point.) On the other hand, a constructivist might say that there are no such substantive constraints and that correctness just is whatever deliberators judge it to be. That would certainly be antirealist. I'll illustrate these points by contrasting two influential views of this sort, one realist and nonnaturalist, the other antirealist and naturalistic.

Scanlon's "Contractualism and Utilitarianism" introduces the idea that rightness and wrongness depend on what could be agreed upon by people who were motivated to regulate their behavior in ways that similarly motivated others could not reasonably reject. He suggests that the shared goal of cooperating on such terms limits what we can reasonably reject. An action is wrong if no reasonably unrejectable system of rules would allow it. An action is permissible if some such systems would allow it. And it is required if no such system or rules would permit refraining from it.

Let me fill in some detail. Suppose some people are in fact motivated to cooperate with others on terms they could not reasonably object to. Having such motivation would make a difference to what such people could reasonably accept or reject as the terms of cooperation. If there is only one option that you could not reasonably reject, and I want to cooperate with you on terms you can't reasonably reject, then I had better not reject that one option. To reject it would be to give up on cooperating with you in that way. So it would be unreasonable to reject that option (given my goal) unless I had really strong reasons of some other sort to reject that option. If you are similarly motivated, wanting to cooperate with me in the same spirit, your reasonable rejection will also be effected by your having cooperation as a goal. Suppose there are two sets of rules or terms of cooperation that leave me tolerably well off, but only one of those leaves you tolerably well off. And suppose also that there are two sets leaving you tolerably well off, but only one of those (the one already mentioned) that also leaves me tolerably well off as well. In that case we each have reason not to reject the single option that leaves both of us tolerably well off. That's the only one neither of us can reasonably reject. So our motivations to cooperate on terms that aren't reasonably rejectable, together with the reasons we might have to reject various terms of cooperation, make it the case that only certain terms of cooperation are acceptable. And the rightness and wrongness of certain actions can then be decided with reference to whether they are allowed by those terms.

This is constructivist in one good sense (O'Neill, 2003). What is right and what is wrong falls out of a certain set of constraints that yield an answer to a collective choice problem. But it is also still only providing a restricted normative-to-normative reduction. What is morally right, wrong, permissible, or impermissible is a function of further normative facts—the reasons people have to cooperate with each other on acceptable terms, and the reasons people have to reject certain terms of cooperation. It is the interplay of these sets of reasons that leads the procedure to generate a result. That only these rules are acceptable to all motivated to cooperate with others on acceptable terms is a wrong-making fact for any actions those terms would disallow. And that these are the only universally acceptable (nonrejectable) terms is itself a function of the reasons people might have to reject them and their strength as compared with the strength of their reasons to cooperate. Insofar as these are reasons, they are themselves normative entities. Scanlon, as he makes clear in later work (Scanlon, 1998, 2014) thinks reasons cannot be further reduced. So he's a kind of nonnaturalist about reasons, and by extension about moral reasons. And, while he wants to avoid heavy duty metaphysics, he does think there are such things as reasons and that what these are is not up to us. So we can see Scanlon's restricted constructivism as generating a form of nonnaturalist realism about morality.

Sharon Street (2008), by contrast, is a thoroughgoing constructivist about all things normative. She thinks that reasons themselves can be given a response dependent and seemingly nonnormative reduction:

> According to metaethical constructivism, the fact that X is a reason to Y for agent A is constituted by the fact that the judgement that X is a reason to Y (for A) withstands scrutiny from the standpoint of A's other judgements about reasons. (p. 223)

Since Street analyses other normative claims in terms of reasons and here analyzes facts about reasons as facts about what one would judge in certain conditions (at least on a natural reading of what withstanding scrutiny comes to), this makes all normative questions be about what one's judgements would be in those conditions. That looks to be a fact about your psychology and in some sense makes normative matters into questions of psychology. There is for Street no second-guessing the judgements of the relevant people about the reasons they have, at least in relevant ideal conditions. "The standards of correctness determining what reasons a person has are understood to be set up by *that person's* set of judgements about her reasons." This view is a view about the entire normative domain, on the assumption that other normative concepts or properties can be analyzed in terms of reasons. So this is a version of reductive naturalism of the general sort discussed in the chapters on cognitivist subjectivism. There is one tiny worry, which is that reason appears in the analysis, since an agent has a reason to Φ iff from her perspective the claim that she has a reason to Φ would survive scrutiny from the standpoint of her judgements about reasons. So we might be worried that we haven't identified the relevant psychological states independently of reliance on our views about reasons. But I think that Street intends us to be able to recognize such judgements without relying on anything normative. So the spirit of her analysis is fully reductive and naturalistic.

It is also antirealist on most people's ways of dividing full-blooded realism from antirealism. People's ideal responses are the truth-makers for all normative claims. There is no further fact that they are tracking with their responses. In a slogan, their responses are truth-making and not truth-tracking. Differently constituted people with a different sense of the upshot of rational scrutiny might make different judgements about their reasons, and be equally correct about the reasons they have just because these are the responses they have in those conditions.

So constructivism too shows up on multiple branches of the taxonomy presented in the previous chapters. It can be naturalist or nonnaturalist, depending on whether it is restricted or thoroughgoing. It can also be cognitivist or noncognitivist. Allan Gibbard's work allows us to locate versions of rationalism and constructivism even on the noncognitivist fork of our taxonomy. He suggests that judgements of morality are about the rationality of responding to various act-types with guilt and resentment (Gibbard, 1990, p. 6). Thus this is a normative-to-normative reduction in the rationalist spirit. It reduced judgements about morality to judgements about rationality. But from here it analyzes judgements of rationality as noncognitivism suggests, as expression of important and systematic noncognitive states. In particular Gibbard suggested these judgements can be understood as acceptance of sets of norms, where accepting a norm comes to something other than believing something about it. This view of Gibbard's is rationalist and noncognitivist. His 2008 book *Reconciling Our Aims* marries this rationalism to a broadly contractualist understanding of common morality. He takes over from Scanlon the idea that morality is about how to live with others on terms they could not reasonably reject. And from there he tries to argue for substantively utilitarian conclusions. It is a little unclear where exactly the metaethics ends and the substantive normative theorizing begins. Perhaps it is fair to say they overlap, so that Gibbard's contractualism is both metaethical and ethical. If that's correct we will have a restricted constructivism of just the same sort as Scanlon's, but in this case partnered with a more basic noncognitivism rather than Scanlon's intuitionism.

The upshot here is twofold. One is just that taxonomies invariably make it harder to locate certain positions, and that ours can make it easy to miss positions that combine metaethical theses restricted to the moral with other metanormative theses that cover the normative in general. The second upshot is just that it can be worth paying attention to these positions that the taxonomy makes harder to locate because they show up on more than one branch. Sometimes we should be interested in commonalities between views even when the views are importantly different in other ways. Theorists who differ about the explanation of normativity in general can learn from and borrow from those with whom they disagree. Similar problems can get similar answers, even when the problems arise within very different frameworks.

14.4. Rationalism and Reasons

Rationalism is an example of a position that can show up on many branches of our taxonomy. It has cognitivist and noncognitivist variants. It is consistent with both naturalism and nonnaturalism. Rationalism, in the present sense, is a normative-to-normative reductive thesis. It reduces facts about morality to facts about practical rationality and/or practical reasons. Typically the strategy is to identify moral facts with facts about practical rationality or reasons that have a certain sort of (distinctively moral) ground, such as altruism or respect and so on. The upshot of such a reduction would be that moral obligation is a species of rational obligation even if every rational obligation is not a moral obligation. Or, to put the point in terms of reasons, morality would favor an agent's following a course of action just when practical reasons of the right sort favor that course of action. So the view immediately entails an indefeasible form of morals/reasons existence internalism.[6]

A rationalist might go on to give a nonnatural account of reasons. Scanlon's position in the previous section is an example of such a view, at least if we read him as thinking that everyone has a reason to try to cooperate with others on terms they can't reasonably reject. But a rationalist could think that reasons can be naturalized, perhaps even in a reductive way. This is Mark Schroeder's (2007) idea. These theories are both minimally realist and cognitivist. But Gibbard's proposal that we briefly considered in section 14.1 implements a noncognitivist version of rationalism. Rationality talk is given a noncognitivist gloss, and all other normative discourse is then analyzed in terms of reasons. And moral judgements are included, although in a somewhat complicated way.

Rationalism is a species of morals/reasons existence internalism. True moral claims are claims about the reasons a person has, so they have the tightest possible connection with reasons. If you think that such internalism is attractive, that's a reason to go in for it. It certainly makes morality worth thinking about. But there can be other reasons to develop a rationalist account. If all normative truths of propositions can be analyzed into claims about reasons or rationality it makes it simpler to generate a global reduction of all such claims. First you show how to analyze other notions in terms of these. And then you offer a naturalistic account of reasons or rationality.

You will thereby have naturalized each part of the normative domain in two steps.

14.5. Conclusion

There's more to say about all of these topics, but no room to say it. I'm hoping readers come away with a good sense of the range of metaethical theories and the common issues to which they are a response. It should be clear that there are a bunch of explanatory *desiderata* that are hard to meet at the same time. I've been trying to show how this generates the diverse range of views people actually hold. My hope is also that some of these issues gripped many of my readers and that some of these will go on to contribute to the lively ongoing discussion.

Reading

Further reading: On supernaturalism, read Robert Adams (1979). On constructivism, read Sharon Street (2008), Carla Bagnoli (2011), and Hille Paakkunainen (2014). Markovits (2014) and Smith (1994) are prominent rationalist treatments of ethics.

Notes

1 My use of 'reductive' here is meant to put the focus on naturalistic theories that identify moral properties with natural properties we can already pick out in nonmoral terms, for we already have terms for divine commands, divine will, and the like. I can't think of any supernaturalist view that is like Sturgeon's (2006) naturalism in suggesting that the properties in question are supernatural but not identical to any we can already pick out in other terms.

2 The original had to do with piety.

3 Schroeder (2005, 2007) calls this the standard model for reasons explanations.

4 We shouldn't put too much weight on the word 'procedure' so that it rules out building substantive constraints into the procedure. What is and isn't correct deliberation could for all that has been said be a very substantive issue.

5 I should warn the reader that many authors use the name 'constructivism' only for anti-realist views (Shafer-Landau, 2003), though Karl Schafer (2015) uses it as I do.

6 Some authors use the term 'rationalism' as a label for this form of morals/reasons internalism; I am not. I prefer to reserve the label for the views that identify or reduce facts about morality to facts about rationality or reasons since in principle there might be necessary connections not explained by such a reduction or identification.

Glossary

This is a set of rough definitions. Often more accurate definitions would qualify these and make them more precise. You'll find the relevant qualifications in the main text where the terms are introduced.

Absolutism—the denial of relativism.

Agent internalism—the view that moral judgements (or reasons) are necessarily connected with the desires or reasons of the agent the judgement is about.

Agent relativism—the view that the truth of moral judgements is relative to some feature of the agent.

Agent subjectivism—the view that moral judgements are about the agent's desires or subjective states.

Analytic truth—a claim that is true in virtue of the meanings of the terms that state it.

Antirealism—the denial of realism.

Appraiser internalism—the view that moral judgements (or reasons) are necessarily connected with the motives or reasons of the one making the judgement.

Appraiser relativism—the view that the truth of moral judgements is relative to some feature of the appraiser.

Appraiser subjectivism—the view that moral judgements are about the desires or subjective states of those making those judgements.

A *priori* knowledge—knowledge that can be or is justified without empirical evidence.

Argument from disagreement or relativity—Mackie's argument from the fact of widespread moral disagreement to the claim that all moral claims are false or inappropriate.

Argument from queerness—Mackie's argument that moral properties or facts (if there were any) would be too odd ("queer") to actually exist. The odd features involve a commitment to some version of strong internalism, the supervenience of the moral on the nonmoral, and an intuitionist epistemology.

Categorical (as applied to reasons)—a reason is categorical if it is a reason for anyone similarly situated regardless of differences in the person's antecedent desires or commitments.

Causal regulation semantics—a theory of meaning according to which terms represent things that causally regulate their use.

Cognitive state—a representational state of mind. Beliefs are supposed to be paradigm cognitive states.

Cognitivism—the view that ethical judgements are or express beliefs.

Composition—a relation between things where one thing composes or makes up the other.

Conative state—a state of mind that is emotional or motivational. A noncognitive state.

Constitution—a relationship between things/properties in which one is made up of or constituted by another.

Cornell Realism—a form of naturalism paradigms that have been defended by certain philosophers associated with Cornell University.

Defeasible—overrideable, or qualifiable in some way.

Direct reference theory—a theory of unmediated reference for terms. (See chapter 11.)

Emotivism—a form of noncognitivism that analyzes moral terms as linguistic devices for the expression of emotion.

Empirical—relying for justification or support on evidence of the senses.

Expressive meaning—the meaning of an expression whose meaning involves expressing a state of mind.

Expressivism—a form of noncognitivism that analyzes moral terms as linguistic devices for the expression of some mental state.

Humean Theory of Motivation—the view that motivation requires noncognitive states that are independent of any belief involved.

Humean Theory of Reasons (or Rationality)—The view that a person's reasons depend on the desires the person in fact has.

Hybrid expressivism—a theory that combines noncognitivist expressivism with the claim that moral judgements also express cognitive states and/or descriptive or representational content.

Hypothetical (as applied to reasons)—depending for its status as a reason on the desires or noncognitive states of the person for whom it is a reason.

Inference to the best explanation—a form of reasoning in which one comes to accept a proposition because it is part of the best explanation of something one has reason to believe.

Internalism—the view that there are necessary connections between moral judgements or truths, on the one hand, and reasons and/or motives, on the other. For example, an internalist about the relationship between moral judgements and motivation might think that such judgements necessarily motivate those who accept them. Also similar views about the relation between reasons and motives. (See chapter 4.)

Intuitionism—an epistemology that requires a faculty capable of giving us knowledge of substantial truths that go beyond ordinary empirical knowledge of our environment. In this context, the knowledge is knowledge of how moral truths are determined by facts about the distribution of nonmoral properties.

Irrealism—antirealism; a position that isn't a form of realism.

Logical Positivist—Philosopher who, among other things, accepts a verification criterion for meaningfulness that requires meaningful nondefinitional claims to be confirmable or disconfirmable by empirical evidence.

Metasemantic—having to do with how terms get their meanings or semantic values.

Minimal realism—my term for the view that moral claims and thoughts are about or represent the world in much the same way that ordinary terms picking out everyday properties do. The realism is only minimal insofar as it need not extend to further commitments about the metaphysics of these properties. So the view is compatible with subjectivism and relativism as well as absolutism.

Modal status—the status of a claim as necessary, nonnecessary, possible, or impossible.

Moral functionalism—an analysis of moral terms that analyzes moral properties as functional role properties.

Moral realism—the thesis that moral language and thought represent the world in much the way that other language and thought do and (typically) which supposes the truth and falsity of such thought and language to be nonrelative and independent of what we think, and which regards a substantial number of such claims as true.

Moral sense theory—a theory that analyzes moral claims in terms of human reactions to the actions and objects they seem to be about.

Naturalism—a view that regards moral knowledge and its subject as importantly similar to scientific knowledge and its subject even to the point of regarding the former as a species of the latter.

Network analysis—a characterization of the nature of moral properties in terms of their position in a network of relations to other properties including other moral and normative properties. (See chapter 12.)

Nomological necessity—something that is necessary so long as the laws of nature remain as they are.

Noncognitivism—The view that moral terms do not (primarily) represent properties as a matter of meaning and that moral thought is not cognitive or representational. Instead, moral thought is portrayed as the acceptance of noncognitive/affective states of mind and moral language as serving to express those states. (See chapter 8.)

Nonnaturalism—the view that moral properties are genuine properties, but not of the same sort as either natural or supernatural properties.

Open Question Argument—Moore's argument that moral properties could not be identical to natural or supernatural properties. The argument traded on it seeming an open question whether some object characterized in natural or supernatural terms also satisfies the relevant moral characterization. (See chapter 2.)

Pragmatics—has to do with how a speaker on an occasion uses these expressions to convey something she means to communicate.

Prescriptivism—a noncognitivist view that treats moral utterances as similar to commands.

Psychological noncognitivism—the claim that moral judgements are not cognitive states.

Quietism—the view that ethics is in no need of any very controversial or metaphysically committing philosophical defense.

Real definition—a definition of what something is that is explained in the first instance by the nature of the thing and not by how we think about it, talk about it, or pick it out. Often opposed to an analytic definition.

Reductive naturalism—naturalism that identifies moral properties with natural properties, most commonly natural properties that can in principle be characterized in other terms.

Reforming definition—a redefinition of a term meant to capture the important part of how it was used up to the present time but that jettisons something possibly problematic or unclear in that prior usage.

Response-dependent—depending on or requiring essential reference to the responses of a subject. Colors are thought to be response-dependent properties by those who think it is of their essence to look a certain way to normal perceivers.

Semantic nonrepresentationalism—one of two constitutive noncognitivist claims. It holds that the meanings of moral predicates in indicative sentences are not (primarily) to represent properties. They do not serve to represent reality.

Semantics—has to do with the conventionally encoded meaning of a term.

Speaker relativism—another label for appraiser relativism.

Speaker subjectivism—another label for appraiser subjectivism.

Speech act—a communicative action using language.

Synthetic *a priori knowledge*—*a priori* (nonempirical) knowledge of substantial (nondefinitional) truths.

Tautology—a (trivial) definitional truth.

Universal prescriptivism—a variety of noncognitivism that treats moral judgements as exceptionless commands addressed to all in appropriate circumstances.

Bibliography

Adams, R. (1979). Divine command ethics modified again. *Journal of Religious Ethics, 7*(1), 66–79.

Aharoni, E., Sinnott-Armstrong, W. & Kiehl, K. (2012). Can Psychopathic Offenders Discern Moral Wrongs? A New Look at the Moral/Conventional Distinction, *Journal of Abnormal Psychology, 121*(2).

Anscombe, G. E. (1958). Modern moral philosophy. *Philosophy, 33*(124), 1–19.

Arpaly, N. (2000). On acting rationally against one's best judgment. *Ethics, 110*(3), 488–513.

Arpaly, N. (2003). *Unprincipled virtue*. Oxford: Oxford University Press.

Ayer, A. J. (1946). *Language, truth and logic* (Rev. ed.). London: Victor Gollancz.

Bach, K. (2011). Meaning and communication. In G. Russell & D. G. Fara (Eds.), *Routledge companion to the philosophy of language* (pp. 79–90). New York, NY: Routledge.

Bagnoli, C. (2011). Constructivism in metaethics. In *Stanford encyclopedia of philosophy* (Spring 2014 Edition), E. N. Zalta (Ed.), http://plato.stanford.edu/archives/win2014/entries/constructivism-metaethics/

Baker, L. R. (2007). *The metaphysics of everyday life*. Cambridge: Cambridge University Press.

Barker, S. (2000). Is value content a component of conventional implicature? *Analysis, 60*(267), 268–279.

Bar-On, D., & Sias, J. (2013). Varieties of expressivism. *Philosophy Compass, 8*, 699–713.

Barry, M. (2007). Realism, rational action and the Humean theory of motivation. *Ethical Theory and Moral Practice, 10*(3), 231–242.

Bedke, M. (2009). Intuitive non-naturalism meets cosmic coincidence. *Pacific Philosophical Quarterly, 90*(2), 188–209.

Bird, A. (1998). Dispositions and antidotes. *Philosophical Quarterly, 48*(191), 227–234.

Blackburn, S. (1984). *Spreading the word*. Oxford: Oxford University Press.

Blackburn, S. (1988). Supervenience revisited. In G. Sayre-McCord (Ed.), *Essays in quasi-realism* (pp. 59–74). Ithaca, NY: Cornell University Press.

Blackburn, S. (1998). *Ruling passions*. Oxford: Clarendon Press.

Boisvert, D. R. (2008). Expressive-assertivism. *Pacific Philosophical Quarterly, 89*(2), 169–203.

Boyd, R. N. (1988). How to be a moral realist. In G. Sayre-McCord (Ed.), *Essays on moral realism* (pp. 181–228). Ithaca, NY: Cornell University Press.

Brandt, R. (1979). *A theory of the right and the good*. Amherst, NY: Prometheus.

Brink, D. (1984). Moral realism and the sceptical arguments from disagreement and queerness. *Australasian Journal of Philosophy, 62*(2), 111–125.

Brink, D. (1986). Externalist moral realism. *Southern Journal of Philosophy, 24*(S1), 23–41.

Brink, D. (1989). *Moral realism and the foundations of ethics*. Cambridge: Cambridge University Press.

Broad, C. D. (1944). Some reflections on moral-sense theories in ethics. *Proceedings of the Aristotelian Society, New Series, 45*, 131–166.

Bromwich, D. (2010). Clearing conceptual space for cognitivist motivational internalism. *Philosophical Studies, 148*, 343–367.

Burge, T. (1986). Intellectual norms and foundations of mind. *Journal of Philosophy, 83*(12), 697–720.

Burgess, J. A. (1998). Error theories and values. *Australasian Journal of Philosophy, 76*(4), 534–552.

Carnap, R. (1962). *Logical foundations of probability*. Chicago, IL: University of Chicago Press. (Original work published 1935)

Copp, D. (2000). Milk, honey, and the good life on Moral Twin Earth. *Synthese, 124*(1), 113–137.

Crisp, R. (2002). Sidgwick and the boundaries of intuitionism. In P. Stratton-Lake (Ed.), *Ethical intuitionism* (pp. 56–75). Oxford: Oxford University Press.

Cuneo, T., & Shafer-Landau, R. (2014). The moral fixed points: New directions for moral nonnaturalism. *Philosophical Studies, 171*(3), 399–443.

Dancy, J. (2006). Nonnaturalism. In *Oxford handbook of ethical theory* (pp. 122–145). Oxford: Oxford University Press.

Darwall, S. (1983). *Impartial reason*. Ithaca, NY: Cornell University Press.

Darwall, S. (1997). Reasons, motives, and the demands of morality: An introduction. In *Moral Discourse and Practice* (pp. 305–312). Oxford: Oxford University Press.

Dowell, J. (2015). The metaethical insignificance of Moral Twin Earth. In R. Shafer-Landau (Ed.), *Oxford studies in metaethics* (Vol. 11). Oxford: Oxford University Press.

Dreier, J. (1990). Internalism and speaker relativism. *Ethics, 101*(1), 6–26.

Dreier, J. (1992). The supervenience argument against moral realism. *Southern Journal of Philosophy, 30*(3), 13–38.

Dreier, J. (1996). Expressivist embeddings and minimalist truth. *Philosophical Studies, 83*(1), 29–51.

Eklund, M. (2009). The Frege-Geach problem and Kalderon's moral fictionalism. *Philosophical Quarterly, 59*(237), 705–712.

Eklund, M. (2011). Fictionalism. In *Stanford encyclopedia of philosophy* (Fall 2011 Edition), E. N. Zalta (Ed.), http://plato.stanford.edu/archives/fall2011/entries/fictionalism/

Enoch, D. (2011). *Taking morality seriously*. Oxford: Oxford University Press.

Falk, W. D. (1945). Obligation and rightness. *Philosophy, 20*(76), 129–147.

Falk, W. D. (1947). "Ought" and motivation. *Proceedings of the Aristotelian Society, New Series, 48*, 111–138.

Finlay, S. (2008). The error in the error theory. *Australasian Journal of Philosophy, 86*(3), 347–369.

Firth, R. (1952). Ethical absolutism and the ideal observer. *Philosophy and Phenomenological Research, 12*(3), 317–345.

FitzPatrick, W. (2011). Ethical non-naturalism and normative properties. In M. Brady (Ed.), *New waves in metaethics* (pp. 7–35). London: Palgrave.

Fletcher, G. (2015). Hybrid expressivism: Pragmatic accounts. *Philosophy Compass, 9*(12), 848–863.

Foot, P. (1958a). Moral arguments. *Mind, 67*(268), 502–513.

Foot, P. (1958b). Moral beliefs. *Proceedings of the Aristotelian Society, 59*, 83–104.

Foot, P. (1961). Goodness and choice. *Aristotelian Society Supplementary Volume, 35*, 45–60. (Reprinted in *Virtues and vices and other essays in moral philosophy*, by P. Foot, 2002, Cambridge: Cambridge University Press).

Foot, P. (1972). Morality as a system of hypothetical imperatives. *Philosophical Review, 84,* 305–316.

Foot, P. (2001). *Natural Goodness.* Oxford: Oxford University Press.

Foot, P. (2002). *Virtues and vices and other essays in moral philosophy.* Cambridge: Cambridge University Press.

Frankena, W. (1958). Obligation and motivation in recent moral philosophy. In A. I. Melden (Ed.), *Essays in moral philosophy* (pp. 40–81). Seattle: University of Washington Press.

Frege, G. (1892). On sense and reference. In *Translations from the philosophical writings of Gottlob Frege* (pp. 126–151), reprinted 1984.

Garner, R. (1990). On the genuine queerness of moral properties and facts. *Australasian Journal of Philosophy, 68*(2), 137–146.

Geach, P. T. (1960). Ascriptivism. *Philosophical Review, 69*(2), 221–225.

Geach, P. T. (1965). Assertion. *Philosophical Review, 74*(4), 449–465.

Gettier, E. (1963). Is justified true belief knowledge? *Analysis, 23*(6), 121–123.

Gibbard, A. (1992). *Wise choices, apt feelings.* Cambridge, MA: Harvard University Press.

Gibbard, A. (2003). *Thinking how to live.* Cambridge, MA: Harvard University Press.

Gibbard, A. (2008). *Reconciling our aims.* Oxford: Oxford University Press.

Grice, H. P. (1991). *Studies in the way of words.* Cambridge, MA: Harvard University Press.

Haji, I. (2002). *Deontic morality and control.* Cambridge: Cambridge University Press.

Hare, R. M. (1952). *The language of morals.* Oxford: Clarendon.

Harman, G. (1965). The inference to the best explanation. *Philosophical Review, 74*(1), 88–95.

Harman, G. (1975). Moral relativism defended. *Philosophical Review, 84*(1), 3–22.

Harman, G. (1977). *The nature of morality: An introduction to ethics.* Oxford: Oxford University Press.

Harman, G. (1978). What is moral relativism? In *Values and morals* (pp. 143–161). New York, NY: Springer.

Harman, G. (1986). Moral explanations of natural facts—can moral claims be tested against moral reality? *Southern Journal of Philosophy, 24*(S1), 57–68.

Hay, R. (2013). Hybrid expressivism and the analogy between pejoratives and moral language. *European Journal of Philosophy, 21*(3), 450–474.

Horgan, T., & Timmons, M. (1991). New wave moral realism meets Moral Twin-Earth. *Journal of Philosophical Research, 16,* 447–465.

Horgan, T., & Timmons, M. (1992a). Troubles on Moral Twin Earth: Moral queerness revived. *Synthese, 92*(2), 221–260.

Horgan, T., & Timmons, M. (1992b). Troubles for new wave moral semantics: The "open question argument" revived. *Philosophical Papers, 21*(3), 153–175.

Horgan, T., & Timmons, M. (2006). Expressivism, yes! Relativism, no! In R. Shafer-Landau (Ed.), *Oxford studies in metaethics* (Vol. 1, pp. 73–98). Oxford: Oxford University Press.

Horgan, T., & Timmons, M. (2009). Analytical moral functionalism meets Moral Twin Earth. In I. Ravenscroft (Ed.), *Essays on the philosophy of Frank Jackson* (pp. 221–236). Oxford: Blackwell.

Horowitz, T. (1998). Philosophical intuitions and psychological theory. *Ethics, 108*(2), 367–385.

Huemer, M. (2005). *Moral intuitionism.* New York, NY: Palgrave.

Hume, D. (1888). *A treatise of human nature* (L. A. Selby-Bigge, Ed.). Oxford: Clarendon Press.

Jackson, F. (1974). Defining the autonomy of ethics. *Philosophical Review, 83*(1), 88–96.

Jackson, F. (1998). *From metaphysics to ethics.* Oxford: Oxford University Press.

Jackson, F. (1999). Non-cognitivism, normativity, belief. *Ratio, 12*(4), 420–435.

Jackson, F., & Pettit, P. (1995). Moral functionalism and moral motivation. *Philosophical Quarterly, 45,* 20–40.

Jackson, F., & Pettit, P. (1996). Moral functionalism, supervenience and reductionism. *Philosophical Quarterly, 46,* 82–85.

Johnson, R.N. (1999). Internal reasons and the conditional fallacy. *Philosophical Quarterly, 49*(194), 53–72.

Johnston, M. (1989). Dispositional theories of value. *Proceedings of the Aristotelian Society,* Supplementary Volumes, 89–174.

Johnston, M. (1992). Constitution and identity. *Mind, 101,* 89–105.

Jones, K. (2006). Metaethics and emotions research: A response to Prinz. *Philosophical Explorations, 9*(1), 45–53.

Joyce, R. (2001). *The myth of morality.* Cambridge: Cambridge University Press.

Joyce, R. (2007). *The evolution of morality.* Cambridge, MA: MIT Press.

Joyce, R., & Kirchin, S. (2010). *A world without values.* New York, NY: Springer.

Kahneman, D., & Tversky, A. (1979). Prospect theory: An analysis of decision under risk. *Econometrica, 47*(2), 263–291.

Kalderon, M. (2004). Open questions and the manifest image. *Philosophy and Phenomenological Research, 68*(2), 251–289.

Kalderon, M. (2005). *Moral fictionalism.* Oxford: Oxford University Press.

Kalderon, M. (2008). The trouble with terminology. *Philosophical Books, 49*(1), 33–41.

Kant, I. (1797). On a supposed right to lie from philanthropy. *Practical Philosophy,* 612.

Kaplan, D. (1979). On the logic of demonstratives. *Journal of Philosophical Logic, 8*(1), 81–98.

Kennett, J. (2006). Do psychopaths really threaten moral rationalism? *Philosophical Explorations, 9*(1), 69–82.

Kim, J. (1989). The myth of nonreductive materialism. *Proceedings and Addresses of the American Philosophical Association, 63*(3), 31–47.

Kirchin, S. (2005). What is intuitionism and why be an intuitionist? *Social Theory and Practice, 31*(4), 581–606.

Korsgaard, C.M. (1986). Skepticism about practical reason. *Journal of Philosophy, 83*(1), 5–25.

Korsgaard, C.M. (1996). *The sources of normativity.* Cambridge: Cambridge University Press.

Korsgaard, C.M. (1997). The normativity of instrumental reason. In G. Cullity & B. Gaut (Eds.), *Ethics and practical reason* (pp. 215–254). Oxford: Oxford University Press.

Kramer, M.H. (2009). *Moral realism as a moral doctrine.* New York, NY: John Wiley.

Kripke, S.A. (1972). Naming and necessity. In D. Davidson & G. Harman (Eds.), *Semantics of natural language* (pp. 253–355, 763–769). Dordrecht: Reidel. (Reprinted in *Naming and necessity,* by S.A. Kripke, 1980, Cambridge, MA: Harvard University Press)

Lavoisier, A. (1777). Memoir on the calcination of tin in closed vessels and on the cause of the gain in weight which this metal acquires in the operation. (Reprinted in *A sourcebook in chemistry 1400–1900,* pp. 154–179, by H.M. Leicester & H.S. Klickstein, Eds., 1952, Cambridge, MA: Harvard University Press)

Levin, J. (2000). Dispositional theories of color and the claims of common sense. *Philosophical Studies, 100*(2), 151–174.

Lewis, D. (1972). Psychophysical and theoretical identifications. *Australasian Journal of Philosophy, 50*(3), 249–258.

Lewis, D. (1989). Dispositional theories of value. *Proceedings of the Aristotelian Society,* Supp., 89–174.

Lewis, D. (1997). Finkish dispositions. *Philosophical Quarterly, 47*(187), 143–158.

Little, M. (1994a). Moral realism I: Naturalism. *Philosophical Books, 35*(3), 145–153.

Little, M. (1994b). Moral realism II: Non-naturalism. *Philosophical Books, 35*(4), 125–133.

Loeb, D. (1998). Moral realism and the argument from disagreement. *Philosophical Studies, 90*(3), 281–303.

Lycan, W. G. (2008). *Philosophy of language: A contemporary introduction.* New York, NY: Routledge.

Mackie, J. (1946). A refutation of morals. *Australasian Journal of Psychology and Philosophy, 24*(1–2), 77–90.

Mackie, J. (1977). *Ethics: Inventing right and wrong.* London: Penguin.

Marcus, R. B. (1963). Modal logics I: Modalities and intensional languages. In *Proceedings of the Boston Colloquium for the Philosophy of Science 1961/1962*, pp. 77–96.

Markovits, J. (2014). *Moral reason.* Oxford: Oxford University Press.

McDowell, J. (1988). Values and secondary qualities. In T. Honderich (Ed.), *Morality and objectivity* (pp. 110–129). London: Routledge & Kegan Paul.

McGrath, S. (2008). Moral disagreement and moral expertise. In R. Shafer-Landau (Ed.), *Oxford studies in metaethics* (Vol. 3, pp. 87–108). Oxford: Oxford University Press.

McGrath, S. (2011). Moral knowledge and experience. In R. Shafer-Landau (Ed.), *Oxford studies in metaethics* (Vol. 6, pp. 107–127). Oxford: Oxford University Press.

McPherson, T. (2008). Metaethics and the autonomy of morality. *Philosophers Imprint, 8*(6), 1–16.

McPherson, T. (2013). What is at stake in debates among normative realists? *Nous, 49*(1), 123–146.

Mead, M. (1954). *Coming of age in Samoa.* New York, NY: Penguin.

Merli, D. (2007). Moral convergence and the univocity problem. *American Philosophical Quarterly, 44*(4), 297–313.

Millikan, R. G. (1984). *Language, thought, and other biological categories.* Cambridge, MA: MIT Press.

Moore, G. E. (1903). *Principia ethica.* Cambridge: Cambridge University Press.

Moore, G. E. (1922). The conception of intrinsic value. In *Philosophical Studies* (pp. 253–275). London: Kegan Paul.

Nagel, T. (1978). *The possibility of altruism.* Princeton, NJ: Princeton University Press.

Nolan, D., Restall, G., & West, C. (2005). Moral fictionalism versus the rest. *Australasian Journal of Philosophy, 83*(3), 307–330.

Nozick, R. (1981). *Philosophical explanations.* Cambridge, MA: Harvard University Press.

Olson, J. (2014). *Moral error theory: History, critique, defence.* Oxford: Oxford University Press.

O'Neill, O. (1975). Lifeboat Earth. *Philosophy & Public Affairs, 4*(3), 273–292.

O'Neill, O. (2003). Constructivism vs. contractualism. *Ratio, 16*(4), 319–331.

Paakkunainen, H. (2014). Vindicating practical norms: Metasemantic strategies. *Oxford Studies in Metaethics, 9*, 45–75.

Parfit, D. (2011). *On what matters.* Oxford: Oxford University Press.

Petrinovich, L., & O'Neill, P. (1996). Influence of wording and framing effects on moral intuitions. *Ethology and Sociobiology, 17*(3), 145–171.

Plato (trans. 2004). *The Republic.* Reeve (tr.) Indianapolis, IN: Hackett.

Plunkett, D., & Sundell, T. (2013). Disagreement and the semantics of normative and evaluative terms. *Philosophers Imprint, 13*, 1–37.

Post, E. (1960). *Etiquette: The blue book of social usage.* New York, NY: Funk & Wagnalls.

Price, R. (1974). *A review of the principal questions in morals* (D. D. Raphael, Ed.). Oxford: Clarendon. (Original work published 1769)

Putnam, H. (1973). Meaning and reference. *Journal of Philosophy, 70*(19), 699–711.

Putnam, H. (1975). The meaning of "meaning." *Minnesota Studies in the Philosophy of Science, 7*, 221–274.

Railton, P. (1986). Moral realism. *Philosophical Review, 95*(2), 163–207.

Railton, P. (1993). What the non-cognitivist helps us to see the naturalist must help us to explain. In J. Haldane & C. Wright (Eds.), *Reality, representation, projection* (pp. 279–300). Oxford: Oxford University Press.

Railton, P. (1998). Moral explanation and moral objectivity. *Philosophy and Phenomenological Research, 58*(1), 175–182.

Richards, K. (2010). *Life.* New York, NY: Little, Brown.

Ridge, M. (2006). Ecumenical expressivism: Finessing Frege. *Ethics, 116*(2), 302–336.

Ridge, M. (2007). Ecumenical expressivism: The best of both worlds? *Oxford Studies in Metaethics, 2*, 51–76.

Rosati, C. S. (1996). Internalism and the good for a person. *Ethics, 106*, 297–326.

Roskies, A. (2003). Are ethical judgments intrinsically motivational? Lessons from "acquired sociopathy." *Philosophical Psychology, 16*(1), 51–66.

Ross, W. D. (1930). *The right and the good.* Oxford: Oxford University Press.

Russell, B. (1905). On denoting. *Mind, 14*(56), 479–493.

Russell, B. (1948). *Human knowledge: Its scope and its limits.* London: George Allen & Unwin.

Russell, B. (1957). Mr. Strawson on referring. *Mind, 66*(263), 385–389.

Sainsbury, R. M. (2009). *Fiction and fictionalism.* New York, NY: Routledge.

Sayre-McCord, G. (1997). "Good" on Twin Earth. *Philosophical Issues, 8*, 267–292.

Scanlon, T. M. (1998). *What we owe to each other.* Cambridge, MA: Harvard University Press.

Scanlon, T. M. (2014). *Being realistic about reasons.* Oxford: Oxford University Press.

Schafer, K. (2015). Realism and constructivism in Kantian metaethics. *Philosophy Compass.*

Schroeder, M. (2005). Cudworth and normative explanations. *Journal of Ethics and Social Philosophy, 1*(3), 1–27.

Schroeder, M. (2007). *Slaves of the passions.* Oxford: Oxford University Press.

Schroeder, M. (2008a). *Being for.* Oxford: Oxford University Press.

Schroeder, M. (2008b). What is the Frege-Geach problem? *Philosophy Compass, 3*, 703–720.

Schroeder, M. (2009). Hybrid expressivism: Virtues and vices. *Ethics, 119*(2), 257–309.

Schroeder, M. (2010). *Noncognitivism in ethics.* New York, NY: Routledge.

Schroeder, M. (2014). *Explaining the reasons we share: Explanation and expression in ethics* (Vol. 1). Oxford: Oxford University Press.

Schroeter, L., & Schroeter, F. (2013). Normative realism: Co-reference without convergence? *Philosophers Imprint, 13*(13), 1–24.

Shafer-Landau, R. (2003). *Moral realism: A defense.* Oxford: Oxford University Press.

Shafer-Landau, R. (2006). Ethics as philosophy: A defense of ethical nonnaturalism. In T. Horgan & M. Timmons (Eds.), *Metaethics after Moore* (p. 209). Oxford: Clarendon Press.

Shepski, L. (2008). The vanishing argument from queerness. *Australasian Journal of Philosophy, 86*(3), 371–387.

Sidgwick, H. (1966). *The methods of ethics.* New York, NY: Dover. (Original work published 1875)

Sinhababu, N. (2009). The Humean theory of motivation reformulated and defended. *Philosophical Review, 118*(4), 465–500.

Sinnott-Armstrong, W. (2006a). Moral intuitionism meets empirical psychology. In T. Horgan & M. Timmons (Eds.), *Metaethics after Moore* (pp. 339–365). New York, NY: Oxford University Press.

Sinnott-Armstrong, W. (2006b). *Moral skepticism.* Oxford: Oxford University Press.

Skarsaune, K. O. (2011). Darwin and moral realism: Survival of the iffiest. *Philosophical Studies, 152*(2), 229–243.

Skarsaune, K. O. (2015). How to be a moral platonist. In Shafer-Landau (Ed.) *Oxford Studies in Metaethics*, Oxford: Oxford University Press.

Smith, M. (1987). The Humean theory of motivation. *Mind, 96*(381), 36–61.

Smith, M. (1994). *The moral problem*. Oxford: Blackwell.

Smith, M. (1995a). Internal reasons. *Philosophy and Phenomenological Research, 55*, 109–131.

Smith, M. (1995b). Internalism's wheel. *Ratio, 8*(3), 277–302.

Smith, M. (1996). The argument for internalism: Reply to Miller. *Analysis, 56*(3), 175–184.

Sobel, D., & Copp, D. (2001). Against direction of fit accounts of belief and desire. *Analysis, 61*(269), 44–53.

Sober, E., & Wilson, D. S. (1999). *Unto others: The evolution and psychology of unselfish behavior*. Cambridge, MA: Harvard University Press.

Stevenson, C. L. (1944). *Ethics and language*. New Haven, CT: Yale University Press.

Stratton-Lake, P. (2002). *Ethical intuitionism: Re-evaluations*. Oxford: Oxford University Press.

Strawson, P. F. (1950). On referring. *Mind, 59*(235), 320–344.

Street, S. (2006). A Darwinian dilemma for realist theories of value. *Philosophical Studies, 127*(1), 109–166.

Street, S. (2008). Constructivism about reasons. In R. Shafer-Landau (Ed.), *Oxford studies in metaethics* (Vol. 3, pp. 207–245). Oxford: Oxford University Press.

Streumer, B. (2011). Can we believe the error theory? *Philosophical Studies, 154*, 325–348.

Strom, S. McDonald's Set to Phase Out Suppliers' Use of Sow Crates, *New York Times* (February 14, 2012), p. B2.

Sturgeon, N. (1985). Moral explanations. In D. Copp (Ed.), *Morality, reason, and truth* (pp. 49–78). Totowa, NJ: Rowman and Allanheld.

Sturgeon, N. L. (1986). Harman on moral explanations of natural facts. *Southern Journal of Philosophy, 24*(S1), 69–78.

Sturgeon, N. (2003). Moore on ethical naturalism. *Ethics, 113*(3), 528–556.

Sturgeon, N. L. (2006). Ethical naturalism. In D. Copp (Ed.), *The Oxford handbook of ethical theory* (pp. 91–121). Oxford: Oxford University Press.

Sturgeon, N. (2009). Doubts about the supervenience of the ethical. In R. Shafer-Landau (Ed.), *Oxford studies in metaethics* (Vol. 4, pp. 53–92). Oxford: Oxford University Press.

Svavarsdottir, S. (1999). Moral cognitivism and motivation. *Philosophical Review, 108*, 161–219.

Swartzer, S. (2013). Appetitive besires and the fuss about fit. *Philosophical Studies, 165*(3), 975–988.

Thomson, J. J. (1983). Parthood and identity across time. *Journal of Philosophy, 80*, 201–220.

Thomson, J. J., & Harman, G. (1996). *Moral relativism and moral objectivity*. London: Blackwell.

Tiberius, V. (2014). *Moral psychology: A contemporary introduction*. New York, NY: Routledge.

Tresan, J. (2006). De dicto internalist cognitivism. *Nous, 40*(1), 143–165.

Tropman, E. (2009). Renewing moral intuitionism. *Journal of Moral Philosophy, 6*(4), 440–463.

van Fraassen, B. C. (1980). *The scientific image*. Oxford: Oxford University Press.

van Roojen, M. (1995). Humean motivation and Humean rationality. *Philosophical Studies, 79*(1), 37–57.

van Roojen, M. (1996a). Expressivism and irrationality. *Philosophical Review, 105*(3), 311–335.

van Roojen, M. (1996b). Moral functionalism and moral reductionism. *Philosophical Quarterly, 46*(182), 77–81.

van Roojen, M. (2002). Should motivational Humeans be Humeans about rationality? *Topoi, 21*(1), 209–215.

van Roojen, M. (2006). Knowing enough to disagree: A new response to the Moral Twin Earth argument. In R. Shafer-Landau (Ed.), *Oxford studies in metaethics* (Vol. 1, pp. 161–194). Oxford: Oxford University Press.

van Roojen, M. (2010). Moral rationalism and rational amoralism. *Ethics, 120*(3), 495–525.

van Roojen, M. (2013). Internalism, Motivational, in LaFollette & Stroud (Eds.), *International Encyclopedia of Ethics*. Oxford: Wiley-Blackwell.

van Roojen, M. (2014). Moral intuitionism, experiments and skeptical arguments. In A. Booth & D. Rowbottom (Eds.), *Intuitions* (pp. 148–164). Oxford: Oxford University Press.

Vavova, K. (2015). Evolutionary debunking of moral realism. *Philosophy Compass, 10*(2), 104–116.

Wedgwood, R. (2001). Conceptual role semantics for moral terms. *Philosophical Review, 110*(1), 1–30.

West, C. (2010). Business as usual? The error theory, internalism, and the function of morality. In R. Joyce & S. Kirchin (Eds.), *A world without values* (pp. 183–198). Dordrecht: Springer.

Westermarck, E. (1932). *Ethical relativity*. New York, NY: Harcourt, Brace.

Wielenberg, E. J. (2010). On the evolutionary debunking of morality. *Ethics, 120*(3), 441–464.

Williams, B. (1980). Internal and external reasons. In R. Harrison (Ed.), *Rational action* (pp. 17–24). Cambridge: Cambridge University Press.

Index

#0176 - 280617 - C0 - 229/152/17 - PB - 9780415894425